metamorphoses

metamorphoses

TOWARDS A MATERIALIST
THEORY OF BECOMING

ROSI BRAIDOTTI

Polity

First published in 2002 by Polity Press in association with Blackwell Publishers Ltd.

Editorial office:
Polity Press
65 Bridge Street
Cambridge CB2 1UR, UK

Marketing and production:
Blackwell Publishers Ltd
108 Cowley Road
Oxford OX4 1JF, UK

Published in the USA by
Blackwell Publishers Inc.
350 Main Street
Malden, MA 02148, USA

A catalogue record for this book is available from the British Library.

Library of Congress Cataloging-in-Publication Data

Braidotti, Rosi.
  Metamorphoses : towards a materialist theory of becoming / Rosi Braidotti.
    p. cm.
  Includes bibliographical references and index.
  ISBN 0-7456-2576-2 (hardback : alk. paper) – ISBN 0-7456-2577-0 (pbk. : alk. paper)
    1. Feminist theory.   2. Becoming (Philosophy)   I. Title.
HQ1190.B737   2002
305.42′01–dc21   01002613

Typeset in 10 on 12pt Times
by Graphicraft Limited, Hong Kong
Printed in Great Britain by TJ International, Padstow, Cornwall

This book is printed on acid-free paper.

For Anneke

Contents

Acknowledgements

My gratitude goes first and foremost to my colleagues in the department of women's studies in the Arts Faculty of Utrecht University who continue to provide a nurturing and stimulating work environment: Berteke Waaldijk, Rosemarie Buikema, Gloria Wekker and Mischa Peters.

I am especially indebted to Dean Wiecher Zwanenburg and Dean Riet Schenkeveld-van der Dussen for granting me sabbatical leave in 1995, which allowed me to do the basic research for this book. I spent the sabbatical as a fellow in the School of Social Studies of the Institute for Advanced Studies in Princeton, USA. I am grateful to the Institute for providing me with a fellowship for that academic year. I also owe thanks to the Netherlands America Commission for Educational Exchanges and especially to the Fulbright Commission and to Jan Veldhuis for awarding me a senior Fulbright Grant that allowed me the year off. In Princeton, at the Institute for Advanced Studies I was most fortunate in having Joan Scott as mentor and point of reference. As ever a source of inspiration, Joan Scott has strongly marked my intellectual development. I also profited immensely from conversations with Michael Walzer, Albert Hirschmann, Clifford Geertz, Evelynn Hammonds, Mary Poovey, Peter Gallison and Carrie Jones. My work at the Institute was facilitated by a fantastic team of librarians, to whom I owe sincere thanks: Elliot Shore, Marcia Tucker, Rebecca Bushby, Faridah Kassim and Pat Bernard.

I also profited greatly from my visit to the Philosophy Department of Melbourne University for several months in 1996. I thank Professor T. Cody, the Arts Faculty of Melbourne University and the postgraduate students for awarding me the official visiting fellowship that greatly facilitated my stay in Melbourne. I also wish to thank the Netherlands Research Organization (NWO) and the Australian Research Council for jointly sponsoring my stay in Australia as part of their bilateral exchanges.

I profited greatly from a month's visit to the Institut für die Wissenschaften vom Menschen in Vienna, in 1996. Dr Cornelia Klinger was extremely supportive and the environment of the Institute very stimulating. Also in 1996 I was fortunate enough to be involved in the symposium 'Sustainability as a Social Science concept', which was held in Frankfurt, at the Institute for Social-Ecological Research and was sponsored by the UNESCO–MOST programme. I thank Professor Egon Becker and Dr Thomas Jahn for their high standards and intellectual leadership.

Being a nomadic scholar, I have also learnt a lot from a shorter but not less stimulating visit to the Instituto Interdisciplinario de Estudides de Genero of the Arts Faculty at the University of Buenos Aires, which I visited for two weeks in October 1998. Dr Nora Dominguez and Dr María Luisa Femenías really made this an unforgettable event. I am also grateful to the Faculty Research Institute on Culture and History (OGC) of Utrecht University for sponsoring this visit.

The two-week visit to the Gender Unit at the University of the Western Cape in Capetown, South Africa, in October 1997, was also very important to me. This was sponsored by the UNITWIN exchanges between UWC and Utrecht University. I wish to thank especially Denise Jones, who made all the difference, Wendy Woodward and Rhoda Kadhali, as well as all the staff and students of the Gender Unit. In Utrecht, Rosemarie Buikema and Renee Römkens were extremely supportive.

From 1998 to date I have had the honour of being appointed Recurrent Visiting Professor at the Gender Institute of the London School of Economics. This appointment was also financially supported by the Research Institute for Culture and History of Utrecht University (OGC), which again I thank. In London I was fortunate in engaging in thought-provoking exchanges with Professors Henrietta Moore, Anne Phillips and Tony Giddens, as well as all the staff and students of the Gender Institute, whom I gratefully acknowledge.

In Utrecht, I depended on several generations of patient and dedicated research assistants who kept the manuscript alive when I was swamped by work: Esther Captain, Yvette van der Linde, Mischa Peters and especially Titia Blanksma and Claire Needler who saw me through the very difficult last phases.

Among my colleagues, I am especially indebted to Veronique Schutgens and Trude Oorschot who, as co-ordinators of the Netherlands Research School of Women's Studies, facilitated my work as director and freed me for research and writing. Thanks also to Esther Vonk and my European partners in the ATHENA network for women's studies, especially Gabriele

Griffin, Nina Lykke, Harriet Silius and Diana Anders. My sister Giovanna provided brilliant insights and high-level scientific information, as well as wit and support. Wiljan van den Akker and Harry Kunneman were present in their criticism and support for my work, as were many other friends and colleagues near and far. A deeply loving thought goes out to Kathy Acker and Clare Duchen, who died far too young. One special friend I do wish to thank is Annamaria Tagliavini in Bologna, who provided constant stimulation, information and challenges to my thinking. Without her inquisitive and fast mind, her wit, and our e-mail discussions, this text could never have been completed.

Last but not least, I thank my life-companion Anneke Smelik, for whom change is a way of life and transformation an ethical issue.

Prologue

'I am rooted, but I flow.'
Virginia Woolf, *The Waves*, p. 69

These are strange times, and strange things are happening. Times of ever-expanding, yet spasmodic, waves of change, which engender the simultaneous occurrence of contradictory effects. Times of fast-moving changes which do not wipe out the brutality of power-relations, but in many ways intensify them and bring them to the point of implosion.

Living at such times of fast changes may be exhilarating, yet the task of representing these changes to ourselves and engaging productively with the contradictions, paradoxes and injustices they engender is a perennial challenge. Accounting for fast-changing conditions is hard work; escaping the velocity of change is even harder. Unless one likes complexity one cannot feel at home in the twenty-first century. Transformations, metamorphoses, mutations and processes of change have in fact become familiar in the lives of most contemporary subjects. They are also vital concerns, however, for the scientific, social and political institutions that are expected to govern and take care of them.

If the only constant at the dawn of the third millennium is change, then the challenge lies in thinking about processes, rather than concepts. This is neither a simple nor a particularly welcome task in the theoretical language and conventions which have become the norm in social and political theory as well as cultural critique. In spite of the sustained efforts of many radical critics, the mental habits of linearity and objectivity persist in their hegemonic hold over our thinking. Thus, it is by far simpler to think about the concept

A or B, or of B as non-A, rather than the process of what goes on in between A and B. Thinking through flows and interconnections remains a difficult challenge. The fact that theoretical reason is concept-bound and fastened upon essential notions makes it difficult to find adequate representations for processes, fluid in-between flows of data, experience and information. They tend to become frozen in spatial, metaphorical modes of representation which itemize them as 'problems'. I believe that this is one of the issues that Irigaray addresses, notably in her praise of the 'mechanic of fluids' against the fixity and lethal inertia of conceptual thinking (Irigaray, 1997). Deleuze also takes up this challenge by loosening the conceptual ties that have kept philosophy fastened on some semi-religiously-held beliefs about reason, logos, the metaphysics of presence and the logic of the Same (also known as molar, sedentary, majority).

The starting-point for my work is a question that I would set at the top of the agenda for the new millennium: the point is not to know who we are, but rather what, at last, we want to become, how to represent mutations, changes and transformations, rather than Being in its classical modes. Or, as Laurie Anderson put it wittily: nowadays moods are far more important than modes of being. That is a clear advantage for those who are committed to engendering and enjoying changes, and a source of great anxiety for those who are not.

One of the aims of this book therefore is both to explore the need and to provide illustrations for new figurations, for alternative representations and social locations for the kind of hybrid mix we are in the process of becoming. Figurations are not figurative ways of thinking, but rather more materialistic mappings of situated, or embedded and embodied, positions. A cartography is a theoretically-based and politically-informed reading of the present. A cartographic approach fulfils the function of providing both ex-egetical tools and creative theoretical alternatives. As such it responds to my two main requirements, namely to account for one's locations in terms both of space (geo-political or ecological dimension) and time (historical and geneological dimension), and to provide alternative figurations or schemes of representation for these locations, in terms of power as restrictive (*potestas*) but also as empowering or affirmative (*potentia*). I consider this cartographic gesture as the first move towards an account of nomadic subjectivity as ethically accountable and politically empowering.

By figuration I mean a politically informed map that outlines our own situated perspective. A figuration renders our image in terms of a decentred and multi-layered vision of the subject as a dynamic and changing entity. The definition of a person's identity takes place in between nature–technology, male–female, black–white, in the spaces that flow and connect in between. We live in permanent processes of transition, hybridization and nomadization, and these in-between states and stages defy the established modes of theoretical representation.

A figuration is a living map, a transformative account of the self – it is no metaphor. Being nomadic, homeless, an exile, a refugee, a Bosnian rape-in-war victim, an itinerant migrant, an illegal immigrant, is no metaphor. Having no passport or having too many of them is neither equivalent nor is it merely metaphorical, as some critics of nomadic subjectivity have suggested (Boer 1996; Gedalof 1999; Felski 1997). These are highly specific geo-political and historical locations – history tattooed on your body. One may be empowered or beautified by it, but most people are not; some just die of it. Figurations attempt to draw a cartography of the power-relations that define these respective positions. They don't embellish or metaphorize: they just express different socio-economic and symbolic locations. They draw a cartographic map of power-relations and thus can also help identify possible sites and strategies of resistance. In other words, the project of finding adequate representations, which was raised to new heights by the poststructuralist generation, is neither a retreat into self-referential textuality, nor is it a form of apolitical resignation, as Nussbaum self-righteously argues (1999). Non-linearity and a non-unitary vision of the subject do not necessarily result in either cognitive or moral relativism, let alone social anarchy, as neo-liberals like Nussbaum fear. I rather see them as significant sites for reconfiguring political practice and redefining political subjectivity. The book will accordingly engage throughout with my cartographic reading of the present, in terms of cultural, political, epistemological and ethical concerns.

In these times of accelerating changes, many traditional points of reference and age-old habits are being recomposed, albeit in contradictory ways. At such a time more conceptual creativity is necessary; a theoretical effort is needed in order to bring about the conceptual leap across inertia, nostalgia, aporia and other forms of critical *stasis* induced by the postmodern historical condition. I maintain that we need to learn to think differently about ourselves and the processes of deep-seated transformation. This quest for alternative figurations expresses creativity in representing the kind of nomadic subjects we have already become and the social and symbolic locations we inhabit. In a more theoretical vein, the quest for figurations attempts to recombine the propositional contents and the forms of thinking so as to attune them both to nomadic complexities. It thus also challenges the separation of reason from the imagination.

One of the central concerns of this book is consequently the deficit in the scale of representation which accompanies the structural transformations of subjectivity in the social, cultural and political spheres of late post-industrial culture. Accounting adequately for changes is a challenge that shakes up long-established habits of thought. Most persistent among those is the habit that consists in dealing with differences in pejorative terms, that is to say, to represent them negatively. Hence my leading question, which has become a

how difference has been corrupted

sort of red thread through all my books: [how can one free difference from the negative charge which it seems to have built into it?] Like a historical process of sedimentation, or a progressive cumulation of toxins, the concept of difference has been poisoned and has become the equivalent of inferiority: to be different from means to be worth less than. How can difference be cleansed of this negative charge? Is the positivity of difference, sometimes called 'pure difference', thinkable? What are the conditions that may facilitate the thinkability of positive difference? What is the specific contribution of poststructuralist philosophies to these questions?

By the year 2000, the social context had changed considerably since the days when the poststructuralist philosophers put 'difference' on the theoretical and political agenda. The return of biological essentialism, under the cover of genetics, molecular biology, evolutionary theories and the despotic authority of DNA has caused both an inflation and a reification of the notion of 'difference'. On the right of the political spectrum, in Europe today, contemporary racism celebrates rather than denies differences. In this reactionary discourse, however, differences of identity are essentialized and attached to firm beliefs about national, regional, provincial or at times (see the French National Front, the Italian Northern 'lega' or the Haider phenomenon in Austria) town-based parameters for the definition of identities. Resting on fixed notions of one's territory, these ideas of 'difference' are deterministic, and also exclusive and intrinsically xenophobic. In this context, moreover, difference is a term indexed on a hierarchy of values which it governs by binary opposition: what it conveys are power-relations and structural patterns of exclusion at the national, regional, provincial or even more local level. It is because of what I consider the political and social regression of this essentialistic notion of 'difference' that I find it important to reset the agenda in the direction of a radical (poststructuralist) critique. The notion of 'difference' is far too important to be left either to the geneticists or to the various brands of nostalgic supremacists (white, male, Christian) who circulate these days.

overview

This is therefore less a book about philosophy than a philosophical book. [It aims at providing a singular cartography of some of the political and cultural forces operative in contemporary culture.] From there on, I will present a number of my own variations on nomadic thought, with special reference to Gilles Deleuze's and Luce Irigaray's philosophies of difference. After surveying the state of contemporary feminist philosophies of the subject in general (chapter 1) and of the nomadic subject in particular (chapter 2), I will go on to explore contemporary culture and cultural studies (chapter 3). I will offer readings of some of the more striking aspects of contemporary popular culture, especially the powerful lure of technology and of techno-bodies (chapters 4 and 5), as well as the Gothic or monstrous social imaginary that so often accompanies their representations (chapter 4). I will argue that the current cultural fascination with monstrous, mutant or hybrid others expresses both a deep anxiety about the fast rate of transformation of identities and also the poverty of the social imaginary and our inability to cope creatively with the on-going transformations. At the centre of it all I will place the social, cultural and symbolic mutations induced by technological culture. Throughout, I will try to stress the important and original contribution that a non-unitary vision of the subject can make to critical theory and cultural practice. Resting on a nomadic understanding of subjectivity, I will attempt to de-pathologize and to illuminate in a positive light some contemporary cultural and social phenomena, trying to emphasize their creative and affirmative potential. By addressing from a variety of angles the issue of nomadic subjectivity, I will attempt simultaneously to produce an adequate cartography of this historical situation and to expose the logic of the new power-relations operative today. This book functions therefore like a walk along a zigzagging nomadic track of my own making, which was inspired by philosophies of difference and more especially by concepts such as embodiment, immanence, sexual difference, rhizomatics, memory and endurance or sustainability.

I will also stress issues of embodiment and make a plea for different forms of thinking about and representing the body. I will refer to this in terms of 'radical immanence'. This means that I want to think through the body, not in a flight away from it. This in turn implies confronting boundaries and limitations. In thinking about the body I refer to the notion of enfleshed or embodied materialism (I use the two interchangeably). I have turned to the materialist roots of European philosophy, namely the French tradition that runs from the eighteenth century into Bachelard, Canguilhem, Foucault, Lacan, Irigaray and Deleuze. I call this the 'materialism of the flesh' school in that it gives priority to issues of sexuality, desire and the erotic imaginary. I connect to it the corporeal feminism of sexual difference. This Continental tradition produces both an alternative vision of the subject and tools of analysis which are useful in accounting for some of the changes and transformations that are occurring in post-industrial societies in the age of globalization. In my critical exegesis of Deleuze's theory of becoming and Irigaray's theory of sexual difference, I will argue that nomadology is not at all incompatible with feminist practices of sexual difference but rather that the two can reinforce one another and strike a productive alliance.

After thirty years of postmodernist and feminist debates for, against or undecided on the issue of the 'non-unitary', split, in-process, knotted, rhizomatic, transitional, nomadic subject, issues of fragmentation, complexity and multiplicity should have become household names in critical theory. The ubiquitous nature of these notions, however, and the radical-chic appeal of the terminology do not make for consensus about the issues at stake, namely what exactly are the implications of the loss of unity of the

subject. Much disagreement and arguments at cross purposes have been
voiced as to the ethical and political issues which the non-unitary subject
raises in contemporary culture and politics (Nussbaum 1999). In other words
the 'so what?' part of the discussion on nomadic subjectivity is more open
than ever, while the contradictions and the paradoxes of our historical condition pile up around us. What exactly can we do with this non-unitary
subject? What good it is to anybody? What kind of political and ethical
agency can she or he be attached to? How much fun is it? What are the
values, norms and criteria that nomadic subjectivity can offer? I am inclined
to think that 'so what?' questions are always relevant, excellent and a welcome relief in the often foggy bottoms of critical theory.

Although it is critical in orientation, this book is never negative. I believe
that the processes of transformation are on-going and that the equivalent
process of transformative repossession of knowledge has just begun. With
that comes also the quest for alternative figurations to express the kind of
internally contradictory multi-faceted subjects that we have become. There
is a noticeable gap between how we live – in emancipated or post-feminist,
multi-ethnic societies, with high technologies and telecommunication,
allegedly free borders and increased controls, to name just a few – and
how we represent to ourselves this lived familiarity. This imaginative poverty
can be read as the 'jet-lag' problem of living simultaneously in different
time-zones, in the schizophrenic mode that is characteristic of the historical
era of postmodernity. Filling in this gap with adequate figurations is the
great challenge of the present. And I cannot think of a bigger one for the
future.

What is adequate about new figurations needs to be the object of a collective discussion and confrontation, and of public debates, and it cannot be
determined by a single individual. I believe that such critical, discursive
exchanges should be at the heart of critical theory today. The first question
that I would consequently like to address to my readers is cartographical:
do you agree with the account of late post-industrial culture I will provide
here? Do we live in the same world? in the same time-zones? How do you
account for the kind of world *you* are living in? Drawing that cartography is
the beginning of philosophical dialogue today. My project consequently
joins forces with other attempts made from different philosophical traditions (Fraser 1996) to reconstruct the public sphere and to develop a public
discourse suitable to the contradictory demands of our times.

The cartographic approach of my philosophical nomadism requires that
we think of power-relations simultaneously as the most 'external', collective,
social phenomenon and also as the most intimate or 'internal' one. Or rather,
power is the process that flows incessantly in between the most 'internal'
and the most 'external' forces. As Foucault taught us, power is a situation,
a position, not an object or an essence. Subjectivity is the effect of the

constant flows or in-between interconnections. What attracts me to French philosophies of difference such as Deleuze's multiple subjects of becoming, or Irigaray's 'virtual feminine', is that they do not stop on the surface of issues of identity and power, but rather tackle their conceptual roots. In so doing, they push the psycho-sociological discussion of identity towards issues of subjectivity, that is to say, issues of entitlement and power. I find it particularly important not to confuse this process of subjectivity with individualism or particularity: subjectivity is a socially mediated process. Consequently, the emergence of new social subjects is always a collective enterprise, 'external' to the self while it also mobilizes the self's in-depth structures. A dialogue with psychoanalytic theories of the 'split' nature of subjectivity is consequently high on my agenda and will run throughout the book.

This brings me back to the emphasis I want to place on issues of figuration. Political fictions may be more effective, here and now, than theoretical systems. The choice of an iconoclastic, mythic figure, such as the nomadic subject, is consequently a move against the settled and conventional nature of theoretical and especially philosophical thinking. Nomadism is also, however, a cross-reference to the 'hidden' face of Western philosophy, to its anti-logocentric undercurrents, which F. Chatelet described as the 'demonic' tradition best symbolized by Nietzsche (Chatelet, 1970). Deleuze banks on this philosophical counter-memory, when he celebrates nomadic thought as a genealogical practice that re-locates philosophy away from the gravitational pull of metaphysics (Deleuze 1973b). Deleuze is particularly intent upon challenging the domination of conscious rationality as a model for the subject, and devotes his energy to re-imagining the philosophical subject altogether. Irigaray's project is analogous: she focuses her critique on the phallogocentric structure of thought and the systematic exclusion of the feminine from theoretical representation. Whereas Irigaray draws inspiration from the untapped resources of a virtual 'feminine', which feminists have to re-configure in their own specific imaginary, Deleuze places all hopes on in-depth transformations of the subject in terms of sexually differentiated processes of becoming (see chapter 2). Nonetheless, there is a point of convergence between Irigaray and Deleuze in their effort in re-inventing the very image of the subject as an entity fully immersed in relations of power, knowledge and desire. This implies a positive vision of the subject as an affective, positive and dynamic structure, which clashes with the rationalist image traditionally projected by institutionalized philosophy.

Thus, my choice of the nomadic figuration is also a way of situating myself vis-à-vis the institution of philosophy as a discipline: it is a way of inhabiting it, but as an 'outsider within', that is to say critically but also with deep engagement. Last, but not least, this figuration has an imaginative pull that I find attuned to the transnational movement that marks our historical situation.

Equally important for nomadic 'becomings' is the quest for a style of thinking that adequately reflects the complexities of the process itself. 'Becoming-animal', for instance is related by Deleuze to a certain approach to writing, to the productions of texts like Kafka's or Woolf's, where the human-centred world view is shattered by other affects, other types of sensibility (more in chapter 4). 'Becoming' is about repetition, but also about memories of the non-dominant kind. It is about affinities and the capacity both to sustain and generate inter-connectedness. Flows of connection need not be appropriative, though they are intense and at times can be violent. They nonetheless mark processes of communication and mutual contamination of states of experience. As such, the steps of 'becoming' are neither reproduction nor imitation, but rather empathic proximity and intensive interconnectedness. It is impossible to render these processes in the language of linearity and self-transparency favoured by academic philosophers. 'Becoming', not unlike Irigaray's 'écriture féminine' calls into question the very performance of a philosophical test, pulling it away from the attraction of logocentrism. Also known as 'de-territorializing', or 'rhizomatic', this nomadic style is an integral component of the concept of 'becoming', and not a mere rhetorical additive.

In order to do justice to these complexities I have opted for a style that may strike the academic reader as allusive or associative. It is a deliberate choice on my part, involving the risk of sounding less than coherent at times. It has to do with my concern for style not as a merely rhetorical device, but as a deeper concept. In choosing to defend the often poetic 'ways' in which philosophers like Irigaray and Deleuze present their theories, I am joining the call for a renewal of the language and the textual apparatus of academic writing but also of public political discussions.

Consequently, I am very committed to the task of reconfiguring a theoretical style in a manner that reflects and does not contradict theoretical nomadism. To attack linearity and binary thinking in a style that remains linear and binary itself would indeed be a contradiction in terms. This is why the poststructuralist generation has worked so hard to innovate the form and style, as well as the content, of their philosophy. This has been greeted by a mixed reception in the academic community. Assessed as 'bad poetry' at best, as an opaque and allusive muddle at worst, the quest for a new philosophical style that rejects the dualism of content and form has clashed with the mood currently dominant in scientific discourse. In the neo-deterministic, pseudo-liberal context of the dawn of the third millennium, a renewed emphasis upon 'scientific clarity' has accompanied the resurgence of genetic, molecular and evolutionary hard-liners for whom 'style' is at best a decorative notion. How the despotic tendency of contemporary scientific discourse joined forces with anti-poststructuralist positions is a phenomenon that deserves more attention than I can give it here. Suffice it to say that such reductions harm not only the 'French' philosophers, but also the implicit definition of 'science' that is systematically opposed to them. Such an aggressive approach reinstates a dogmatic vision of science that does no justice to the state of contemporary research. It is a regression all along the line. Thinking nomadically means also taking the risk of oblique and allegorical cross-references. My quarrel with linearity, therefore, remains open.

In a more feminist vein, as Linda Alcoff so generously noted, this choice of style expresses my desire 'to find value in multiple feminist modes of theory. . . . This is a difference not just in style but, importantly, in political understanding, in part based on a different view of discourse that appreciates the fact that, because it is not coherent or stable, our modes of resistance need not be either' (Alcoff, 2000: 870). Indeed, my choice of a nomadic style is intended as a gesture of rejection of the competitive, judgemental, moralizing high tone that so much feminist theory has come to share with traditional academic writing. In turn, this has to do with my refusal to embrace the 'image of thought' that is conveyed by such a judgemental exercise of critical reason. I do not support the assumption of the critical thinker as judge, moral arbiter or high-priest(ess). Nothing could be further removed from my understanding of the task of the critical philosopher than such a reactive deployment of protocols of institutional reason. My decision to adopt an unconventional – albeit risky – style of thinking is related to such convictions. My hope is that what appears to be lost in terms of coherence can be compensated for by inspirational force and an energizing pull away from binary schemes, judgemental postures and the temptation of nostalgia. Whether this succeeds or not, it is important that my readers keep in mind the reasons that led me to adopt this style in the first place.

My refusal to separate reason from the imagination also alters the terms of the conventional pact between the writer and his or her readers. If the philosophical text is to be approached on the model of connection, it is relinquished into the intensive elements that both sustain the connections and are generated by them. The writer/reader binary couple is recombined accordingly, and a new impersonal mode is required as the appropriate way of doing philosophy. This impersonal style is rather 'post-personal' in that it allows for a web of connections to be drawn, not only in terms of the author's 'intentions' and the reader's 'reception', but rather in a much wider, more complexified set of possible interconnections. The complexity of the network of forces that come to bear on the subject is such that it blurs established, that is to say hegemonic, distinctions of class, culture, race, sexual practice and others. The question of style is crucial to this project. As readers in an intensive mode, we are transformers of intellectual energy, processors of the 'insights' that we are exchanging. These 'in'-sights are not to be thought of as plunging us inwards, towards a mythical 'inner' reservoir of truth. On the contrary, they are better thought of as propelling us in the multiple directions of extra-textual experiences. Thinking is living at a higher degree, a faster pace, a multi-directional manner.

I dedicated *Patterns of Dissonance* to the figuration of the acrobat walking a tight-rope across the postmodern void. In *Nomadic Subjects* I danced through a set of musical and territorial variations. *Metamorphoses* is neither a tight-rope nor a web, but rather the rope of a bungee-jumper, dangling in a tantalizing way in the void, making quick excursions into it, but always bouncing back to safety. It reads like a road-map, marking idiosyncratic itineraries and paradoxical twists and turns around a number of central ideas, hopes and yearnings of mine. It is a map that draws the trajectory of changes, transformations and becomings. The chapters grow from but also apart from each other in a direction that is not always linear. The readers may have to be patient at times and bear with the stress of a journey that has no set destinations. This is a book of explorations and risks, of convictions and desires. For these are strange times and strange things are happening.

I

Becoming Woman, or Sexual Difference Revisited

'I am a violent being, full of fiery storms and other catastrophic phenomena. As yet I can't do more than begin this and begin again because I have to eat myself, as if my body is food, in order to write.'

Kathy Acker, 'The end of the world of white men', p. 66

'Imagine, if you will, a lesbian cross-dresser who pumps iron, looks like Chiquita Banana, thinks like Ruth Bader Ginsburg, talks like Dorothy Parker, has the courage of Anita Hill, the political acumen of Hillary Clinton and is as pissed off as Valerie Solanis, and you really have something to worry about.'

Marcia Tucker, 'The attack of the giant Ninja mutant Barbies', p. 28

Feminism shares with poststructuralist philosophies not only the sense of a crisis of the Logos, but also the need for renewed conceptual creativity and for politically informed cartographies of the present. One of the aims of feminist practice is to overthrow the pejorative, oppressive connotations that are built not only into the notion of difference, but also into the dialectics of Self and Other. This transmutation of values could lead to a re-assertion of the positivity of difference by enabling a collective re-appraisal of the singularity of each subject in their complexity. In other words, the subject of feminism is not *W*oman as the complementary and specular other of man but rather a complex and multi-layered embodied subject who has taken her distance from the institution of femininity. 'She' no longer coincides with the disempowered reflection of a dominant subject who casts his masculinity in a universalistic posture. She, in fact, may no longer be a she, but the subject of quite another story: a subject-in-process, a mutant, the other of the Other, a post-Woman embodied subject cast in female morphology who has already undergone an essential metamorphosis.

Feminist philosophies of sexual difference are historically embedded in the decline and crisis of Western humanism, the critique of phallogocentrism and the crisis of European identity. The philosophical generation that proclaimed the 'death of Man' led to the rejection of humanism, marked the implosion of the notion of Europe, and also contributed to disassembling the package of geo-political specificity of Western discourses and especially of philosophy. Irigaray broadens the range of her intervention to cover spatio-temporal co-ordinates and a number of many constitutive relations, including ethnicity and especially religion. The fact that the notion of 'difference' as pejoration goes to the heart of the European history of philosophy and of the 'metaphysical cannibalism' of European thought makes it a foundational concept. It has been colonized by hierarchical and exclusionary ways of thinking, which means that historically it has also played a constitutive role not only in events that Europe can be proud of, such as the Enlightenment, but also in darker chapters of our history, such as in European fascism and colonialism. Because the history of difference in Europe has been one of lethal exclusions and fatal disqualifications, it is a notion for which critical intellectuals must make themselves accountable. Feminist ethics and politics of location can be of inspiration in meeting this challenge.

The politics of location refers to a way of making sense of diversity among women within the category of 'sexual difference' understood as the binary opposite of the phallogocentric subject. In feminism, these ideas are coupled with that of epistemological and political accountability seen as the practice that consists in unveiling the power locations which one inevitably inhabits as the site of one's identity. The practice of accountability (for one's embodied and embedded locations) as a relational, collective activity of undoing power differentials is linked to two crucial notions: memory and narratives. They activate the process of putting into words, that is to say bringing into symbolic representation, that which by definition escapes consciousness.

A 'location', in fact, is not a self-appointed and self-designed subject-position. It is a collectively shared and constructed, jointly occupied spatio-temporal territory. A great deal of our location, in other words, escapes self-scrutiny because it is so familiar, so close, that one does not even see it. The 'politics of location' consequently refers to a process of consciousness-raising that requires a political awakening (Grewal and Kaplan 1994) and hence the intervention of others. 'Politics of locations' are cartographies of power which rest on a form of self-criticism, a critical, genealogical self-narrative; they are relational and outside-directed. This means that 'embodied' accounts illuminate and transform our knowledge of ourselves and of the world. Thus, black women's texts and experiences make white women see the limitations of our locations, truths and discourses. Feminist knowledge is an interactive process that brings out aspects of our existence, especially our own implication with power, that we had not noticed before. In Deleuzian language, it 'de-territorializes' us: it estranges us from the familiar, the intimate, the known, and casts an external light upon it; in Foucault's language, it is micro-politics, and it starts with the embodied self. Feminists, however, knew this well before either Foucault or Deleuze theorized it in their philosophy.

Where 'figurations' of alternative feminist subjectivity, like the womanist, the lesbian, the cyborg, the inappropriate(d) other, the nomadic feminist, and so on, differ from classical 'metaphors' is precisely in calling into play a sense of accountability for one's locations. They express materially embedded cartographies and as such are self-reflexive and not parasitic upon a process of metaphorization of 'others'. Self-reflexivity is, moreover, not an individual activity, but an interactive process which relies upon a social network of exchanges. The figurations that emerge from this process act as the spotlight that illuminates aspects of one's practice which were blind spots before. By extension, new figurations of the subject (nomadic, cyborg, Black, etc.) function like conceptual *personae*. As such, they are no metaphor, but rather on the critical level, materially embedded, embodying accounts of one's power-relations. On the creative level they express the rate of change, transformation or affirmative deconstruction of the power one inhabits. 'Figurations' materially embody stages of metamorphosis of a subject position towards all that the phallogocentric system does *not* want it to become.

A range of new, alternative subjectivities have indeed emerged in the shifting landscapes of postmodernity. They are contested, multi-layered and internally contradictory subject-positions, which does not make them any less ridden with power-relations. They are hybrid and in-between social categories for whom traditional descriptions in terms of sociological categories such as 'marginals', 'migrants', or 'minorities' are, as Saskia Sassen (1994) suggests, grossly inadequate. Looked at from the angle of 'different others', this inflationary production of different differences simultaneously expresses the logic of capitalist exploitation, but also the emerging subjectivities of positive and self-defined others. It all depends on one's locations or situated perspectives. Far from seeing this as a form of relativism, I see it as an embedded and embodied form of enfleshed materialism. Put in a more feminist frame with Irigaray, the differences proliferating in late postmodern or advanced capitalism are the 'others' of the Same. Translated into a Deleuzian perspective, these differences, whether they are large or quantitatively small, are not qualitative and consequently do not alter the logic or the power of that Same, the Majority, the phallogocentric master-code. In late postmodernity the centre merely becomes fragmented, but that does not make it any less central, or dominating. It is important to resist the uncritical reproduction of Sameness on a molecular, global or planetary scale. I don't want to conceptualize differences in a Hegelian framework of dialectical interdependence and mutual consumption of self and other. I do see them instead as being disengaged from this chain of reversals in order to engage in quite a different logic: a nomadic, or rhizomatic one.

The work on power, difference and the politics of location offered by post-colonial and anti-racist feminist thinkers like Gayatri Spivak (1989b), Stuart Hall (1990), Paul Gilroy (1987; 1993), Avter Brah (1993), Helma Lutz et al. (1996), Philomena Essed (1991), Nira Yuval-Davis and Floya Anthias (1989) and many others who are familiar with the European situation helps us illuminate the paradoxes of the present. One of the most significant effects of late postmodernity in Europe is the phenomenon of trans-culturality, or cultures clashing in a pluri-ethnic or multicultural European social space. World-migration – a huge movement of population from periphery to centre, working on a world-wide scale of 'scattered hegemonies' (Grewal and Kaplan 1994) – has challenged the claim to the alleged cultural homogeneity of European nation-states and of the incipient European Union. Present-day Europe is struggling with multiculturalism at a time of increasing racism and xenophobia. The paradoxes, power-dissymmetries and fragmentations of the present historical context rather require that we shift the political debate from the issue of differences between cultures to differences *within* the same culture. In other words, one of the features of our present historical condition is the shifting grounds on which periphery and centre confront each other, with a new level of complexity which defies dualistic or oppositional thinking.

Feminist theory argues that if it is the case that a socio-cultural mutation is taking place in the direction of a multi-ethnic, multi-media society, then the transformation cannot affect only the pole of 'the others'. It must equally dislocate the position and the prerogative of 'the Same', the former centre. In other words, what is changing is not merely the terminology or metaphorical representation of subjects, but the very structure of subjectivity, social relations and the social imaginary that support it. It is the syntax of social relations, as well as their symbolic representation, that is in upheaval. The customary standard-bearers of Euro-centric phallocentrism no longer hold in a civil society that is, among others, sexed female *and* male, multicultural and not inevitably Christian. More than ever, the question of social transformation begs that of representation: what can the male, white, Christian monotheistic symbolic do for them? The challenges, as well as the anxieties, evoked by the question of emerging subjects-in-process mark patterns of becoming that require new forms of expression and representation, that is to say socially mediated forms which need to be assessed critically. Feminist theory is a very relevant and useful navigational tool in these stormy times of locally enacted, global phenomena, i.e. 'G-local' changes.[1]

Whether in relation to media cases such as that of Princess Diana, or of social phenomena such as poverty and marginalization, one often hears the term 'the feminization' of postmodern and post-industrial cultures. A highly problematic term, if ever there was one; it is symptomatic, in so far as it expresses the crisis of masculinity and of male domination, but it also refers to a normative level of 'soft values', such as flexibility, emotionality, concern or care. These 'soft' qualities clash against but are not incompatible with the rather rigid protocols which still govern the public sphere and reflect not only its male-dominated structure, but also the masculine-saturated imaginary that supports it. That these 'transformations of intimacy' (Giddens 1994) can be expressed in terms of 'feminization', though their relationship to real-life women and their experiences is far from direct, or transparent, is an endless source of wonder for me. I would therefore prefer to translate this allegedly 'feminized' process into the need to develop socially more flexible, multi-layered approaches to access and participation in contemporary technological culture. At both the micro- and the macro-levels of the constitution of subjectivity, we need more complexities both in terms of genders and across ethnicities, class and age. This is the social agenda that needs to be addressed. The inflationary discourse of the 'feminine' has never proved particularly helpful for women and 'others', unless it is supported by a healthy dose of feminist consciousness.

Black, post-colonial and feminist critics have, however, rightfully *not* spared criticism of the paradoxes as well as the rather perverse division of labour that has emerged in postmodernity. According to this paradox it is the thinkers who are located at the *centre* of past or present empires who are actively deconstructing the power of the centre – thus contributing to the discursive proliferation and consumption of former 'negative' others. Those same others, however – especially in post-colonial, but also in post-fascist and post-communist societies – are rather more keen to reassert their identity, rather than to deconstruct them. The irony of this situation is not lost on any of the interlocutors: think for instance of the feminist philosophers saying: 'how can we undo a subjectivity we have not even historically been entitled to *yet*?' Or the black and post-colonial subjects who argue that it is now their historical turn to be self-assertive. And if the white, masculine, ethnocentric subject wants to 'deconstruct' himself and enter a terminal crisis, then – so be it! The point remains that 'difference' emerges as a central – albeit contested and paradoxical – notion, which means that a confrontation with it is historically inevitable, as we – postmodern subjects – are historically condemned to our history. Accounting for them through adequate cartographies consequently remains a crucial priority.

In this chapter I will continue building my cartography by focusing on issues of embodiment and immanence, reading especially Irigaray with Deleuze so as to compose my own brand of enfleshed materialism.

Materialism: embodiment and immanence

The body strikes back

If I were to think in figurations and locate the issues of embodiment in my cartography, so as to stress some of the paradoxes of political sensibilities of this end of millennium in Europe, I would pick two contradictory ones: the public's schizoid reaction to the death of Diana, Princess of Wales, and the nameless bodies of thousands of asylum seekers in the European Union today.

Alternatively labelled – depending on one's politics – as 'a phenomenon of mass hysteria', or as 'the floral revolution' – analogous to the Eastern Europeans' 'velvet revolution' – the events surrounding the death of Princess Diana have already entered the realm of political mythology. They were also one of the biggest ever media events focused on a single individual. What is most extraordinary about the com/passionate reaction of the British public is the fact that it consisted of an overwhelming majority of young women, gays and people of colour. The excluded or marginal social subjects, those whom Thatcherism had forgotten or swept aside, bounced back in to the political and media arena with a vengeance. It was the return of the repressed, not with a bang but a whimper. It formed a suitable complement to the landslide that had brought 'New Labour' to power in the UK a few months before and to a renewal of respect for emotions, affectivity and the role they can and should play in public and political life. It was also a powerful expression of the continuing potency of the white Goddess as an object of collective worship (Davies and Smith 1999). That it was subsequently denied and repressed as a ritual of collective bonding and outpouring of emotions merely confirms the symptomatic value of the event. One of the things I find relevant about Princess Diana is the fact that she was a woman in full transformation. In other words, she was more interesting for what she was becoming than for what she actually was. I think this dynamic and transformative dimension is crucial to understanding Diana's charisma. As Julie Burchill put it: 'She was never a plaything: she was always a work in progress' (Burchill 1998: 44). This was not lacking in opportunism, as Rushdie suggested, in a less charitable vein: 'Diana was not given to using words like "semiotics", but she was a capable semiotician of herself. With increasing confidence, she gave us the signs by which we might know her as she wished to be known' (Rushdie 1997: 68).

By way of counterpoint, and in order not to confine the cartography of the body within the parameters of the dominant cultural code, I want to turn to another significant case. The second image therefore is that of endless and nameless women, men and child refugees, or asylum-seekers, who have been uprooted from their homes and countries in the many micro-wars that are festering across the globe, including in Europe, at the dawn of the third millennium. The century-old virus of nationalism combines, in contemporary Europe, with the destabilizing effects created by the post-communist world order, as well as the globalization process. The end result is an influx of refugees and a rise in violence, exclusion, racism and human misery that has no equivalent in post-war Europe. These two examples represent for me two sides of the same coin, which is the saturation of our social space by media images and representations.

This results in positioning embodied subjects, and especially the female ones, at the intersection of some formidable locations of power: visibility and media representations produced a consumeristic approach to images in a dissonant or internally differentiated manner. Female embodied subjects in process today include interchangeably the highly groomed body of Princess Diana (like Marilyn Monroe before her) *and* the highly disposable bodies of women, men and children in war-torn lands.

At both the macro and the micro levels the body is caught in a network of power effects mostly induced by technology. This is the driving force of the globalization system and the trans-national economy which engender continuous constitutive contradictions at the 'g-local' level. Manuel Castells (1996), in his seminal work on network societies, argues that technology is absolutely crucial to the changes that have structured the global societies. Post-industrial societies are operating under the acceleration of digitally-driven 'new' cyber-economies. Whether we take bio-technologies, or the new information and communication technologies, the evidence is overwhelming. Capital flow, undeterred by topological or territorial constraints, has achieved a double goal. It has simultaneously 'dematerialized' social reality and hardened it. Suffice it to think of media events such as Princess Diana's funeral, or the Serbs' ethnic cleansing of Kosovo – which are experienced in the relative quiet of one's living room via the television set – as virtual happenings. The 'virtual' reality of the migrants, asylum-seekers or refugees is not high tech, but rather comes close to an over-exposed kind of anonymity, or social invisibility. The virtual reality of cyberspace is a highly contested social space, or rather a set of social relations mediated by technological flow of information.

Consequently, cyberspace and the 'cyborg' subjectivity it offers are no longer the stuff of which science fiction is made. On the contrary, the blurring of the boundaries between humans and machines is socially enacted at all levels: from medicine, to telecommunication, finance and modern warfare, cyber-relations define our social framework. What I want to emphasize, however, is that the cyborg as an embodied and socially embedded human subject that is structurally inter-connected to technological elements or *apparati*, is not a unitary subject position. The cyborg is rather a multi-layered, complex and internally differentiated subject. Cyborgs today would include for me as much the under-paid, exploited labour of women and children on off-shore production plants, as the sleek and highly trained physiques of jet-fighter war-pilots, who interface with computer technologies at post-human levels of speed and simultaneity. As a political cartography, or figuration, the cyborg evokes simultaneously the triumphant charge of Schwarzenegger's *Terminator* and the frail bodies of those workers whose bodily juices – mostly sweat – fuel the technological revolution. One does not stir without the other. The cyborg is also, however, an empowering political myth of resistance to what Haraway calls 'the informatics of domination', about which more in chapter 5.

On a more philosophical level, in relation to the embodied subject, the new technologies make for prosthetic extensions of our bodily functions: answering machines, pagers and portable phones multiply our aural and memory capacities; microwave ovens and freezers offer timeless food-supply; sex can be performed over telephone or modem lines in the fast-growing area of 'teledildonics'; electric tooth-brushes and frozen embryos enlarge other bodily functions; video and camcorders, Internet networks and a plethora of simulated images open up a field that challenges the Platonic notion of 'representation' that has been sedimented by centuries of practice. Media images are the never dead, forever circulating reflections of a haunted postmodern vacuum. The technologies have affected the social space of postmodernity by bringing about a dislocation of the space–time continuum. Technologies freeze time in a discontinuous set of variations determined by speed and simultaneity. They thus induce a dislocation of the subject, allowing not only for deferred or virtual social and personal relations, but also for a pervasive social imaginary of ubiquity and timelessness. Hyper-mobility and virtual communities do not fail to make a visible impact on the social fabric – including labour relations – as well as on the culture and the social imaginary.

In such a context it is inevitable that the body of the 'others' will strike back. On an everyday sociological level, the body is striking back with a vengeance. An estimated two million American women have silicon breast implants – most of which leak, bounce off during bumpy airplane flights or cause undesirable side-effects. Millions of women throughout the advanced world are on Prozac or other mood-enhancing drugs. The hidden epidemic of anorexia–bulimia continues to strike a third of females in the opulent world – as Princess Diana so clearly manifested. Killer-diseases today don't include only the great exterminators, like cancer and AIDS, but also the return of traditional diseases which we thought we had conquered, like malaria and TB. Our immune system has adjusted to the antibiotics and we are vulnerable again (Griggers 1997). There is no question that what we still go on calling – somewhat nostalgically – 'our bodies, ourselves' are abstract technological constructs fully immersed in the advanced psycho-pharmacology chemical industry, bio-science and the electronic media. What is equally clear for me is that we need to be vigilant. The techno-hype is over and we need to assess more lucidly the price that we are paying for being so 'high tech'. We got our prosthetic promises of perfectibility – now, let's hand over our pound of flesh, shall we?

Jackie Stacey points out the paradoxes as well as the strengths of contemporary 'body'-culture in her study of cancer. Discourses and social practices around cancer share with other aspects of today's culture both a fear of and fascination with the monstrous, the hybrid, the abject or mutant body. The Gothic parallel between the proliferation of cancerous cells and the centuries-old fear of monstrous births is imaginatively powerful, as well as intellectually stimulating. Cancer is a death-directed proliferation of cells, almost a cruel parody of reproduction. Secondly, as a social phenomenon, cancer engenders a number of significant practices of power. Stacey argues that medical practices of disciplining the body have been applied in a perverted variation on Foucault's theme of 'bio-power'. They have shifted the emphasis to a form of hyper-individualism which places the responsibility for one's well-being squarely into one's own hands. Illness today is related to 'self-management'. This marks the end of the seventies' linguistic paradigm of 'illness as metaphor', which politicized one's lived experience and socialized the sense of both responsibility for and grief about illness. Nowadays, illness is interiorized and socially controlled to the extreme. This paradox of social normativity and of hyper-individualism is linked to the privatization of health and the dismantling of the welfare state in postindustrial societies. This form of micro-management of one's health results in the social currency of medical prevention, which in turn link illness to social practices such as lifestyle, diet, fitness, etc. The 'body' thus emerges as a target for managerial practices of self-health which in turn requires of the social and cultural critic new skills in 'body-literacy' that go beyond what social theory can grant us.

The immediate social consequences of this are, according to Stacey, a decline of public health standards and a free hand for private financial and insurance companies, that is, a return to liberal individualism in the most exploitative sense of the term. In this regard, and in juxtaposition to Stacey's account of her successful recovery from cancer in the UK, I would situate the tragic and premature cancer-related death of Kathy Acker in the USA. Unable to afford private health insurance, Acker succumbed to cancer after having tried a number of cheaper, 'alternative' and highly ineffective therapies. This suggests to me that the health management of the self in post-industrial 'liberalized' societies on the one hand is progressive in that it rests on contemporary biological and bio-molecular redefinitions of the embodied subject.

On the other hand, it is quite regressive in the social implementations and repercussions in so far as it makes for brutal exercises in power and exclusion. These tend to perpetuate some of the more classical forms of discrimination along variables such as class, race, age and gender. As I pointed out at the start, the simultaneous appearance in the social sphere of well-cared-for, expensive bodies like Princess Diana's and the uncared-for bodies of multiple asylum-seekers are two faces of the same coin. They reinstate the body at the centre of contemporary concerns, but they do so in a manner that also re-inscribes them in some of the most persistent power-relations and structural exclusions.

Bodily materiality

The notion of the embodied or enfleshed subject is central to my understanding of the kind of philosophical materialism which I support. Historically I see it as one of the most fruitful aspects of Continental philosophy, namely the extent to which it highlights the bodily structure of subjectivity and consequently also issues of sexuality and sexual difference. This tradition offers complex models of analysis for interrelations between the self and society, the 'inside' and the 'outside' of the subject. Reactivated by the social movements of the late sixties and seventies, this tradition of embodied materialism lays the grounds for a radical critique of power and for the dissolution of the humanist subject.

The impact of psychoanalysis has been significant here, and it has resulted in a radical deconstruction of the subject by splitting subjectivity from the supervision of rationality. As a result, the subject is no longer identified with consciousness: 'desidero ergo sum' must replace the old 'cogito'. In other words, the activity of thinking is enlarged to encompass a number of faculties of which affectivity, desire and the imagination are prime movers. Deleuze and Irigaray are especially committed to thinking through the radical immanence of the subject after the decline of metaphysics and of its phallogocentric premises. Equally central to Deleuze's philosophical project, however, is the joyful affirmation of positive and multiple differences, of loving irreverence towards the stately institution of philosophy and the creative empowerment of new ideas and forms of thought.

Foucault, Deleuze and Irigaray emphasize the crucial importance of sexuality – of the subject's 'libidinal economy' – to an understanding of contemporary subjectivity. What matters to me are the implications of this notion for political practice. Politics in this framework has as much to do with the constitution and organization of affectivity, memory and desire as it has with consciousness and resistance. I will return throughout this book to the importance of the embodied self, sexuality, memory and the imagination to the making of political subjectivity. The embodiedness of the subject is a form of bodily materiality, not of the natural, biological kind. I take the body as the complex interplay of highly constructed social and symbolic forces: it is not an essence, let alone a biological substance, but a play of forces, a surface of intensities, pure simulacra without originals. This 'intensive' redefinition of the body situates it within a complex interplay of social and affective forces. This is also a clear move away from the psychoanalytic idea of the body as a map of semiotic inscriptions and culturally enforced codes. I see it instead as a transformer and a relay point for the flow of energies: a surface of intensities.

The body has also come back with a vengeance in social practices and discourses as well as in science and bio-technology, in contemporary evolutionary theory, under the impact of information technologies. How to combine all these insights into one coherent theory of embodiment is beyond the means of our historicity. The body remains a bundle of contradictions: it is a zoological entity, a genetic data-bank, while it also remains a bio-social entity, that is to say a slab of codified, personalized memories. As such it is part animal, part machine but the dualistic opposition of the two, which our culture has adopted since the eighteenth century as the dominant model, is inadequate today. Contemporary science and technology in fact have reached right into the most intimate layers of the living organism and the structures of the self, dissolving boundaries that had been established by centuries of humanistic thinking. This means that we can now think of the body as an entity that inhabits different time-zones simultaneously, and is animated by different speeds and a variety of internal and external clocks which do not necessarily coincide. Hence the renewed importance of the issue of temporality, or of bodies-in-time. More on this in chapters 3 and 5.

The embodied subject is thus a process of intersecting forces (affects) and spatio-temporal variables (connections). I take the concept of the body as referring to the multifunctional and complex structure of subjectivity. This is the specifically human capacity for simultaneously incorporating and transcending the very variables – class, race, sex, nationality, culture, etc. – which structure it. This in turn affects the notion of the social imaginary. The process of becoming-subject requires sets of cultural mediation; the subject has to deal with material and semiotic conditions, that is to say institutional sets of rules and regulations as well as the forms of cultural representation that sustain them. Power is negative (*potestas*) in that it prohibits and constrains. It is also positive (*potentia*) in that it empowers and enables. The constant negotiation between the two poles of power can also be formulated in political terms in the notion of subjectivity as power and desire. This view posits the subject as a term in a process, which is co-extensive with both power and the resistance to it. Narrativity is a crucial binding force here, but I interpret it as a collective, politically-invested process of sharing in and contributing to the making of myths, operational fictions, significant figurations of the kind of subjects we are in the process of becoming. This notion of narrativity cannot be adequately contained within the semiological paradigm but needs to be embedded and embodied in a form of neo-materialism.

In this perspective, 'subjectivity' names the process that consists in stringing the reactive (*potestas*) and the active instances of power (*potentia*) together, under the fictional unity of a grammatical 'I'. The subject is a process, made of constant shifts and negotiations between different levels of power and desire, that is to say wilful choice and unconscious drives. Whatever semblance of unity there may be, is no God-given essence, but rather the fictional choreography of many levels into one socially operational self. It implies that what sustains the entire process of becoming-subject is the will to know, the desire to say, the desire to speak; it is a founding, primary, vital, necessary and therefore original desire to become.

Body materiality and sexual difference

Sexual difference theory, far from being a reactive or critical kind of thought, is also an affirmative one in that it expresses the feminist political passion for both social change and in-depth transformations of the subject. In my vision, feminists posit themselves as female subjects, that is to say not as disembodied entities but rather as corporeal and consequently sexed beings. The female feminist subject starts with the revaluation of the bodily roots of subjectivity, rejecting any universal, neutral and consequently gender-free understanding of human embodiment. The feminism of sexual difference should be read as emphasizing the political importance of desire as opposed to the will, and of its role in the constitution of the subject. Not just libidinal desire, but rather ontological desire, the desire to be, the tendency of the subject to be, the predisposition of the subject towards being. More on this in chapter 4.

The subject of feminism is thus sexed; he or she is motivated by the political consciousness of inequalities and is committed to asserting diversity and difference as a positive and alternative value. The feminist subject of knowledge is an intensive, multiple subject, functioning in a net of interconnections. I would add that it is rhizomatic (that is to say non-unitary, non-linear, web-like), embodied and therefore perfectly artificial; as an artifact it is machine-like, complex, endowed with multiple capacities for interconnectedness in the impersonal mode. It is abstract and perfectly, operationally, real, and one of the main fields of operation is sexual difference. The 'feminine' for Irigaray is neither one essentialized entity, nor an immediately accessible one: it is rather a virtual reality, in the sense that it is the effect of a project, a political and conceptual project of transcending the traditional ('Molar') subject-position of Woman as Other of the Same, so as to express the other of the Other. This transcendence, however, occurs through the flesh, in embodied locations and not in a flight away from them.

The material/maternal roots of subjectivity

Central to sexual difference theory is the insight that the root of the term materialism is *mater*. This implies that the material as the primary and constitutive site of *origin* of the subject, is also the instance that expresses the specificity of the female subject, and as such it needs to be thought out systematically. In the perspective of radical feminist bodily materialism, it is the primary matter and the foundation stone, whose silent presence installs the master in his monologic phallogocentric mode. The feminism of sexual difference argues that women have borne both materially and symbolically the costs of the masculine privilege of autonomous self-definition: they have been physically and symbolically dispossessed of a place from whence to speak. This led to Irigaray's assertion (1974) that sexual difference is that last utopia of our culture, that is to say *u-topos*, the nowhere, or that which so far has had no place for expression. Irigaray has a different emphasis: she reminds us that the material/maternal is the instance that expresses the specificity of female sexuality (Whitford 1991), the sense of a female humanity, and also of her divinity.

Irigaray also significantly points out, however, that the term 'utopia' also contains a temporal dimension, i.e. it means 'not yet', that which has not yet come to pass. This 'not yet' is for Irigaray the virtual feminine, the 'other of the Other', the collectively empowered, self-defined feminist subject. This is embedded in the collective feminist practice which aims at making a difference, that is to say at turning difference into the positive, empowering affirmation of alternative subject-positions for and by female feminist women. The quest for an alternative female genealogy is crucial to this project (Irigaray 1987, 1989), by immersion into the maternal imaginary. For Irigaray this takes the form of the exploration of images that represent the female experience of proximity to the mother's body. This opening out of the feminine towards religious or mystical experiences is central to Irigaray's notion of the 'sensible transcendental', to which I will return.

There is no sentimentality involved in this reappraisal of the maternal/material feminine. Irigaray acknowledges that motherhood is also the site of women's capture into the specular logic of the Same, which makes her subservient to the Masculine. Maternity, however, is also a resource for women to explore carnal modes and perception, of empathy and interconnectedness that go beyond the economy of phallogocentrism. I see this 'other' maternal feminine in Irigaray as linked to the political project of providing symbolic representation for the female feminist subject as a virtual subject-position that needs to be created and activated. Tamsin Lorraine (1999) quite rightly sees it as the expression of Irigaray's committment to rethinking the 'corporeal' as well as the 'conceptual' logics of the subject and to harmonize them within an immanent subject of 'becoming-woman' (1999: 222): 'For Irigaray the intrauterine space is an anoedipal space, a space of plenitude rather than lack, singularity rather than universality, and the interactive attunement of singularities rather than the grid of social positioning that pertains to all. The umbilical cord represents desire for this anoedipal space.' As Rouch had suggested (1987), the material/maternal feminine can provide alternative figurations of intersubjectivity, for instance through the complex symbiotic relationship between mother and child. The placenta as well as the umbilical cord can function as an alternative way of figuring interconnectedness. The latter has not escaped the attention of science-fiction writers and filmmakers who have projected the foetus into outer space, superimposing it on the image of the human attached to the spaceship as he floats in the immensity. Thus even the most traditional image, that of mother and child, can be repossessed by strategic repetitions or revisitations, for Irigaray, and by becoming de-stratified and de-territorialized, for Deleuze. The matrix, never static at any point in history, is now set in nomadic motion both in mainstream culture and in the many oppositional counter-cultures of today. I shall return to this in chapters 4 and 5.

Poststructuralist theories of sexual difference become clearer if contrasted to other brands of feminist philosophy. For instance, in the high Hegelian mode of the previous generation of feminist theory, for Beauvoir, Woman as the antithesis of the system carries a *yet unrepresented* value, which is misrepresented by male-dominated culture. Deconstructing the dialectical mode of representing gender through the binary Masculine/Feminine couple amounts to a critique of the false universalism of the masculine subject. In poststructuralism, in fact, the subject-position is seen as coinciding with consciousness, universality, masculine agency and entitlement. By dialectical opposition, Woman as the Other of this subject is deprived of all these attributes. She is thus reduced to unrepresentability within the male symbolic system, be it by lack, by excess or by perennial displacement of her subject-positions. Even feminine sexuality is defined by Irigaray (1997) as not-one, that is to say multiple and complex and ex-centric to phallic genitality. This theoretical premise leads to a political conclusion: through the strategy of mimetic repossession of the feminine by feminist women, a political process is set up that aims at bringing the 'other of the Other' into representation. This is what I have called the 'virtual feminine' of sexual difference feminism. In poststructuralist or sexual-difference feminism, materialism is linked both to embodiment and to sexual difference, and the link is made by the political will and determination to find a better, a more adequate, representation of female corporeal reality, not as given but as virtual, that is as a process and a project. In this line of feminist thought, great care is taken to disengage the question of the embodied subject from the hold of both orthodox Lacanian psychoanalysis and Marxism – the two fundamental intellectual bureaucracies of the last century (as Deleuze so rightly calls them). A vision of materialism as embodied materiality is proposed instead. In so doing, Irigaray intersects with the Deleuzian project, especially his concept of the an-organic body, or body without organs.

As Chanter put it, Irigaray 'brings the body back into play, not as the rock of feminism, but as a mobile set of differences' (Chanter 1995: 46). The body is then an interface, a threshold, a field of intersecting material and symbolic forces; it is a surface where multiple codes (race, sex, class, age, etc.) are inscribed; it is a cultural construction that capitalizes on energies of a heterogeneous, discontinuous and unconscious nature. The body which, for Beauvoir, was one's primary 'situation', in reality is now seen as a situated self, as an embodied positioning of the self. This renewed sense of complexity aims to stimulate anew a revision and redefinition of contemporary subjectivity. This vision of the body contains sexuality as a process and as a constitutive element.

I want to stress the importance of sexuality in feminist thought, where it is perceived critically as the site of power, struggles and contradictions. But it is re-visited creatively precisely because of its crucial importance as a site of constitution of the subject. In other words, the sexed female feminist is both the subject around which feminists have gathered in their recognition of a general condition, and it is also the concept that needs to be analysed critically and eventually deconstructed.

This means that the quest for a point of exit from phallogocentric definitions of Woman requires a strategy of working through the images and representations that the (masculine) knowing subject has created of Woman as Other: the strategy of 'mimesis'. Irigaray mimes the undifferentiated universalist bias of the subject. She consequently recognizes the positions to which 'the feminine' has been assigned by patriarchal thought – the eternal 'Other (of the Same)' – but only in order to undo it. She refuses to separate the symbolic, discursive dimension from the empirical, material or historical one and thus does not dissociate the debate about the 'feminine' from the presence of real-life women. Her mimetic relationship to the subject, far from being biologically deterministic, exposes and critiques the essentialism of phallogocentric discourse. Irigaray's politics assumes that the subversion of identity acquires sex-specific connotations and that consequently it requires sex-specific strategies. In my adaptation of Irigaray's textual and political strategy of 'mimesis', I have argued that it is an affirmative form of deconstruction. That means that it amounts to a collective repossession of the images and representations of Woman as they have been coded in language, culture, science, knowledge and discourse and consequently internalized in the heart, mind, body and lived experience of women. Mimetic repetition of this imaginary and material institution of femininity is the active subversion of established modes of phallogocentric representation and expression of women's experience which tend to reduce it to unrepresentability. The mimetic reassertion of sexual difference challenges the century-old identifications of the thinking subject with the universal and of both of them with the masculine. The feminism of sexual difference challenges such encompassing generalizations and posits as radically other a female, sexed, thinking subject, who stands in an asymmetrical relationship to the masculine. Repetition engenders difference, for if there is no symmetry between the sexes, it follows that the feminine as experienced and expressed by women is as yet unrepresented, having been colonized by the male imaginary. Women must therefore speak the feminine, they must think it and represent it in their own terms; read with Deleuze, this is an active process of becoming. Under the heading of the 'double syntax', Irigaray defends this irreducible and irreversible difference and proposes it as the condition of possibility for an alternative vision of women's subjectivity and sexuality. What then becomes central is the political and conceptual task of creating, legitimating and representing a multi-centred, internally differentiated female feminist subjectivity, without falling into relativism or fragmentation. The politics of location come into play here: if it is the case that the material/maternal site is primary and constitutive of the subject, it can also be turned in to a location of resistance.

Here the distinction between will and desire becomes fundamental: because the implications of the phallogocentric institutionalization of sexuality are written on or in our bodies, they are complex in that they are enfleshed. Feminists cannot hope therefore merely to cast off their sexed identity like an old garment. Discursive practices, imaginary identifications or ideological beliefs are tattooed on bodies and thus are constitutive of embodied subjectivities. Thus, women who yearn for change cannot shed their old skins like snakes. This kind of in-depth change requires instead great care and attention. It also needs to be timed carefully in order to become sustainable, that is to say in order to avoid lethal shortcuts through the complexities of one's embodied self. In this respect, the analysis of *W*oman in opposition to but also in complicity with real-life women activates the distinction that separates institution or representation (*W*oman) from experience (women). This distinction opens up a space for a feminist repossession or redefinition of subjectivity. This amounts to no less than a change of civilization, of genealogy, of a sense of history. Feminist counter-genealogies are the inroads to a new symbolic system by women. As Irigaray put it: it is not a matter of changing specific items within a horizon already defined as 'our common humanity', but rather of changing the horizon itself. It is a matter of understanding that our interpretation of 'identity' is theoretically and practically incorrect (Irigaray 1991: 167).

This is the 'virtual feminine' which I set in opposition to Woman as Other-than or different-from, that is to say, specularly connected to the Same as its devalued Other. Sexual difference as a political practice is constructed in a non-Hegelian framework whereby identity is not postulated in dialectical opposition to a necessarily devalorized other. There is no such negation: it rather rests upon the working through of many differences between, among and within women. I see 'differences among women' as being constitutive of the category of sexual difference and not exterior or antithetical to it (Frye 1996).

The sexual politics of this project are clear, albeit complex. For Irigaray it is about how to identify and enact points of exit from the universal mode defined by man, towards a radical version of heterosexuality, that is to say the full recognition of the specificities of each sexed subject position (Irigaray 1990, 1993). More specifically, she wonders how to elaborate a site, that is to say a space and a time, for the irreducibility of sexual difference to express itself, so that the masculine and feminine libidinal economies may co-exist in the positive expression of their respective differences. This positivity is both horizontal/terrestrial and vertical/celestial and it entails the (re)thinking through of gender-specific relations to space, time and the interval between the sexes, so as to avoid polarizing oppositions. Issues of 'other differences', notably religion, nationality, language and ethnicity are crucial to this project and integral to the task of evolving towards the recognition of the positivity of difference. Figurations are essential to this political project.

This radically heterosexual project, however, is not heterosexist, nor does it imply the dismissal of homosexual love. E. Grosz for instance refers to Irigaray's advocacy of a 'tactical homosexuality modeled on the corporeal relations of the pre-oedipal daughter to the mother' (Grosz 1994b: 338). This mother-daughter bond aims at exploring and reclaiming bodily pleasures and contacts that have been eradicated from their memory. It thus becomes a tool for undoing the Oedipal plot and allows them to experiment with different approaches to their morphology. Grosz concludes: 'It provides a model of homosexuality not as a substitute for heterosexuality but as its disavowed prerequisite. It makes explicit the intolerable threat of women's desire within a culture founded on its denial' (Grosz 1994b: 338). Although this can be empowering for female homosexual identity, I think it important to stress that Irigaray remains a heterosexual thinker. This constitutes the core of Wittig's and Butler's critique of Irigaray, to which I will return later.

Irigaray is especially keen to prevent the assimilation of female homosexuality to a phallic mode of dialectical opposition to the other and thus of masculine identification. Nor is she dupe to the illusion that a mere choice of another woman as object of desire is enough to allow a woman to escape from the phallic clutches. In either case (homo or hetero), Irigaray is not prescriptive – she just emphasizes the need for a space of experimentation by women of their desires and specific sexual morphology. Men are called upon to do the same: to reclaim a non-phallic sexuality and re-signify their desires. Sexual difference cuts both ways. The real difference – which produces the ethical passion of 'wonder' (Irigaray 1984) – is the escape from sexual sameness, i.e., identification with male phallicity.

I want to defend sexual difference as a theory and a political practice that rests upon and exploits a number of constitutive contradictions, the answer to which can be formal in a logical sense (Frye 1996), but also practical in the sense of pointing to a solution in praxis, in 'doing'. In my reading, Irigaray's version of materialism deliberately and self-consciously addresses a number of paradoxes that are constitutive of feminist theory at the turn of the century. Sexual difference theory simultaneously produces and destabilizes the category 'woman'. It binds together both the notions of embodiment and of sexual difference and the link between the two is made by the political will and determination to find a better, a more adequate, representation of embodied female subjectivity. In this line of thought, great care is taken to disengage the question of the embodied subject from the hold of naturalistic assumptions and to emphasize instead the social and discursive formation of embodied materiality.

Feminist affirmation of sexual difference goes hand in hand with the rejection not only of essentialist identities, but also of the dialectics of negation as the logic of constitution of the subject. Sexual difference thus brings into representation the play of multiple differences that structure the subject: these are neither harmonious nor homogeneous, but rather internally differentiated. Therefore sexual differences force us to think the simultaneity of potentially contradictory social, discursive and symbolic effects. These multiple 'differences within' can and must be analysed in terms of power-relations; they constitute overlapping variables that cut across any monolithic understanding of the subject: class, race, ethnicity, religion, age, lifestyle, sexual preferences. In other words, one 'speaks as' a woman in order to be politically empowered to act as one, according to the terms of the paradox outlined above. It is a way of acknowledging an identity which can then be put to the task of its own emancipation. The political gesture consists firstly in situating oneself at the crest of the contradictions that are constitutive of the social and symbolic position of women, and secondly in activating them towards the destabilization of the socio-symbolic system and more especially of the asymmetrical power-relations that sustain it. Because of this, I see it as perfectly suitable to a nomadic vision of subjectivity.

The transatlantic disconnection

Considering the wealth, political charge and sophistication of sexual difference theory, I do wonder why its reception has been so mixed. Sexual difference is a very pragmatic political philosophy of the subject, which takes sexuality as a major point of reference. In the light of this commitment to empowering women, it seems very puzzling to me that so many feminists have rejected the emphasis on the feminine as alternatively too obvious, too deterministic or too irrelevant. It makes me think that 'femino-phobia' is alive and well, even among feminists. By the late 1990s, in academic and especially philosophical circles, the theory was marginal at best, half-forgotten and in general assessed negatively. As Tina Chanter (1995) brilliantly argues, the ideas of Irigaray and of sexual difference have received quite a superficial reception in the USA; opposition to it generally coalesced around the concept of 'gender', which was constructed in direct opposition to Continental theories of sexual difference. I find that the charges made against sexual difference (Felski 1997) are very similar to the general critiques that are made of poststructuralism across the big transatlantic divide. They rest on three crucial points: essentialism (sexual difference is allegedly a-historical and deterministic and thus leaves no room for social change); universalism (it makes over-general claims and disregards cultural diversity) and heterosexism (it plays down the creative subversive force of lesbian and homosexual desire). I do think it important to stop and ponder about the nature of the opposition to sexual difference instead of just putting it down to 'misreadings' and basic lack of familiarity with Continental philosophy.

Some contextual considerations come immediately to mind. The North American reception of sexual difference in philosophy – as opposed to literary and cultural theories – was often reductive and often ill informed. Tina Chanter makes this point:

> The likes of Hegel, Heidegger, and Derrida were regarded at best, with mild suspicion, at worst as charlatans who had little to say about the real world – little more than a series of self-indulgent esoteric musings. The result was that Kristeva and Irigaray were judged in terms of the liberal discourse of equal rights and the ideal of sameness that, however inexplicit, tended to accompany it. Not surprisingly, French feminists were found wanting by these standards. (Chanter 1995: 35)

Moreover, the historical context for the philosophical reception of these theories in the USA was far from ideal. Whereas the 1980s in Europe was a period of expansion of social democracy that saw the collapse of the Berlin Wall, in the USA it was the era of Reagan and Star Wars: a period of generalized backlash which was hardly favourable to critical thought. While on the Continent feminism was experimenting with writing, eroticism, and the exploration of ways and means of making difference as effective tools for social policy and legislation, in the USA the 1980s was the era of the feminist 'sex-wars'. Documented by scholars like Hester Eisenstein (1983), Carol Vance (1984) and Ann Snitow (1983), the American feminist discussion on sexuality took a very negative turn. Monopolized by the quarrel over pornography and prostitution, sexuality came to be identified with issues of violence and domination, that is to say negatively. This was the case with campaigners like Andrea Dworkin, as well as in the polemical and often parodic reappraisal of sexual transgression by the lesbian sado-masochists and eloquently expressed by Pat Califia (1988) and other sexual radicals. The mainstream 'liberal feminist' organizations like NOW (National Organization of Women) increasingly skirted the issue, focusing instead on the socio-political and economic agenda. Exit sex.

In her analysis of the backlash feminism, significantly called 'American Gothic', Margaret Walters (1997) singles out the repressive moralism and the anti-sexuality campaign initiated by MacKinnon and Dworkin (1976) as a specific form of internal backlash and a threat against feminism. In Walters' estimate, American feminism through the nineties made sexuality the sole and central source of women's oppression. This results in under-playing the more structural elements of patriarchal power; it also denigrates women's capacity for sexual agency and self-determination.

This left all issues related to bodies, pleasures, eroticism and the specific ways of knowing of the human flesh hanging nowhere. Jane Gallop (1997), in one of the most remarkable cartographies of the era of the sexwars, denounced the situation. She criticizes the extent of the sexophobic approach to the body which led some of the anti-pornography feminist campaigners to strike an alliance with the right-wing Moral Majority in order to ban pornography and criminalize prostitution. Gallop also points out that this wave of aggression could not fail to affect the women's movement from within. Gallop defends a position that I partly share, namely that in the USA in the 1990s, sexual harassment has replaced pornography as the key feminist issue. Both have produced what strikes me as a dogmatic and primitive type of feminist practice, which stigmatizes sexuality. I share the belief that this is yet another form of repressing women's desires.

The other significant point Gallop makes, though she pushes it to conclusions about sexuality in the classroom that I do not share entirely, is that the feminist pursuit of knowledge mobilizes the whole of the woman's self – body as well as mind. There is a fundamental aspiration towards non-dualistic thinking in feminist theory, a rejection of binaries on theoretical as well as political grounds. Feminist consciousness re-unites that which has been disconnected under patriarchy; knowledge and/as pleasure therefore become all one. 'I learnt that desire, even desire unacted upon, can make you feel very powerful. And the place where I learned desire – where it filled me with energy and drive – I call feminism' (Gallop 1997: 19).

In his analysis of Gallop's case of lesbian sexual harassment, Patton (2000) adopts a Deleuzian frame, which produces an interesting and positive assessment of the case. Arguing, with Spinoza and Deleuze, that the empowering notion of sexuality which Gallop defends entails a positive experience of power, Patton concludes that desire, in such a collective encounter between teacher and students, coincides with a mutual increase in the capacity to act in the world: a kind of rise in the degree of one's *potentia*, or joyful affirmation of one's enjoyment of being of and in the world alongside others. Patton concludes with a very ethical statement:

> Gallop's experience shows how the feeling of power obtained by contributing to the power of others may be indistinguishable from an intense experience of desire, and vice versa. If this is so, then it matters little whether we speak of desire or the feeling of power. What matters is the manner in which we act upon the actions of others, and the kinds of assemblage in which and through which we desire.

Unfortunately, this not being the best of all possible worlds, Gallop's joyful experimentation with desire, knowledge and power resulted in a law-suit against her. *Potestas* and its corollary of negative passions strike back. Gallop emphasizes that it is an aberration to target feminist knowledge practices and the sexual experimentation which they entail for sexual harassment lawsuits. After all, such legal action was intended to stop abuses of power and disadvantage, not as an end to sexuality and pleasure. Sexual harassment cases are all the more violent when they take place among women, especially feminist women across the generational student–teacher divide.

I must admit that a European feminist reading Gallop's account of a sexual harassment law-suit by lesbian students against their bisexual professor does lead one to wonder if she has landed on a different planet. As a matter of fact, throughout the nineties sexuality in the USA lost ground in the political arena but it scored highly in the courts of law. Racialization was built into this script: witness the escalation of sexual harassment lawsuits from Mike Tyson to O.J. Simpson, to culminate in the string of White House 'white trash' sex scandals up to the Monica Lewinsky case. Be this as it may, if I were to attempt a translation of this into the language of feminist theory, I would say that 'the body' in USA feminism cannot be positively associated with sexuality in either the critical or the public discourse. Sexuality, which is the fundamental paradigm in the critical discourses of psychoanalysis and poststructuralism, simply has no place in American political discourse: it became side-lined, erased or strangled. Moreover, by virtue of the climate of political conservatism on the one hand, and on the other the increasing importance of legal litigation in American public and political life, the debate around sexuality was cast in the USA almost exclusively in terms of social rights. However crucial issues of right and entitlement may be to the discussions of sexuality, I think they are far from providing adequate cover for the complexities and the diversity of feminist discourses and practices of sexuality. In such a context it is not surprising that Europe-based theories of sexuality, psychoanalysis and sexual difference, which proved so inspirational in literary theory, struck at best a marginal, 'radical chic' note in philosophical and social theory circles. What chance, then, did Irigaray have?

The state of gender theory did the rest. In mainstream American feminist discourse, the sex/gender dichotomy swung with a vengeance towards the pole of gender, embracing it under the joint cover of liberal individual 'rights' and social constructivist 'change'. Neither sex nor sexuality were high on the list. It was left to the gay, lesbian and queer campaigners to try to rewrite sexuality into the feminist agenda. In this framework, sexuality is almost always synonymous with transgression. For instance, T. de Lauretis (1994) returns to issues of psychoanalytic desire in order to provide a foundational theory for lesbian desire as something specific in its 'perverse' and non-procreative or non-maternalist logic. Judith Butler (1990) also makes an important intervention, pointing out that the distinction sex/gender is, in fact, untenable. If anything, argues Butler, it is the always already sexualized matter that constructs the possibility of this dichotomy in the first place. I will return to this point.

A proper, scholarly, comparative analysis of the transatlantic disconnec-tion about sexuality in the eighties and nineties and of the ways in which it fuelled the opposition between 'gender' and 'sexual difference' would deserve more time and care than I can give it here.[2] In any case, at the dawn of the new millennium, it is accepted that gender has become too polyvalent as a concept to be universally really helpful (Hawkesworth 1997). This implies that the understanding of 'sexual difference' that emerges from American poststructuralist feminism, be it Butler, de Lauretis or Scott – and that which generates from the Continental tradition – are not merely polemically at odds with each other, but also conceptually different. The term 'sexual difference' in each of these traditions neither means the same, nor refers to similar theoretical assumptions. As Butler recently noted (1999), her own poststructuralist reflection grows from and feeds on the Anglo-American sociological and anthropological tradition of sex/gender. It thus differs con-siderably from the French accounts of sexual difference. This constitutive ambivalence makes for an interesting case of a location that appears as Eurocentric in the USA and as highly Americanized in Europe. Far from pleading for any purity in the matter, I think that these nomadic streaks in contemporary feminist theory are very positive and could be explored and exploited further. In order to do this, however, I think we need cartographies, that is to say embedded and embodied genealogical accounts of our own respective theoretical practices. We also need open and fair discussions. This could lay the grounds for a new set of transatlantic exchanges in the context of a culture that is becoming 'g-local' also within feminism.

The American reception of sexual difference is framed by reference to gender theories and more especially on the sex/gender paradigm best exemplified by Gayle Rubin's interpretation of Levi-Strauss's paradigm of the exchange of women and its role in the constitution of the patriarchal order. In this conceptual framework, 'gender' refers specifically to the heterosexist matrix of power which constructs personal identities, social relations and symbolic representations. As Butler put it: 'normative sexuality fortifies normative gender' (1999: xi), hence her politically-minded question of analysing how gender hierarchy supports compulsory heterosexuality. Accordingly, 'sex' becomes an effect of gender and therefore sexual difference is just a consequence of large power-relations that encompass all kinds of other variables. This framework differs considerably from classical social-constructivist definitions of gender. It is also noticeably antagonistic, however, to poststructuralist emphasis on the primacy of *sexuality* and therefore of sexual difference as a socio-symbolic institution that effects the subject-construction. Gayle Rubin's focus on the heterosexist matrix of power differs seriously from my understanding of sexuality and of its role in shaping identities. In the Continental tradition I claim as my legacy, the Anglo-American 'sex/ gender' distinction is far less relevant than the complex, interactive and power-driven web of relations around the sexuality/sex nucleus.

In her important critique of the sex/gender distinction, Moira Gatens (1996) stresses the extent to which gender theory tacitly assumes a passive body on which special codes are imprinted. Thus, the social-psychology-inspired model of gender is diametrically opposed to the insights of psychoanalysis. The points of divergence concern firstly the structure of human embodiment: passive for gender theory, dynamic and interactive for poststructuralist theory. Secondly, the notion of sexuality and of its role in the constitution of subjectivity which is of great importance for poststructuralism, is not so for social-psychological gender theories. I think it is precisely the priority given to the sexual as the site of subject-formation that makes feminist thinkers like Irigaray, Grosz, Chanter, Gatens, myself and others state the constitutive and primary importance of sexual difference.

In my reading of poststructuralist philosophies of difference, from Foucault to Irigaray and Deleuze, the main emphasis falls on the material, sexualized structure of the subject. This sexual fibre is intrinsically and multiply connected to social and political relations; thus, it is anything but an individualistic entity. Sexuality as a social and symbolic, material and semiotic institution is singled out as the primary location of power, in a complex manner which encompasses both macro- and micro-relations. Sexual difference – the sexualized bipolarity, is merely a social implementation of the political economy of sexualized identities, which is another word for power in both its negative or repressive (*potestas*) and positive or empowering (*potentia*) meaning. Sex is the social and morphological assignation of identity and suitable form of erotic agency to subjects that are socialized and sexualized in the polarized dualistic model of the special institutions of Masculinity/Femininity. Gender is a generic term to describe the kind of power-mechanisms involved in this complex interplay of forces. With Deleuze, I would say that gender dualism is the position of the Majority, who thus consolidate the interests of an Oedipalized political economy that structures our material and imaginary social framework. I will return to this.

The point here is that, far from marginalizing sexuality, in my conceptual framework it is a central point of reference which acts as the matrix for power-relations in the broad but also most intimate sense of the term. The theoretical genealogy that I claim runs from Levi-Strauss through to Lacan and beyond. In this line, sex/gender is not as relevant a distinction as sexuality/sex, and consequently also sexual difference as a distributor and organizer of social and symbolic differences. Again, the comparison with social-psychologically-inspired gender theories is important. For poststructuralist thought, sexuality is the constitutive socio-symbolic cast in which human subjectivity is thrown. It is dynamically interrelated to cultural codes and therefore co-extensive with questions of power, in both the reactive (negative) and affirmative (positive) sense. I do think that this conceptual dissymmetry is crucial to the transatlantic exchanges around the paradoxes of materialism. I would like to propose that instead of letting this important discussion sink into stale polemics, more attention should be paid to the respective differences between the sex and gender and the sexuality and sex paradigm. What is at stake is a hard-core theoretical difference, not just a matter of terminology. It is a divergence well worth exploring.

Gender materialism

The tradition of gender materialism refers back to Simone de Beauvoir, who made significant interventions to disengage materialism from the double burden of its opposition to idealism and its dependence on Marxist theories of historical materialism. Caught in the transatlantic disconnection, Beauvoir's work becomes framed in ways which are often contradicted by her own texts (Moi 1994). Beauvoir's work is also caught in the debate which, since the 1980s (Duchen 1986), has opposed the neo-materialism of Monique Wittig (1973, 1979a and b) and Christine Delphy (1975 and 1984) to the strategic essentialism of the sexual difference theorists Hélène Cixous (1975, 1977, 1986a and b, 1987) and, more importantly, Luce Irigaray (1974, 1977, 1980, 1984, 1987a, 1987b, 1989, 1990). I shall explore this in more detail.

Wittig is one of the major spokeswomen of the French materialist school which launched the campaign of denigration of sexual difference (Fuss 1989). She was among the first to coin the term 'essentialism' to refer pejoratively to the kind of feminism that took into account the unconscious, sexual difference and feminine writing, that is to say the whole repertoire of feminist poststructuralism. Paradoxically enough, her work as a creative writer, especially her novel *Le Corps lesbien* (Wittig 1973), contributed greatly to the radical redefinition of female sexuality and lesbian desire. She is, however, opposed to the emphasis that both Cixous and Irigaray place on what they carefully define as 'female homosexual libidinal economy', and the specificity of feminine morphology, sensibility, sexuality and creativity, especially writing that goes with it.

Wittig builds on the classic sex/gender distinction and turns it into a radical critique of heterosexism. She emphasizes the need to free female sexuality from its subjugation to the signifier *W*oman. In her view *W*oman as the privileged other of the patriarchal imaginary is an idealized construction of the same order as the Phallus: it is a man-made notion and as such is ideologically contaminated and untrustworthy. Wittig radicalizes de Beauvoir's point about the constructed nature of femininity. She proposes that we dismiss the signifier woman as epistemologically and politically inadequate, and suggests that we replace it with the category of 'lesbian'. The lesbian is not a woman because a lesbian has subtracted herself from identities based on the Phallus.

Wittig's position, while attractive in that it aims at empowering women, is problematic in that it universalizes the lesbian into a new model of normativity. This leaves no room for alternative definitions of lesbianism, such as, for instance, A. Rich's idea of the lesbian continuum (1985) and Irigaray's notion of a 'female homosexual libidinal economy' (1977). Moreover it certainly excludes a priori the possibility of freely chosen or optional heterosexuality. This option is seen as co-extensive with domination and it consequently leads to voluntary servitude, a position that is reminiscent of Andrea Dworkin (1976) and the most extreme anti-sexuality wing of USA feminism.

As Antoinette Fouque (1982) astutely observed, the opposition is paradoxical: on the one hand female sexuality as the foundational theory for a new vision of subjectivity (sexual difference) and on the other, a radical anti-foundationalism that results in the ultimate dismissal of the feminine (lesbian neo-materialism). I prefer to define these as two opposing strategies of deconstruction of traditional femininity: on the one hand, the strategy of extreme sexualization through embodied female subjectivity: Irigaray's 'transcendence via radical immanence', on the other hand the rejection of femininity as the heterosexual power-matrix in favour of a position 'beyond gender'. To these different positions there correspond different understandings of 'materialism': for Irigaray it has to do with *mater*/matter and the sexed body, hence her emphasis on morphology, but also verticality or transcendence; for Wittig it is a naive social constructivism which paradoxically works with an idealist position on language and social changes.

Both the gender materialism and the bodily materiality of sexual difference aim at empowering women to act as authoritative speaking subjects, but they do not go the same way about it. Irigaray works through affirmative deconstruction, Wittig through her conviction of the potentials of the plasticity of language. Contrary to Irigaray, who sees the subject-position as structurally masculine, Wittig believes that women can enter into the subject-position and repossess it and redefine it for their own purposes. Wittig therefore encourages women to use language to express their own meanings, without falling into the deconstructive complexities of Irigaray's 'écriture féminine' or quests for an alternative symbolic. In other words, she is vehemently anti-poststructuralist in rejecting two key ideas: the structure of the non-unitary or split subject and the constitutive non-transparency of language.

Wittig's work has proved inspirational for the lesbian and queer theories that have developed in the USA. Thus, Butler emphasizes the fact that for Wittig 'gender' is not a substantive reality, but rather an activity. Inspired by Rubin, she then proceeds to re-interpret Wittig's notion of 'gender' as a performative utterance that constructs categories such as 'sex', 'women', 'men', 'nature' for the specifically political purpose of reproducing compulsory heterosexuality. Gender is the process by which women are marked off as 'the female sex', men are conflated with the universal and both of them are subjugated to the institution, as defined by Foucault (1977a), and of compulsory heterosexuality, as defined by Rich (1985). In so far as the lesbian refuses this process, she is subversive because she problematizes the whole scheme of sexuality. The strategy supported by Wittig is, according to Butler, to allow other kinds of gendered identities to proliferate: the lesbian is the first step towards exploding the monolithic structures of gender.

All other differences notwithstanding, Butler retains from Wittig two crucial notions, which she opposes to the feminism of sexual difference. The first one is that gender is performative: it creates the very categories and sexed identities which it purports to explain. Having taken over from Wittig the idea of the co-extensivity of gender with the regulatory discourse of heterosexuality, Butler develops a hermeneutics of suspicion against the notion of 'gender' – and more especially towards the category of 'women' as the foundation of feminist politics. Butler emphasizes both the normativity and the limitations of the category 'women' which fails to be exhaustive simply because gender intersects with 'racial, class, ethnic, sexual and regional modalities of discursively constituted identities' (1991: 3).

Consequently, Butler aims at elaborating a 'critical genealogy of the category woman' to contest and prevent the reification of female identity. The key question then becomes: 'what kind of subversive repetition might call into question the regulatory practice of identity itself?' (1990: 32). Butler proposes a strategy of parodic repetition, that is, the politically motivated exposure of the masquerade. Differently from Wittig, though in the same vein, – Butler proposes that we explode the category 'women' by letting many other alternative genders proliferate: not one, not two, but as many genders as there are individuals. Not just lesbian, the ex-woman will be trans-sexually dislocated in many possible directions: if biology is not destiny, if the body is construction, then any sex goes. Butler concludes in a more cautious tone, speaking in the conditional tense about the politics of the parody, and asking what feminist politics *would* look like if genders *were* allowed to proliferate so as to explode the classical binarism. She takes her distance from Wittig, as she does from Irigaray; for reasons of universalism, both universalize something: Wittig the lesbian, Irigaray the woman. What Butler longs for is a strategy by which she can leave behind the regulatory fictions of sexuality – this is her particular brand of political utopia. In the long run, she may be closer to Foucault than to any feminist thinker.

Recently Butler has re-adjusted her position and, with the privilege of hindsight, has shown much more sensitivity to the role that fantasies, personal histories and unconscious factors play in fastening an embodied subject on a certain kind of sexuality. She has stated (1999: xiv): 'The performance of gender subversion can indicate nothing about sexuality or sexual practice. Gender can be rendered ambiguous without disturbing or reorienting normative sexuality at all. Sometimes gender ambiguity can operate precisely to contain or deflect non-normative sexual practice and thereby work to keep normative sexuality intact.' It would be indeed naive to believe that the mere rejection or destabilization of gender dualism is exclusively or necessarily a subversive position. I think that a great deal of contemporary conservative or neo-liberal discourse takes the form of a spurious celebration of 'differences' in the pluralistic mode. Often cross-referring to biological or genetic sciences, the praise of plural differences is neither a sufficient nor a necessary pre-condition for the subversion of identity predicated on the sovereignty of the One and the political economy of the Same.

A telling example of what I would define as a conservative rejection of gender dualism for the purpose of erotic pleasures is Mario Vargas Llosa's diatribe against it (1997) in a chapter significantly called 'The rebellion of the clitorises'. Varga Llosa makes an interesting – albeit contradictory – argument: on the one hand he deflates the over-emphasis that is usually placed on morphological differences between the sexes. Having a penis or a clitoris is thus reduced to mere biological accident, or statistical data. On the other hand, Vargas Llosa turns gender pluralism into a weapon to defend the uniqueness of the individual as a socio-political entity.

Enlisting in support of his position the leading feminist epistemologist Anne Fausto-Sterling, Vargas Llosa defends at least five different genders, including different degrees of intersexuality. Faithful to his liberal attachment to individualism, Vargas Llosa takes gender plurality, or intersexuality, as evidence of the rich variety of the human species whose fundamental entitlement is to liberty.

In what strikes me as a flawed argument, Vargas Llosa wants his cake and eats it too: his defence of multiple genders barely conceals the sexual dualism that is intrinsic to the definition of the individual and of individual rights, which he defends. This indicates to me that there is nothing inherently subversive or even transformative at stake in this otherwise noble and erotic praise of multiple sexual pleasures. The numerical multiplication of gender options does nothing to alter the balance of power and the political economy of sexual dialectics, which is one of the motors of the phallogocentric regime. Moreover, I think that both sexuality and sexual difference are so central to the constitution of the subject that they cannot be eradicated merely by reversing socially-enforced gender roles. Instead, in-depth transformations or metamorphoses need to be enacted.

Against the revival of phallocentric gender pluralism, I think it important to move beyond polemical divides within feminism. Thus, I want to stress that the alleged distinction between the sex–gender and the sex–sexuality traditions of thought within feminism is not one between heterosexuality and lesbian theory, but it rather takes the form of a disagreement within lesbian theories and practices of female homosexuality. Sexual difference theorists like Cixous and Irigaray posit lesbian desire in a continuum with female sexuality, starting with the attachment to the mother. In the case of Irigaray, this is referred to the anti-Freudian tradition in psychoanalysis which tends to defend both the specificity of the female libido and, contrary to Melanie Klein's theory of aggression against the mother, the continuity between mother-love and lesbian desire. Cixous and Irigaray radicalize the idea suggested by Horney and Klein about the structuring power of the pre-Oedipal relationship to the mother, and also eroticize it fully. They break away from the Freud–Lacan line that over-emphasizes the figure of the father and the power of the Phallus in the constitution of human desire. In this tradition, female homosexuality is a necessary moment in the development of female sexual identity.

Of course, the various brands of this theory have quite different aims. Cixous argues for a magnificent and somewhat grandiose brand of female homosexual aesthetics rich in cosmological appeal. Irigaray, on the other hand, pleads for a radical brand of heterosexuality based on the mutual recognition of each sex by the other: in other words, a new feminist universal. They both agree, however, on the rejection of lesbianism as a separate identity, a distinct sexuality and a political subjectivity. Wittig, however, and recent works inspired by Wittig, such as de Lauretis, argue for the specificity of lesbian desire. This is disengaged from the continuum with female sexuality, psychoanalytic feminist renditions of female homosexuality and also desire for the mother. The disagreement rests on the notion of lesbian desire as the site of a possible epistemological break, or categorical divide. Wittig is militant about it: her assertion that the lesbian is somewhat outside the binary gender system and thus does not count as a woman being provocative at best. After this outrageous statement split the collective *Questions Féministes* in Paris, throwing historical Beauvoir-inspired feminists like Christine Delphy into the greatest disarray (Duchen 1986), Wittig emigrated to California and engaged in a very productive dialogue with de Lauretis, Butler and others.

Psychoanalysis minus the unconscious

Throughout the nineties, as Jacqueline Rose had predicted (1986), feminist theory has mastered the jargon of psychoanalysis while turning its back on the unconscious, thus taking a rationalistic and voluntaristic turn. Psychoanalysis is crucial in theorizing and representing a non-unitary vision of the subject, but in my reading it also highlights the enfleshed, sexed and contradictory nature of the human subject. Fantasies, desires and the pursuit of pleasure play as important and constructive a role in subjectivity as rational judgement and standard political action. I would like to try to reconnect the wilful agency required of politics with the respect that is due, both theoretically and ethically, to the affective, libidinal and therefore contradictory structures of the subject. Sexuality is crucial to this way of thinking about the subject, but unless it is coupled with some practice of the unconscious, though not necessarily of the Freudian kind, it cannot produce a workable vision of a non-unitary subject which, however complex, still hangs somehow together. Unconscious processes, memories, identifications and untapped affectivity are the invisible glue that sticks together that bundle of contradictions that is the subject.

I am not arguing here that psychoanalysis has all the answers, far from it, but it does leave some space for unconscious processes to play their role. Anticipating the anti-Freudian move that Deleuze and Guattari make in relation to the unconscious, I would like to point out, however, that whereas in the psychoanalytic tradition these internal crevices are often the stuff that nightmares and neuroses are made of, they need not be so. I would like to take the risk of arguing that internal or other contradictions and idiosyncrasies are indeed constituent elements of the subject, but they are not such a tragedy after all.

If it is the case that paradoxes and contradictions are historically constructed and socially embedded in practices of power and resistance, we may accept them with less anxiety (Scott 1996). I take the unconscious as the guarantee of non-closure in the practice of subjectivity. It undoes the stability of the unitary subject by constantly changing and redefining his or her foundations. I see it as a constant return of paradoxes, inner contradictions and internal idiosyncracies, which instill instability at the heart of the self. A nomadic subject is marked by a structural non-adherence to rules, roles and models. Taking unconscious structures into account is crucial for the whole practice of feminist subjectivity precisely because they allow for forms of disengagement and disidentification from the socio-symbolic institution of femininity.

How does dis-identification work? By opening up intervals, a sort of internal distance that allows one to take stock of one's position; a moment of stasis, an interval between the predictability of social models and the negotiations with one's sense of self. These in-between spaces, these spatial and temporal points of transition, are crucial to the construction of the subject and yet can hardly be rendered in thought and representation, given that they are what supports the process of thinking in the first place. The intervals, or in-between points and processes, are facilitators and, as such, they pass unnoticed, though they mark the crucial moments in the whole process of becoming a subject.

Social and cultural norms or normative models are external attractors, stimulants or points of reference. They act like magnets that draw the self heavily in certain directions and stimulate the person accordingly. The social imaginary functions in terms analogous to discursive glue that holds the bits and pieces together, but in a discontinuous and contradictory manner. I will not however approach the working of these 'ideological' formations following the classical Althusserian mode. Nor will I follow the schemes of social psychology and the kind of gender theory it has inspired. Thus, I do not see the impact of images or representations in terms of 'internalization', because I find this theory too dualistic in the way it splits the self from society, the 'inside' from the outside of the subject. I am far more interested instead in thinking about the extensive web of interconnections between the two. Power in the coercive or negative sense (*potestas*) as well as in the empowering or positive sense (*potentia*) is another name for this web of co-extensivity of self with society.

Accordingly, I would agree that a great deal of the 'appeal' of social roles or norms is clearly due to their coercive impact, but it is also the case that a lot of psychic space is willingly surrendered by the subject in the pursuit of social visibility and acceptance. This affects my understanding and assessment of the role and impact of the 'social imaginary' as a process of two-way flows between a nomadic subjectivity and a web-like field of social actualizations of potentially contradicting desires. By extension, interpellations of the conscious and the unconscious kind are heterogeneous and internally contradictory, but nonetheless formidable. Non-unitary identity implies a large degree of internal dissonance, that is to say, contradictions and paradoxes. Unconscious identifications play the role of magnets, building blocks or glue. They can also become equally active, however, in processes of resistance to social roles and norms. A political strategy of affirmative feminist mimesis requires the open-ended unconscious structures as an element that may be mobilized to enable the subject to take some distance from the socially imposed models. Desires are political and politics begins with our desires.

In other words the recognition of the non-coincidence of the subject with his or her consciousness need not be played back to the old familiar tune of anguish and panic at the thought of incipient psychosis or imminent implosion. Orthodox Lacanians like Kristeva have excelled of late in these panic exercises, whether it is in her analysis of horror and monstrous others, of ethnic diversity and, inevitably, of loss and melancholia. There is often a semi-religious tone of tragic solemnity in these accounts of the dangers of the collapse and destabilization of the self – not to speak of civilization – under the attack of the abject others who seem to creep in from everywhere. Any spectator of David Cronenberg's films will know, however, that this knee-jerk conservative reaction is eminently comic and it can be dispelled as easily as an outburst of laughter. Nostalgia is not merely politically conservative, but is also a deterrent to serious analysis of contemporary culture, as I will try to show in chapters 4 and 5.

I want to go on to defend the sexual difference approach because, as I have argued before, it combines wilful and unconscious elements in a manner that does justice to the complexity of the subject. Following Irigaray, the most adequate strategy consists in *working through* the stock of cumulated images, concepts and representations of women, of female identity, such as they have been codified by the culture we are in. If 'essence' means the historical sedimentation of many-layered discursive products, this stock of culturally coded definitions, requirements and expectations about women or female identity – this repertoire of regulatory fictions that are tattooed on our skins – then it would be false to deny that such an essence not only exists, but is also powerfully operational. History is everyone else's and hence also women's destiny. In other words, because of this history and because language is all we have, before we relinquish the signifier 'woman' we need to re-possess it, to revisit its multi-faceted complexities. These complexities define the one identity we share – as women. And that is the starting-point, however ambiguous and limited it may be. Consequently, the theoreticians of the radical dismissal of the signifier 'woman' in favour of lesbian or of multiple sexuality, strike me as being in a psychoanalytically *perverse* position – that is to say a position of wilful denial. Wittig should know that identity is not just volition, that the unconscious structures one's sense of identity through a series of *vital* (even when they are lethal, they are vital) identifications. The unconscious is imbued with traces of bodily morphology; thus feminists who are committed to bodily materialism should know better than to confuse wilful choice – political volition – with unconscious desire. Wittig's and Butler's attempt to undo the foundations for the politics of identity does not answer the question of subjectivity, i.e. of how one is also and primarily the subject of one's own unconscious. The corollary is that the way out of this psychic reality is not by wilful self-naming (at best that is an extreme form of narcissism, at worst it is the melancholic face of solipsism) but by careful repetitions, by working through.

In her more recent work, Judith Butler pursues and clarifies her position on identity, sexuality and power. In keeping with the earlier premises of her work on queer theory, she defends a vision of the subject which, however much in process and non-essentialized, requires the workings of consciousness as a regulatory entity. Hegel casts a long and maybe even growing shadow over Butler's work. Thus, for instance, the question of the separation between the psychic and the social, and the complex task of joining them or setting them in relation, emerges as central to Butler's political project of recasting agency in the mode of performative subversions. A Derridian definition of repetition is at the heart of this notion of performativity as alternatively (1993: 2): 'the reiterative and citational practice by which discourse produces the effects that it names' and that which 'describes the relations being implicated in that which one opposes' (p. 241). If the frame of reference is deconstructivist, however, Butler's passion is fundamentally political. Hence the recurrence of the question of how the subject can be subjected to the kind of interpellations which constitute her or him in power. I read Butler's work primarily as a determined and self-conscious effort to seek for a correspondence between the psychic and the social. This becomes also a quest for interconnections between the psychoanalytic theory of desire as lack and the social practices of enforced normativity, prohibitions and exclusion. In ways which at times strike me as hasty or even reductive, Butler sets up an equation between psychic foreclosure and social repression. She can thus ask the key question: how did certain social practices, like heterosexuality, come to acquire a symbolic primacy? For Butler, following Rubin and the gender paradigm that is dominant in US feminism, power in fact is cast as the heterosexual matrix which attributes sexed identities on a hierarchically ordained binary scale aiming at the disavowal of homosexual desire.

Butler's question concerns not only an analytic dimension: how did the symbolic inscription of heterosexuality come about? It also implies a normative aspect – on how effective change can be achieved. Because Butler's work is framed by a discourse about social and legal rights, this normative dimension is dominant in her thought, which means that Butler at times sacrifices conceptual consistency for the sake of political effectiveness. One significant example of this is the discussion on the transferability of the phallus. In outlining Butler's case I want to argue that her deconstruction of the political myth of phallic supremacy, coupled with the social practice of compulsory heterosexuality, paradoxically ends up down-playing the embodied nature of the subject. Let me explain.

Butler's argument runs as follows: Lacan's notion of the Phallus as the symbolic operator of differences constitutes a radical disjunction from the conventional notion of the penis as empirical referent. For Butler this confers on the Phallus a sort of plastic quality, a transferability which leaves it open to appropriation and re-signification by others, especially lesbians (1992: 168, note 19):

> Although I am clearly in some sympathy with the project of deauthorizing the male Imaginary, my own strategy will be to show that the Phallus can attach to a variety of organs, and that the efficacious disjoining of Phallus from penis constitutes a narcissistic wound to phallomorphism and the production of an anti-heterosexist sexual Imaginary. The implications of my strategy would seem to call into question the integrity of either a masculine or a feminine Imaginary.

For Butler the Phallus is merely the idealization and inflated representation of morphology. It aims to reinstate the primacy and insuperability of heterosexuality and of heterosexist identifications and the necessary erasure and defilement of lesbianism and homosexuality.

The very notion of the transferability of the Phallus suggests moreover an ease about changes and in-depth transformations of the self, which I find problematic both conceptually and ethically. As far as I am concerned, psychoanalysis is not only another philosophical system, but also a cure, that is to say an intervention in the complexity and pain of one's subjectivity. This implies that such interventions are neither easily accessible, nor free of pain. In other words, changes hurt and transformations are painful; this does not mean that they are deprived of positive and even pleasurable side-effects, of course.

My position consists in stressing that the pain involved requires respect and that I find insufficient respect for the pain of in-depth changes in Butler's account of the transferability and negotiability of the Phallus. I see in it a sort of reduction not only of the Phallus to its penile support, but also of the erotic body as a whole to the status of a prosthetic device. Accordingly, Butler reduces morphology and body contours to discursive practices, namely to the views of biology, physiology, and hormonal and bio-chemical disciplines. These act as interpretative matrices which both affect and limit access to bodily materiality. This means that organs are mere 'imaginary effects and that the relation between language and materiality is an undecidable unity of elements that are neither fully identical nor fully different' (Butler 1992: 151). The imaginary here stands for the Marxist idea of false consciousness, something intrinsically unreliable. Because the imaginary is both constitutive and false, Butler cannot entrust it with the political mission of activating change or resisting hegemonic formations of the subject as Irigaray does. She thus falls back on a classical equation of the political subject with wilful, conscious activity. This begs the question for me of how a feminist political subject can achieve change at the in-depth levels of her sexual economy. Gender trouble is indeed no guarantee of sexual subversion.

I find Butler's position both on sexual difference and on psychoanalytic theories of the original/originary loss that lies at the heart of the subject to be quite contradictory. I think Butler both acknowledges and denies the insight of psychoanalysis, namely that at the origin of the subject there is the constitutive loss of the primary object of desire – the mother. As I argued earlier, however, for Irigaray motherhood, and the maternal-feminine site of subjectivity, is never only the reactive specular other of the same. In her political project of re-configuring the corporeal materiality of alternative feminist subjects, the maternal is the laboratory for the elaboration of the 'other of the Other', that is to say the virtual feminine which is activated by feminists in a process that is both political and conceptual. Butler does not agree with this reference to an 'other' corporeal or embodied maternal feminine which escapes or is in excess of adequate representation within the phallogocentric economy.

This is a very consistent move by Butler, in keeping with the gender-framework which I outlined earlier, especially Gayle Rubin's interpretation of Levi-Strauss and the theory of the heterosexual matrix (Rubin 1975). In opposition to this I want to stress again that poststructuralist thinkers like Irigaray and Deleuze, propose quite a different reading of the subject. Bodily matter, sexuality and reproduction are indeed central to their way of think-ing, but they are also de-essentialized. The emphasis on sexuality and filiation, or the materiality of human reproduction, lies at the heart of the discussion of both the kinship system and the social field. In this tradition of thought, issues of sexuality and filiation are so fundamental that they cannot be reduced to a sociology of gender roles. I would rather say that the difference rests on one crucial point: we need to consider the co-presence of morpho-logical and social power-relations and their joint impact on the positioning of the subject.

Thus, Butler takes her leave from poststructuralist theories of sexual difference because she does not recognize the transformative power of the feminine in subverting the representational economy of phallogocentrism. For Butler, as for Rubin, de Lauretis and others, the exclusion of the fem-inine and/as the rejection of the maternal is accordingly neither primary nor foundational. It is rather presented as an *a posteriori* hallucinatory projec-tion that covers the sense of loss, and this sustains the subject in the delusional quest for coherence and self-consciousness.

My position on this issue is aligned to the psychoanalytic insight that the split from or the loss of the mother is a crucial step in the process of constitution of the subject. With Irigaray I would argue that the loss of the mother's body entails for the little girl a fundamental lack of primary narcissism as the scar of the wound due to the separation. This originary loss also forecloses access to the mother as primary object of desire, thus depriving the female subject of fundamental ontological grounds for self-assurance. The little boy, on the other hand, is 'compensated' later for the loss of the mother by having his desire deferred to, and displaced to another woman. He may lose the original love object, but inherits the earth in return: men draw all sorts of advantages from their position of representatives of the phallic signifier. For the little girl, however, there is only economic and symbolic misery.

The implication for me of this view of the original separation is that it is the whole of female subjectivity and eroticism, the entirety of her body, that is short-circuited in the process. As Deleuze would say, the little girl's body is 'stolen' from her, as the whole of her sexuality is coerced into the phallogocentric regime. I think it important to stress here the extent to which Deleuze and Irigaray share the same conceptual matrix and of how radically it differs from the paradigm of gender in Gayle Rubin, who is the main source of inspiration for Butler. The little girl's 'stolen body', according to Deleuze, marks her exclusion from symbolic representation. It is the 'capture' of her body by the Oedipalizing vampire of phallogocentrism. Both Irigaray and Deleuze stress that it is the specific materiality of the female flesh that is erased by the phallic regime. This primordial erasure is the condition of possibility for the subsequent kidnapping of the Symbolic order by the masculine.

Butler, on the other hand, interprets this ontological kidnapping of the little girl's erotic subjectivity exclusively in terms of the foreclosure of homosexuality. This is the direct and coherent implication of the theory of gender that Butler works with, one which assumes the constitutive and *a priori* erasure of homosexuality by a gender system which invents (hetero)sexual normativity and imposes it on living bodies. This is in my eyes, however, both a reduction of the psychoanalytic insight and an unfounded theoretical assumption about the process of sexualization of the subject.

Butler shares the Lacanian assumption that entry into language or access to the Symbolic requires the separation from and loss of the maternal body. She goes on, however, to the next step of her argument (1992: 145): 'Insofar as language appears to be motivated by a loss it cannot grieve, to repeat the very loss it refuses to recognize, we might regard this ambivalence at the heart of linguistic iterability as the melancholy recesses of signification.' From this originary loss, which can only be rendered *a posteriori* as the fantasy of a lost origin, Butler derives the – for me unfounded – conclusion that materiality of the body as a whole denies any pre-discursive validity. For Butler it is an *a posteriori* construction, which is always already sexed.

The fact that such loss is always and already caught within language has the paradoxical effect of depriving it of any foundational materialist value for Butler: if all is language, then anything goes. From here there follows a systematic devaluation of the feminine as the site of loss and consequently as genesis of the subject.

The implication inherent in Butler's position is that the 'mother' in question in this originary loss is in fact the site and the object of homosexual love. This is true as far as it goes, but in my opinion that is not far enough. This discussion needs in fact to take into account the impact of fantasy in any account of the 'origins' of the subject. To accept that any theory concerning the origins is fantasmically-loaded may not make it any less fantasmic, of course, but at least it would have the advantage of self-reflexivity. I find such self-reflexivity lacking in Butler's critique of psychoanalysis, with the result that her interventions can easily be challenged by alternative accounts, which are not less fantasmic, but more self-consciously so. For instance, let me evoke a counter-hypothesis in reaction to Butler's lesbian reading of the originary loss of grounding for the subject.

It is the case that most mothers are somebody else's lovers – and this fundamental triangulation of the couple and the child alone lends complexity and ambiguity to the alleged 'exclusiveness' of the mother–child/daughter bond. Moreover, at least statistically and for the time being, most mothers' partners tend to be men – humans of the opposite sex. The presence of the sexual other is not negligible: even if the mother is alone, or is actually a lesbian, the morphological, biological and symbolic presence of the other sex in her – be it just sperm or semen – is not nothing. Taking once again the risk of strategic essentialism, I think it important to inscribe at the heart of the narrative of the subject's origin the principle of not-One, that is, of incommensurable difference.

Regardless of the sexual identity and the gender of one's partner, the traces of heterosexuality on us all are undeniable. One can clearly choose to disguise this fact, to avoid all the morphological wrappings of sexual difference, such as a penis actually attached to a desiring male body, biblical-style penetration, fecundation of the ovum via penetration of sperm-carrying penis into the vagina. One can sing the praises of masquerades and polyvalence, such as lesbian cross-dressers who pump iron; one can choose to emphasize all kind of prosthetic or technological alternatives, such as women with strap-on dildos and penis-less men, but that will not suffice to erase sexual difference. A mere shift in the empirical referent cannot alter the somatic and psychic traces of sexual otherness. These traces are encrypted in the flesh, like a primordial memory, a genetic data-bank that pre-dates entry into linguistic representation. In the beginning, there is difference in the positive sense of 'not-One', that is to say there is flesh that is engendered as the effect of the encounter of two others, whatever their sexual morphology and gender identity may be. In the beginning, there is live flesh that longs for living, breath that yearns for breathing. Although the temptation to cast this into Christian iconography is strong, I would plead for resisting and for attempting instead a secular, bodily materialistic account of this process. The implication is clear: the virtual possibilities which have been foreclosed by entry into a phallic regime of signification which has kidnapped the little girl's body and sexuality cannot be retrieved by mere parodic repetitions: a much deeper, more affirmative type of mimesis is needed, to mobilize more archaic structures. This return to the flesh stresses the limits of semiological or linguistically-based models of repetition and subjectivity. This is one of the main reasons why I appreciate Irigaray's sober appeal to a radical re-appraisal of heterosexuality as the recognition of incommensurable differences, outside the dialectical scheme of hegemony by a sovereign consciousness. All that sexual difference stands for, here, is the fundamental importance of the principle of 'not-One' at the origin of the subject.

Whereas Butler would take such a statement as further evidence of the constituting force of heterosexuality and the *a priori* erasure of homosexuality from our psychic horizon, I see it as pointing instead to the enfleshed and highly material foundations of our bodily selves. Butler takes the linguistic turn, I go nomadically the way of all flesh. I think that sexual difference is written on the body in a thousand different ways, which includes hormonal and endrocrinological evidence. This discussion raises the issue of the limits of embodiment and of how much liberty we can take with the empirical, embodied self. Just how 'negotiable' is one's embedded and embodied subjectivity, considering that the subject is an assemblage of constitutive relations supported by social conventions and power structures? As Deleuze asks, what can a body do? I want to argue that the empirical is the specific location of an entity: it is spatial, even geo-political, but also temporal, both in the sense of linear, historical time (*Chronos*) and of circular, genealogical time (*Aion*). Each entity has its own in-built temporality as an organism, as well as its more complex, forward-looking temporality as a nomadic subject; more on this in chapter 2.

Moreover, the psychoanalytic scheme of triangulation of desire argues for the importance of the mother as the fantasmic love-object for *both* homo- and heterosexual love. If Freud's much-discussed (and for Butler highly suspicious) remark that all humans are polymorphous and perverse means anything, it points to the constitutive, all-encompassing sensual presence of the mother and the primacy of the bond with the mother in the life of the subject. But there is no evidence or necessity for this love and the bond that ensues from it to be homosexual or lesbian, *or to ever have been so*. We need to re-instate here the notion of fantasy.

I think that the function of the Law signified by the phallus is not only to provide a sense – albeit delusional – of coherence for the subject through inscription into the culturally dominant codes. It is also and primarily a principle of management of the phantasy of the original loss. This means that we need to re-inscribe at the heart of human subjectivity the presence of a third dimension, a third party, an 'outside' that is constitutive precisely because it is not bilateral, but plural. This triangulation of desire is the centre-piece of the Hegelian core of psychoanalysis. The third party intervenes between the mother and the child and it multiplies the subject's sense of splitness accordingly: it literally floods the subject with the 'outside', the social, the symbolic, the cultural, and all the avalanche of affects which they convey.

Whether this 'other' – the object of the mother's attention and desire – is a man or another woman changes little in the function of the third party as the psychic organizer of differentiation between mother and child. This third party merely expresses the fundamental psychic truth that the mother's desire is elsewhere, that it does *not* coincide with the child's total demand and totalizing expectations of it. Hence the delusional character of the child's wish to be the mother's Phallus, that is to say to be 'everything' for her. Recognizing this delusion is a necessary step in the process of constitution of an autonomous and well-functioning self, and as such it marks the subject's capacity to distinguish between fantasy and reality. This shock of recognition entails loss, mourning and melancholia. But this is the price to pay, the pound of flesh to be sacrificed for entering ethical and emotional adulthood. Literally, you can't always have what you want.

Kaja Silverman offers an interesting alternative angle here; she points out (1992) that the Phallus may well be a monological system, but it functions differentially, that is to say by producing complementary binary sets. Thus, what Lacan significantly defines as 'The name-of-the-father' also and simultaneously expresses the desire of the mother. This desire is not merely for the penis, though it is part of it, but for all it represents erotically – the promise of plenitude and *jouissance* – as well as culturally and socially – namely privilege and security. On all these accounts, the symbolic Law of the father will split the child from the mother and force *both* to surrender the fantasy of plenitude which marks their bond. The symbolic function of separating mother from child is considered by Lacan as the gateway to psychic sanity in so far as it breaks through the potentially totalitarian hold of the one over the other. It does so by installing the Phallus as the marker of the loss of the child's desire to be the total object of desire for the mother. I think it important to stress the fact that feminist critics of Lacan like Irigaray do not challenge the psychic function of a symbolic signifier as a principle of order, separation or differentiation. Conservative Lacanians like Kristeva consider such a symbolic function as vitally necessary, moral and even sacred. Irigaray's quarrel is with Lacan's insistence that this symbolic function can only and must be fulfilled by the Phallus. As we shall see in the next chapter, Deleuze and Guattari are the most radical critics of the concept of the symbolic, which they consider as the despotic signifier of an exploitative political economy of desire. This is not, however, Irigaray's position; she argues that the Lacanian Phallus is the imaginary referent for the penis; it is the symbolic operator of the necessary division of the subject from his or her mother, which inaugurates his or her entry into language. Last but not least it is also the inscription of the paternal metaphor at the heart of the social contract. On all these scores, the Phallus is neither plastic nor easily transferrable, as Butler would have it.

I think Butler confuses and condenses – for political purposes – three separate issues, which are crucial to the process of differentiation or separation from the mother. There are amalgamated:

- separation from the mother
- realization of the heterosexual imperative
- constitutive loss of homosexuality.

These 'moments' in the constitution of the subject neither coincide, nor are they bound together: they require a more sequentially ordained temporal scale in order to unfold. Time needs to play a role here. The loss of the original object is far too total and fundamental a trauma to lead to further speculation on the part of the infant subject who has much to cope with. The realization of sexual difference does occur, of course, but much later. In fact, as far as realizations go, this one will need to be reconstructed *a posteriori* as a fantasy of a forever always-already lost origin. It is a narrative infused with self-protective fantasies about oneself. The separation from the mother as the main organizer of the spatio-temporal co-ordinates of the subject does not coincide with the realization of the impossibility of homosexual love, or with the stunned realization that the mother is not homosexual/gay/queer, but a forever-lost heterosexual desiring subject. I want to plead for another temporal sequence between these different moments, one which would allow for some psychic space between the primary loss and subsequent repression of the maternal body and the assignation of sexual difference. Unless such a psychic space is granted, in fact, I do not see how *any* feminist project of transformation of the in-depth structures of female subjectivity can take place. Like Irigaray, I think that the maternal body provides both the site of destitution and of recovery for female feminist subjectivity, understood as a virtual reality of a collectively re-negotiated referential bond. It is the seed of the virtual feminine. The motor of the transformation, however, is temporal. Time, fortunately, is on our side.

Following on from the above, let me turn to the strategic implications. I am with Irigaray and Deleuze in taking the erasure of the feminine, its kidnapping by the Oedipal regime, as the sign for the foreclosure of women's subjectivity as a whole. The feminine as the foreclosed site of loss becomes the sign for all other kinds of excluded, by now 'virtual only', possibilities. This psychic and symbolic division of labour between symbolic presence (M) and absence (F) comes to construct the social field and the respective role and status of men and women as the empirical referents for the imaginary constructions of masculinity and femininity. This state of affairs has no necessity other than that which emerges from its own long-standing history. With Deleuze you may want to call it an established habit, a sedimented custom, or an institutionalized addiction. This is how I read Lévi-Strauss's statement that exogamy and the exchange of women by men had neither logical nor psychic necessity: it just was so by virtue of historical sedimentation. Of course it could have been the other way around, and the excluded possibilities – say the exchange of men by women – can be raised as a hypothesis, or become retrieved as virtual realities. The problem of how to retrieve them and gain access to them as well as the hypothesis of virtual alternatives, of different locations of subjectivity, amounts to questioning their historically embedded material locations. One cannot change without the other.

For Butler, beyond the maternal feminine there is the always-already lost object of desire: the homosexual same-sex other who plays the role of the constitutive outside. The feminine merely points towards this foreclosed homosexuality, like a road-sign in the middle of the Gobi desert, indicating some living settlement situated thousands of kilometres away. A signifier for the unreachable, a sign of loss and destitution, a recipe for despair, Butler's 'feminine' is reduced to a pathetic effort at simulating signification on the road to nowhere. I clearly disagree with this depreciation of the feminine, both on conceptual and strategic grounds. I think that Butler's argument is very closely modelled on Irigaray's theory, but, whereas Irigaray promotes a deconstructive type of mimesis that would allow both women and men to retrace the steps of the original loss and to retrieve it away from mourning and melancholia, Butler proposes a performative notion of gendered iden-tity which fails to account for unconscious processes.

Biddy Martin has commented on the 'femino-phobia' (my terminology) of Butler's theories and has expressed concern at the erasure of the feminine that is taking place in queer theory (Martin 1994:108): 'First, it limits the scope of feminist inquiry. And second it associates the cross-gender identified lesbian with sexuality, the lesbian-feminist with gender identifications and makes the lesbian femme completely invisible. . . . The woman-identified woman, in much lesbian feminist work, was/is as repressive of femmeness as it is of cross-gender identifications.' It is indeed spectacular how lesbian and queer theories in the USA have eclipsed any notion of 'woman-identified women'. Feminine identifications are really out of the picture; even the feminine-looking/passing lesbian or 'femme' has been censored, unless she be inscribed in the butch-femme couple. Martin finds the opposition between 'queerness' and the feminine lesbian or woman as too extreme and pleads for more permeable boundaries between the inside and the outside of sexed, embodied subjects. Though body and psyche are shot through with the effects of power, they are not reducible to it; thus a more complex frame of analysis is necessary.

This takes me to my next point: the political implications. The project of sexual difference consists in trying to shift the grounds for the constitution of female subjectivity for both hetero-and homosexual people and thus to re-think the full range of sexual agency for women and men. Irigaray's point about the 'sensible transcendental' is of the greatest relevance here. An essential counterpart of this re-investment of sexuality and the subsequent process of radicalizing heterosexuality concerns the role of men. In order to understand the importance of this point, let me recall my earlier argument concerning the effect of the 'sex wars' in USA feminism: sexuality exited from mainstream feminist agendas. It also returned with a vengeance under the cover of 'minority' sexualities, by women of colour, and especially by lesbian and queer sexualities, in opposition to the moralism and the silence of the liberal majority. The paradoxical result of this is that both hetero-sexuality and the role of men are doubly silenced: by the liberal feminist majority because, as in the Clinton–Lewinsky case, they literally do not know what to say about white American masculine sexuality; and by queer theorists because they assimilate heterosexuality to power, domination and exclusion. Butler's position shares in some of this: her emphasis on the heterosexual matrix of power has the paradoxical effect of silencing any possible role for heterosexual men, even potentially liberatory ones.

Kaja Silverman, by contrast, pleads for new theorizations of mascu-linity, by paying more attention to the symbolic function fulfilled by the 'Name-of-the-father' and the ways in which desire is organized through a binary set of signifiers. Whereas Lacan is happy to accept the relocation of male Lack as the site of the female subject in all her symbolic misery, radical Lacanian feminists like Silverman plead for a different sort of wisdom: (1992: 114): 'The only immutable law of desire is the one which denies to each of us the possibility of wholeness and self-presence – the Law, that is, of language. Let us attempt to devise other ways of living this Law than through the differential distribution of Lack.'

Irigaray instead strikes on both registers: firstly she relocates the mother away from the privileged signifier of lack and reconfigures female sexuality as multiplicity and porosity, in opposition to oneness and rigidity. Second, not only does she interpellate men directly, but also empowers them to play their sexuality differently: they can also try to re-embody and re-embed their sexuality in a non-phallic manner. Unless both sexes join in the effort to implement non-phallic sexuality, to re-write the script of sexuality away from the violence of the Phallus, nothing will change. Translated into the language of Deleuze, the majority needs to become minoritarian: we need a polyvalent, fluid, becoming minoritarian of both sexes, men and women included. The alternative would be to assume that heterosexuality is a dirty word and an obsolete practice which needs to be laid to rest once and for all, but what kind of a feminist message would that be for most women?

I find Butler reductive about heterosexual desire, as if it had to do only with domination and exclusion (traces of Wittig) or with the possession of certain organs. I understand that some of this reductive thinking is contextual: in the USA the influence of feminists like MacKinnon and Dworkin has resulted in assimilating heterosexual gender identity with sexual subordination and even victimization. By contrast, I find that Irigaray offers a sober and workable alternative in her attempt to radicalize heterosexuality. Her goal is that of turning the heterosexual encounter into a suspension of dialectical games of domination, a multi-layered space of encounter, admiration and love of the multiple differences embodied in the other. Deleuze offers instead the alternative of polysexuality, as we will see in the next chapter. In any case heterosexuality cannot be reduced only to the desire for a penis or the pursuit of social respectability and normality. For female feminist subjects especially, heterosexuality encompasses a much wider and more wide-ranging perspective of sexual otherness. This need not be a static or hegemonic model, but rather the process of encounter between nomadic sexed positions. I think the patriarchal sexual regime has denied the fullness and symmetry of two sexual economies, confining them both under the burden of phallogocentrism. It follows that for me it is also a radical project to envisage the recomposition of another type of heterosexuality, which would respect the incommensurable difference of a virtual 'two' which needs to be explored and shaped in a dialogue with sexual 'sames' and sexual 'others'.

Beyond mourning and melancholia

In the previous section, questions of repetition and mimesis have repeatedly been raised. Let me explore them further. Butler emphasizes performances, but chooses to play the compulsion to repeat back on to the refrain of negativity and bad conscience. Repetition is not understood in any mimetic, non-Hegelian sense of the term, but in a Derridian sense of the unavoidability of the eternal return of the violence of the signifier. Admittedly, desire does play a role in Butler's thought, but it is a negative, mournful theory of desire, which understates the role and the impact of pleasure on the constitution of the subject and side-steps the question of the unconscious.

Melancholia is crucial to Butler's notion of desire as mortal; her thesis in fact rests on the assumption that 'gender' incorporates the foreclosure of homosexual love, which can only be experienced as always-already lost and beyond reach. This reflects and deflects Irigaray's idea that the subject is constituted across the original loss of the mother's body and that entry into the symbolic requires the erasure of that primary bond. For Butler the heterosexual matrix is instead such that it requires the repudiation of homo-sexuality; this traces a psychic itinerary made of constitutive loss. Hence also her emphasis on the death-drive.

Melancholia is characterized by the internalization of constitutive loss. Women, homosexuals, people of colour and post-colonial subjects, who are marginal within the phallogocentric symbolic, are particularly prone to melancholia. This problem goes beyond individual pathology and captures a political dimension, which centres on one's attachment and loyalty to a forbidden or socially unpresentable and unrecognized love-object. In the absence of a public language and ritual of recognition and hence also of mourning, melancholia assumes a social and political dimension. The unspeak-able and unspoken lost object of desire – which for Butler is the homosexual loved one – withdraws into the psyche as a remainder of insoluble grief. To analyse the insoluble nature of such grief amounts to calling into question the political economy of compulsory heterosexuality which engenders it.

This concern for death and loss is problematic. However central it may be to the Hegelian–Lacanian vision of the constitution of the subject, I find that with Foucault, Irigaray and feminist psychoanalytic theories, some empowering alternatives have been offered, for instance the emphasis on pleasure as a constitutive element of subjectivity. What if what kept the subject bound to the power *apparati* which simultaneously construct and constrain it was precisely the surplus value of pleasure? It is pleasure, especially the excessive, transgressive and boundary-breaking pleasure of *jouissance*, that provides the glue which fixes the socially-driven imaginary upon the subject and vice-versa. Žižek understands this addictive force as the irresistible impact of ideology upon the subject. Thinking this through with Irigaray and Deleuze I want to raise instead another possibility: what if the 'fixer' of the psychic landscape were the over-flowing plenitude of pleas-ure, rather than the melancholy discourse of debt and loss? I think this more Spinozist option has a great deal to offer and I will explore it further in the next chapters.

Admittedly, this emphasis on mourning and melancholia is motivated to a great extent by Butler's concern for the deaths caused in the gay com-munity by the AIDS crisis. More particularly, her work is informed by the question of how to formalize a gay discourse about death and loss in the public sphere. Public rituals of mourning are needed, so as to enforce the recognition of gay grief and have it accepted socially. I think this worthy and humane concern lies at the heart of Butler's investment in the political economy of mourning and loss. It also attaches her more firmly to the Lacanian tradition of thought than her own work would actually allow.

For end-of-millennium Lacanians and psychoanalytically-invested decon-structionists, desire is the margin of excess which is necessarily foreclosed in the instance of structuring meaningful utterances, that is, of making sense. In the Hegelian scheme which dominates Lacan's concept of desire, however, there is an inescapable debt of negativity, an ontological deficit which can never be repaid, or filled up. There is clear evidence of this in Žižek's work on negativity in the socio-political public sphere. 'Fantasy' is for Žižek both the hidden motor of the apparatus of subjectivity and that which cannot be assimilated within it. Akin to Kristeva's 'abject', this notion of fantasy refers to that which cannot be integrated into the symbolic structure, or rather, that whose function is to resist assimilation into the symbolic. Thus 'fantasy' is defined with reference to Hegel's concept of 'negativity' as a systematic and necessary *défaillance* (a failure, or deficiency) at the core of the subject. The fantasy element functions for Žižek like a creative void, the ghostly or spectral foggy bottom of His unsubstantiality. The Gothic imagery is not coincidental: Žižek's texts are full of it, which partly connects to his interest in contemporary cinema and especially low-class genres such as horror and science fiction (about which more in chapter 4), and partly to his vampiristic understanding of the subject. The fantasy element, in fact, feeds upon the plenitude of the subject, sapping it away into a series of delusional and compensatory manifestations of the self.

What is being forced upon the subject is the overwhelming and therefore irresistible forms of compensation or 'enjoyment' of ideologically-conveyed meanings and cultural products which aim at deluding him or her into a coherent and masterful image of Himself. In this respect, I think Žižek stresses the gloomiest aspects of Lacan's theory of subjectivity, by applying to it something which I would describe as an overdose of Hegelian dialectics. The end result is a sad and cynical vision of a subject for whom the lack, guilt and the subsequent discontent are structural, that is to say necessary and therefore inescapable. Peter Dews sums up the situation with admirable clarity when he argues that, contrary to Hegel, for Žižek: 'the loss of the loss does not involve the cancellation, or even relativization, of a limit or a lack, but rather an acceptance of the fact that what appeared to be a reparable loss is in fact a constitutive lack' (Dews 1995: 24).

Predictably enough, such a conservative reading of Lacan has the effect of emphasizing the most traditional definitions, positioning and consquences for Woman as an imaginary construction and, as a consequence, for real-life women. In terms of thinking the feminine, Žižek's work represents an anti-feminist regression that reiterates the whole array of symbolic invisibility and specularity which feminists have been arguing against since the early days of Lacan's work. Butler (1993) has commented critically on this aspect of Žižek's thought, stressing the negative impact of the over-emphasis he places on the register of fantasy and consequently on the Lacanian 'Real', to the detriment of a more dynamic and positive vision of the subject. I think this has everything to do with the specific notion of 'ideology' that is at work in Žižek's exasperated Lacanianism and which contributes to the depoliticization of psychoanalysis.

The constitutive void that lies at the core of subjectivity and which in turn generates the self as a delusional and compensatory entity has implications for what Althusser used to call the ideological production. This becomes inclusive of absolutely everything and thus it loses any sharp edge of definition. What emerges here is the paradox of the evanescent, disappearing or dead subject which all of poststructuralism brings to the fore of critical theory (contrary to Žižek, I see Lacan as a major poststructuralist thinker). For instance, Deleuze reinscribes this paradoxical non-existence of the subject into the circular logic of proliferation of differences and consequently into a self-contradictory movement of dispersion of the self into a range of consumable others, which is the schizophrenic logic of advanced capitalism. Irigaray analyses the same phenomenon in terms of the growing vampirism of the contemporary subject on a notion of the feminine that has to carry the full burden of materiality, the flesh, birth and mortality, while he dwells upon the misty depths of his ontological crisis. Far less imaginative, Žižek starts by defending the anti-representational vision of ideology, but then retreats into an even worse sense of disempowerment of the subject.

The 'object' of ideology does not quite exist; it is a creative empty place, and what it creates is the illusion of a coherent decisional self. The point is that ideological representations work, whether their content is 'true' or 'false'. The success of ideology, therefore has nothing to do with the truth or falsity of its representation; what matters instead is the subjective position that ideology implicitly creates in the process of enunciation. With this move, Žižek actualizes at the subjective level Lacan's brand of structural linguistics: just as there is no logical or necessary connection between the signifier and its signified content, there is no necessary relation between the content of ideology and its effect. No matter what it represents, the effect is to create a 'slot' or a place of enunciation for the subject, and for Žižek there is no escape from this infernal circular machinery. It is all the more infernal as its operations are non-transparent; although Žižek attempts to define three moments of ideological production: ideology as a complex of ideas and texts, as the external materiality of the state apparatus and the general and widespread production of society at large and especially the media, I think he pushes to extremes the banalization of the notion of ideology to cover all and any forms of representation.

Žižek argues that the 'false' element in the 'false consciousness' induced by ideology is due to a structural impossibility, that of translating into human/social/public language the underlying libidinal forces. Žižek expresses it in the notion of 'fantasy', which is simultaneously driven to seek fulfilment

– and necessarily fails to do so. Both Butler and Žižek share a rather static understanding of the materiality of the embodied subject: matter has neither memory nor dynamic force of its own, certainly none outside a symbolic that is ruled by lack and negativity. The political implications of this infernal circularity are significant: for Žižek we are within ideological space the moment any content, be it 'true' or 'false', is functional with regard to social relations. Therefore, even attempts at stepping out of what we perceive as ideology is the very form of our enslavement to it, in that our attempts are no less 'ideological'. Žižek quotes as examples of this circularity the rhetoric of 'humanitarian wars' in the Balkans or the self-contradictions involved in trying to beat the media at their own game. The consequence is that in order to be effective, both relations of domination and of resistance to ideology must remain concealed. We can only denounce ideology from a place that must stay empty, not determined by any positive reality, otherwise we would fall back into ideology. As this special place is, for Žižek as for Lacan, that of psychoanalysis, the function of which is to make the subject accept his necessary enslavement, the political double-bind closes upon itself and the end result is a recipe for disempowerment.

The whole capitalist-infused economy of deficit and lack, which invests the Lacanian conceptual machinery and marries it to a certain view of Hegel, is perpetuated by Žižek with a smug pretence at debunking. The 'illusion' of consciousness comes down to its intrinsic link with – and unpayable debt to – the 'Real': the primordial libidinal matter which constructs social activity by providing the necessarily silenced foundations for what – if anything – can be spoken. This structuring lack is central to Lacan's ontology of negativity, and gives rise to what Derrida describes as the 'spectral economy' of the subject: a constitutive, undecidable present absence, or structurally necessary absence as the only mode in which the subject can be present to him- or herself. As Kear astutely points out (1999: 183): 'If Ego equals Ghost, then "I am" would mean "I am haunted"' – in other words, 'I' am simultaneously constructed by the introduction of the desire and by the failure of it. This forces 'me' performatively to repeat the 'hauntologically' primal scene which marks the site of 'my' constitutive foundation in loss and lack. I do find this a perfectly Gothic scene, in tune with *fin-de-siècle* gloom. It invites us to wallow in a prolonged and at times ecstatic glorification of loss, mourning and melancholia, thus bringing Lacan's delusional vision of the subject to some point of implosion. This slightly hallucinated mode of both erasing and affirming the subject strikes me as central to both Lacan's and Žižek's melancholic view of subjectivity. Because this concept allows for a performative view of the subject – as the flawed entity that forever pursues that which evades him or her in the very act of constitution of his or her place of enunciation – a strange resonance has emerged between Žižek and Butler. I find the emphasis on the structurally aporetic and fundamentally failed attempt by the subject to affirm his or her libidinal intensity – this emphasis on lack and negativity – tainted with a comic touch of tragedy. Against the negative passion and the seduction of the aporetic, there has to be an alternative. Translated into nomadic language: I actively yearn for a more joyful and empowering concept of desire and for a political economy that foregrounds positivity, not gloom. Butler's explicit rejection of Deleuze's theory of desire (1987), however, positions her as antithetical to this vision.

What I find even more problematic in this melancholia-oriented twilight of psychoanalytic theory is its blatant obliteration of the radical materialism of both Irigaray and Deleuze. Yet, as early as 1968 (in *Différence et répétition*) in the case of Deleuze and 1974 for Irigaray (in *Spéculum. De l'autre femme*), the objection to the theory of desire as lack had been raised. Namely that desire, this structurally silenced libidinal sub-stratum, was neither of the order of an undecidable temporality, nor of a logical impossibility. The originary moment is in the constitution of the desiring subject as sexed or gendered, in that it displays a strong link to the maternal feminine (Irigaray). It is also however historicized, in that its phallogocentrism reflects an instrumental relation to the material-affective roots of the subject (Deleuze); as such it marks a specific moment in the historicity of subject-construction under capitalism (Deleuze) and patriarchy (Irigaray). I cannot help wondering why the path-breaking agendas of radical materialists like Irigaray and Deleuze are being ignored or silenced by the post-Lacanian discourses about negativity, which triumphed at the end of the second millennium. Why is it that loss, failure, melancholia and the ontological lack continue to dominate views of the subject both inside and outside feminism?

Again, contextual considerations come to mind. The social imaginary of feminism in the 1990s was dominated by the notion of fetishism and the figuration of the trans-sexual body, queer sexuality or in-between genders (Grosz and Probyn 1995). Since the mid-1980s trans-sexuality had been heralded (Baudrillard 1987) as the dominant figuration for contemporary sexuality. This indicates a sort of play with sexual indifferentiation which simultaneously, in my eyes, displaces and confirms the gender polarity. Technology provides a powerful mode of cultural mediation of the trans-sexual imaginary. Prosthetically enhanced, self-consciously artificial, the trans-sexual body is the prototype of the cyborg in that it signifies the symbiosis between the organic, the biochemical, the technological and the surgical. I will return in chapter 5 to analysis of the anthropological but also morphological mutation that seems to be taking place in the organization of postmodern sexualities. For the moment it is important to stress that in gender theory especially, a collective becoming-trans-sexual is a dominant *topos* in the cultural representations of the sexed body. Appeals to Deleuze's body-machines are crucial to this trans-sexual imaginary, as I will argue in the next chapter. Like the character Vaughan in James Ballard's novel *Crash*, a deep wound seems to mark the contemporary sexual body, making it like: 'a deranged drag queen revealing the leaking scars of an unsuccessful transsexual surgery' (Ballard 1973: 201). Postmodern Gothic and post-gender sexualities are haunting the imaginary of post-industrial societies. While acknowledging this phenomenon, I want to argue that far from erasing sexual difference, it makes it for me a more urgent question than ever.

Conclusion: the sensible transcendental

Sexual difference requires opening out towards issues of transcendence and universality – not in the sense of erasing other differences, but rather in the formulation of alternative subject-positions of a more general appeal and value. In my view, the paradox of Irigaray's position is that, while it is based on a notion of materiality that I find very de-essentialized, it seems to move ineluctably towards issues of transcendence and incorporeal immateriality. Colebrook (2000b: 121) helps to elucidate this point:

> Irigaray's 'transcendental sensible' . . . short-circuits the closure of representationalism by showing that the condition which the subject repeats and refigures as his own ground can never be fully comprehended by the subject, precisely because the subject is nothing other than an effect of this repetition. In presenting the origin as object the subject is produced as subject. But this repetition of the origin as presence can never itself be presented. In order to be fully present to himself the subject must negate his corporeal facticity.

As I indicated earlier in this chapter, this negation of material grounds or 'corporeal facticity' constitutes metaphysics and founds it on a concurrent rejection of corporeality. This originary violence is sexualized or genderized, and it is intrinsic to the authority of the classical subject in that it grounds him on consciousness. The burden of embodiment is projected on to the maternal feminine and immediately erased. This erasure constitutes the subject and founds phallogocentrism, understood as the empire of the One and the objectification of the Other. Hence Irigaray's insistence that this 'difference' is internal to the logic of the Same and her political determination to disengage the feminine from this one-dimensional road so as to redefine it as the other of the other, that is to say a constitutive not-One.

Although a great deal of this project aims at postulating a social and political contract by and for women, it also contains an equally powerful transcendental charge. By advocating a feminine form of transcendence through 'radical immanence', Irigaray postulates a definition of the body not only as material, but also as the threshold to a generalized notion of female being, a new feminist humanity. Irigaray's work seems to move ineluctably towards issues of incorporeal materiality. This tendency is explicit in her work on the sensible transcendental and 'the woman divine'. The embodied materialism of sexual difference, in other words, is the assertion of the importance of a multiplicity that can make sense, by granting symbolic recognition to women's way of being. Irigaray's 'divine' aims at materializing the *a priori* conditions needed to achieve changes in our symbolic as well as material conditions. It implies re-thinking space, time, nature, the earth and the divine. The issue of the sensible transcendental is crucial to this project. It situates the female embodied subject in a space between transcendence and immanence. This kind of materiality connects the subject to a number of differences within herself and also between herself and others. It does so, moreover, in a non-dialectical and non-oppositional manner.

The female subject can recognize and enact her specificity by granting symbolic importance to her bond to other women as fundamental mediators between herself and the world: this is the idea of a feminine universal as mediation. Colebrook puts it clearly: for Irigaray, 'the sensible is proximate. Neither the full presence of experience, nor the radical anteriority of a transcendental condition, the sensible is given as the other body whom I recognize as another form of becoming, as a "concrete universal" ' (2000b: 123). Like the first stone of a new civilization, Irigaray's 'divine' aims at materializing for feminist practice the *a priori* conditions to achieve changes in our symbolic as well as material structures. No bodily materialism without transcendence; no female embodied subject without incorporeality. I think that the position of strategic essentialism invites the reader to dwell on this paradox and not to seek for hasty ways out of this ontological vicious circle.

Olkowski captures this vein in Irigaray's work (2000: 107):

> Woman as becoming is thus anomic, against and outside the rule, the principle and the structure. Her molecules are a powerful contagion, spread by symbiosis and mucosity. And if we succeed in depathologising everything associated with women by constituting a logic and a language of fluidity, all those words that are so distasteful because they express the body of woman – the uteral, the vulvar, the clitoral, the vaginal, the placental, or woman's luminous body itself – may then enter, for the first time ever, into our knowledge.

The diffuse, flowing, transgressive and cosmic nature of this eroticism codes it culturally as 'feminine' – and thus, once again, there is no avoiding the feminization of this theory of desire. Nor is there a way to resolve its in-built contradictions: they have to be enacted and worked through.

On the issue of alterity, Irigaray's radical heterosexuality postulates the need for a female homosexual nucleus – a primary homosexual bond that is required to re-compose women's primary narcissism, which has been badly wounded and damaged by the phallocentric symbolic. The love of another woman is crucial to this process of laying the foundations for the pre-history

of a possible future, which is a complex way of referring both to surviving –
in a reactive mode – and to living – in an active and creative manner. The
other woman – the other of the Other – is the site of recognition of one's
effort at becoming in the sense of pursuing a process of transformation, of
deeply-rooted change, of in-depth metamorphoses. This primary narcissism
must not be confused with secondary narcissistic manifestations – of which
women have been richly endowed under patriarchy. Vanity, the love of
appearances, the dual burden of narcissism and paranoia are the signs of
female objectification under the power (*potestas*) of the Same. Nor is it *per
se* the prelude to a lesbian position: it simply states the structural significance of love for one's sex, for the sexual same, as a crucial building block
for one's self-esteem. It is important to emphasize therefore the importance
of primary narcissism as some fundamental threshold of sustainability that
allows a female subject to undertake first the process of self-assertion and
then of transformation. As I have often argued in my work – before one can
undo, deconstruct, redefine, or relinquish subjectivity, one has to be a subject to begin with, otherwise, this would be a recipe for self-annihilation.
What Irigaray argues is that this process of re-building the foundations
(primary narcissism) necessarily requires another woman – this is because
we are all of woman born, and the imprint of the mother upon us is of
lasting and fundamental importance. Whereas under phallogocentrism, the
maternal marks the lack or absence of symbolic recognition, in the 'virtual
feminine' proposed by Irigaray, it can be turned into an empowering and
affirmative gesture.

Whether in the queer or the radical heterosexual way, I think that a
subversive approach to sexual identity and to sexuality is one of the legacies
of a feminist, nomadic becoming-woman process. In other words, the
object-choice (homo/hetero/'perverse') or the choice of sexual lifestyle is far
less important than the structural shifts entailed by this process in the structures of the desiring subjects. I tend to see the erotics of 'becoming-woman'
as a vitalistic sensuality, that remains deeply attached to the embodied subject. This is in keeping with the tradition of 'enchanted materialism' that
both Deleuze, Irigaray and a great deal of French and Continental culture
belong to. That a lot of this tradition is close to libertine literature, or to the
ars erotica that Foucault regretted had left mainstream culture, only makes
it historically all the more interesting. Two key ideas are worth stressing
here: firstly the emphasis on the specific intelligence of the enfleshed subject;
secondly both the continuity and the quarrel with psychoanalysis and the
project to disengage desire from lack and negativity to think of it instead as
plenitude and abundance. These two conceptual axes make the transcendental empirical of Luce Irigaray and other voices in the sexual difference
tradition compatible with the sensualist erotics of 'becoming-woman' in
Deleuze. I will pursue this in the next chapter.

This in turn posits feminism as a political and ethical passion, and consequently the feminist subject-position not as a given, but as a project, as something that some women can yearn for and work towards, for the good of all. I would call this an 'intensive' reading of feminist politics which assumes a non-unitary, nomadic subject equally opposed to classical humanism and to liberal notions of the individual. Accordingly it posits the instance of the political not merely in the wilful commitment to the basic pursuit of decency, social justice and human rights, though these remain unfulfilled and desirable aims to date. Politics can also be defined in terms of the passions and values that underscore it. This 'typology' of ethical passions is an approach inspired by Nietzsche and read with Deleuze. It allows us to see volitional choices not as transparent, self-evident positions, but rather as complex, contradictory multi-faceted ones. A dose of suspicion towards one's own 'motivations' or intentionality does not condemn one to cynicism, nihilism or relativism. On the contrary, by injecting affectivity, self-reflexivity and joy in the political exercise, it may return political beliefs to their full inspiration.

I have often argued that what feminism ultimately liberates in those who partake of it is a yearning for freedom, dignity, justice, lightness and joyfulness. These values can be translated into rational beliefs and policies, but they also form a substratum of desire that motivates the entire exercise in the first place. Politics begins with our passions. This was quite clear in the early militant days of the women's movement when laughter and joy were profound political weapons and statements. Not much of this Dionysian force seems to be left in these days of postmodern Gothic gloom, but we do well to recall it. Deleuze has typified the spirit of May 1968 – but I think any radical or transgressive movement would fit the bill – as a lightness of touch, a sense of opening up of possibilities, a profound empowerment of the potentials of life. This heightened sensibility both accompanies and makes possible social change, political and epistemological and other wilfully chosen political measures. In feminism as elsewhere it is crucial however to move beyond the deadly-serious priests of revolutionary zeal and revalorize the merry-making aspect of the processes of social change.

I think this emphasis on positive, empowering passions is another point of intersection between Irigaray's 'virtual feminine' as sensible transcendental and Deleuze's vision of the subject as empirical transcendental. The points in common, as well as the divergences, illuminate the ways in which feminist positions today appeal to Deleuze's thought. That Irigaray criticizes Deleuze's notion of multiplicity and the dispersion of sexed identities as interfering with the affirmation of a new female subjectivity, while Wittig on the contrary welcomes it as a way out of the sexual polarizations of the gender system, gives us a measure of the problem. The point for me, however, is that this 'captation' of Deleuze's work is very welcome and empowering for contemporary critical theory and cultural studies.

The emphasis Irigaray, Deleuze and Guattari place on the embodied and embedded nature of the subject – through the notion of radical immanence – gives to their philosophy a political edge related to power issues. It also opens critical theory to an ethical and an ecological dimension which embeds the subject in social relations of power. Knowledge claims rest on the immanent structure of subjectivity and must resist the gravitational pull towards abstract transcendentality. For Irigaray, this amounts to a radical exploration of the dissymmetrical forms of embodiment enjoyed respectively by men and women. It is a path of transcendence that goes via and through the body, not away from it. According to Deleuze and Guattari, on the other hand, the knowing subject has been re-thought in material terms: territories, resources, locations and forces. This is a break from the spatio-temporal continuum of classical humanism. Similarly, it is important to move beyond the reductivism of social constructionism, which tends to underplay the continuity of factors that provide the empirical foundations of the subject and which are mostly related to biology, but also include affectivity and especially memory and desire.

Moreover, a poststructuralist philosophy which assumes a subject that is both non-unitary and embodied/embedded in multiple power-relations also grants to temporality and memory a much more central place in the structuring of the subject. For instance, Irigaray pleads for the specific temporality of women (cyclical, repetitive, fluid) in order to find adequate social representations and applications for it. She also sees feminism as a laboratory for the consumption and transformation of women's genealogies into sources of experimentation, from past symbolic misery into an empowered alternative imaginary. Deleuze's 'nomadology' as a philosophy of immanence, on the other hand, rests on the idea of sustainability as a principle of containment and development of a subject's resources, understood environmentally, affectively and cognitively. A non-unitary subject thus constituted inhabits a time that is the active tense of continuous 'becoming'. Deleuze defines the latter with reference to Bergson's concept of 'duration', thus proposing the notion of the subject as an entity that lasts, that is to say that endures sustainable changes and transformation and enacts them around him or herself in a community or collectivity. In this perspective, even the Earth/Gaia is posited as a partner in a community which is still to come, to be constructed by subjects who will interact with the environment – both social and ecological – differently. Deleuze and Guattari turn to Spinoza to find philosophical foundations for a vitalistic yet anti-essentialistic brand of immanence. They rethink continuities between the subject and his or her context both socially (power-relations) and ethically (contiguity with the Earth). They do so without reference to humanistic or holistic worldviews, in so far as these are the pillars on which the humanist subject used to stand, dialectically opposed to His 'others'.

In this respect, I see in these philosophies of radical immanence a shift of emphasis away from anthropocentrism in favour of biocentric egalitarianism. I shall return to this in chapters 3 and 4. They differ from deep ecology, however, in not underplaying the contradictions and discontinuities between the human and the non-human universe and thus in not romanticizing the interaction between them. Even the most convinced social constructivists today argue that the performances of bodies cannot be ascribed exclusively to social codes or to symbolic and imaginary orders – nor can they be read back into the Holy Scriptures of the DNA Scrolls. Both 'nature' and 'the body' are slippery categories that tend to slide towards essentialism or get caught into positivist reductions – or in their opposite, new-age naive celebrations. In the age of the politics of bio-diversity, the interdependence of the natural and the social, the distinction mind–body needs to be explored outside classical, dualistic habits of thought. The key term here is 'radical immanence', that is to say a deeply embedded vision of the embodied subject. As a materialist theory it can provide an answer in so far as it encompasses the body at all levels, also, and maybe especially, the biological one. In the light of contemporary genetics and molecular biology, it is more than feasible to speak of the body as a complex system of self-sustaining forces. The DNA and the cells communicate effectively with each other, transferring vital information. In terms of bio-diversity, we humans are actively and destructively involved in manipulating our environment. Neuro-sciences have increased our understanding of memory and the extent to which the storage and retrieval of information is essential to the progress of the self. This is evidence which can no longer be ignored by critical, Left-leaning intellectuals. Nor need it be left to the delusions of grandeur of professional scientists and their industrial, financial backers. Feminist philosophical nomadism is a relevant and significant attempt to come to terms with both embodiment and sexual difference as processes of transformation, while foregrounding issues of power, empowerment and accountability.

Consciousness needs to be redefined accordingly in terms of flows of variations, constantly transforming within patterns of continuity. The old mind–body liaison needs to be reconstructed in terms which are not nationally driven, top-down and hierarchical. Processes, flows, in-between-status have to be taken into serious account, that is, into conceptual representation. Continuities and discontinuities alike need to be considered. Internal complexities and non-sequential effects have to be accepted in the order of our thought. To live up to these complexities, we need conceptual creativity and a healthy, non-nostalgic detachment from traditional beliefs about what counts as 'the knowing subject'.

A feminist project that mobilizes such forces and aspirations will mix them up with the fiery energy of post-Woman subjects with the brains of Hillary Clinton, the looks of Madonna, the courage of Anita Hill and the talent of Kathy Acker. This is also likely, however, to involve the readers in increasing degrees of complexity. It is my passionate conviction, however, that because, and not in spite of, these difficulties, the issues of sexual difference and the quest for alternative feminist subject-positions, not unlike the Princess of Wales, simply won't go away.

2

Zigzagging through Deleuze and Feminism

'A kind of order or apparent progression can be established for the segments of becoming in which we find ourselves; becoming-woman, becoming-child, becoming-animal, -vegetable, or -mineral; becoming-molecular of all kinds, becoming-particles.'

Gilles Deleuze and Felix Guattari, *A Thousand Plateaus*, p. 272

'In order to become, one needs a gender or an essence (necessarily sexed) as horizon; otherwise the becoming will be only partial or multiple without a future of one's own leads to abdicating responsibility for this process, to the other or the Other of the other. Becoming means achieving the fullness of all that one could be. This process is obviously open-ended.'

Luce Irigaray, *Sexes et parentés*, p. 73

This chapter expands in new but parallel directions the discussion of identity, sexuality and sexual difference. I will argue that most of the uses that Deleuzian philosophy is put to are still polemical and ambivalent towards feminist theory, especially among his, mostly male, followers. Yet a growing *corpus* of Deleuzian feminism is taking shape with remarkable rigour. I will situate Deleuze's work so as to clarify the many positive feminist uses to which his philosophy can be put. The purpose of this chapter is consequently to mirror, pursue and complexify the previous one.

Deleuze's legacy

The pleasures of un-Oedipal thinking

The co-author of the *Anti-Oedipus* leaves his readers in a double-bind: how to do justice to our admiration for his work without putting ourselves in the very Oedipal position of philosophical orphans. Nothing could be more unDeleuzian, in so far as Deleuze criticized the institution of philosophy for being a monumental, intimidating machine that makes us all feel inadequate. Deleuze took on this issue theoretically and went on to attack systematically the extent to which philosophy promotes negative, resentful, Oedipalized feelings. He opposed to this necrophilic cult of dead white men, a vision and a practice of philosophy that emphasizes the empowering force of affirmative passions. Thus, Deleuze engages in a quarrel with the canonized version of the history of philosophy, which he argues is dominated by the holy trinity of Hegel, Husserl and Heidegger. Deleuze opposed to them a counter-genealogy based on the empiricists, Spinoza, Leibnitz, Nietzsche and Bergson.

More importantly in terms of the ethical project of overturning Oedipalized (negative) into affirmative (positive) affects, Deleuze refuses to canonize his favourite authors. He thus presents them exactly for what they are: dearly beloved texts. Joyfully disrespectful of tradition in his philosophical passions, Deleuze practiced very un-Oedipal relations with his favourite philosophers. In some ways very faithful to their spirit – to the passions that animated them – Deleuze is also capable of bending them to his own ends and purposes. The co-author of the *Anti-Oedipus* will not be caught merely rehearsing his masters' voice. A 'bachelor machine' through and through, Deleuze picks and chooses, enacting with bravado the art of 'bricolage' and of conceptual pickpocketing. Thus, he retains philosophical monism from Spinoza, but only to hijack it away from the concept of a divinely-ruled, rational substance. From Bergson he picks the notion of duration but rejects the monism of his idea of time. In both cases, however, he remains extraordinarily faithful to the affective structures of their project, that is to say, to the degree of *potentia*, intensity or positivity which their ideas express. What Deleuze retains, repeats and enhances is the most affirmative aspects of his favourite thinkers' philosophy. In so doing he experiments with a philosophical style that leaves behind the drudgery on endless commentaries over commentaries on commentaries. This breaks with the bureaucratic protocols to which the institutions have reduced philosophy. The discipline is redefined, accordingly, as a radical, upbeat and extremely stimulating archive of life-enhancing texts. What I value in philosophical nomadism is that it views thinking in terms of the potency of thought, the joyful explosive intelligence of an embodied mind that actually enjoys the activity of thinking. Philosophical texts act therefore like fragmentation bombs of enthusiasm. This emphasis on pleasure as a leading principle in intellectual life, which I refer to as the 'epistemophilic' dimension of thinking, clashes frontally with the canonized worship of the dead which still constitutes the heart of philosophical teaching. In this respect, Deleuze's emphasis on the erotics of thinking is nothing short of a scandal.

The implications for those who come after him are daunting. If being Oedipalized – made to feel inadequate and having resentful, jealous, envious, negative affects instilled in one – is the kind of 'love' that philosophy extols from its followers, what forms of resistance are possible? Deleuze preached and practiced conceptual insurrection against the theoretical fathers; a sort of joyful and generous disobedience instead of the tragic solemnity that marks Oedipal respect for the elders. How should his own followers behave, I wonder: will his male heirs manage to combine the urge to mourn his loss with the commitment to de-Oedipalizing the practice of philosophy? How will they experience this tension and how will the potentially contradictory positions affect their views of both femininity and feminism?

I find that Deleuze's brand of loving disrespect could not be more different from the strategy of 'double displacement' (Spivak 1983) of the subject which is favoured by deconstruction. This is a strategic move that allows for resistance to the rigid patterns of imitation that are imposed by the phallogocentric subject, also known as the Oedipalization process. For Derrida, as for Spivak, a subject can avoid the lethal pitfall of the dead-serious repetition of the Law only by taking up a feminine position, that is to say through hysterical displacement (Derrida 1980). This amounts to shifting the grounds from under the feet of the Oedipalizing master. Hence Derrida's celebration of the feminine as a form of resistance to his powers, in spite of the fact that the price the feminine pays for this kind of resistance is symbolic absence. In a sort of apotheosis of the aporetic, Derrida then proceeds to pitch the undefinable feminine against the alleged Phallicity of all feminists (Derrida 1987), thus adding insult to injury.

Philosophical nomadism takes a different route. Deleuze's style of philosophy differs from this quite considerably, in that it does not start from the psychoanalytic premise of the feminine as symbolic absence at all. On the contrary, it accomplishes a reversal of this dialectics of negativity which for Deleuze is implicit in psychoanalytic theory and practice. Determined to disengage the operations of thinking from the trappings of the dialectics of sex, Deleuze practices an ethics of transformation of the kind of passions that are involved in and supportive of phallogocentrism. In so doing Deleuze strikes an alliance with the subversive and irreverent strands of feminist thought.

The sense of tragic Phallic solemnity is exploded by the joyful laughter of Alice in Wonderland, who proclaims that it is all a pack of cards and that the emperor is naked. The transcendence of the negative passions that are induced by the Oedipalizing economy of the Phallus – that 'fascism of the soul' as Deleuze calls it – is the engine of the transformation. Another name for this process of transformation is: 'becoming'. Becoming is the actualization of the immanent encounter between subjects, entities and forces which are apt mutually to affect and exchange parts of each other in a creative and non-invidious manner. The notion of 'forces' accomplishes a double aim, which is central to Deleuze's emphasis on radical immanence: on the one hand it gives priority to affectivity in his theory of the subject, and on the other it emphasizes the embodied structure of the subject and the specific temporality of the embodied human. A force is a degree of affectivity or of intensity, in that it is open and receptive to encountering other affects. The transformation that occurs in the process of becoming asserts the affirmative, joyful affects over and above the negative ones.

In so far as feminism is a hermeneutics of suspicion it functions as a factor of disengagement from the Masters' and Mistresses' voice. Consequently, as a feminist Deleuzian, that is to say an anti-Oedipal yet passionately undutiful daughter of one of the few philosophers who preached conceptual disobedience, I find myself, quite simply, in an ideal position. What could be more Deleuzian, in fact, that this structural – that is, externally induced (by feminism) – distance from his master's voice? From this location, I find myself looking with increasing amazement at the deadly serious style of neo-Deleuzian philosophers, wondering how they can be so Oedipalized and get away with it. Let me suggest as a starting-point therefore that the appropriate way to mourn this anti-Oedipal non-master may well be the joyfully disrespectful affirmation of positive and multiple differences, even and especially among his followers. A loving kind of irreverence – even towards his own philosophy – is one of the ways of empowering new forms of thought and new rituals of mourning, of becoming-Deleuzians in an un-Oedipal manner.

References to Deleuze have grown enormously in feminist theory. In the earlier phase of reception the tone was more polemical.[1] More and more positive voices, however, have emerged in the feminist readings of Deleuze. For instance, Bray and Colebrook (1998) argue that Deleuze's work offers feminism the possibility of a positive, active and affirmative ethics. Although the authors do not go into further details about the concrete norms and measures which would be enabled by such an ethics, I do share their appraisal of Deleuze and their preference for positivity. In the recent volume *Deleuze and Feminist Theory* (Buchanan and Colebrook 2000), Colebrook brings out the point that Deleuze's legacy is not and maybe could not be simple, yet it remains immensely inspirational for feminism. The issue of the becoming-woman remains a clear stumbling-block: 'Should the women's movement be told that it must be "molar" or concerned for identity only for a moment on the way to "molecular" becoming?' (Colebrook 2000a: 2). However, the impact of Deleuze's re-working of the concept of sexual difference is so deep that the polemic pales by comparison. Colebrook is very eloquent in arguing that ultimately, the way we understand difference, and especially sexual difference, affects how we understand philosophy itself.

Deleuze's work is of high relevance for feminism: not only does he display a great empathy with issues of difference, sexuality and transformation, but he also invests the site of the feminine with positive force. Conveyed by figurations such as the non-Oedipal Alice, the little girl about to be dispossessed of her body by the Oedipal Law, or by the more affirmative figure of the philosopher's fiancée Ariadne, the feminine face of philosophy is one of the sources of the transmutation of values from negative into affirmative. This ethical metamorphosis allows Deleuze to overcome the boundaries that separate mere critique from active empowerment. Last but not least, Deleuze's emphasis on the 'becoming woman' of philosophy marks a new kind of masculine style of philosophy: it is a philosophical sensibility which has learned to undo the straight-jacket of phallocentrism and to take a few risks. In Deleuze's thought, the 'other' is not the emblematic and invariably vampirized mark of alterity – as in classical philosophy. Nor is it a fetishized and necessarily othered 'other', as in deconstruction. It is a moving horizon of exchanges and becomings, towards which the non-unitary subjects of postmodernity move, and by which they are moved in return.

I am tempted to say that at some level the interrelation between Deleuze and feminist theory is simply a question of affinity – an epidermic sort of thing. The unconventional, provocative, non-linear style of nomadism appeals to the anarchic spirit of feminists, who are trying to break out of a mimetic relationship to the dominant scientific discourse. The issue of figurations can constitute an important bond here, as it marks a shift of emphasis away from the propositional content of ideas to the charge, quality and degree of the intensity they express. This cannot fail to appeal to feminist theorists who have asserted the proximity between the thinking process, life and the lived experience. Feminism has contributed in fact to re-thinking the living processes of existence, literally the spaces in between the mental and the physical, the theoretical and the experiential. Feminist philosophers (Lloyd 1985) have also connected this shift to the task of overthrowing centuries-old dichotomies. It is this quest for overcoming dualism and reconnecting life and thought that constitutes the bottom line of a possible alliance between feminism and nomadic thinking: it is a joint commitment to re-thinking subjectivity as an intensive, multiple and discontinuous process of interrelations. I would express this as the radical edge of postmodernism (hooks 1990), namely to move beyond critique and to bring about a community of historically located subjects seeking for interconnections in a non-ethnocentric and non-phallocentric manner. If this strikes you, the readers, as a mouthful, no doubt it is so.

Deleuze redefines the practice of theory-making in terms of flows of affects, and the capacity to draw connections. Accordingly, Deleuze describes the subject as an affective or intensive entity and ideas as events, active states which open up unsuspected possibilities of life. The truth of an idea, in other words, is in the kind of affects and the level of intensity that it releases. Ideas are noble or lowly, active or reactive, depending on whether they mobilize one's powers of affirmation and joy, over the forces of denial and negation. Affectivity governs the truth-value of an idea. In juxtaposition with the linear, self-reflexive mode of thought that is favoured by phallogocentrism, Deleuze defines this new style of thought as 'rhizomatic' or 'molecular'. These new figurations of the activity of thinking are chosen for their capacity to suggest web-like interaction and interconnectedness, as opposed to vertical distinctions. Deleuze defends this view of the subject as a flux of successive becomings by positing the notion of a 'minority' consciousness, of which the 'becoming-woman' is somehow emblematic.

On the concept of becoming

The concept of 'becoming' is central to both Irigaray's and Deleuze's philosophical concerns. Nomadic embodied subjects are characterized by their mobility, changeability and transitory nature. Their power of thinking is not the expression of in-depth interiority, or the enactment of transcendental models: it is a tendency, a predisposition which expresses the outward-bound nature of the subject. Thinking is a way of establishing connections with a multiplicity of impersonal forces. Following from this I think that the most fruitful starting point for an alliance between feminist concerns and Deleuze's thought is precisely the effort to imagine the activity of thinking differently.

In his determination to undo the Western style of theoretical thought, Deleuze moves beyond the dualistic oppositions that historically have conjugated the monological discourse of phallogocentrism. Deleuze – the most 'philosophical' of the poststructuralist philosophers – attacks especially the binary logic of the logocentric system and proposes to overcome the structure of thought on which the dichotomous oppositions are based, rather than simply reversing the terms of the opposition. The point is to move beyond dialectics. Quoting Scotus, Deleuze stresses the extent to which in Western thought Being is univocal, it is One, the Same and asserts its sameness through a series of hierarchically ordained differences. The classical notion of the subject treats difference as a sub-set of the concept of identity as sameness, that is to say equating it to a normative idea of a Being that remains one and the same in all its varied qualifications and attributes. This univocity has been captured by the moral discourse of Western metaphysics, which therefore rests on an inherently normative image of thought, this norm being the Being of a subject who coincides with consciousness, rational judgement and who is endowed with an immortal soul. Hence the importance of thinking 'difference' so as to disengage it from the reactive pole of a binary opposition which is organized to affirm dialectically the power and primacy of the Same. What Deleuze aims at is the affirmation of difference in terms of a multiplicity of possible differences; difference as the positivity of differences.

As I argued earlier, in trying to define the conceptual and ethical landscape of modernity and in his determination to move beyond the stale binary oppositions of phallogocentrism, Deleuze goes back to the classical roots of materialism. In so doing, he gives a genealogical line of thinking that, through Lucretius, the empiricists, Spinoza and Nietzsche, emphasizes activity, joy, affirmation, dynamic or molecular becoming. Deleuze opposes it to the Majority: the sedentary, guilt-ridden, life-denying, moralizing tone of most Western philosophy: a dogmatic image of thought which perpetuates itself with unerring regularity.

Deleuze tracks the continuity of this vision of the subject through Hegel into contemporary psychoanalysis. Adopting Nietzsche's figurative style of speech, Deleuze (Deleuze and Guattari 1980) dubs as 'slave morality' Lacan's negative vision of desire, his metaphysical notion of the unconscious as the black box of deep 'inner' truths, and the emphasis on castration and lack. He prefers to posit the unconscious in terms of displacement and production, and desire as affirmation. As I argued in the previous chapter, I understand the unconscious as marking the structural non-coincidence of the subject with his or her consciousness. This non-coincidence is a disjunction that separates the thinking subject from the illusion and delusion of plenitude and self-transparence, the monolithic, identical image of the self that supports the phallogocentric system.

In this perspective therefore, the construction of a thinking subject cannot be separated from that of a desiring subject: affectivity and intellectuality grow together in such a way as to make it difficult to separate reason from the imagination. The key idea here is that desire is the first and foremost step in the process of constitution of a self. What makes the entire procedure possible is the will-to-know, the desire to say, the desire to speak, to think and to represent. In the beginning there is only the desire to know – the knowledge about desire, a yearning, a predisposition, a gravitational pull.

In developing this idea in his philosophical nomadology, Deleuze operates a double displacement. The first is in relation to the Platonic theory of representation, which is dominant in philosophical thinking. Deleuze reverses the qualitative distinction between 'original' or 'real' ideas – the regime of Sameness – and the 'simulacra' or copies – the regime of Difference. Instead of following the century-old tradition of prioritizing the One/Same by linking it dialectically with the Other/Different, philosophical nomadism accomplishes a transgression. Deleuze argues that Sameness/Difference are not specular and therefore dialectically linked by negation, but rather they are of an altogether different qualitative kind. They are *two* positively different others or sames, de-linked from dialectical interconnection. This reversal of Platonism allows Deleuze to conclude that Sameness/Difference are not two sides of the same coin, but rather two incommensurable and highly specific modes of being. The following ideas are crucial here: that the subject is a complex, heterogeneous, non-unitary entity and that accordingly the Other is not a simulacrum, a specular reflection caught in the centuries-old 'metaphysical cannibalism' of the subject. The Other is a matrix of becoming in his or her own right and it generates a new kind of entity on which the same actually depends for their own self-definition. What matters is what occurs in the in-between spaces, the intervals, the transitions between their respective differences. This is not a 'heterogeneous brand of monism' (Halberstam and Livingston 1995: 10) but the unfolding of positive difference.

The second displacement occurs, as I indicated earlier, in relation to psychoanalysis. In clear opposition to Lacan, Deleuze explodes the myth of interiority and rejects the omnipotence of a symbolic system that indexes the subject on a scale of lack, signifier and negativity. This encompasses the constitutive loss of embodied materiality in the form of the maternal site of origin and bequeathes to the subject a negative symbolic capital of mourning and melancholia. Psychoanalysis also asserts the sovereignty of the Phallus, with its traditional entourage of specular others. Last but not least it affirms the power of the linguistic signifier – with its in-built logic of absence, deferral and differential assignation of meanings. In other words, philosophical nomadism moves to a post-Lacanian emphasis on the materiality of the body, which is redefined as a pre-reflexive re-collection of embodied matter. This 'somatic' dimension is understood in vitalistic terms, freely borrowed and adopted from Spinoza's *conatus*, namely as living matter yearning to become and to go on becoming. In this respect, the term body/ *soma* only makes sense in a binary opposition to the mind/*psyche*, and thus it is inadequate in a rhizomatic scheme.

In his nomadology Deleuze explicitly and purposefully attacks the Hegelian legacy within both psychoanalytic theory and philosophy, with its luggage of lack and negativity and the mournful self-referentiality of the semiological apparatus. I would call this a philosophy of priests, judges, censors, confessors and pornographers: all of them rely on negative, resentful, disavowed affects and thus reject *potentia* as an affirmative and vital force. Deleuze concentrates on disengaging the patterns of repetition, which are constitutive of the subject, from the infernal machines of Dr Hegel, thus freeing them from dialectical oppositions. If sameness and difference are indeed posited as altogether 'other' regimes of truth, their interrelation needs to be thought anew and, if possible, with some conceptual creativity. The punchline of this highly philosophical argument, in fact, should be quite familiar to my readers by now. It comes down to a plea for more innovative and creative energy in thinking about the structures of subjectivity at a time in history when social, economic, cultural and symbolic regimes of representation are changing very fast.

The empirical transcendental

Joining together creativity with the activity of thinking, Deleuze's work is marked by the positivity of thinking as a process of becoming. This transcends the boundaries of both classical philosophy in the institutional sense of the dutiful administration of the symbolic capital of phallocentrism, and of critical theory as an exercise of negation. Throughout the different phases that mark his extraordinarily cohesive body of work, Deleuze never ceases to emphasize the empowering force of affirmative passions and thus redefines the embodied subject as an empirical transcendental entity.

In so doing Deleuze goes further than any social constructivist attack on the 'myth' of human nature, while also moving beyond the ways in which psychoanalysis 'sacralizes' the sexual body. Deleuze's philosophy aims instead at replacing both these views with what I would call a high-tech brand of vitalism, the respect for bio-organisms and also for bio-diversity. This engenders also the 'intensive' style of writing which is his trademark. This results in a project that aims at alternative figurations of human subjectivity and of its political and aesthetic expressions. Rhizomes, bodies-without-organs, nomads, processes of becoming, flows, intensities and folds are part of this rainbow of alternative figurations which Deleuze throws our way.

As I stated in the previous section, for Deleuze thought is made up of sense and value: it is the force, or level of intensity, that fixes the value of an idea, not its approximation to a pre-established normative model. An idea is a line of intensity, marking a certain degree or variation in intensity. An idea is an active state of very high intensity, which opens up hitherto unsuspected possibilities of life and action. An idea is that which carries the affirmative power of life to a higher degree. The force of this notion is that it puts a stop to the traditional search for ideas or lines which are 'just' (in theory and politics alike). For if ideas are projectiles launched into time they can be neither 'just' nor 'false'. Or rather, they can be either 'just' or 'false', depending on the degree and levels of intensity of the forces, affects or passions that sustain them. Philosophy as critique of negative, reactive values is also the critique of the dogmatic image of thought which they sustain. It expresses the thinking process in terms of a typology of forces (Nietzsche) or an ethology of passions (Spinoza). In other words, Deleuze's rhizomatic style brings to the fore the affective foundations of the thinking process.

Thinking, in other words, is to a very large extent non-conscious, in that it expresses the desire to know, and this desire is that which cannot be adequately expressed in language, simply because it is that which sustains it. Through this intensive structure of the thinking process, Deleuze points to the pre-philosophical foundations of philosophy: its embodied, fleshy starting-block.

We are faced here with the problem of what is ontologically there but by necessity propositionally excluded in the philosophical utterance. There is the unspoken and the unspeakable desire for thought, the passion for thinking, the epistemophilic substratum on which philosophy later erects its discursive monuments. This affective stratum makes it possible for Deleuze to speak of a pre-discursive moment of thinking. Pursuing this insight in a Spinozist mode, Deleuze rejects the phantoms of negation, putting thought at the service of creation. In this perspective, we shall call philosophy all that expresses and enriches the positivity of the subject as an intensive, libidinal thinking entity. As I argued in the previous section, this definition of philosophy clearly clashes with the one embodied and perpetuated in institutional practice. Deleuze attacks the academic power-base (*potestas*) of a discipline which he aims to nomadize, that is, to de-Oedipalize so as to make it able to express the potency (*potentia*) of the subject.

Deleuze's analysis of thinking (Deleuze 1962 and 1968a) points in fact to a structural aporia in philosophical discourse. Philosophy is both logo-philic and logo-phobic, as Foucault had already astutely remarked (1977b). Discourse – the production of ideas, knowledge, texts and sciences – is something that philosophy relates to and rests upon, in order to codify it and systematize it; philosophy is therefore logo-philic. Discourse being, however, a complex network of interrelated truth-effects, it far exceeds philosophy's power of codification. So philosophy has to 'run after' all sorts of new discourses, such as women, post-colonial subjects, the audio-visual media and other new technologies, in order to incorporate them into its way of thinking; in this respect philosophy is logo-phobic. It is thus doomed to accept processes of becoming, or to perish.

I find that the strength of the philosophy of immanence that I am defending here is also its social and historical relevance. It assumes that the overcoming of dialectics of negativity is historically and politically necessary in the framework of a poly-centred, post-humanist and post-industrial world. I would also like to add that it is conceptually necessary to get over the in-built pessimism of a philosophy of eternal returns which does not trigger any margins of empowering difference. I maintain that whereas Derrida, confronted with the same challenges, ends up glorifying the vicious circle of undecidability and endless reiteration, and whereas Irigaray invests in the feminine as the force that can break the eternal return of the Same and its classical Others, rhizomatic thinking encourages each subject to empower him- or herself as a multiplicity and along multiple axes. Only such a qualitative leap can accomplish that creative overturning of the melancholia of negativity, bad conscience, law and lack. 'Just do it!' sums up quite well the brand of vitalistic pragmatism that I find in Deleuze's philosophy. It is an instigation to empower positively the difference that each and everyone can make. It has nothing to do with voluntarism and all to do with a shift of grounds, a change of rhythms, a different set of conceptual colours. Resonances, harmonies and hues intermingle to paint an altogether different landscape of a self that, not being One, functions as a relay-point for many sets of intensive intersections and encounters with multiple others. Moreover, not being burdened by being One, such a subject can envisage forms of resistance and political agency that are multi-layered and complex. It is an empirical transcendental site of becoming.

Resting on Spinoza, whom he decidedly recasts out of the Hegelian mould, Deleuze opens a whole dimension to the debate about the politics of desire and the desirability of an enfleshed subject who may actually yearn for change and transformation. Not happy with accommodation, and well beyond the libidinal economy of compensation, this subject which is not One actively desires processes of metamorphosis of the self, society and of its modes of cultural representation. This project of undoing the Hegelian trap that consists in associating desire with lack and negativity results in a radical new ethics of enfleshed, sustainable subjects. How could this non-unitary subject, this subject which is not One avoid a confrontation with the feminine?

Discontinuous becomings

Although philosophical nomadism and the feminist theories of sexual difference share a number of crucial assumptions, which I have outlined in the previous chapter, they also differ considerably. The dividing line between them is the emphasis on sexual difference understood as the dissymmetrical relationship between the sexes. Where Deleuze and Irigaray differ, in other words, is on the priority that they are willing to grant to the elaboration of adequate forms of representation of subjectivity. The difference is conceptual as well as political, and it focuses on the notion of 'becoming-woman'.

For Irigaray, as for Deleuze, the subject is not a substance, but rather a process of negotiation between material and semiotic conditions that affect one's embodied, situated self. In this perspective, 'subjectivity' names the process that consists in stringing together – under the fictional unity of a grammatical 'I' – different forms of active and reactive interaction with and resistance to these conditions. The subject is a process, made of constant shifts and negotiations between different levels of power and desire, constantly shifting between wilful choice and unconscious drives. Whatever semblance of unity there may be is no God-given essence, but rather the fictional choreography of many levels into one socially operational self. It implies that what sustains the entire process of becoming-subject is the will-to-know, the desire to say, the desire to speak, as a founding, primary, vital, necessary and therefore original desire to become.

In her defence of sexual difference against its hasty dismissal as part of the deconstruction of the subject, Luce Irigaray refers negatively to the Deleuzian diagram of the desiring machines (Irigaray 1974, 1977, 1980, 1984, 1987a, 1989, 1990). The notion of 'the body without organs' is for Irigaray reminiscent of a condition of dispossession of the bodily self, a structurally splintered position which is historically associated with femininity as a symbolic mark of absence and with women as its empirical referent. She points out that the emphasis on the machine-like, the inorganic, as well as the notion of loss of self, dispersion and fluidity are all too familiar to women: is not the 'body without organs' women's own historical condition (Irigaray 1977: 140)? Irigaray's critique of Deleuze is radical: she points out that the dispersal of sexuality into a generalized 'becoming' results in undermining feminist claims to a redefinition of the female subject.

There is a tension therefore between Deleuze's theories of multiplicity and becoming-minority and feminist theories of sexual difference. This tension highlights the difficulties involved in freeing the subject Woman from the subjugated position of Other, that is to say, the self-effacing servant at the banquet of the Socratic club. As I stated earlier, the issue at stake in the redefinition of female subjectivity is how to make the feminine express a 'different difference', released from the hegemonic framework of oppositional, binary thinking within which Western philosophy had confined it. In a feminist perspective, the focus is as much on the deconstruction of the phallogocentric representations of the feminine as on the experience and the potential becoming of real-life women, in their diverse ways of inhabiting the subject position of Woman. In other words, the feminist issue is how to activate political and epistemological agents, capable of alternative definitions of female subjectivity. The philosophy of Luce Irigaray has convinced me that it is unthinkable that the question of the deconstruction of phallogocentrism could be disconnected from the concrete changes taking place in women's lives. Yet the quest for a different, positive vision of female subjectivity entails a redefinition of human subjectivity in general.

Moreover, Deleuze and Irigaray share a common root in their stated desire to move beyond Lacanianism. Not surprisingly, their critique of Lacanian psychoanalysis takes different forms. Irigaray concentrates her work on attacking the Lacanian assumption of the psychic and historical inevitability of the phallogocentric system centred on the phallic signifier. She proposes to replace it with a female symbolic, expressed in an imaginary that is no longer mediated by the Phallus. Deleuze on the other hand suggests that we rethink subjectivity without reference to any one symbolic system. Vitalist empiricism in its link to affectivity; desire as positivity, not as lack; theoretical practice as a cartography of positions; subjectivity as a passions-driven network of impersonal or machine-like connections are Deleuze's key ideas. They also constitute the backbone of Deleuze's critique of Lacan who, in his eyes, overemphasizes dialectical oppositions, the metaphysical illusion of substance and the teleological structures of identity.

Compared to feminist discussions of gendered identity, Deleuze's work does not rest on a dichotomous opposition of masculine and feminine subject positions, but rather on a multiplicity of sexed subject-positions. The differences in degree between them mark different lines of becoming, in a web of rhizomatic connections. It is a vision of the subject as being endowed with multiple sexualities.

> For us . . . there are as many sexes as there are terms in symbiosis, as many differences as elements contributing to a process of contagion. We know that many beings pass between a man and a woman; they come from different worlds, are born on the wind, form rhizomes around roots; they cannot be understood in terms of production, only in terms of becoming. (Deleuze and Guattari 1987b: 242)

These different degrees of becoming are diagrams of subject-positions, typologies of ideas, politically informed maps, variations on intensive states. Multiplicity does not reproduce one single model – as in the Platonic mode – but rather creates and multiplies differences. This has dire consequences for sexual difference.

There is an unresolved knot in Deleuze's relation to the becoming-woman and the feminine. It has to do with a double pull that Deleuze never solved, between on the one hand empowering a generalized 'becoming-woman' as the prerequisite for all other becomings and, on the other hand, calling for its dismissal. On the one hand, the becoming-minority/nomad/molecular/ bodies-without-organs/woman is based on the feminine, on the other hand it is posited as the general figuration for the kind of subjectivity which Deleuze advocates. Deleuzian becomings emphasize the generative powers of complex and multiple states of transition between the metaphysical anchoring points that are the masculine and feminine. But they do not quite solve the issue of their interaction. Deleuze's work displays a great empathy with the feminist assumption that sexual difference is the primary axis of differentiation and therefore must be given priority. On the other hand he also displays the tendency to dilute metaphysical difference into a multiple and undifferentiated becoming, which prompts my question: what is the relation between feminist theories of sexual difference and Deleuze's philosophy of difference?

Is molar to molecular as masculine to feminine?

In identifying the points of exit from the phallocentric modes of thought, towards a new, intensive image of philosophy, Deleuze stresses the need for new images for these subject-positions. This results in the elaboration of a set of post-metaphysical figurations of the subject. The notion of the *figural* (as opposed to the more conventional aesthetic category of the 'figurative') is central to this project:[2] figurations such as rhizomes, becomings, lines of escape, flows, relays and bodies without organs release and express active states of being, which break through the conventional schemes of theoretical representation.

Alternative figurations of the subject, including different feminine and masculine subject-positions, are figural modes of expression, which displace the vision of consciousness away from phallogocentric premises. Deleuze's central figuration is a general becoming-minority, or becoming-nomad, or becoming-molecular. The minority marks a crossing or a trajectory; nothing happens at the centre, for Deleuze, but at the periphery there roam the youthful gangs of the new nomads:

> All becomings are already molecular. That is because becoming is not to imitate or identify with something or someone. Nor is it to proportion formal relations. Neither of these two figures of analogy is applicable to becoming: neither the imitation of a subject nor the proportionality of a form. Starting from the forms one has, the subject one is, the organs one has, or the functions one fulfils, becoming is to extract particles between which one establishes the relations of movements and rest, speed and slowness that are *closest* to what one is becoming, and through which one becomes. (Deleuze and Guattari 1987b: 272)

The space of becoming is one of affinity and symbiosis between adjacent particles. Proximity is both a topological and a quantitative notion, which marks the space of becoming of subjects as sensitive matter. The space of becoming is one of dynamic marginality.

In so far as man, the male, is the main referent for thinking subjectivity, the standard-bearer of the Norm, the Law, the Logos, Woman is dualistically, that is, oppositionally, positioned as his 'other'. The consequences are that:

1 there is no possible becoming-minority of man
2 the becoming-woman is a privileged position for the minority-consciousness of all.

Consistent with his critique of the phallogocentric appropriation of symbolic subjectivity, Deleuze agrees with Irigaray that Man as the privileged referent of subjectivity, the standard-bearer of the norm/law/logos, represents the majority, the dead heart of the system. The consequences are on the one hand that masculinity is antithetical to the process of becoming and it can only be the site of deconstruction or critique. On the other hand, the becoming-woman is a fundamental step in the process of becoming, for both sexes.

Deleuze states that all the lines of deterritorialization go necessarily through the stage of 'becoming-woman', which is not just any other form of becoming minority, but rather is the key, the precondition and the necessary starting-point for the whole process. The reference to 'woman' in the process of 'becoming-woman', however, does not refer to empirical females, but rather to topological positions, degrees and levels of intensity, affective states. The becoming-woman is the marker for a general process of transformation: it affirms positive forces and levels of nomadic, rhizomatic consciousness.

> There is a becoming-woman, a becoming-child, that do not resemble the woman or the child as clearly distinct entities. . . . What we term a molecular entity is, for example, the woman as defined by her form, endowed with organs and functions and assigned as a subject. Becoming-woman is not imitating this entity or even transforming oneself into it. . . . Not imitating or assuming the female form, but emitting particles that enter the relation of movement and rest, or the zone of proximity, of a microfemininity, in other words, that produce in us a molecular woman, create the molecular woman. (Deleuze and Guattari 1987b: 275)

Clearly, the woman occupies a troubled area in this radical critique of phallocentrism: in so far as woman is positioned dualistically as the other of this system, she is also annexed to the Phallus – albeit by negation. Deleuze, not uncharacteristically ignorant of basic feminist epistemological distinction between *W*oman as representation and women as concrete agents of experience, ends up making analogous distinctions internal to the category of woman herself. At this point his relationship to Irigaray becomes quite paradoxical, because Deleuze supports a clearly feminist position:

> It is, of course, indispensable for women to conduct a molar politics, with a view to winning back their own organism, their own history, their own subjectivity. . . . But it is dangerous to confine oneself to such a subject, which does not function without drying up a spring or stopping a flow. (Deleuze and Guattari 1987b: 276)

In spite of such evident support for women's uphill struggle towards achieving full subjectivity, with human and citizenship rights, Deleuze, like Derrida and other poststructuralists, opposes to the 'majority/sedentary/molar' vision of woman as the structural operator of the phallogocentric system, the woman as 'becoming/minority/molecular/nomadic'. Deleuze argues that all becomings are equal, but some are more equal than others. As against the molar or sedentary vision of woman as an operator of the phallogocentric system, Deleuze proposes the molecular or nomadic woman as a process of becoming. In the following sections I will explore this notion further and attempt an assessment.

In so far as the male/female dichotomy has become the prototype of Western individualism, the process of decolonizing the subject from this dualistic grip requires as its starting-point the dissolution of all sexed identities based on this gendered opposition. In this framework, sexual polarizations and gender-dichotomy are rejected as the prototype of the dualistic reduction of difference to a sub-category of Being. Thus, the becoming-woman is necessarily the starting-point in so far as the over-emphasis on masculine sexuality, the persistence of sexual dualism and the positioning of woman as the privileged figure of otherness are constitutive of Western subject-positions. In other words, 'becoming-woman' triggers off the deconstruction of phallic identity, through a set of deconstructive steps that re-trace backwards, so as to undo them, different stages of the historical construction of this and other differences.

Sexuality being the dominant discourse of power in the West, as Foucault taught us (1975b, 1976, 1984a, 1984b),[3] it requires special critical analysis. The generalized becoming-woman is the necessary starting-point for the deconstruction of phallogocentric identities precisely because sexual dualism and its corollary – the positioning of Woman as figure of Otherness – are constitutive of Western thought. It is because of historical and not biological reasons that sexed identities are foregrounded in the process of deconstruction. By virtue of the economic, cultural and symbolic importance that Western culture has attributed to sexuality, it follows that gender and sexual difference have historically evolved as a primary – though by no means unique – site of constitution of subjectivity. Sexuality is a major element in the complex technologies of the self and the complex networks of power to which they connect. Through this route, Deleuze's thinking comes to intersect with feminist critiques of sexuality. However, Deleuze's next step, his ultimate aim with respect to sexual difference, is to move towards its final overcoming. The nomadic or intensive horizon is a subjectivity 'beyond gender' in the sense of being dispersed, not binary, multiple, not dualistic, interconnected, not dialectical and in a constant flux, not fixed. This idea is expressed in figurations like 'polysexuality', the 'molecular woman' and the 'bodies without organs' to which Deleuze's de-phallic style actively contributes.

Deleuze uses also his theory of the becoming-woman of women as the basis for a critique of certain kinds of feminism. To Deleuze, some feminists display the irritating tendency to refuse to dissolve the subject 'woman' into a series of transformative processes which should instead pertain to a generalized and 'gender-free' becoming. In other words, feminists are conceptually mistaken, though their political heart may be in the right place, in their assertion of specific rights and entitlements for women. They are even more misguided when they argue for a specifically feminine sexuality: emphasis on the feminine is restrictive. Deleuze suggests that they should instead draw on the multi-sexed structure of the subject and reclaim all the sexes of which women have been deprived.

Ultimately, what Deleuze finds objectionable in feminist theory is that it perpetuates flat repetitions of dominant values or identities, which it claims to have repossessed dialectically. This amounts to perpetuate reactive, molar or majority-thinking: in Nietzsche's scale of values, feminists have a slave-morality. As an anonymous ICA artist put it recently: 'ironic mimesis is not a critique, it is the mentality of a slave'.[4] For Deleuze, feminists would be subversive if, in their becoming, they contributed both socially and theoretically to constructing a non-Oedipal woman, by freeing the multiple possibilities of desire meant as positivity and affirmation. Women, in other words, can be revolutionary subjects only to the extent that they develop a consciousness that is not specifically feminine, dissolving 'woman' into the forces which structure her. This new general configuration of the feminine as the post-, or rather un-Oedipal subject of becoming, is explicitly opposed to what Deleuze constructs as the feminist configuration of a new universal based on extreme sexualization or rather an exacerbation of the sexual dichotomy.

This position is for me theoretically problematic, because it suggests a symmetry between the sexes, which results in attributing the same psychic, conceptual and deconstructive itineraries to both. This alleged symmetry is challenged most radically by Irigaray, as I argued in the previous chapter. In her perspective, sexual difference is a founding, structural difference, which cannot easily be dissolved, without causing psychic and social damage. This perspective is determined by Irigaray's acute sense of the historicity of women's struggles. Colebrook shares my concern: 'Just what are Deleuze and Guattari doing when they take Woolf and the women's movement away from the concepts of identity, recognition, emancipation and the subject towards a new plane of becoming?' (Colebrook 2000a: 3).

Deleuze proceeds *as if* there was clear equivalence in the speaking positions of the two sexes: he misses and consequently fails to take into account the central point of feminism. I would argue that the dissymmetry functions as a re-vindication of radical difference at the psychic and conceptual but also at the political level. Politically, it implies that the identification of points of exit from the phallogocentric mode takes dissymmetrical forms in the two sexes. The assertion of the positivity of sexual difference challenges the centuries-old identification of the thinking subject with the universal and of both of them with the masculine. It posits a female, sexed, thinking subject, who stands in a dissymmetrical relationship to the masculine. The feminine thus defined is not the structural 'other' of a dualistic system, but is radically and positively other. In the feminist analysis, in other words, women's position as designated other is radicalized into a speaking stance that is incommensurable with that of man.

Clearly, this radical dissymmetry has been covered up by being coded as devalorized difference and naturalized as such. It has been made to rest on a linear, teleological sense of time. History as we have come to know it is the master discourse of the white, masculine, hegemonic, property-owning subject, who posits his consciousness as synonymous with a universal knowing subject and markets a series of 'others' as his ontological props.

Developing this insight further, I have argued (Braidotti 1991a) that one cannot deconstruct a subjectivity one has never been fully granted control over; one cannot diffuse a sexuality which has historically been defined as dark and mysterious. In order to announce the death of the subject, one must first have gained the right to speak as one. I concluded that Deleuze gets caught in the contradiction of postulating a general 'becoming-woman' which fails to take into account the historical and epistemological specificity of the female feminist standpoint. A theory of difference which does not acknowledge sexual difference leaves me as a feminist critic in a state of sceptical perplexity. Or, to put it differently, Deleuze's critique of dualism acts as if sexual differentiation or gender dichotomies did not have as the most immediate and pernicious consequence the positioning of the two sexes in an asymmetrical relationship to each other. He gets stuck on a fundamental ambivalence about the position of sexual difference within his own project of 'becoming-woman', which is both one of many possible becomings and the one through which all other becomings are possible: it is both foundational and accessory, originary and accidental.

I do not mean to suggest, of course, that Deleuze does not have excellent reasons for doing so. Quite on the contrary, as stated earlier, the critique of psychoanalytic discourse, which he shared with Guattari, is a systematic deconstruction of the institution of sexuality and sexed identities as our culture has constructed them. It is therefore no wonder that in his theory of the becoming-minority Deleuze argues for the dissolution of all identities based on the Phallus, even the feminine as the eternal other of this system. Nevertheless, in a feminist perspective based on sexual difference, the problems remain.

Moreover, Deleuze is not consistent in thinking through the problem of the 'becoming-woman'; he rather proceeds in a contradictory manner about it. It is the position of 'yes, but . . .', 'I know what you mean, but . . .'; this is the mode of denial, that is to say of wilful disavowal, which expresses a structural and systematic indecision. A similar naivety about sexual difference is expressed in *Qu'est-ce que la philosophie?*, in which Deleuze contemplates the possibility of the crucial conceptual character in philosophy being a woman: 'What might happen if woman herself becomes a philosopher?'

(Deleuze and Guattari 1991: 69). May I be so bold as to venture that only a non-woman would contemplate this possibility as a great novelty, an unprecedented event or a catastrophe internal to the philosophical order and capable of subverting it? Since the 1970s, and especially in French-language cultures, women have been raising exactly this question. They have enacted a collectively-driven repossession of the subject-positions by and for politically motivated women. I would expect this rather large corpus of work and experience, which I see as a real symbolic capital of female femin-ist intelligence, to be taken into account whenever the otherwise politically naive question, 'what happens when women start thinking for themselves?' is actually asked.

I have argued earlier that transformations and Deleuze's processes of becoming cannot be created by sheer volition and are not just a matter of judgement and choice. Given the co-extensivity of the psychic and the social in the radically immanent theories of the subject defended in different ways by both Deleuze and Irigaray, transformations do not include only 'inter-nalized' reality – that would be a form of narcissism and paranoia. They also include radically de-essentialized forms of embodiment (Deleuze) or strategically re-essentialized embodiments (Irigaray). In any case, becomings or transformations are external and interrelational.

Minorities and minoritarian subjects

A nomadic becoming-woman entails an opening outwards of the process of redefining female subjectivity. In turn that calls for a broadening of the traditional feminist political agenda to include, as well as the issue of women's social rights, a larger spectrum of options, which range from cul-tural concerns related to writing and creativity, to issues which at first sight seem to have nothing to do specifically with women. That is precisely the point: the co-existence of feminine specificity with larger, less sex-specific concerns. Nomadic feminism is about tracing a zigzagging path between them.

As an illustration of the general principle of becoming minoritarian, I would paraphrase Griggers (1997), who in turn paraphrases the Chiapatas movement, and argue that nomadic subjects could be any of the following: gays in Cuba, blacks in South Africa, a Palestinian in Israel, an illegal migrant in the EU, a gang member in any slum of the world's metropolises, a communist in the post-cold war era, an artist without gallery or portfolio, a pacifist in Bosnia, a housewife alone on Saturday night in *any* neighbour-hood in *any* city, in *any* country, a single woman on the metro at 10.00 pm, a peasant without land, an unemployed worker, a dissident amidst free-market fetishists, a writer without books or readers. In other words, the nomadic subject signifies the potential becoming, the opening out – the transformative power of all the exploited, marginalized, oppressed minorities. Just being a minority, however, is not enough: it is only the starting-point. What is crucial to becoming-Nomad is undoing the oppositional dualism of majority/minority and arousing an affirmative passion for and desire for the transformative flows that destabilize all identities.

Becoming-minority is a task *also* for the minorities, who too often tend to be caught in the paralysing gaze of the master – hating and envying him or her at the same time. Becoming nomadic means that one learns to re-invent oneself and one desires the self as a process of transformation. It is about the desire *for* change, for flows and shifts of multiple desires. Deleuze is no Romantic. Nor is he prone to the theoretical orientalism that plagues so much of the deconstructivist generation. He does *not* suggest that 'homelessness' and 'rootlessness' are the new universal metaphors of our times. This level of generalization is not much help. What he does theorize, however, is a non-unitary yet politically engaged and ethically accountable nomadic subject. What Deleuze does attempt is to de-territorialize the fixity and scramble the unitary structure of the classical view of the subject. Nomadology stresses the need for a change of conceptual schemes altogether, an overcoming of the dialectic of majority/minority or master/slave. Both the majority and the minorities need to untie the knots of envy (negative desire) and domination (dialectics) that binds them so tightly. In this process, they will necessarily follow asymmetrical lines of becoming, given that their starting positions are so different. For the majority, there is no possible becoming – other than in the undoing of its central position altogether. The centre is void, all the action is on the margins.

For the real-life minorities, however, the pattern is different: women, blacks, youth, post-colonial subjects, migrants, exiles and homeless may first need to go through a phase of 'identity politics' – of claiming a fixed location. This is both inevitable and necessary because, as I have often argued, you cannot give up something you have never had. Nor can you dispose nomadically of a subject-position that you have never controlled to begin with. I think consequently that the process of becoming-nomad (-minority, -woman) is internally differentiated and depends largely on where one starts off from. The politics of location is crucial. In other words, heterogeneity is injected into both poles of the dialectical opposition, which are undone accordingly. The 'Molar' line – that of Being, identity, fixity and *potestas* – and the 'Molecular' line – that of becoming, nomadic subjectivity and *potentia* – are absolutely not the same. They are two 'others'. Within phallogocentrism they have been captured in a dualistic mould. They are differentiated by structural inequalities that impose Sameness in a set of hierarchical relations. Deleuze defines the Molar/Majority as the standard and the Molecular/Minority as the other in the sense of 'the other of the same'. The central challenge of Deleuze's philosophy however is how to undo this dualistic mode and redistribute the power-relations of the two terms. More important than either of them, therefore, is the Line of Flight or of becoming. This is always and only a becoming-minoritarian as in woman/child/animal/imperceptible.

The differences in the starting-positions are important in that they mark different qualitative levels of relation. Thus, if one starts from the Majority position (the Same) there is only one possible path: through the Minority (the Other) – hence the imperative to become woman as: the first move in the deterritorialization of the dominant subject (also known as the feminization of Man). For those who start from the position of empirical minorities, on the other hand, more options are open. If the pull towards assimilation or integration into the Majority is strong for the minorities (hence the phenomenon of phallic women), so is the appeal of the lines of escape towards minoritarian becomings. In other words, you can have a becoming-woman that produces Margaret Thatcher and one that produces Kathy Acker, neither of whom is 'feminine' in any conventional sense of the term and yet they are as different from each other as the workhorse is from the racehorse.

What matters here is to keep open the process of becoming-minoritarian and not to stop at the dialectical role-reversal that usually sees the former slaves in the position of new masters or the former mistresses in the position of dominatrix. The point is to go beyond the logic of reversibility. This is especially important for those social subjects, women, blacks, post-colonial and other 'others', who are the carriers of the hopes of the Minorities. The process of becoming nomadic in the rhizomic mode favoured by Deleuze is not merely anti-essentialistic, but a-subjective, beyond received notions of individuality. It is a trans-personal mode, ultimately collective.

As I argued earlier, the question about nomadic thought is not *what*, but *where* it is and who can gain access to it. The old ontological questions about philosophy's meaning, function and corporate identity cannot possibly be answered philosophically any more. In this impossibility lies the evidence of the terminal crisis of philosophy as a discipline of thought; the historical decline of the 'master' narratives – and the opening-up of new possibilities. Nomadic thought marks a radical break from the Oedipal legacy at work within Western philosophy. It breaks especially from the established model of representing subjectivity. Dorothea Olkowski (1999a) argues that a feminist approach to Deleuze's philosophy entails taking on the broader conceptual concerns of his work, namely what she defines as 'the Ruin of Representation': that is to say, a nomadic, anti-representational re-arrangement of forces.

I would relate this to my concern for style and Deleuze's love of the creative enhancement of life through writing. I do not think it is possible to render the full impact of philosophical nomadism in the traditional and – to my mind – worn-out language of theoretical thought. An effort needs to be made to 'translate' the propositional content into a language that is adequate to its innovative force. If I were to do so, I would say that nomadism is a resolute vote of no-go thrown against the fortress of Western Reason. It is a view of subjectivity that rejects the phallo-logo-Eurocentric idea of a triumphant conscious subject whose task is supposed to be the supervision of your actions, thoughts and agency. The maniacal sleepless eye of Reason brooding over its empire is the reflection of this obsessional neurosis we still call 'our rational self', the biblical tree of knowledge allegedly encompassing in its vertical immobility all possible ramifications of human science, fixity and the imperialism of the Phallus: sedentary, monolithic and nostalgic of its old hegemony. In reaction to this, the nomadic subject is shifting, partial, complex and multiple. It exists in the shifts and the patterns of repetitions – the opposite of the tourists, the antithesis of the migrant, the nomadic subject is flows of transformation without ultimate destination. It is a form of intransitive becoming; it is multiple, relational, dynamic. You can never *be* a nomad, you can only go on trying to *become* nomadic.

Whose becoming is it, anyway?

Philip Goodchild (1996), in his useful introduction to Deleuze and Guattari's philosophy, sums up the present climate of the discussion on the 'becoming-woman' among Deleuze's followers. Goodchild reiterates a tendentious argument against feminist interpretations of Deleuze's becoming which shows far less sympathy for or understanding of feminism than Deleuze's texts ever did. Blaming feminism's paradoxical views of subjectivity without even attempting to appreciate their complexity, while glossing over Deleuze's no less manifest paradoxes, Goodchild practices double standards while enacting with distressing seriousness the position of dutiful son.

The central case made against feminist philosophy is that it is Majority-bound, linked to the Phallus by negation and totally unaware of itself. For the new generation of Deleuzians, feminism is at best a dialectical recuperation within the phallocentric/molar scheme of representation. 'They castrate desire once more' (Goodchild 1996: 177). Feminists are confined to the side of castration and negativity, to Nietzschean slave morality, to negative passion feeding on neurosis and resentment. I find that Goodchild has more of Derrida than of Deleuze in this, the former having explicitly cornered feminism into Phallic monomania.

This position operates a double reduction: of feminism as well as of Deleuze's thought. Firstly, feminism is reduced to a maniacal obsession with monolithic sexual difference, to the detriment of all other differences. Showing no real knowledge of feminist philosophies of difference, Goodchild then proclaims that all feminist readings of Deleuze are simply wrong. Adopting a priestly, holier-than-thou, approach, Goodchild proceeds to straighten out the situation, dictating the proper line of interpretation of His master's voice.

Conclusion? Goodchild saves it for a footnote, though it is the real punchline:

> It may appear to be the case that a multiplication of sexualities, losing a specific feminine identity, is historically dangerous for women – and indeed, it certainly would be in the short term – but closing off the critical routes by which the dominant power structures in thought can be analyzed and overthrown has more serious long-term historical consequences for women and minorities, who always bear the brunt of social ills. Deleuze and Guattari's revolutionary aim is to overthrow the most insidious, molecular and imperceptible power-machines that exist within the social field. (Goodchild 1996: 177)

Is feminism potentially one of these? It follows by extension that what is most insidious and consequently potentially reactionary within the social field is feminism's stubborn and – for Goodchild – unintelligent insistence that women's issues should not be marginalized or delegated to an improbable future. Moreover, both Deleuze and Foucault praised feminism as the only social movement that had reconnected life to thought, politicizing the living, the private, all that Marxism had left unquestioned. Far from being behind the times, feminism proved, for Deleuze's generation, a true laboratory of ideas, concepts and practices. This makes Goodchild's reduction especially disappointing and, in my opinion, dangerous. The danger consists essentially in relegating to a distant future the test of Deleuze's theory of becoming, thus turning it away from its immanent charge and making it into the last utopia of a century that has had far too many of them.

I do think that if this nomadic philosophy does not manage to get on its side those minorities – whom Deleuze explicitly acknowledged as the motors of the transformations which he theorized – then neither this nor any other century will ever become Deleuzian. What is really running out of time is the possibility of inscribing Deleuze's radical project into contemporary culture *at all*.

More orthodox Deleuzians, however, play it a lot harder, accusing feminist Deleuzians alternatively of incompetence or of extreme political correctness. 'I suspect yours is a molar/moral argument', emailed me one of them recently, 'are you speaking on behalf of the ministry of feminism? I think you are very prejudiced against Deleuze & Guattari or you would not speak the way you do. You are just influenced by what you heard about them by others.' The sting is there: a feminist reading of Deleuze is either unoriginal, or inadequate and off-the-point. In any case, the feminist Deleuzian remains a target of violence and contempt by over-enthusiastic, Oedipalized zealots.

Faced with such negativity, the feminist undutiful Deleuzian daughter is left wondering whether all critical judgement has left the mind of her peers, so that the only possible response to Deleuze is one of mindless adoration? Such an Oedipal response to Deleuze strikes me as a contradiction in terms.

I see no reason why feminism should be singled out for cleansing of its potentially sedentary, molar or hegemonic tendencies. Although it does encompass processes of institutionalization, canonization and stock-taking, feminism is clearly not alone in this. All social movements are subjected to fluxes of activity, flows of disintegration and even implosion, as well as sedentarization. No political empowerment is possible without these variations of political intensity. Without giving in to the cheap anti-feminism of the Left, or the facile post-feminist sound-bites of Camille Paglia, I prefer to situate this danger of molar/sedentary/institutional feminism in a historical context of change and transformation. Feminism operates both on the linear time-frame of social change and progress and on the more discontinuous time-sequence of deeper changes in the structures of the self. The paradoxical interdependence of the two motions is the driving force of this movement; it is also, in my opinion, the key to its far-reaching success. Both aspects of feminism are alive and well today: on a global scale, the pursuit of Majority-based basic rights is advancing. The case of 'women's rights are human rights', explicitly stated in 1995 at the Beijing UN conference is highly significant here. Patricia Williams (1993) has made the case for women's rights in the framework of diversity and multiplicity quite explicit.

Equally strong, however, is the case for feminist nomadism which implies a critique of the specific brands of 'Molar' or equality-minded identity politics that feminism itself has contributed to creating. Thus, Irigaray (1987b) and her generation critiqued an emancipatory model of feminist politics whose aim can be perhaps too hastily summed up as wanting to integrate women as first-class citizens in the system of power which had traditionally confined them to a secondary position. In her critique of Beauvoir, Irigaray noted how this would be a mere reversal of the sexual dialectics. This may benefit women in the short range, but in the long run it would basically confirm the existing structures of power. As such it is likely to create as many exclusions as inclusions, especially among 'minority' women. In other words, feminists developed their own scepticism of the majority and of his paralyzing gaze, as well as the pitfalls and limitations of homologation into a masculine model. These developments were both historically and conceptually parallel to the philosophical itinerary of Irigaray, Deleuze and their generation.

The accounts of feminism and of feminist theory that are emerging from the rank and file of the new Deleuzians are puzzling in that they neglect the turn toward difference which marked the feminist poststructuralist generation. They are unhistorical and decontextualized in their reception of Deleuze.

This may well be one of the effects of the relative occultation and marginalization of this brand of feminism through the 1990s – the era of the hegemony of 'gender'. It may also simply mark a generation gap and the specific forms of selective memory that such gaps entail. Another significant example of this new scholarship is the rather cursory treatment of difference-minded feminism in Patricia Pisters's study of Deleuze (1998). Although it is true that Pisters's specific field, film theory in general and feminist film theory in particular, have been dominated by semiotics and psychoanalysis, that seems to me no reason to dismiss them and their feminist versions as irrelevant only because not 'Deleuzian enough'. Again, this approach relies far too totally and uncritically on Deleuze to solve all of the problems and issues facing critical theory today. I think Deleuze can help and even do a lot, but I would never advocate total reliance on his, or for that matter any other, theoretical framework. This seems to me to be the age of hybridity, transversal and transdisciplinary connections and non-Oedipal creativity also and maybe especially in media and cultural studies where the intersection of feminist with Deleuzian theories can be most enriching for both (MacCormack 2000).

The becoming-minoritarian of men

Fortunately, however, other voices are also present: Paul Patton's comments on Deleuze's concept of 'becoming' (1999; 2000) strike me as more useful and cogent. Patton argues that Deleuze and Guattari explicitly declined to assess the usefulness or validity of their theoretical tools. That would amount to indexing their thought on a self-referential theory of truth and this is completely against their philosophical premises. Like Foucault, they saw themselves as providers of tools which others had to put to the test. It is consequently up to the rest of us to pick and choose out of their archive, and see what we can invest theoretically and politically for the purposes of our projects. The implication is clear: if a certain tool does not work, then it can either be remodelled or cast out and replaced with a more suitable one. The process of coming to terms with this is the hard labour of thinking. One usually thinks with one's hands, and they are seldom clean.

More importantly, Patton points out a serious fallacy in current debates between feminists and Deleuzian theorists of the becoming-woman/animal, etc.: namely, the tendency to read the becomings as necessarily or even preferably leading to the destruction of gender. Quoting Massumi, Patton introduces a very important and much needed shift in perspective. Translated into my language, I would say that we need to disengage the nomadic processes of becoming from the conceptually misguided attempt to go 'beyond gender'. What becomes central instead is the process of undoing, recomposing and shifting the grounds for the constitution of sexed and gendered subjectivities. Patton is careful in stressing the non-teleological nature of becomings: they are processes without beginning or end, origin or destination. They aim at nothing other than transformations, redistribution and displacement. They are 'open to all at any time' (Patton 2000: 83). It is consequently futile to try to index processes of becoming to the general aim of human or women's liberation.

I would personally extend this argument further and suggest that becoming/woman/animal, etc., can play a significant role in redefining feminist politics in a historical era when sexual difference is a more multi-layered notion than ever. The implication is that the whole discussion about the compatibility between Deleuze and feminist theory can be laid to rest at long last and a more pragmatic approach can be adopted. The question for me would then become what kinds of distribution and recomposition of masculinities and femininities are possible here and now? And how can they be activated in the direction of nomadic becomings and positive experimentations with difference?

Another cluster of contemporary Deleuzians by-passes the pitfalls of Deleuze's feminist legacy and his structural contradictions about the feminine, or the becoming-woman, by embracing fully the creative charge of philosophical nomadology. Brian Massumi (1992), for instance, offers a splendid example of how the cartographic mode, and consequently the quest for new figurations, can be put to the task of elaborating a creative, non-Oedipalized relationship to Deleuze's texts themselves, as well as to the *corpus* of feminist theory. The double emphasis on the need for conceptual creativity and the quest for new images of thought or alternative figurations combine in stressing the importance of philosophical style. Massumi is one of the Deleuzian thinkers who takes the greatest care of writing in a form that both reflects and reinforces the content. Highly creative, Massumi's work functions as an on-going experiment which illustrates simultaneously the relevance of Deleuze's thought and the futility of trying to imitate him.

Alphonso Lingis's work is an interesting comparison to Massumi's (Lingis 1994, 1998). Equally creative, but far more hysterical in his assimilation of the master's voice, Lingis's texts strike me as exacerbations of Deleuze's style. They push some of his premises to the extreme, often with great poetic force, which however reads at times like a parody. Lingis reminds me of another loyal Deleuzian, the Italian Bifo (Franco Berardi), former leader of the 1977 political anarchical movements. In his recent writings on globalization, nomadology and the politics of the new technologies (Berardi 1997), Bifo adopts a rather prophetic or visionary mode. Inspired by Nietzsche, like Lingis, Bifo mixes poetic with theoretical voices within the same text. This (in my opinion) healthy disregard for coherence goes hand-in-hand with a flair for discontinuities in graphic lay-out and chronological sequences. At times his texts take on an apocalyptic tone, mostly however they run at a high level of intensity. They constitute singular expressions of a nomadic sensibility that laughs with tragic seriousness at 'Splatterkapitalismus' (Berardi 1997: 7) as a horror show and at the no less horrific inertia of its lawful subjects sealed in 'Prozacnation' (1997: 21). Significantly, whereas Lingis incorporates and mimes the feminine, Bifo leaves it alone and highlights instead the relevance of male nomadic subjects in quest for a radical politics in an era that seems to want to yield none.

Massumi's work, on the other hand, differs from both Lingis's and Bifo's in that he is mercifully free of any self-referential constraints: he is, as it were, ego-less. This allows Massumi to trace patterns of becoming that are less representational and hence higher in creative energy. Intrinsically political, Massumi's texts are constructed both geologically and genealogically as multi-layered strata that do not fit into any predictable symmetry. His political theory texts (Massumi, 1992a and 1992b) enact diachronic interventions upon the social unconscious and the kind of flows of desire that both constructs it and sustains it. Massumi's work is diagrammatic in that he draws the flow-charts of desiring subjects, both the Majority-subject and His 'others' or minorities. He also underscores the interconnections between single events or actors, texts, historical contexts and other effects.

This focus on the effects of the text, of the affectivity it enacts, and on the material interrelations that sustain it, are all central to the cartographic concerns that I value so highly. It triggers off what I consider the most important effect of all: it destabilizes the readers and, like a diagonal line in Mondrian's paintings, it evokes the becoming-minoritarian, it makes the readers yearn for it. This desire is crucial to the Deleuzian diagrams or 'abstract machines' which function in this cartographic mode of flow-charts. In his disobedience, or rather, his disregard for orthodoxy, Massumi does not even attempt Oedipal loyalty and dutiful imitation, thus expressing perfectly the conceptual core of Deleuze's philosophy.

Not surprisingly, perhaps, there is something of the lexicographer in Massumi's relationship to Deleuze's texts: he indexes the key-terms and organizes them in a synoptical overview (Massumi 1998) with a precision and exactitude which express loyalty in a definitely un-Oedipal fashion. The indexical, lexicographic, geometric precision of Massumi's engagement with Deleuze's thought brings out another dimension of philosophical nomadism: a logical structure of the non-linear kind which makes it into a suitable candidate for digitalization. Rhizomatic texts are best served by information technologies which open up, at a touch or a click, a web of multiple possible connections. I believe this aspect of the rhizomatic sensibility is most alive in music, especially the technology-based experiments with sound that explicitly cross-refer to Deleuze.[5] I shall return to them in the next chapter. For now, let me stress that Massumi's geometrical accuracy is 'just' as in justness and not only justice, that is to say it does justice to Deleuze's philosophy while by-passing specular mimicry or banal repetition. Significantly, Massumi is extremely careful with the whole 'becoming-woman' theory and takes some critical distance from it, thus resisting facile assimilations of the feminine into the general nomadology. By avoiding the hysterical mode of identification with Deleuze, Massumi spares him the posthumous humiliation of being constructed as the Master he never wanted to be, that is to say a despotic ruler of the 'truth', a position which Deleuze abhorred and repudiated. The operation, however, is not without its perils: Massumi's books are hardly more accessible that Deleuze's own, or Spinoza's. They can only appeal to the kind of readers who are fascinated by mappings or charts, that is to say by non-linearity and extra-verbal communication through graphics or visuals. It is through precision and indexical exactitude that Massumi skilfully avoids repetition and enacts an impressive example of continuity without negative passions.

Writing intransitively

'Writing does not have an end in itself, simply because life is not something personal. Or rather: the aim of writing is to lift life to the state of an impersonal force.'

Deleuze and Parnet, *Dialogues*, 61

What seems to be emerging is a disturbing form of masculinism in the reception of Deleuze and Guattari's work. For instance, in the comparative work currently being done there is a tendency to ignore Luce Irigaray, the philosopher whom I think is the most obvious term of comparison for Deleuze. Moreover, in the aftermath of Deleuze's work, very genderized selection of his *corpus* is taking place among his followers. A great deal of emphasis is placed on his socio-political texts by the – mostly male – admirers, whereas the cultural or aesthetic texts – with the possible exception of the two volumes on cinema – are either neglected or left to the restricted number of female Deleuzians. As a result, at this stage, a re-compartmentalization of his work is taking place, along the lines allowed for and even required by academic institutions of higher learning. One can speak of a 'cultural studies' approach to Deleuze, which centres on his literary, theatre and film texts and which runs parallel to and often unaware of philosophical commentaries on his work. The effects of this very genderized division of labour strike me as negative for the appreciation and the understanding of Deleuze's work.[6] After all, Deleuze's critique of 'representation' is the over-arching concern that unifies the different moments of his work, without effacing its heterogeneity.

I think that the aesthetic aspects of Deleuze's philosophy are often downplayed.[7] For instance, although the cross-references to literature in general and science fiction in particular in Deleuze's work, and more especially *Mille Plateaux*, have been noticed by commentators,[8] they have not yet been the object of systematic analysis. Part of the problem here is the specific and wide-ranging erudition that Deleuze displays and for which even the term 'interdisciplinarity' is inadequate. An omnivorous reader with enormous memory capacity, Deleuze represents in this respect the best of an old-style French education system where broad knowledge of the humanities was both encouraged and rewarded. Unfortunately, the same humanistic sweep of competence and scholarship is not always present among his followers and commentators.

I think that precisely because his philosophy attempts to recode and re-configure the image of thought by a series of rigorous interventions on the representation of the pre-discursive and pre-conceptual groundwork of subjectivity, with emphasis on embodiment and immanence, it is impossible to separate the 'cultural' from the 'conceptual' aspects of his work. In this respect, as I have argued before, I do think that 'minority subjects of subjugated knowledges', such as feminist, black and post-colonial queer and other theorists are in a privileged position as readers of Deleuze's transgressive philosophical phantasmagoria.

It is important to emphasize, in this respect, that Deleuze was a very multi-layered writer, an acute commentator of literary and cultural texts; a lover of contemporary art and a fascinated spectator of the modern version of Plato's cave, which is how he saw cinema. His was a mobile and yet rigorous intelligence that effused the classical disciplinary distinctions imposed by the nineteenth-century institution that is the European university. Deleuze signifies for me the capacity for a paradoxical and deep love for philosophical thinking: not uncomplicated, because great loves never are, but in some ways unquestionable because it is so fundamental. Thinking is like breathing: you do it unreflexively, or not at all. And if you happen to want to do it reflexively, or with full awareness, it becomes a full project of its own. Deleuze marks for me the deployment of the philosophy of multiple becomings, which goes much farther than the critique of metaphysics. It is rather a vote of confidence in philosophy's capacity for self-renewal. An essential element of the vitality of Deleuze's philosophy is his wilful shedding of disciplinary grandeur in favour of dialogical exchanges with other disciplines – like physics, genetics and mathematics – but also with contemporary cultural and artistic practices such as cinema, art and techno-culture.

Thus, under the impact of affirmative creativity, philosophy renews itself by becoming an enlarged notion. I think that the becoming-creative of philosophy itself is Deleuze's fundamental legacy. Philosophy is redefined as the activity that consists in reinventing the very image of thinking, so as to empower the active, positive forces and disengage it from the reactive or negative passions. Central to this creative impetus is Deleuze's love for writing and for literature in so far as it enhances the intensity (*potentia*) of life.

The theories and processes of becoming in the radically immanent mode proposed by Deleuze and, in an analogous but dissymmetrical manner, by feminist theories find their clearest expression in writing and especially in literary texts and the kind of cultural effects which they interact with. Writing parallels for Deleuze the process of becoming-minority and of becoming-woman; consequently it is in literature and the arts that Deleuze finds the best illustrations for this process. Trinh T. Minh-ha (1989: 19) describes most effectively the molecularization of the self that occurs in writing: 'To write is to become. Not to become a writer (or a poet), but to become, intransitively. Not when writing adopts established keynotes or policy, but when it traces for itself lines of evasion.' Writing can be for Deleuze, and maybe it even ought to be, the primary vehicle for de-territorialization or becoming-minoritarian. It is a line of escape from phallogocentrism not in a metaphorical sense, but as a process of unsettling binarism, linearity and other sedimented unitary habits. Writing is about transiting in in-between spaces, cultivating transversality and mutations.

The literary texts which are favoured by philosophical nomadism are potent affirmations of life's virtual possibilities. Writing at this level of intensity is absolutely not the diligent activity that consists in capitalizing on the paranoia, narcissism and other negative passions that mark the triumphant sovereignty of the 'I'. I rather find that the authors Deleuze celebrates destabilize the 'I' by sabotaging the nest of negativity on which it erects itself. What is affirmed in the process is the impersonal voice of a self that is not One, but rather a cluster of multiple becomings. *Potentia* is a non-personal state of potency which engenders a radically immanent form of singularity. This affirmation is all the more singular as it is quite impersonal, that is to say it expresses the immanence of *a* life, not of *Life* as a metaphysical idea. This is the point where writing joins in with vital processes of becoming-animal, from the roach of Kafka to the moths, dolphins and porpoise of Virginia Woolf.

Another point worth raising here concerns the importance of multilinguism to Deleuze's approach to literature. This is not simply linguistic pluralism, but rather the flair for and the sense of heterogeneous dialects and idioms that resist unification. I take it therefore as constitutive of a concept and practice of nomadism that breaks from mono-linguism as from other forms of monolithic linearity. Moving between languages, speaking several and mastering none, living in constant simultaneous translation, is a possible location for the nomadic sensibility which best expresses itself in creative writing. One has to learn to stutter, to look for words, to hesitate, even and especially in one's so-called 'mother' tongue. As I stated elsewhere (Braidotti 1994a), there are no mother tongues, only linguistic sites from which one takes one's departure. Emphasis is placed on the general becoming-minority of language, of *not* settling into one linguistic *humus*. Deleuze lived and wrote in the historical period of the decline of French as a world language and in some ways his work reflects a becoming-minoritarian of the grand French imperial linguistic tradition. In this respect, Deleuze is a deeply multicultural thinker: his philosophy envisages and calls forth a world in linguistic turmoil, where mixity and hybridity are the norm, where even English, the world language, is breaking down in a variety of dialects, black English being a good case in point.

Last, it is important to note the emphasis Deleuze places on the superiority of Anglo-American literature as a vehicle of becoming and deterritorialization (especially in the much quoted work of Woolf, Kerouac, and Henry James). Deleuze explicitly opposes this American line of flight to the ego-centred, rationalistic and rather stuffy deterritorialization, becoming and tradition of the French novel. This will not fail to strike English-speaking readers as a very stereotypical portrait of French literature, which expresses by contrast a very European perception of the United States as the open frontier and the tradition of 'on the road again'. This is certainly the case, and I think the informed reader should approach Deleuze's rendition of 'Anglo-American' literature very much as his own location, that is, his affective map, or set of selected snapshots, and respect the singularity of the connections that Deleuze draws among them. In other words, contrary to those critics who single out Deleuzian nomadology for attack because of alleged lack of scholarly objectivity, I want to defend his account of literary and artistic works as specific cartographies of his own engagements with certain texts and authors. Instead of longing for an objective account of Deleuze's method of textual interpretation, I think that what matters is to see it precisely as the refusal of interpretation, that is to say as an anti-hermeneutical move.

For philosophical nomadism, texts are not semiotic-linguistic apparati that need to be entered following the logic of the signifier. Deleuze is especially clear in his rejection of psychoanalytically-inspired literary criticism, with its inherent belief in latency and the power of repressive mechanisms at work in the text. This approach also expresses an equally passionate belief in the powers of unveiling or processing them, so as to bring them into a manifest level. Deeply materialist, like Foucault, Deleuze considers all texts as impersonal, machine-like, connection-making devices. Tool-boxes at worst, transformative carriers at best, texts are to be approached according to the principle of affinity or sympathy: you try them on and either they work or not. This is not a naive belief in the spontaneity of one's approach to artworks. Nor is it a sort of anarchical relativism. It rather stresses the importance of affective interconnections; the unity of the aesthetic with the cognitive and their joint contribution to an ethics of empowerment.

Concretely, it produces a pragmatic approach to texts, which rests on the assumption that authors and readers are not the privileged 'knowing' subjects who can always locate the hermeneutical keys that will open the secret chambers of a text's deeper truths. Deleuze attacks this notion of the sovereignty of the author–reader couple with the same passion that he devotes to the critique of the humanist subject-position. In so doing, as I stated earlier, he calls for a new partnership between authors and readers, which would be based on mutual displacements and consensual rejection of their traditional prerogatives as 'owners' of the text's 'true' interpretation. To reduce this to relativism would be to miss the point altogether, because what is at stake here is the reinscription of the text into a set of discontinuous variations that mark the tempo of a subject's becoming. Reading and writing are consequently redefined as moments in the process of becoming-minoritarian. Texts are not here to be interpreted, but rather to be assimilated, consummated, used – or not.

Accordingly, texts are accounted for like territories, regions, or embodied areas of enframed and formatted intensity. Hence the importance of constitutive elements that Deleuze singles out in the texts of his choice: speed, fluidity, quality of the air, bodily motion and so on. A Deleuze-inspired approach to literature is more like a geography of affects, a map of elemental forces, than a conventional piece of critique; as such it requires radical readjustments in the reader. I think these adjustments, far from being of an undescribable or erratic kind, are distinct interventions aimed at throwing the reader out of the text and back into his or her embodied location. The aim is to trigger processes of transformation, or of becoming. Deleuze's texts are powerful, in the sense more of *potentia* than of *potestas*. Accordingly, the literature Deleuze loves and cross-refers to has the same force: it transports us out of the immediate confines of our daily consciousness. Literature for Deleuzian readers is a vehicle of deterritorialization. 'Style', consequently, is all-important, but in a materialist mode, as the specific speed or level of intensity which one adopts in order to engage with certain textual effects so as to engender processes of becoming. The hermeneutical mode is replaced by a pragmatic materialism that emphasizes the importance of the perception–consciousness nexus as opposed to the representation–consciousness model of interpretation.

What I find interesting about Deleuze's contribution to 'cultural studies' is a sort of pragmatics of the affective forces that shape certain texts. It is a typology of textual passions, a sort of applied affective meteorology which traces the grids of possible lines of becoming, that is to say of deterritorialization of the subject, across the texts. This approach expresses the intensive, non-unitary and yet sexualized structure of the nomadic subject. The cartography of affective forces in Deleuze's philosophy rests upon his complex understanding of both time and memory, to which I will return.

The process of writing is a vehicle by which this affective reorganization or scrambling of the subject takes place.

I want to suggest that for me, Deleuze's philosophical nomadology is a variation on the theme of 'écriture féminine' and as such it is intimately connected to his theories of the becoming-woman. A call for more conceptual and imaginative creativity is built into the notion of the becoming-woman as in the becoming-animal, so much so that it can also be read as an aesthetic and literary concept. Irigaray calls for the constitution of an alternative imaginary that would adequately express the unrepresentable aspects of female sexuality: fluidity, porosity, mucosity. Deleuze invites us to confront the sexual, the animal other, the physical and the unrepresentable object and learn to express its positive strength, its glorious non-familiarity. Whereas Irigaray stays within the linguistic constitution of the subject and thus calls for a female feminist re-appropriation of language and representation, Deleuze takes the plunge into the ruins of representation and the sensibility of the post-human. He wants us to confront the kaleidoscope of affects and desires that one is deliberately not socialized into becoming. As a consequence, Deleuze's philosophical nomadology is not only conceptually charged, but also culturally very rich. In so far as he invests creativity with a nomadic force, Deleuze raises issues of sensibility, affectivity and, ultimately, desire. It is on this field, therefore, that his encounter with feminist allies is the most resoundingly vocal.

Alternative patterns of desire

Throughout, the different versions of the 'becoming-woman' issues related to sexuality and sexual identity are central. As I argued in the previous section, Deleuze, working with Spinoza and Nietzsche, stresses the element of affectivity and desire which constitute the structural core of subjectivity. Thus, the subject is off-centre in relation to the flow of affects that invest it. Psychoanalysis starts from the same assumption that the subject is not master in his or her house, but according to Deleuze it fails to destabilize the power of consciousness as the moral and rational control agency. In a conceptual vein, Deleuze praises the psychoanalytic emphasis on the primacy of the 'drives' but he also argues that psychoanalytic theory and practice end up closing the very door they had initially opened. The whole economy of the unconscious is in fact re-subjugated in the name of the Father and under the moral and political supervision of a self-regulating, socially-enforced conscious and moral rationality. Freud's moment of genius, according to Deleuze, is the discovery of the theory of the the drives. Freud's failing, however, is to have indexed them back towards a regulatory and normative scheme of the subject, governed by compulsory heterosexuality, Oedipal reproduction and the cost-effective transmission of property best guaranteed by the socio-economic and legal structure of the family. In other words, according to Deleuze, psychoanalysis re-invests the affective foundations of the subject into a libidinal economy dominated by the phallogocentric principle which equates consciousness with control or the despotic domination of the 'dark continents within'.

To me it is liberating to critique the theoretical impact of Lacanian psychoanalysis in the light of Deleuze's theory of rhizomatic desire, which is informed by Guattari's schizo-analysis. Deleuze skilfully avoids the position of disavowal of unconscious processes, into which, in my opinion, Foucault falls. Deleuze focuses not only on the 'external' socio-political mechanisms of psychoanalysis as an institution which historically perpetuates disciplinary and normative practices of construction of subjects. He rather addresses the conceptual core of the issue, which consists of the embodied structure, the temporal foundations of subjectivity and the primacy of affectivity and desire. In his own work on the philosophy of 'becoming', Deleuze is especially committed to rescuing the concept of 'memory' from the metaphysical trappings into which psychoanalysis had thrown it. With reference to Bergson, Spinoza and Nietzsche, Deleuze radicalizes and unhinges the role of memory in subject-formation.

Essentially, Deleuze and Guattari's case against Lacan rests on what they consider his semi-religious attachment to a concept of desire and lack. This incorporates and capitalizes on the one hand on the centuries-old tradition of Christian guilt and on the other hand on the Hegelian tendency to define desire as the fulfilment of structural needs which are experienced as omissions and lacks. Both are related to the emphasis psychoanalysis places on 'interiority' as the location of the subject's 'true self'.

As I argued in the previous section, if I read this in Spinozist terms, that is to say in terms of affectivity, intensity and speed, psychoanalysis expresses a very negative set of forces: it is the morality of the confession, the priestly or 'pastoral' guidance so dear to Foucault, but distasteful to Deleuze's posthumanist secular mind-set. It smacks of the boudoir, the brothel and the bourgeois drama of the nineteenth century. For Deleuze, the same assessment applies to Lacanian psychoanalysis as to the French novel, which is claustrophobic, closeted, closed-in upon itself to the point of onanistic jubilation and neurotic self-obsession. Flaubert's much-celebrated 'Emma Bovary, c'est moi!', and Sartre's commentary on it, would be perfect examples of what Deleuze has in mind in his criticism. The woman-identified sensibility of this classical writer conveys a sexuality that is simultaneously titillating and denied, exposed and disavowed. It is exemplified by the agony and the ecstasy of Bernini's rendition of Saint Theresa, modelled on the passion of Christ. It infuses the erotic imaginary of the nineteenth century, where the

Dame aux camélias (and the cinema version of the same – *Camille* – played by Greta Garbo) embodies the excesses and the virtues of this kind of sexual passion – a passion which, as feminists from Germaine Greer (1999) to Naomi Wolf (1991) have pointed out, is predicated on the ill and decaying body of the 'femme fatale' whose sinfulness and delights turn into the living symbol of the *fleurs du mal* and the perverse *jouissance* they engender. This vision of the feminine as a sexualized imaginary is decadent and as such it is quite mainstream in European culture.

I find in nomadic philosophy the inspiration for an altogether different erotic imaginary, perhaps slightly more cruel, but thankfully more unsentimental as well; less sacrificial and more upbeat, because it is turned outwards, not inwards; a more secular approach to intensity and passion, free of the constraints of the confessional and the brothel and more attuned to the technologically mediated forms of desire that are experienced and experimented with nowadays. This eroticism is cosmic and eco-logical and hints at transcendance, but always through and not away from the flesh.

Desire is for me a material and socially enacted arrangement of conditions that allow for the actualization (that is, the immanent realization) of the affirmative mode of becoming. Desire is active in that it has to do with encounters between multiple forces and the creation of new possibilities of empowerment. It is outward-directed and forward-looking, not indexed on the past of a memory dominated by phallocentric self-referentiality. Unconscious processes are central to the discontinuous temporality of this non-unitary subject. The emphasis falls on the non-coincidence of the subject with his or her conscious self. Deleuze proposes instead a multi-layered, dynamic subject that is embodied but dynamic, corporeal and in-process. It has to be built up over and over again, and its expression is therefore concomitant with the constitution of the social field. This is central to the notion of enfleshed materialism I defend in this book. A body is, spatially speaking, a slice of forces that have specific qualities, relations, speed and rates of change. Their common denominator is that they are intelligent matter, endowed with the capacity to affect and be affected, to interrelate. Temporally speaking, a body is a portion of living memory that endures by undergoing constant internal modifications following the encounter with other bodies and forces. In both cases, the key point is the embodied subject's capacity for encounters and interrelation. As such, desire and yearning for interconnections with others lies at the heart of Deleuze's vision of subjectivity.

This ontological vision of the primacy of desire, however, is expressed also as a critique of the psychoanalytic reduction of desire to (hetero) sexuality and of both to (preferably reproductive) genital activity. On this point the authors of the *Anti-Oedipus* are quite ruthless: they 'nomadize' desire because they want to free it from the normative cage within which psycho-analysis has enclosed it. This radical nomadism, however, is not merely a recipe for the sexual anarchy which Western culture has amply experimented with since the eighteenth century. On this point, Foucault's work on the history of sexuality and especially on the fallacy of the 'sexual repression hypothesis' remains fundamental. Sexuality, far from being repressed in European culture, has been discursively and socially produced in a very creative manner. Even Lacan noted ironically the complementarity as well as the play of echoes between the 'divine' Marquis de Sade and the awesome Immanuel Kant. I think that Deleuze's view of desire carries a broader appeal which re-inscribes it as the fundamental and the fundamentally pos-itive passion, using Spinoza as the leverage point.

Thus, a nomadic or Deleuzian Spinozist approach stresses that the affectivity (*conatus*) is indeed at the heart of the subject, but that it is equally the case that this desire is not internalized, but external. It happens in the encounter between different embodied and embedded subjects who are joined in the sameness of the forces that drive them. Intensive, affective, external resonances make desire into a force that propels forward, but also always remains in front of us, as a dynamic, shifting horizon of multiple other encounters, of territorial and border crossings of all kinds. Hegel criticized Spinoza for his positive theory of desire, arguing that negativity is important for self-realization. In a Hegelian scheme of things in fact the actualization of desire implies the death of the object in order to realize the self-fulfilment of the subject. In their appeal to a more positive theory of desire, Deleuze and Guattari argue that the idea of desire as lack reflects the specific historicity and the socio-economic conditions of a moment of capitalist domination. It is historically located and consequently dated. The nineteenth-century phase of capitalist appropriation through binary opposition having been replaced with the informatics of domination (Haraway 1990b) and boundary-free flows of capital, a different notion of desire is being enacted today. Deleuze and Guattari want to think and act within the boundaries of the *here and now* and try both to reflect the new historical conditions and try to subvert them by disengaging desire from capitalist cumulation. Resting on Nietzsche and Spinoza, Deleuze proclaims a notion of desire that no longer rests on the dualistically split subject of modernity, but rather on the intensive entity that is activated by eternal returns, constant becomings and flows of transformations in response to external promptings, that is to say sets of encounters with multiple others. Crucial to this redefinition is the rejection of any categorical distinction between the material and the symbolic, or the social and the semiotic. In the age of the Internet and globalization, these distinctions are especially problematic and difficult to uphold.

I see Deleuze as redefining the interface between intentionality and desire at a historical time when the subject is dismembered and re-located along multiple axes, marked simultaneously by globalization and fragmentation, as I argued in chapter 1, an era when critical self-awareness is held in check by the forcefully installed amnesia of changes that are sweeping over us with too much speed and simultaneity. It is the changing historical scenario that engenders the urge for – if not the conditions of possibility for – a radical restructuring of the subject as a desiring entity. In other words, the move from negative to positive schemes of desire has to do with the necessity to shift political paradigms in changing historical conditions, that is to say in late postmodern capitalism.

Mutant Ninja Barbies: lesbian feminist Deleuzians

Feminist theorists have been most receptive to Deleuze's notion of desire and his critique of psychoanalysis. For instance, in her vehement rejection of sexual difference, Monique Wittig was among the first to call upon Deleuze to defend her politico-epistemological hypothesis of a multiple, lesbian, non-phallic sexuality. Speaking on behalf of the gay and lesbian movement, Wittig starts from the assumption that 'the official discourse on sexuality is today only the discourse of psychoanalysis that builds on the *a priori* and idealist concept of sexual difference, a concept that historically participates in the general discourse of domination' (Wittig 1979b: 119). Paraphrasing Deleuze, she consequently argues that: 'for us there are, it seems, not one or two sexes but many, as many sexes as there are individuals. For though they have enclosed us in a sexual ghetto, we do not accord to sexuality the same importance as heterosexuals' (Wittig 1979b: 119). In this perspective, Deleuze and Guattari's notion of 'polysexuality' is taken as an apology not only for gay and lesbian politics, but also for the seemingly anti-psychoanalytic hypothesis of 'as many sexes as there are individuals'. This idea was to prove extremely popular.

In her most Deleuzian text, though it singularly lacks all reference to Deleuze's work, Wittig (1982: 111)[9] reiterates her rejection of anything specifically feminine, let alone 'une écriture féminine'. She argues: 'woman cannot be associated with writing, because "woman" is an imaginary formation and not a concrete reality, she is the enemy's old brand-mark, which now some relish as a long-lost and hard-won attire.' Dismissing as biologically deterministic and 'naturalistic' all reference to feminine specificity, Wittig confronts the problem of the masculine appropriation of the universal with the subsequent confinement of the feminine to the particular. The question is: how can then a feminist woman express notions of a general human value?

In attempting to answer this question, Wittig proposes Deleuze's category of minoritarian subject. As we know by now, in order to gain access to this minoritarian position, one has to be a member of a minority, but that alone does not suffice. 'A text written by a minority writer is operational only if it manages to pass off as universal its minority viewpoint' (Wittig 1982: 116).[10] For instance, a writer like Djuna Barnes is literarily and politically subversive in that, starting from her lesbian existence, she formulates views of general value for all, the non-lesbians included. This kind of consciousness is what Wittig wants to defend, against the emphasis on and over-investment in the feminine proposed by the sexual difference theorists.

I find this argument similar to Deleuze's defence of the becoming-minoritarian; it is also, however, paradoxically opposed to his vision of the subject as a non-unitary entity. Wittig supports both the notions of polysexuality, and that of becoming as the de-territorialization of the subject, but she cannot share the conceptual premises on which these notions rest. I think Wittig uses the language of poststructuralist theory, especially Deleuze, while still believing in the humanist philosophy of presence. Wittig seems quite happy to simply replace the old phallic subject and his annexed feminine with the lesbian as the next authoritative, sovereign subject. This continues to support the position that valorizes the speaking subject as autonomous and universal, whereas Deleuze is committed to displacing the speaking subject from the centre of discursive power. Judith Butler points out, quite rightly in my opinion, that Deleuze's post-Lacanian reading of the subject as a libidinal entity situates desire not only as a positive force, but also as the point of vanishing of the wilful conscious self. This is why Butler, who is a rationalist at heart, disagrees with Deleuze. Butler differs radically however from Wittig's pre-psychoanalytic definition of sexuality as 'self-determined articulations of the individual subject' (Butler 1990: 167), and of desire as the ideological transcription of social codes. Wittig is a humanist who is still caught in the metaphysics of substance, that is to say the belief that the category of 'sex' directs the expression of pre-gendered identities which are disciplined by heterosexual desire. Wittig mistakes volition for desire.

It seems to me that, although she quotes extensively Deleuze's defense of polysexuality and multiple sexualities, Wittig's line of argumentation is alien to the insights of poststructuralism. By being so simplistic about the *locus* of social power and so relentlessly dismissive of 'women' as 'female sex' Wittig ends up with a paradoxically *idealist* notion of both 'women', or the female sex, and of sexed identities. The latter being for Wittig the direct result of social imprints, they are reduced to mental constructs: identity is an idea sustained for the purpose of social control.

As I argued in the previous chapter, philosophical nomadology seems to be functioning like a magnet that attracts a relatively broad range of queer, perverse, in-between positions which coalesce around the project of destroying, overcoming or abolishing the gender system. As Patton rightly suggests, this position is modelled on Marxist discourse about the abolition of 'class' and of class-relations. Deleuze's philosophy is thus read in the framework of the trans-sexual social imaginary of post-industrial culture. Confronted with this femino-phobic coalition and rather amused by the idiosyncracies and contradictions of the different positions and the ways in which they cross-refer to Deleuze, my line of questioning remains steady. I take consciously the risk of naivity, or the lesser one of being accused of philosophical incompetence by any number of 'holier-than-thou' neophytes. Going deliberately against the grain of most contemporary hyper-loyal reception of the co-author of *the Anti-Oedipus*, I shall never tire of asking the debunking question: 'that's all very well, but whatever happened to sexual difference understood as the dissymmetrical power-relations between the sexed subjects?'

This question has been asked also in other quarters, where the dialogue between Deleuze and feminism has produced, in my opinion, more creative border-crossings. For instance, Elizabeth Grosz is an eminent feminist Deleuzian who has made significant contributions to discussions of nomadic desire. Grosz, not without some hesitation, practices the very schizoanalysis she preaches and thus proposes to 'suspend feminist judgment in order to enter the project(s) articulated in Deleuze and Guattari's *A Thousand Plateaus*, (Grosz, 1994a: 191). I think that Grosz's point of entry is an effect of political resonance, in keeping with that affective sympathy, empathy or sense of connection which I described earlier as one of the deeper points of intersection between Deleuze and feminism. She argued that rhizomic politics 'theorizes, in a clearer and more direct form than rival or alternative political philosophies (including Marxism, socialism, liberalism and anarchism) the kinds of theoretical and political struggles in which feminists are involved' (Grosz 1994a: 193). Although Deleuze seldom acknowledges his debt to the practice of feminism, a positive connection is created here. Grosz attempts to combine the empowering aspects of psychoanalytically-inspired sexual difference theory (Irigaray) with an interest in lesbian desire as a brand of nomadology or becoming-minoritarian of women.

A sensualist thinker with a great deal of interest in sexuality, Grosz emphasizes the Deleuzian vision of subjectivity as multiplicity, poly-centredness, collectivity, dynamism and transformation. What attracts her especially is the rejection of the psychoanalytic notion of desire as lack and the possibility of reconceptualizing other assemblages of desire. In this respect Grosz's brand of 'queer' theory is of an altogether different conceptual fibre than either that of Wittig (idealist), de Lauretis (psychoanalytic) or Butler

(Derridian). Grosz's reading of Deleuze focuses on the creative potential of his concept of difference as pure positivity disengaged from the dialectics of hierarchical ordering and negation. Grosz (1995a) explores the Spinozist aspects of Deleuze's philosophy of the body in relation to self-destructive forms of bodily behaviour such as anorexia-bulimia. Resting on Deleuze's transcendental empiricism, Grosz develops a feminist approach to the philosophy of affects and relations which implies a desire to understand and to empathize with behaviours that mainstream culture considers as deviant, pathological, addictive or quite simply sick.

Just a reminder: affects are the body's capacity to enter relations – to be affected. Relations therefore are the virtual links that a body can form with other bodies. A body here indicates merely a dosage and an assemblage of forces, a portion of spatio-temporally framed affects: it is a multiple phenomenon. Grosz (1995a) expands feminist anti-humanism into the analysis of sex and sexuality, with reference to Deleuze and Guattari. She thus reads heterosexuality as a compulsory and dominant instance of power, and forces like misogyny and homophobia in terms of Molar or Majority formations that deny, diminish and humiliate a body's potential to express its intensity, or level and degree of desire. This allows Grosz to argue that homophobia can be described as the negative, reactive force that separates a body from 'what it can do', from a level of activity and *potentia* that is considered excessive or transgressive. Coding lesbianism as the path of becoming, Grosz emphasizes the challenge it throws to the status quo. Essence being nothing more than the sedimentation of repeated habits, the repetition of the familiar sexual gestures is socially encouraged over experimentation and risk. In contrast to this, Grosz points to gay and lesbian sexualities as expressions of becoming-minoritarian, which show great promise for the project of dislocating the humanistic subjects. She however avoids lesbian essentialism by stressing that what matters for the politics of sexual radicals is not merely to claim counter-identities, albeit identities they taught us to despise. What matters is how one lives and renders one's straightness as queer, one's lesbianism as queer. It is the processual becoming that matters here. Far more committed to re-figuring queer sexuality than to philosophical nomadism, however, Grosz takes her distance from the psychoanalytic organization of desire round the nucleus of fantasy, and pleads instead for multi-located pleasures.

Grosz (1995a) goes further and argues that for Hegel, as for Freud and Lacan, however, the 'proper' object of desire is the desire of the other. To be able to subjugate the other, to impose one's desire upon the other so that she or he becomes the object of that desire, is the constitutive moment of subjectivity. This is the much discussed 'master-slave' dialectics which is central, among others, to Beauvoir's philosophy of love. Although there have been important feminist attempts to reconfigure this mortal double-bind of self and other and its role in seduction and fantasy life, such as for instance Jessica Benjamin's sophisticated mix of object-relations theory and feminist ethics (Benjamin 1988), Grosz prefers to move on. Psychoanalysis is contaminated by an ontology of lack and guilt which persists in postulating the logic of desire in terms of have/have not (Freud), or in the Lacanian mode of to be/to have the Phallus. Disengaged from her Lacanian origins, Grosz returns to Spinoza as providing an alternative source for conceptualizing desire on a monist and not dualistic mode. Although Spinoza's monism is not without problems for feminism (Gatens 1996) the univocity of matter and the centrality of desire make him a viable alternative to Hegelian dialectics. As I argued earlier, desire as production, the unconscious as a process of expression of multiple and polymorphous interconnections, fantasy as invention of myriads of flows and pleasures: this is the new scenario made possible by a nomadic approach to sexuality.

On this score, of special significance is the alliance and the affinity that connects Grosz to Alphonso Lingis. In a remarkable set of mimetic renditions of Deleuze's style of thinking, Lingis rests on Deleuze to fuel his own project of recasting sexuality in a nomadic mode. Lingis enacts in his highly controversial texts one of the most powerful renditions of schizoanalysis. His nomadic polysexuality is the heir to the tradition of homosexual desire inaugurated by Guy Hocquengem, one of the first gay activists in Europe (with Lotringer in New York), to refer to Deleuze and Guattari's polysexuality in a politically empowering manner.[11] Hocquengem takes the category 'homosexual' as a sub-category of the Majority or dominant subject, in the same way as Woman is the Other of the same according to Irigaray's deconstructive analysis. What interests Hocquengem is to disengage the category of homosexuality from this Oedipalized system and to make it into a site of experimentations and flows of an anti-Oedipal variety. Because the dialectics of object-choice governs the production of desire, constructing binary oppositions only to integrate them into a system that favours One and the Same, Hocquengem argues that homosexual desire that would be disengaged from proper objects can be a crack in the system and it can inject into it a heavy dose of polymorphous perversity and flows. Nomadic desire is object-loose and fancy-free. Totally male-dominated, Hocquengem however has neither time nor concern for female homosexuality. Yet his defence of queer desire as not-one echoes Irigaray's reconfiguration of female sexuality as multiple, and complex within itself. Irigaray remains attached to the 'proper' object choice, as well as to the idea of the symbolic, thus recasting heterosexuality in a polymorphous mode, whereas Hocquengem privileges the 'improper' object choice, which he detaches from the Hegelian-linguistic scheme of signification.

I find these attempts at reconciling 'femino-phobic' and 'femino-philic' approaches to desire both fascinating and unconvincing. For me, the central

issue is the status of the material/maternal feminine and the many, potentially contradictory, ways in which it continues to affect the constitution of
female subjectivity and sexualities. Equally important to me is the politics
of locations, actualized in the method of cartographic accounts of one's
position. In this regard, I find that one of the striking paradoxes of the philosophy of embodiment proposed by Grosz is that it is disembedded from
contextual, historical and geo-political concerns. The real groundings of
Grosz's thought are textual and though issues of corporeality are thematically
central to her *corpus*, they suffer from a systematic neglect of the geo-politics
of their own power-locations. In this sense, I consider Grosz as a utopian
writer, caught in the 'no-place' and 'not yet' of poststructuralist theories of
difference and quite contented with this position.

Tamsin Lorraine (1999) argues that both Deleuze and Irigaray addressed
that which is unrepresentable within Western philosophy, respectively for
Deleuze a nomadic, fluid notion of thinking that bridges the constitutive
gap between mind and body, reason and imagination, being and becoming,
and for Irigaray, a fluid, multiple feminine disengaged from the specular
logic of masculine/feminine, active/passive, signifying/lacking. I want to
argue that the multi-centred, enfleshed subject is the site of intersection
between philosophical nomadism and sexual difference feminism. The
key road-signs of this intersection are Deleuze's empirical transcendental
and Irigaray's 'sensible transcendental'. They offer the most fruitful border-
crossing between their respective systems of thought and their political
projects. I would not want to disengage either of them, however, from the
politics of location and the specific modes of accountability they propose.
Deleuze and Irigaray itemize the enfleshed subject and issues of difference in
the framework of their vision of philosophy as the cartography of the present.
That implies renewed and constant attention to the shifting grounds of
socially mediated power-relations.

The white face of femininity in post-industrial societies

I think that the minoritarian spirit is alive and well, not only amidst the
ranks of the cyber-feminists and cyber-girls, but also in critical philosophy,
music, the arts, the ecological movement and the construction of multicultural spaces. It is indeed very crowded on the margins and the novelty
is never where one would expect it. But equally strong and even more
vibrant is the strand that aims at a becoming-minoritarian within theoretical
discourse.

In her acute and upbeat rendition of 'becoming-woman', for instance,
Camilla Griggers (1997) looks critically at the construction of femininity
and the post-feminist woman in late twentieth-century USA as the 'abstract
machine' of late capitalist technologies:

Her forms of expression are determined by optical and electronic media, psychopharmacology, the war machine, the chemical industry, plastics technology, bioscience. In this sense, the abstract machine of femininity could not be more real. She is the gaze smiling at you from the page; she is the voice calling to you in electronic transmission. She is the one who turns her head indifferently from you to stare into the camera eye, or into the radar screen as she runs bombing missions over the desert. In private, she cannot help vomiting what she has consumed into the toilet. Her womb is a politics, as is her face. (Griggers 1997: x)

Femininity is caught in the double-bind of late postmodernity by being simultaneously 'Other' (of the same) and integrated in the Majority. In late post-industrial societies this dominant femininity functions as the site of proliferating and commodified differences. Like Princess Diana, she is both the pathetic and 'despotic face of white femininity' and the scapegoat sacrificial victim. The iconic value of Princess Diana's face as white, imperial and sacrificial at the same time is a relevant figuration for the paradoxes of one brand of contemporary femininity. Diana has received renewed critical attention of late. The notion that recurs most regularly is that of the powers of identification that Diana triggers and evokes. Johnson (1999), for instance, argues that Diana was a gay icon, because of the tale of oppression and redemption which marked her existence. Her spectacularly pathetic 'coming out' as a bulimic – closeted by definition – also contributes to her gay appeal, as does Diana's undeniable affinity for the glamour and attractiveness of gay men in show-business. The AIDS activism and her unhappy quest for emotional and erotic fulfilment are part of the same configuration: she is abject and glorious at the same time.

Equally important to Diana's evocative, queer power, as Spurlin argues (1999), is her brave and desperate denunciation of gender politics within the British royal family (Campbell, 1998), her refusal to 'go away quietly', her stepping out of the codified conventions of loveless upper-class marriage and her defiance of heterosexual normativity in the realm of male infidelities and female subservience and passivity. Diana transgresses and exceeds the heterosexual matrix, and thus joins forces with queer politics, though she is clearly not gay herself. Valerie Walkerdine (1999) sees another pattern of identification with Diana on a broader, 'mass' level. Diana's struggle for survival reflects and represents the ordinary struggle for self-definition that most human beings have to go through in order to become psychological subject. Diana embodies the dynamic, pain-drenched nature of becoming-a-subject.

That most of the people mourning her were women, youth, gay and blacks is a telling tale about the shifting grounds on which Sameness and Difference are related and pitched against one another. In the age of the post-industrial transformation of the UK, and the erosion of traditional working-class values and identities, masculinity is far from immune from this crisis. Walkerdine adds (1999: 103):

> At the moment of Diana's self-transformation many women were economic-ally as well as domestically and personally having to remake themselves. This process, sometimes referred to as the 'feminization of the economy', produces not only a huge change in class relations but a huge shift of gender as well. It may be that many of the men who had to face the terrible mourning of their work and manhood began to have to face the emotionality and self-transformation that Diana embodied too.

The becoming-woman of these men and the becoming-women of these women run along parallel but dissonant lines. In what looks like a game of role-swapping, or of 'gender-bending', the 'softening' of the former Masters echoes the sharpening of the self-definition of the former Others. Read with reference to nomadic becomings, I would argue that what matters in this process is less the rate of success in attaining access to functional psycho-logical subjecthood, or masterful subject-position, than its opposite, the dismantling of both. In other words, it is the potential for dislocation of the very groundworks of identity that provides an element of active transforma-tion or subversive becoming in what would otherwise be merely a role-reversal in the sense of a rearrangement of terms within the same unaltered framework.

Diana as a socio-symbolic event is a subversive subject in so far as she grows increasingly aware of the ways in which she simultaneously inhabits and challenges or disrupts the many facets of her social identity as princess/mother/wife/celebrity/sexualized female flesh/bulimic/desiring subject/single woman/philanthropist and so on. It is a multiplicity at odds with itself that makes her strike out on her own, but as a dissonant, fragmented and rather messy subject – a leaky body, a less-than-perfect image. I think the mix of pathos and privilege is an integral part of her appeal and also of her strange charisma. Millions identified with this, partly because it is a less-than-perfect whole, a partial success only.

In this respect, it is essential to racialize the process and think of the white despotic and pathetic face of Princess Diana – as the contested and contra-dictory site where transformation must occur. This takes place, as I argued earlier, in the global contest of the dissolution of imperial entities and the generalized spreading of diasporic identities in postmodernity. According to Jatinder Verma (1999), Princess Diana stood out from within the general-ized 'bleaching' (1999: 121) or whitening processes (Frankenberg 1993) that go on in the constitution of contemporary identities.

The iconic value of Princess Diana's face prompts a number of comments about the political economy of late postmodernity and the location of whiteness within it. Camilla Griggers, for instance, rests on Deleuze's work to analyse the social production of faces as landscapes of power and passports to normality. Possessing the 'right' face is a social process of subjectivization that functions by binary exclusions: 'is she black or white? straight or lesbian? The face will tell' (Griggers 1997: 3). Following Canguilhem's and Deleuze's definition of normality as the zero-degree of deviancy or monstrosity, Griggers analyses the production of white femininity as the site of schizoid contradictory trends: privilege and commodification.

In chapter 1 I juxtaposed the white iconicity of Princess Diana's body to the anonymous faces of endless female victims that stare at us from the television screen in a quest of aid for survival. These are two sides of the same coin of hyper-inflated femininity of the era of postmodernity. They are also opposite in terms of power-locations, entitlement and privilege. The case of Princess Diana is significant in that she at times manages to combine elements of both the sacrifice and the triumph, thus causing great turmoil in the register of representation.

Griggers also applies a differential treatment to the production of white femininity on white women, and of the many 'others' or minorities. The despotic white face on a white woman is the sign of her Molarity and Normality; on a black woman it is a measure of racism, an attempt to integrate difference into the logic of sameness. Michael Jackson's whitening effects come to mind here, as the widespread use of bleaching/whitening products on black bodies, hair and faces especially, throughout most of the globe today. There are several on-going attempts at situating and re-locating whiteness, and not all of them go in the direction of the Molar: some entail anti-racist processes of becoming-minoritarian. Thus, a white face imposed on a drag queen, as in the fashion of the lesbian radical chic, can be an act of subversion. This points to asymmetrical and differentiated paths of becoming which unfold from dissymmetrical and ultimately irreconcilable starting-off subject-positions. The dissymmetry needs to be kept in mind in order to make sense of the patterns of both negative and affirmative deconstruction, undoing or becoming, that flows from it.

Griggers argues that the political stance consists in becoming-minoritarian or molecular in a radical materialist, pragmatic philosophy of multi-layered transformations. The becoming-woman is subversive in that it works actively towards the transformation of the signs, the social practices and the embodied histories of white institutionalized femininity. A Deleuzian approach calls for relinquishing this quest for identity modelled on the Molar/sedentary subject, to activate instead multiple becomings, away from identity. Some of these transitions are happening already in the fact that so many bodies are malfunctioning or ceasing to produce the programmed codes, of which the use of Prozac, the spreading of anorexia and bulimia are clear symptoms. These breakdowns are not enough, however, to disrupt the machine. Griggers is especially intrigued and concerned about the position of the lesbian body in this economy of commodification. For lesbian identity is no exception to the rule of postmodern fragmentation. It is even situated in one of the zones of highest turbulence.

In so far as lesbianism, especially in the anti-Woman, trans-sexual mode preached by Wittig and other radical lesbians, embodied the blurring of the classical gender dualism and the explosion of the differences between the masculine and the feminine, Griggers argues that it fails to be subversive. It is actually situated at the crest of the wave of exposure and commodification of the sexed body. The proliferation of differences for the sake of the market economy being one of the distinctive traits of postmodernity, as I argued in chapter 1, lesbianism runs an even higher risk of commodification than other brands of sexuality today. This is made manifest by notions such as the lesbian Phallus, lipstick dykes, lesbian S/M, phallic lesbian mothers, Madonna's fifteen-minute burst of fame as Sandra Bernhardt's lesbian lover, and a general marketing of in-between gender identities in advanced post-industrial societies. Griggers concludes that, in the USA, under the pressure of 'family values' ideology: 'The lesbian can appear as porn at the same time as she must be censored as the obscene' (Griggers 1997: 40).

This is the kind of play with identity that Cindy Sherman offers to gallery crowds and the art people, and it is offered as sexualized services by sex activists like Susie Bright/Sexpert who deterritorialize standard sexed identities and queer sexuality in the quest for subversion and fun. Lesbians are caught in the same historical contradictions as everyone else: they are simultaneously within and without the Majority. The emphasis falls on the pursuit of transformations and changes. The lesbian faces the task of assembling disorganized, monstrously hybrid disruptive bodies, while being simultaneously within the system she is trying to subvert. The point about desire, in fact 'is to ask not to which drives desires correspond, but to ask into which assemblage various blocks of becoming enter' (Griggers 1997: 114).

Nomadic feminism thus enlargens the definition of female sexuality and the subject to encompass more global power-relations than the ones determined by gender alone, with special concerns for issues of military violence, war and lethal technologies of death. I shall return to these in chapter 5. The only way to resist this death-bound machinery is to elaborate hybrid, transformative identities working both inside and outside, on the majority and the minoritarian front simultaneously. The sexual politics of this feminist appropriation of becoming-woman rests on a sober reading of the logic of advanced capitalism and of the contradictory locations of femininity within it. The mark of Deleuzian feminists across the board is:

1 Their radical attachment to cartographic, i.e. materialist, mappings of
   contemporary power-relations, with special attention to technology;
2 the emphasis on the flesh, embodiment, affectivity and the positivity
   of sexuality;
3 the priority they give to processes of becoming, assemblages, connections, rather than to identity politics;
4 a healthy disregard for the distinction between high and low culture,
   with special emphasis on creativity, artistic expression and the active
   enactment of their theories in the space of writing and the production
   of nomadic texts;
5 a zigzagging relationship to sexual difference.

Conclusion

I find it one of the more regrettable aspects of feminist theory throughout
the last decades of the last millennium that, while it grew progressively more
seduced by nomadology, rhizomatics and Deleuze's conceptual machinery,
it confined to marginality the analogous, pioneering and equally powerful
conceptual apparatus of sexual difference feminist theory. I think that
Irigaray's 'feminine' can be read alongside Deleuze's concept of the 'virtual'
as a process of simultaneous exiting from the phallogocentric premises and
of asserting and thus creating new territories. As I have argued earlier, there
are very cogent historical and political reasons why Irigaray holds on to the
relativity classical dialectical scheme of the subject which Lacanian psychoanalysis perpetuates. I think no feminist who is committed to political work
on behalf of the status of women can afford to move altogether out of this
scheme. If it appears at first as a delay, a kind of in-built theoretical backlog
that confines feminism to outdated theoretical frameworks, I want to argue
that: firstly, this paradox of the feminist subject does not necessarily or
inevitably condemn it to molarity and therefore to despotic normativity. As
I stated earlier, I think that this anti-feminist line, which is favoured by so
many younger Deleuzians today, does not do justice to Deleuze's philosophy,
let alone to feminist theory. Secondly, I argue that this paradox endows
sexual difference with a political platform, the capacity to be translated into
action, into concrete policies. Deleuze's more conceptually subversive framework, however, suffers from a lack of possible applications.

  I found it most surprising to see, for instance, that serious Deleuze
scholars such as Holland (1999) when attempting to apply Deleuze to feminism, automatically apply it to queer theory and especially Butler's notion of
performativity, without as much as scratching the surface of the debate.
Although Holland draws some useful and significant comparisons between
classical feminist materialism and thus raises issues related to labour,

family-structure, etc., on a more conceptual level, I think he takes a few shortcuts. Not only has Butler openly rejected Deleuze's theories in her work (Butler 1987), but it is clear to anyone who has seriously engaged with her work, that she cannot sustain any theoretical comparison with rhizomatic or nomadic philosophies. Butler's philosophical roots and theoretical agenda are of an altogether different kind. The hasty way in which Holland tackles the intersection of feminism with Deleuze fails to do justice to both. It also corners Butler into the impossible role of stand-in for the most diverse and disparate theories, even those which manifestly have little to do with her work.

Confronted with this vulgarization effort, let me state once again that devoted Deleuze scholars who are convinced that a productive dialogue can be established with feminism, need to look again at the early Irigaray corpus. In her recent work Olkowski (2000) revisits the American reception of Irigaray, especially the charge of essentialism, and wonders how it both echoes and confirms the equally ambivalent reception of Deleuze. Pursuing Tina Chanter's critique, Olkowksi argues that American dismissals usually either enforce or instantiate the very dichotomies that Irigaray is putting into question. The points of intersection between Deleuze and Irigaray are, according to Olkowski, an interest in pragmatics and praxis, social activism, literary language and practices, and a new philosophical framework that 'embraces multiplicity without creating binaries' (Olkowski 2000: 5). Central to their philosophical alliance is the notion of morphology and more especially of the morphological expression of embodied subjects. Irigaray's emphasis on fluidity and fluid mechanics, on mucosity and interstitial humidity such as the placenta, blood and other bodily fluids, expresses the creation of alternative figurations of the self – and the necessity to find adequate expressions for them.

Olkowski suggests that all these morphological interventions by Irigaray re-state the idea of the feminine sex as not-one, that is to say as multiple within itself. This is comparable to the language of becoming in Deleuze, though it is clear that for him the feminine is only the term in a series. For both of them, the dominant concept is an open whole, a flux. I think that for Deleuze the aim is to prevent the molar sedentarization of the woman into a castrated man. For Irigaray it is the more humble task of repossessing the wholeness of the woman and empowering her to enter a collective process of self-expression. Both of them aim to de-pathologize the female and make it into a dynamic force of transformation of the whole framework of subjectivity, not merely of gendered or sexed identity. Irigaray's 'sensible transcendental' is fully embedded and embodied. As Goicoechea has argued, this 'transcendental sensuotics' is grounded in 'the porosity and mucosity of a female desire that can open to a desire and wonder between the sexes' (Goicoechea 1999: 6). As such it marks a positive, joyful ground for encountering the other. By comparing this favourably to Deleuze's rhizomatics, Goicoechea emphasizes that Irigaray's mucosity/porosity dynamic of desire is not mono-directional and consequently not incompatible with nomadic desire. The 'virtual feminine' of Irigaray is also an open multiplicity, a bodily immanent singularity constitutionally linked to a collectivity.

Moreover, the becoming-minoritarian/woman of the subject does not stop at the empirical level, but it rather would force a re-alignment of the basic parameters of subjectivity: the power of *potestas* (constraint, negativity, denial) would have to confront the equally powerful impact of *potentia* (plenitude, intensity, expression). I find this one of the strongest points of the radical philosophies of immanence I have explored here: the extent to which they resist the separation of self from society, the psychic from its outsides, the symbolic from the material. Irigaray's multiple, non-one feminine sexuality and Deleuze's theory of the folded and unfolding intensive subject of becoming constitute a serious challenge to both the liberal vision of the autonomous subject and to the psychoanalytic dialectics of lack, loss and signification. Irigaray and Deleuze, moreover, agree that the very condition of possibility for a separation of the symbolic from the material – the inflated, universalistic posture that flies into abstraction and leaves the embodied subject gasping for air – the sheer thinkability of this separation is the mark of the patriarchal, cash-nexus of power.

The phallogocentric regime cannot be separated from the Majority, that is, a material process of masculine colonization of social space. This starts from the theft of the bodies of women and 'others' and their confinement into a binary, Oedipalizing cage of negation. This hyper-inflated masculine colonizes the basic 'symbolic' functions of the West – the religious, military and political structures – and segregates them in the phallic mode. To deal with this, a materialist politics of affirmation as well as critique is necessary. The problem with liberalism is its undue glorification of the self, given as at the same time centralized, unitary and plural. The problem with psychoanalytic theory, on the other hand, is that it fails to acknowledge the political economy of its vision of the subject. Deleuze and Guattari consequently see psychoanalysis as an expression and manifestation of the political economy of capitalist production. As Massumi eloquently put it, the Freudian unconscious is 'an individualization of a despotic political structure (rather than despotism being the result of a projection of a personal unconscious structure)' (Massumi 1992: 52). Deleuze then goes on to redefine desire as interdynamic affectivity that flows in the in-between spaces. Affect, yearning or tendency is 'a self-propelling drive inscribed in matter' (Massumi 1992: 73). Although on this point Irigaray is closer to Lacan than to Deleuze, in that she respects the notion of the symbolic as the organizer and distributor of significant differences, she still aims to recombine that which patriarchal power had separated, namely the embodied subject from her or his *potentia*, all she or he could become. Irigaray calls for the meltdown of that frozen slab of history that is the patriarchal symbolic and calls for radical re-enfleshments of men and women according to alternative systems, which need to be negotiated and collectively applied. All other differences notwith-standing, Irigaray, like Deleuze, has explicitly stated that the production of new desiring subjects requires massive reorganizations and changes in the material fabric of society.

This is where I feel a great deal of attraction for Lichtenberg's (1992: 177) concept of 'met(r)amorphosis' which she defines as 'the becoming-thresholds of borderlines'. Following Irigaray, she proposes to disengage the symbolic function from the Phallus, so as to leave open a space, both in terms of a psychic space and a temporal span, in which the symbolic may be reconfigured in a manner more suitable to female feminist subjects of the nomadic kind. Lichtenberg pleads for non-phallic systems of representation of the symbolic function and freely adapts Deleuze to her project of destabilizing the Oedipal machinery. As a counter-figuration, she proposes the 'Matrix' in its classical inception of a uterine space, which however is de-territorialized so as to engender the virtual feminine as positive difference. This process of refiguring the subject through a non-Oedipal matrix engenders 'met(r)amorphoses'. These point to not-oneness, multiplicity, plurality, prediscursive and even prenatal connections among non-unitary subjects. This co-existence of opposites is set up against the totality and sameness of the historically dated Phallic signifier. Cross-referring to Deleuze and Guattari's fascination for borderline cases but also to Irigaray's emphasis on porosity and mucosity, 'met(r)amorphoses' invest fluidity and flows with signifying powers. Like the umbilical, the uteral, the vulvar, the clitoral, the placental, this repossession of the matrix offers yet another interesting interconnection between the feminism of sexual difference and philosophical nomadism. Again, the question of style emerges here.

Thinking in figurations, the cartographic, intensive and creative way that I am defending throughout this book, implies a leap out of the kind of mental habits which philosophical reason seems to cling to as if its life depended on them. This seems to me what is ultimately at stake in the becoming-woman of theoretical and critical practice. It includes the rejection of the holy principles of philosophical practice: the emphasis on critique, rather than the elaboration of alternative conceptual frameworks; a binary mode of positing the problems, which favours dialectical oppositions over horizontal interconnections; a long-established reliance on negativity rather than affirmation. I would want to propose that these very mental habits can be historicized, that is to say they can be seen as reflecting changing social and historical conditions. They can also be embedded and thus be made accountable for their own premises. For instance, the tendency to separate the mental from the social, the symbolic and the material, is in itself the expression of a historical regime of truth for which there is no authority other than the force of habit. In the specific case of Lacanian psychoanalysis and the forms of deconstruction that emerge from it, their paradigm is a semiotic and linguistically-based theory of signification and a negative theory of desire as lack. To this tradition, I am opposing the philosophies of radical embodied immanence, and the strategic ways in which they re-position the feminine.

I do so out of sheer pragmatism and of a concern to make philosophy relevant to today's world. As I argued in the previous chapter: in the age of global telecommunications and world-wide campaigns, of transnational capital flow, of world migration and mass refugee problems, of Internet and global computer pornography, of narco-dollars and the largest increase in sexual slavery of women and children in decades – in other words, in an age when power coincides with the blurring of borders but also their closing down and the spread of visualization technologies on a global scale, it follows that politics is also and maybe primarily the management of the social imaginary. If that is the case, how on earth can the distinction between the symbolic and the socio-material, the psychic and the social, the cultural and the political be kept up at all? As Deleuze and Guattari argue in their double volume on *Capitalism and Schizophrenia* (1972, 1980) the material and symbolic conditions of our existence overlap to a degree that is almost problematic. Consequently, we need new theories and practices that encompass the speed and the simultaneity of the semiotic and material practices that surround us, not those that perpetuate their disconnection. We need to think those in-between spaces and practices.

This is where the intensive or rhizomic approach is an inspiration: I would like to return the activity of thinking to its embodied emotional, memory-driven and imagination-based structures. We cultural critics may all gain by acknowledging that the struggle over theory is transported by a multiplicity of non-theoretical factors that make it imperative to destabilize the sovereign image of the philosopher as legislator of knowledge. We may gain a lot by speaking instead of the seductive powers of theory-making, and of its deadly bite as well. This nomadic image of thinking has a female face that points in several contradictory directions at once. I choose to emphasize the non-dominant figuration. This becoming minoritarian/molecular/woman is not one *topos* but a highly differentiated and turbulent space of multiple and dissymmetrical becomings. Some concern a transformation internal to the rules and practice of philosophy and critical theory itself. They disconnect it from the universal pretension of the Hegelian-Marxist figure of the intellectual, and also illuminate possible strategies of critique of and resistance to power as *potestas*. Others concern subversive, creative, esoteric, opaque and often undetectable processes of transformation of our social field and of the subjects that sustain it.

Becoming is a question of undoing the structures of domination by careful, patient revisitations, re-adjustments, micro-changes. A long apprenticeship to minute transformations, through endless repetitions, will replace the illusion of a royal road to the revolution or of one single point of resistance, and assert instead the constant flows of met(r)amorphoses. Becoming is a nomadic kind of revisitation or remembering which traces empowering transversal lines that cut across the staticity of sedimented memory, activating it by de-programming it out of the dominant mode. Becomings are creative work-in-progress processes. Like a text by Gertrude Stein, set to music by Philip Glass and performed by Diamanda Galas, it is the kind of refrain that sticks and keeps on returning: the sort of thing that one, quite simply, forgot to forget.

3

Met(r)amorphoses: becoming Woman/ Animal/Insect

'If we had a keen vision and feeling of all ordinary human life, it would be like hearing the grass grow and the squirrel's heart beat, and we should die of that roar which lies on the other side of silence. As it is, the quickest of us walk about well wadded with stupidity.'

George Eliot, *Middlemarch*, p. 226

'I look at my face in the bathroom mirror. I want to see something different. I take off my clothes. I stand naked. I want to be changed. Nothing is impossible, not for she-devils. Peel away the wife, the mother, find the woman, and there the she-devil is. Excellent! Glitter glitter. Are those my eyes? They're so bright they light up the room.'

Fay Weldon, *The Life and Loves of a She-Devil*, p. 44

'You have the individuation of a day, a season, a year, a life (regardless of its duration), a climate, a wind, a fog, a swarm, a pack (regardless of its regularity). A cloud of locusts carried by the wind at five in the evening; a vampire who goes at night, a werewolf at full moon. . . . It's the entire assemblage in its individuated aggregate that is a haecceity.'

Deleuze and Guattari, *A Thousand Plateaus*, p. 262

Introduction

Postmodernity is marked by the return of the 'others' of modernity: woman, the sexual Other of man, the ethnic or native Other of the Eurocentric subject and the natural or earth Other of techno-culture emerge as counter-subjectivities. Given the structural importance of these 'others' as props that confirm the 'same' in His dominant subject-position, their 'return' coincides with a crisis of the structures and the boundaries of classical subjectivity, which challenges its very foundations. Poststructuralist philosophers address directly this crisis of humanism; Foucault for instance points out that modern philosophy and social sciences have responded to the challenge of postmodernity by developing discourses that are attuned to the emerging subjectivities of the 'others'. Thus, psychoanalysis encapsulates the instance of the unconscious, the critique of rationality and the question of the feminine or of woman's desire; anthropology and especially ethnology mirror the ethnic others and the discourses about nature explode from Darwin onwards into a cluster of fast-growing sciences and technologies of 'life'. It is worth stressing however, that these emerging others were far from content with being incorporated in a variety of discourses in modernity, albeit critical ones. They also produced discourses of their own and voiced their increasingly visible and focused subjectivities. Thus, feminist and post-colonial native or black theorists produced discourses and practices of their own which challenged His Master's voice. Around the notion of nature or earth a number of counter-discourses emerged, ranging from ecology to the new biological sciences of today, all the way to the information technologies. More on these in the next chapter.

I want to argue now that Deleuze's theory of subjects-in-becoming develops alongside the discourses and practices of the 'others' of postmodernity and engages with them in a very creative manner. I stated that philosophical nomadology requires a high degree of self-reflexivity; that is to say it does not merely engage with discourses and practices of otherness in a mimetic or consumeristic manner. Nomadology cuts a more creative path through these discourses in a non-dialectical manner. It does so by giving priority to the undoing of the formerly dominant model of subjectivity and thus putting on the spot the discourse of the Same, the One: rather than stressing those of the others, it is the Master's discourse that takes the heat. This is what is at stake in the nomadic theory of becoming.

Becoming works on a time sequence that is neither linear nor sequential, hence the emphasis Deleuze places on the notion of depersonalized memory. Processes of becoming, in other words, are not predicated on a stable, centralized Self who supervises their unfolding. They rest rather on a non-unitary, multi-layered, dynamic subject. The post-humanist approach to differences is the chosen strategy to express this vision of the subject. Becoming woman/animal/insect is an affect that flows, like writing, it is a composition, a location that needs to be constructed together with, that is to say in the encounter with, others. To speak of becomings as 'eternal returns', following Deleuze's rendition of Nietzsche, refers to the discontinuous regularity which marks the continuous present of energetic flows. They push the subject to his or her limit, in a constant encounter with external, different others. The nomadic subject as a non-unitary entity is simultaneously self-propelling and hetero-defined, or outward-bound. All becomings are minoritarian, that is to say they inevitably and necessarily move into the direction of the 'others' of classical dualism – displacing them and re-territorializing them in the process, but always and only on a temporal basis. The nomadic subject thus engages with his or her external others in a constructive, 'symbiotic' (Pearson 1999) block of becoming, which bypasses dialectical interaction. I have argued in chapter 2 that 'becoming' is a persistent challenge and an opposition to Molar, steady identities: it functions on an anti-Hegelian, anti-developmental, anti-teleological model.

These patterns of becoming can be visualized alternatively as sequential modes of affirmative deconstruction of the dominant subject-position (masculine/white/heterosexual/speaking a standard language/property-owning/ urbanized), or else, as stepping stones to a complex and open-ended process of de-personalization of the subject. Internally self-contradictory becoming can best be expressed by figurations: the wasp and the orchid; the woman and the turning of the waves; the sound and the fury, signifying nothing. The process of becoming-woman/animal, in fact, is not about signification, but rather the opposite: it is about the transcendence of the linguistic signifier. What it asserts is the potency of expression. Expression is about the non-linguistically coded affirmation of an affectivity whose degree, speed, extension and intensity can only be measured materially, pragmatically, case by case.

The different stages or levels of becoming trace an itinerary that consists in erasing and recomposing the former boundaries between self and others. In a different philosophical tradition one could say that the becoming-woman/ insect/imperceptible/molecular are deconstructive steps across the boundaries that used to separate qualitatively Self/same from others. In philosophical nomadology, on the other hand, these are not deconstructive steps, as they do not feed upon themselves, in the way that Irigaray's strategic mimesis does. As Tamsin Lorraine put it: 'one lesson of Deleuze & Guattari's anti-psychoanalytic stance, however, is that destratification does not necessarily have to retrace the route of one's personal history' (1999: 202).

Therefore, it is in the worst possible conceptual taste to even think of being able to separate out the becoming-woman from the other unfolding and deploying of multiple becomings. As I argued in the zigzagging itinerary of the previous chapter, in fact, the 'becoming-woman' marks the threshold of patterns of 'becoming-minoritarian' that cross through the animal and go into the 'becoming-imperceptible' and beyond. Nonetheless, for the sake of the argument, but also to facilitate the linearity of the process of reading/ writing, I will distinguish and address separately a number of specific instances of becoming, for instance, in this chapter, the 'becoming-animal'. In so doing, I want to defend a multi-layered argument: firstly, that the concept of becoming is crucial to Deleuze's philosophy of immanence. Secondly, that the 'becoming-woman' is both integral to the concept and process of becoming and also uncomfortably written into it as a constitutive contradiction of Deleuze's nomadic subjectivity. Thirdly, that there are no systematic, linear or teleological stages or phases of becoming; each plateau marks a framed and sustainable block or moment of immanently actualized transformations. Fourthly, I want to investigate further the hypothesis that the process of becoming may not be as sexually undifferentiated as Deleuze and Guattari suggest. This will pursue the line of argumentation that I started to outline in the previous chapter, namely that the becoming woman/ animal, far from marking the dissolution of all identities into a state of flux where different connections will merge, may instead display sexually differentiated forms. I am well aware that such a hypothesis is anathema to orthodox Deleuzians, but as I argued earlier I am mercifully free of the Oedipalized ties that seem to bind some of today's neo-Deleuzians. Practicing instead the brand of conceptual disloyalty I learned from Deleuze, I will pursue my cartographic exercise, to play the politics of locations. I have argued that dispersing Phallic sexuality and identity into undifferentiated flows may take different forms and speeds depending on one's geo-political, sexual and other locations. Let me now test this hypothesis in the case of the becoming-animal.

To demonstrate my case I will attempt several potentially contradictory things: to track down contemporary cultural manifestations of multiple becomings; to assess these against my transformative reading of nomadic philosophies; to show that sexual difference continues to play a role in the ways in which contemporary culture tries to live with and represent the fast changes it is going through, and to assess them in the light of Deleuze's concepts. The corpus I will use for this cartographic exercise is mostly literary, artistic and cultural, in keeping with Deleuze's contention that the process of becoming entertains intimate ties with that of writing or creativity.

On animals

Of the traditional 'others' that mark the outward boundaries of the classical vision of the subject, the animal, natural or organic other is in some ways the hardest to analyse. Maybe because it is too close for comfort, especially ever since Darwin. Deleuze's theory of the 'becoming-animal' addresses this uncomfortable familiarity through some of the dominant discourses of animality: evolutionary theory and genetics; psychoanalysis, which simultaneous unveils and disavows the 'beast within' and the long tradition of literary representation of animals. I will concentrate first on the latter, in order to move on towards other, more complex issues.

Animals, according to Borges, come in three categories: those we humans eat; those we watch television with and those we are frightened of (wild, exotic or untamed ones). This facetious account expresses clearly the high level of lived familiarity which characterizes Wo/man's interaction with the organic, animal others. The phenomenon of pets alone is enough to confine the Wo/man-animal link within the most classical parameters of Oedipal relationships. Deleuze's problem consequently is how to engage in an animal relationship with animals – the ways hunters do and anthropologists do not. That is to say that how to engage with them outside the Oedipal cage of consumption of otherness in which they have been historically caught. How to deterritorialize, or nomadize, the human–animal interaction thus becomes the challenge. It covers not only what goes on between Wo/man and animal, but also the notion of the animal within. This is a way of desacralizing the concept of human nature and the life which animates it.

Anti-metaphysics

The animal is traditionally defined as the metaphysical other of man. Deleuze is taking up issues with a long-established philosophical tradition that upholds categorical distinctions between Man and His others. Heidegger is a special case in point, and in some ways Deleuze's theory of the becoming-animal is a direct response to the Heideggerian concept of 'the world' as that towards which the human subject has the ability to spin a web of work, intentional activity and hence of belongings, or of interconnections. For Heidegger this capacity is crucial and exclusive to the human and separates him from the rest of living beings. Thus, in 'The origin of the work of art' (1993: 231) Heidegger argues: 'A stone is worldless. Plant and animal likewise have no world; but they belong to the covert throng of a surrounding into which they are linked. The peasant woman, on the other hand, has a world because she dwells in the overtness of beings. . . . a work as work sets up a world.' For Heidegger the essential difference between Man, animal and plant rests on the human being's ecstatic capacity to stand outside himself, to open up the space of the world and to be thrown out of the present into the temporal continuum that is his ek-sistence. This temporal continuity makes Man into the ek-sistent, i.e. that which is essentially connected to the truth of Being even and especially in his capacity to stand outside Being. Heidegger (1993: 230) says:

> Of all the beings that are, presumably the most difficult to think about are living creatures, because on the one hand they are in a certain way most closely akin to us, and on the other are at the same time separated from our Ek-sistent essence by an abyss. However, it might also seem as though the essence of divinity is closer to us than what is so alien in other living creatures,

closer, namely, in an essential distance which, however distant, is nonetheless
more familiar to our Ek-sistent essence than is our scarcely conceivable, abysmal
bodily kinship with the beast.

Heidegger considers the definition of Man as a rational animal not only a
genuine misnomer, but also one of the most pernicious legacies of metaphysics, analogous to locating human essence in an immortal soul or an
innate power of reason. Man's essence is his 'Ek-sistenz', that is to say his
capacity for 'representational positioning' (231), or his ecstatic inherence in
the structure of Being. This is the abyss that separates man from beast.

Philosophical nomadology is exactly the opposite of all this. For instance,
Shaviro (1995) turns this point into a passionate, neo-Nietzschean attack
on the concept of consciousness. Against Heidegger he argues firstly that
language does not represent the world or contain the hermeneutical keys to
the essence of the world. On the contrary, language 'intervenes in the world,
invades the world, appropriates the world' (1995: 42). The model is not
Heidegger's 'ek-sistenz', but the mode of viral contamination, or parasitic
appropriation. The embodied subject is shot through with relational link-
ages of the symbiotic, contaminating/viral kind which interconnect it to a
variety of others, starting from the environment or habitat. Consequently
consciousness itself, far from being an act of vertical transcendence, rather
functions as a push downwards, almost like an act of inner invasion. It
constitutes literally the folding and holding within of forces originating
from the outside. As such, consciousness is rapacious, predatory, unthankful
and self-obsessed. It is constructed in Western cultures with reference to
the guiding principles of narcissism and paranoia, which are the keys to the
sacred institution of individual identity. For philosophical nomadism, the
subject is fully immersed in and immanent in a network of non-human
(animal, vegetable, viral) relations.

From an altogether different philosophical tradition, Seyla Benhabib
pointed out (1996) in her study of Hannah Arendt's critique of 'existenz
philosophy' that Heidegger is quite contradictory. On the one hand he
argues that being-in-the-world and sharing it with others is constitutive of
the human. On the other hand, the fundamental condition through which
the meaning of being human is revealed is by 'being-unto-death, the awareness of Dasein's temporality and finitude' (Benhabib, 1996: 53). Heidegger
thus ends up denying plurality and collectivity while he embeds the subject
in just such a setting. As Arendt put it, Heidegger denies that we share the
world with others and thus he ends up with an atomized definition of the
subject. Irigaray makes an analogous critique of the self-referential and
claustrophobic Heideggerian universe in *L'Oubli de l'air* (1983).

The central issue that Deleuze takes up in opposition to phenomenology
is the emphasis on transcendence. This connects to his stated need to redefine

a sense of attachment and connection to a shared world, a territorial space. In philosophical nomadology this quest is addressed precisely through the notion of the becoming-animal. This is a spatial and temporal mode of enhancing a common life-space which the subject never masters nor possesses, but merely crosses, always in a pack, a group, or a cluster. It is an embodied subject, but by no means one which is suspended in an essential distance from the habitat/environment/territory. On the contrary, the nomadic subject is radically immanent to it. Deleuze pushes the quarrel with phenomenology further and brings it to bear on the very notion of embodiment and embeddedness.

In the metaphysics of substance, the bodily equivalent of the 'power of reason' is the notion of Man as 'rational animal' which is expected to inhabit a perfectly functional physical body. All other modes of embodiment, being zoomorphic, disabled, malformed or ill-functioning, are pathologized and classified on the other side of normality, that is to say monstrosity. This process is inherently racialized in that it upholds aesthetic and moral ideals based on white European civilization. The morphological normativity that works in the established ideas of normality as anthropocentric, standard white embodiment is best exemplified in Leonardo's figure of the naked, male, white body which allegedly constitutes the measure of all things. As Foucault argued, this is a major exercise in disciplining the body and in inscribing such discipline at the heart of the human and social sciences. In other words, normative discourses about normality are also at work in the production of knowledge, science and forms of cultural expression. Foucault singles out especially psychoanalysis as perpetuating this legacy of normalization. Let me expand on this point.

In a psychoanalytic perspective, the bodily self with its multiple functions is disaggregated according to organs, how they relate to the drives and contribute to successful, socially acceptable, object choices. Disciplining the body means socializing it into acceptable, 'normal' behaviour in terms of choices of love-objects and modes of externalization of the drives. I would render this psychoanalytic process as follows: identity is coded on the body by a process of psychic mapping which functions by indexing certain organs on to specific functions, so as to produce operational sequences: eye/vision/sign/reading/scopic verification; ear/voice/acoustic signification; desire/object/appropriation/pleasure, and so forth. Organs and functions, desires and 'proper' objects need to be 'joined' in socially acceptable assemblages. In this process of inscription, pleasure and pleasure zones play a fundamental role. The libidinal force of pleasure acts as the psychic 'glue' that fixes sensations on to organs and maps them out psychically. I would moreover describe pleasure like an invisible ink that writes out the chain of signifiers on to the sensible matter of the flesh.

In so far as psychoanalysis proves the anatomy of this psychic process, it is a theory which aims at explaining, not at transforming, the data. Foucault assesses it consequently as a very conservative discipline, which upholds a normative, normal, heterosexual vision of the desiring subject. Deleuze's philosophical nomadism will push this criticism further and turn it into a conceptual objection. Deleuze wants to free the flows of desire from their dependence on a normative vision of the embodied subject. As I argued in the previous chapter, the morphological frame of the nomadic body is open-ended, interrelational and trans-species. It explodes the boundaries of humanism at skin level. It also frees the subject from his or her enslavement to a linguistic model of development, based on the power of signification. In turn this implies also the rejection of the psychoanalytic model of transcription of sensations into data which get mapped out psychically and provide the subject with some sense of corporeal cohesion or unity. The power of language, for Deleuze and Guattari, reveals the despotic power of the Phallic signifier, which is the historical expression of a specific moment in the organization of capitalism. This is imprinted on the subject as an internalized form of despotism which is exemplified by the power of conscious self-reflexivity over the heterogeneous, surging and potentially chaotic mass of libidinal affects.

Under the influence of Guattari, Deleuze proposes instead a vision of the body as un-organic: a body-without-organs, a body freed from the codes of phallogocentric functions of identity. The un-organic 'body without organs' is supposed to create creative disjunctions in this system, freeing organs from their indexation to certain prerequisite functions: this is the process of becoming-animal. In some ways, this calls for a generalized perversion of all bodily functions, not only the sexual ones; it is a way of scrambling the master-code of phallocentrism and loosening its power over the body. I find in Deleuze's work a sort of joyful anarchy of the senses, a pan-erotic approach to the body which blossoms out in his theories of both the 'becoming-woman' and even more in the 'becoming-animal'. The figurations make concrete and actual the rejection of the principle of adequation to and identification with a phallogocentric image of thought, which lies at the heart of the nomadic vision of subjectivity. Deleuze proposes them as the new, post-metaphysical figuration of the subject. In his work on the becoming-animal Deleuze acts upon the idea that the activity of thinking cannot and must not be reduced to reactive ('sedentary') critique. Thinking can be critical if by critical we mean the active, assertive process of inventing new images of thought – beyond the old icon where thinking and Being joined hands together under the sphinx-like smile of the sovereign Phallus. Thinking, for Deleuze, is instead life lived at the highest possible power. Thinking is about change and transformation. Thinking is enfleshed, erotic and pleasure-driven.

It is important to stress that the anti-metaphysics of the subject proposed by Deleuze is inherently political: it is the kind of thought that aims at reconnecting theory with daily practices of change, transformation and resistance. Foremost among Deleuze's concerns is the idea that the philosophy and the politics of difference must take into account not only the negative aspects of power, that is to say the experiences of oppression, exclusion and marginality, but also the need to redefine the positive structures of the subject. Politics has to do with the elaboration and implementation of structural changes within and without the subject, starting with his or her desires. Politics has to engage with *potentia*, as well as with *potestas*.

Deleuze thus stresses the importance of affectivity as a force that structures subjectivity. As I argued earlier, this move is intended to disengage the subject from the traditional framework of reference to which the phallogocentric regime had confined it. It thus stresses the non-coincidence of the subject with his or her consciousness. Philosophical nomadology shifts the balance of power away from the mind and on to the body. Even more significantly, it favours the unity of mind and body, not their binary opposition. The emphasis on affectivity here marks a pre-discursive moment in which one thinks without thinking about it, a phase in which thinking is just like breathing. Thinking precedes self-reflexivity and rational thought. It rests on the human being's predisposition, receptivity, capacity as well as the yearning for thinking. The tendency of the subject towards thinking, representing him or herself in language, is the pre-philosophical basis of philosophy; it is a pre-discursive element (Violi 1987) which is in excess of and nevertheless indispensable to the act of thinking as such. It is an ontological inscription, a pre-disposition that is neither thinking nor conscious and which by virtue of social conventions inscribes the subject into the web of discursivity, that is to say into language, and therefore into power.

Anti-metaphors

Animals are also living metaphors, highly iconic emblems within our language and culture. We normally and fluently metaphorize them into referents for values and meanings. Leonardo da Vinci (1988) canonizes the repertoire: the merriness of the rooster, the sadness of the raven, the rage of the bear, the nobleness of the eagle, the foresight of ants, the deceit of foxes, the cowardice of rabbits and hares, the humility of lambs, the lust of the bat and the hypocrisy of the crocodile are only some of the *topoi* which since da Vinci have become part of our mental and linguistic habits. Leonardo picks up the tradition that Aesop inaugurated and La Fontaine pursued. Hannah Arendt (1968), in one of her rare moments of admiration for another woman, reminds us that Rosa Luxemburg was considered by Lenin to be an 'eagle' because of her intelligence and integrity. On his part Isaiah Berlin (1978) used animal metaphors to indicate major ethical traits in the human species. Thus, the distinction between the hedgehog and the fox has the force of a qualitative and ethical indexation system. The former only knows one big, thick, dense thing but it knows it to death, so to speak. The fox, on the other hand, is mercurial and quick in picking up many varied sources of information and adapting them to its purposes. Hedgehogs rest on single, universalizing principles, whereas foxes pursue many ends, albeit unrelated and contradictory ones, without ever trying to fit them into a unitary scheme. Isaiah Berlin is happy to rest on the animal analogies to make his moral point, and yet it does not take much to give a nomadic twist to his words. Centripetal versus centrifugal, multiple as opposed to monolithic: these two are qualitatively apart not only as species, but in terms of the ethology of forces that animate them. As Deleuze would put it: they differ just as the workhorse differs more from the racehorse than from the ox. This way of approaching the issue, however, implies that the animal is not interpreted metaphorically, but is taken in its radical immanence as a field of forces, a quantity of speed and intensity.

Historically, other attempts have been made, of course, to approach animals in an energetic mode, not exactly along the nomadic lines I have in mind, but rather in a technological-industrial mode. Since antiquity, animals have been associated with technology and machines not only because they allegedly lack an innate rational soul and consequently a will and a sovereign subjectivity of their own, but also because they are industrial workers. Not only are the bodies of animals used for their capacity to produce primary material: think of the tusks of elephants, the hides of most creatures, the wool of sheep, the oil and fat of whales, the silk of caterpillars and then, of course, milk and their edible meat. The taxonomy of animals reads at times like an industrial production plant: animals are used as prototypes for engineering, especially insects, to which I will return in the next section. For the moment the point is that, for Deleuze, animals are neither functional to teleological systems of classification, nor are they about metaphors: they are rather about metamorphoses.

And yet, as I pointed out in the previous chapter, writing is for Deleuze a sort of becoming animal. Loyal to his anti-phallogocentric vision of creativity, Deleuze praises the nomadic force of writing, which implicates one into the spatio-temporal co-ordinates of the field of yet unknown perception and experience. Writers, like animals, are committed creatures who live on full alert, constantly tensed up in the effort of captivating and sustaining the signals that come from their plane of immanent contact with other forces. This kind of becoming, and the specific memory that accompanies it, also provides, therefore, a new classification for literary and cultural texts. Deleuze, especially in his analysis of Kafka's work, defines as 'minor literature' the kind of text which is disengaged from the linear sequence of memory. This sort of memory is located within the molar order and, as such, it is a reservoir of negative and reactive forces. According to Bensmaia (in Boundas et al. 1994), the main traits of 'minor literature' are its deterritorializing force, or its potential for multiple becomings. This is related to the capacity of art to politicize every aspect of one's existence even and especially the most intimate aspects (memories, loves, etc.) and its intrinsically collective force. In all these respects, 'minor' literature – even and especially when it consists of 'great works of literature', as Kafka's works uncontestably are – is anti-Oedipal, in so far as it resists the colonizing force of the molar system and the totalizing influence of narrative closure.

That there is a powerful and I daresay vital link between the literary text and the different moments of 'becoming' is clear. Charles Stivale offers a cartographic reading of the different becomings in Deleuze's work and of the literary texts and authors to which they refer (Stivale 1984).[1] It seems to me, however, that Deleuze writes these cross-references very much in the mode of 'souvenirs', without claiming the kind of exact faithfulness to the texts that is so dear to literary critics and other brands of textual specialists. Similarly, he worked 'from memory' and did not watch again the films he discussed in his two-volume study of cinema. I would like to propose consequently that we take Deleuze's textual references not in the conventional mode of academic bibliography, but rather in the mood of the rhizomatic and nomadic philosopher: as co-ordinates which set the longitude and the latitude of his project of becoming.

As I argued in chapter 2, in my commentary on Massumi's work, there is something of the cartographer and the lexicographer in Deleuze's system of classifying and organizing texts. Authors as diverse as Kerouac, Woolf or Sarraute can be placed on the same level, stratified and coalesced, following criteria of indexation that ignore the standard tools of literary theory. Deleuze focuses instead on the geological, geometrical and geo-political frames which are set by these authors' texts. I find that Deleuze's favourite writers, not unlike his beloved philosophers, trace itineraries of liberation of the subject, of many, even potentially contradictory, becomings. Most of them open up towards a cosmic dimension, which in the old humanistic language used to be called 'the infinite'. These texts yearn to capture the last breath which marks the point of exit from the human, into the all-too-human, the post-human, the magnetic field of cosmic resonance. That is to say, the human engages in the intensity of becoming at the cost of his or her becoming imperceptible. Like Virginia Woolf's *Waves*, sound, heat, and liquid waves bypass the human and thus connect to larger forces. A secular form of spiritual inter-connectiveness is at work in philosophical nomadism.

Women who run with (Virginia) woolf

The case of the wolf is emblematic of Deleuze's theory of the becoming-animal. It contains the basic elements of his quarrel with psychoanalytic notions of the unconscious, the ethics of affects and his literary and cultural theories. In the fast track of processes of becoming, one metamorphosis leads to, or melts into, another without much restraint. Thus, the figure of the wolf, werewolf or she-wolf can also be rendered in classical Gothic mode, as demon, vampire or satanic lover. The best example of this sequence in popular culture is the stage show and film *Cats* where the hybrid morphological creature – half female, half panther – stands simultaneously for ethnic mixity, moral ambiguity, sexual indeterminacy and unbridled erotic passion. The process of trans-species nomadism, or morphological hybridity, is loaded with sexuality in that it entails the erasure of and the transgressing of bodily boundaries. This 'explosion' of the civilized confines of one's 'self' re-asserts some raw corporeality of the subject, which is often rendered in the mode of the orgasm, of the ecstatic erotic encounter with radical otherness. The *topos* of the wolf incorporates a great deal of these elements, with speed, fur, blood and violence thrown in for extra thrills.

Popular culture here has impeccable literary credentials. The werewolf, or *lycanthropos*, wolf-man or she-wolf is a well-established figure in classical as well as in Scandinavian and Teutonic mythologies. Ancient mythologies display zoomorphic gods and consider all in-between, monstrous or hybrid creatures as *teras*: objects of adoration as well as aberration. After all, it is in the shape of a she-wolf that Roman civilization cast the myth of its divine origin. She-wolves, like cat-people of all sorts (leopards, panthers, jaguars) have distinguished cultural backgrounds and literary credentials, from Petronius' *Satyricon* to Ovid's *Metamorphoses* and Apuleius' *Golden Ass*. Pliny gives a careful description which testifies that the wolf stands for blood-thirsty violence; he reports an Arcadian legend that at the sacrifice of a human victim, one tasted the vitals of the sacrificial boy and immediately turned into a wolf, roaming the earth for ten long years. The image of a human mutated into a furry four-legged predator roaming the moonlit landscape in a pack, in search of prey and copulation, is a *topos* that pre-dates the currency it has received in the postmodern Gothic genre of which Angela Carter's 'The company of wolves' (1985) is a major example. It has a long-standing literary legitimacy. Moreover, the wolf as a metaphor for male violence and more especially for his sexual aggression has also been canonized both in folklore and in fairy-tales. The sexual connotations of the wolf, especially the werewolf, have been extensively analysed by Propp (1968), Bettelheim (1972) and Marina Warner (1995): the wolf is the dangerous and irresistible seducer who haunts the helpless female victims.

The homicidal tendencies of the werewolf are explored with comic and very sexually specific violence in Fay Weldon's *The Life and Loves of a She-Devil* (1983). The exemplary tale of the betrayed, dutiful wife who turns murderous in revenge illustrates two features of the wolf that endear it to Deleuze, as much as to feminist, transformative writers like Weldon. Firstly, that an animal is a war-machine; it is an organism 'that strikes back when and where it is stricken' (Massumi, 1992: 51). Secondly, in order to reach such precision in striking, it disposes of a formidable memory. This is an embodied and embedded memory, capable of recording sensorial or physical data and storing their impact upon oneself. Significantly, Weldon's novel foregrounds unforgetting jealousy and its side-effects. It also plays on issues related to the political economy of body-management in late capitalism, namely: fatness and slimness, good looks and sexual attractiveness as well as the cash-flow. Food is a major indicator of power-relations, and in some ways the she-wolf is the antithesis of the despotic/pathetic face of the bulimic/anorexic victimized female.

The Estonian writer Aino Kallas, in her short story 'The wolf's bride', narrates the metamorphosis of a female werewolf. It describes in a moving manner the freedom and the exhilaration as well as the voluptuousness, of giving up the human form. The process of physical transformation marks also the shifts of consciousness of the woman, who gradually discovers her commonality or sameness with the leading wolf, the leader of the pack. 'And she melted away into the murmur of the forest spruce, was pressed in golden drops of resin from the red sides of the pines, and vanished into the green dampness of the marsh moss, as she now belonged to *Diabolus Sylvarum*, she was in the clutches of satan' (Kallas 1990: 133–4). The ecstatic melting of boundaries that takes place in the becoming-wolf of Aalo delivers and expresses a deep eroticism. In her commentary on this short story, Lea Rojola (1995) traces the historical and literary genealogy of this myth in Estonian culture. She also stresses the highly sex-specific structure of the story: at night this woman runs and mates with the wolves, but during the day is a gentle and obedient wife. Only after she gives birth to the child of sin is she found out and is burnt in a sauna by the women of the village. After this ritual cleasing, her human husband kills a great grey wolf with a silver bullet melted down from his wedding ring. Aalo's soul dwells within this wolf. Rojola reads this tale as a case of split or double life which reflects the social schizophrenia of emancipated women in Nordic countries in the 1920s. The conflict between the archaic and the new is reflected in the different locations of the female werewolf. As an emblem, the she-wolf represents therefore the monstrousness of liberated female sexual desire. That the expression of her desire cost her her life does not detract from the intensity or value of it.

Considering the importance of female desire and *jouissance* to the *topos* of the female werewolf, let me stress that the nomadic theory of the becoming-wolf has nothing in common with archetypal Jungian thinking. According to Jung, the collective unconscious contains archetypes or primordial images that keep on recurring in the course of history. They convey universal and essential truths through their psychic re-occurrence. Clarissa Pinkola Estés (1992) offers the best Jungian-inspired coding of the archetype of the wolf in relation to the female psyche. Her approach is a quantitative accumulation of common traits between women and wolves, such as complicity with the wild; familiarity with wilderness; pleasure in the outside, especially the forest; hunting; bleeding and the taste of blood; copulating in the moonlight and other forms of wild sexuality. Represented through various artforms and present trans-historically in a variety of cultures, they constitute a cultural constant.

This strikes me, however, as antithetical to Deleuze's notion of the becoming-animal. The Jungian collective unconscious is a quantitative plurality within a one-dimensional and mono-directional system, not a qualitative multiplicity in an open-ended set of complexities, as in philosophical nomadism. In other words, the realization of the archetypes fixes the ego within a firm frame of references and attributes; it does not operate the qualitative reframing of perception and immanence that are sought after in nomadic thinking.[2]

In his critique of Jungian archetypes Baldick (1987) puts it admirably: the Jungian myth is granted anteriority over its own literary and cultural manifestations and consequently it enjoys a higher authority over modern scientific culture, in so far as it pertains to a more ancient, timeless rhythm of nature. This results in an over-emphasis on the authority of the myth itself, which over-invests 'mythic consciousness' with greater importance than modern-day living and in distinct opposition to the experiences of history. In the case of Jung's archetypes, this becomes a semi-religious belief which categorically distinguishes the myth (immutable and healing) from history (changeable and anxiety-ridden).

> The archetype itself is empty and purely formal, nothing but a *facultas praeformandi*, a possibility of representation which is given *a priori*. The representations themselves are not inherited, only the forms, and in that respect they correspond in every way to the instincts, which are also determined in form only. (Jung 1982: 106)

It is this essentialism and the opposition to historical change that makes the Jungian archetypes into a disturbing dogmatic methodology. By assuming that all myths belong to the same timeless sphere and psychic plane, the most banal interpretations of these myths are being circulated.

Todorov (1975) argues that, on the issue of the myth and the imagination, in modern continental thought there are two schools of thought. One draws from structuralism and is inspired by Lévi-Strauss, Freud and Marx. This school singles out constitutive rational elements even in unconscious processes and pre-scientific thought. The other school is inspired by Bachelard, Jung and Frye. They stay closer to a thematic approach in reading the products of human consciousness. They also trust the resources of the sensuous imagination and emphasize it over and above the structural elements of human thought. I think Deleuze's approach is historically closer to the structuralist, but it ultimately moves beyond the useful distinction made by Todorov. The nomadic subject is not split along the traditional axes of mind/body, consciousness/unconscious, or reason/imagination. On the contrary, the notions of embodiment and immanence posit it as one energetic, forever-shifting entity, fundamentally driven by desire for expansion towards its many-faceted exterior borders/others.

In this regard, I do not see a possible reconciliation between Jung and Deleuze on the issue of the imagination or on the structure and function of myths such as the were-wolf. In the case of Jung as in that of Heidegger, I must also own up to a serious difficulty on my part to forget that this (socially encouraged and even rewarded) tendency of an allegedly 'great' thinker to take a flight outside history, towards the abstract heights of timeless re-occurrence of the Same, became politically enacted in the banality of evil. The fact of both Heidegger's and Jung's collaboration with Nazism is neither coincidental nor is it external to their systems of thought, as Arendt said of Heidegger: it is embedded in the very conceptual fabric of their thinking. I neither want to judge, nor to draw hasty conclusions. But I am not about to add insult to injury by paying myself the luxury of forgetting, either. History does matter, as do the historical manifestations of *any* locations, positions, meaning or beliefs. A materialist philosophy would not have it any other way.

Dorothea Olkowski gives a very interesting reading of the differences between a psychoanalytic and a Deleuzian concept of the becoming-animal in a paper significantly called: 'Writers are dogs' (1999b). Taking Freud's Wolf-Man as her main case, Olkowski stresses the intensive structure of the experience. Noting that the Wolf-Man dreamt of a whole pack of wolves and not just a single one, Olkowski argues that Freud imposes a spurious kind of unity on the heterogeneity and multiplicity of the Wolf-Man's affectivity. Re-interpreted as neurosis, re-packaged around a unitary – albeit shaky – subject, the whole episode is confined to the dialectics of pathology–normality, with the psychoanalytic cure as the main switch. Olkowski, on the other hand, reads the Wolf-Man with Deleuze as a case of qualitative expansion of the self into a creative multiplicity, whereby speed, the company of other wolves or collectivity are crucial elements. Cross-reading this with Artaud's *oeuvre*, she compares the writing process to a trip through variations of intensity that are simply 'too much' and can flip into schizophrenia, the dark depths of the unspeakable, the absence of signification.

Bio-centred egalitarianism

The animal is also man's genetic brother: *zoe* links them in an unstoppable web of interconnections. *Zoe*, of course, is the poor half of a couple that foregrounds *bios* defined as discursive or intelligent life. Centuries of Christian indoctrination have left a deep mark here. The relationship to animal life, to *zoe*, rather that *bios*, constitutes one of those qualitative distinctions upon which Western reason erected its empire. I believe that one of the most persistent and unhelpful fictions that is being told about human 'life' is its alleged self-evidence, its implicit worth. *Zoe* is second best, and the idea of life carrying on independently of, even regardless of and at times in spite of, rational control is the dubious privilege attributed to the non-humans. These cover all of the animal kingdom, down to its smallest aquatic and aerial variants.

Since Darwin and evolutionary theory, however, it has grown to encompass increasingly large and central zones of the human organism. The distress and disarray that the triumph of what Ansell Pearson dubs 'germinal life' has caused for classical rationalist schemes of thought cannot be underestimated. Traditionally, the self-reflexive control of life is reserved for humans, whereas the mere unfolding of biological sequences is for non-humans. The former is holy (*bios*), the latter quite gritty (*zoe*). That they intersect in the human body turns the physical self into a contested space, a political arena. The mind–body dualism has historically functioned as a shortcut through the complexities of this in-between contested zone. Artists have crowded into this in-between area, offering a number of interconnections.

For instance, Kafka's metamorphosis of a human into an abject insect is a trip to the limit of one's ability to endure, also known as sustainability. It is touching the bottom of some inhumanity that connects to the human precisely in the immanence of its instances. What you see is what you get; this is the bottom line: a scaly and fast-fading body that cannot even adequately express what it needs for the pain to stop. This obscenity, this life in me, is intrinsic to my being and yet so much 'itself', that it is independent of the will, the demands and expectations of the sovereign consciousness. This *zoe* makes me tick and yet escapes the control of the supervisory agency of the Self – built on the twin pillars of narcissism and paranoia. *Zoe* carries on relentlessly and is cast out of the holy precinct of the 'me' that demands control and fails to obtain it, ending by being experienced as an alien other. It is experienced as in-human, but only because it is all too human; obscene, because it lives mindlessly on. This scandal, this wonder, this *zoe*, that is to say an idea of Life that is more than *bios* and supremely indifferent to *logos*, this piece of flesh called my 'body', this aching meat called my 'self' expresses the abject/divine potency of a Life which consciousness lives in fear of. Nomadic subjectivity is, by contrast, in love with *zoe*.

The point is confirmed by other bodily experiences; it is the case, for instance with pregnancy or with other fast proliferation of cells, for better or for worse, as Stacey pointed out in her study of cancer, which I quoted in chapter 1. The experiences in which the ego-bound human organism is experienced as the host of life-processes which it does not control and which carry on ruthlessly and regardlessly, expresses the force of *zoe*. Traditionally this power has been rendered in terms of a hierarchy that privileges *bios* and reflects a reason–matter, control–chaos binary scale of values. This potency (*potentia*) of Life is experienced as 'other' by a mind that cannot do anything else but fold upon itself and go on patrolling its own constitutive elements as if it were in charge of them. This inner inversion by negative passions is a deeply-seated, uneasy form of mild schizophrenia, which we gloriously call 'consciousness'. The life in me, however, is not under the empire of law, signifier and lack: life just is. Consciousness is only the socially recognized, allowed and encouraged form of capturing the specific slice of life which constitutes me. Conscious self-representation is a social convention which fulfils the important aim of trying to bind together different human beings who negotiate their social bonds by installing an economy of symbolic exchanges among themselves. It is not the site of truth or agency, or rather if it is so, it is due to its function as the site of intersecting and conflicting forces. As Freud put it more conservatively, the self is a clearing-house that breeds the kind of neurosis that the socialized, urbanized dwellers of Western civilization are tied to. Civilization and its discontents extol their pound of flesh as the price to pay for not being a pack of werewolves howling, mating and killing in the moonlight. Thus, the self is politics by another name, it is the micro-fascism of a dominant vision of the subject which serves the purposes of a vampire-like economic system based on stock and exchange, accumulation and profit.

For philosophical nomadology the strength of animals lies precisely in not being-one which is expressed in their attachment to and interdependence on a territory. They rely on a small and highly confined or defined slice of environment to which they relate sensorily and perceptively. Insects, especially spiders and parasites like ticks, are among Deleuze's favourites. Like artists, animals mark their territory physically, by colour, sound or marking/framing. In order to mark, code, possess or frame their territory, animals produce signals and signs constantly; insects buzz and make all sort of sounds; upper primates practically talk (just ask Jane Goodall); cats, wolves and dogs mark the lands with bodily fluids of their own production, dogs bark and howl in pain and desire. They are immanent to their gestures aimed at coping with needs and environments. In the process of recognizing, coding and coping they transcend their sheer animality, joining up with the human in the effort of expressing, inhabiting and protecting their territory. Orienting oneself in a strange territory; finding food and water, let alone a mate, expressing all this so that the others in the collective pack or group can get the idea – that is a model of radical immanence that needs to be revalued. It is non-verbal communication at its best.

In this respect, humans may have more in common with their genetic neighbours, the animals, than they may care to admit, and in some ways they are less constructive. This point about a structural proximity between the human and its genetic neighbours is eloquently driven home in popular culture by Agent Smith in the film *The Matrix*:

> every mammal on this planet instinctively develops a natural equilibrium with its surrounding environment. But you humans do not. You move to an area and you multiply. You multiply until every natural resource is consumed. The only way you survive is to spread to another area. There is another organism of this planet that follows this pattern. A virus. Human beings are a disease of this planet. You are a plague.

Contemporary writers like Angela Carter and Martin Amis are shrewd trackers of the kind of genetico-ethical mutations that are currently taking place in post-industrial urban landscapes, and in the psychic horizons of those human and post-human subjects that inhabit them. More on this in the next chapter.

This proximity, however, is not to be taken in the classical, benevolent mode of caring for 'our four-legged friends'. The culture of pets in some ways constitutes the epitome of humanism: pets are indeed those Oedipalized entities we watch television with. In philosophical nomadism, on the other hand, the proximity is trans-species and transgenic material in the sense of matter/*mater* which I discussed in chapter 1. It has to do with a chain of connections which can best be described as an ecological philosophy of non-unitary, embodied subjects. Thus, I do not wish this discussion to slip in the direction of 'animal rights' or other on-going anthropocentric discussions on animal ethics. What is at stake for me here is precisely the critique of anthropocentrism and of liberal individualism, both in the light of recent scientific developments in genetics and molecular biology and also in view of the cultural manifestations they engender. Mette Bryld and Nina Lykke's recent work on *Cosmodolphins* (1999) offers a splendid example of the novelty of this approach. They combine a 'technophilic' attitude with ecological concerns, feminist ethics of sexual difference and a lively dialogue with contemporary biological sciences and bio-technologies, all of it framed by an intense participation in and enjoyment of contemporary post-industrial culture, in both its 'high' and its popular forms.

In order not to confuse the becoming of the animal with the becoming-animal, it is important to distinguish the discourse of physiology, which deals with organic functions, from that of ethics. Nomadic ethics, inspired by Spinoza, is related to the physics and the biology of bodies. That means that it deals with the question of what exactly a body can do and how much it can take. This is the issue that I code as 'sustainability': how much a body can take in pleasure or enhancement of its potentials, as in pain or impoverishment of its *potentia* (or *conatus*). This implies an equation between ethical virtue, empowerment, joy and the understanding. To represent adequately to oneself one's own good amounts to understanding it. Such an act of understanding, however, is not the mere mental acquisition of certain ideas. It rather coincides with a bodily process, i.e.: an activity that enacts or embodies what is good for the subject, the actualization of his or her *potentia*. Mind and body act in unison and are glued together by what Spinoza calls *conatus*, that is to say the desire to become and to increase the intensity of one's becoming.[3]

This approach is made explicit in Keith Ansell Pearson's work on Deleuze's philosophy of the body (1997). By reading Nietzsche and Darwin with Deleuze, Pearson explores the interconnections between ethics of values and the nature of bodies; he thus emphasizes the continuum of becomings as well as the transmutation of values that is implied in a nomadic concept of 'life' that is simultaneously materialistic and vitalistic. In so doing, Pearson uses Deleuze's insights to 'begin to map non-human becomings of life' (p. 109). Combining in a skilful manner biology and technology, Pearson envisages a 'trans-human' space of pure, processual metamorphoses that asserts the infinite powers of a life that does not require the supervision of the human mind in order to endure.

Deleuze's bio-philosophy is therefore also a topology of affects, based on the selection of these forces. This process of unfolding affects is central to the composition of radically immanent bodies and thus it can be seen as the actualization of enfleshed materialism. Deleuze follows Spinoza here. The selection of the forces of becoming is regulated by an ethics of joy and affirmation which functions through the transformation of negative into positive passions. These imply the repetition of pleasure and the avoidance of sadness and of the relations that express sadness. The selection of the composite positive passions constitutes spaces of becoming or corporeal affects. These are essentially a matter of affinity: being able to enter a relation with another entity whose elements appeal to one produces a joyful encounter. They express one's *potentia* and increase the subject's capacity to enter into further relations, grow and expand. This expansion is time-bound: the nomadic subject by expressing and increasing its positive passions empowers itself to last, to endure, to continue through and in time. By entering into relations, nomadic becomings engender possible futures, they construct the world by making possible a web of sustainable interconnections. This is the point of becoming: a collective assemblage of forces that coalesce around commonly shared elements and empower them to grow and to last.

The becoming-animal functions accordingly through constant mutations, affects and relations. On this point Deleuze works with both Spinoza and Nietzsche to defend his positive vision of the subject against the captivating, belittling influence of social codes and norms, which are upheld by a repressive notion of the State. Nietzsche is especially influential on the issue of anti-humanism and the critique of the negativity that is built into accepted notions of consciousness. Nomadic subjectivity wants to undo this. It aims at putting consciousness back into its rightful place, as one form – albeit a hegemonic one – of expression of the subject, a form that is structured around a tightly held bundle of negative passions, retentive tendencies, festering suspicion: the ego is a temple to narcissism and paranoia. In opposition to this, the nomadic subject aims to become, to split at the seams the neatly formatted version of Man as 'rational animal', to explode its in-built contradictions.

What if consciousness were, in fact, an inferior mode of relating to one's own environment and to others? What if consciousness were no cognitively or morally different from the pathetic howling of wolves in the full moonlight? What if, by comparison with the know-how of animals, conscious self-representation were blighted by narcissistic delusions and consequently blinded by its own aspirations to self-transparency? What if consciousness were ultimately incapable of finding a remedy to its obscure disease, this life, this *zoe*, an impersonal force that moves me without asking for my permission to do so? After all, mortality is there as the limit and the horizon and there is no hubris of the conscious mind that can prevent death from the swift completion of its appointed rounds. Becoming-animal is a brush with the bottom line, with the outsider-within. There is no creativity without it. And yet it is not a mere reversal of the dialectics into irrationality, it is a different path of becoming.

Towards the post-human

As I stated earlier, it is the degree and speed of intensity of the affects that determines the power (*potentia*) of a body and consequently also the level of interactivity with other entities. This ethical approach is also at the heart of Deleuze's quarrel with the determinism of contemporary genetic theories. Life, as a project that aims at affirming the intensity and positivity of desire, rests on the materialist foundation of the enfleshed subject. By stressing this biological aspect, Deleuze is simultaneously accepting the lesson of contemporary biology and also disagreeing with the neo-determinism of social biologists and evolutionary psychologists. Deleuze disagrees with many molecular biologists as to the reductive vision of the subject which they endorse. By interpreting contemporary biology with reference to the 'enchanted materialism' of empirical philosophies of immanence, Deleuze attempts to disengage biology from the structural functionalism and neo-determinism of DNA-driven linearity and to veer it instead towards the zigzagging patterns of nomadic becoming. As Halberstam and Livingston put it (1995: 3) 'the human body itself is no longer part of "the family of man", but a zoo of posthumanities.'

Elizabeth Grosz has recently stressed the importance for feminists of rethinking the biological structure of the human. This call for a return to the biological roots of the body reiterates the rejection of social constructivism which is crucial to feminist theory in the third millennium. In her recent work on Darwin, Grosz sets the agenda as follows: 'What are the virtualities, the potentialities, within biological existence that enable cultural, social and historical forces to work with and actively transform that existence?' (1999). I find this appeal to be invested by the kind of radical immanence and the 'enchanted enfleshed materialism' that both Irigaray and Deleuze defend, in parallel but analogous ways.

There is, however a specific philosophical touch to the 'return to Darwin' proposed by Grosz and other contemporary Deleuzian thinkers. In other research fields, such as science studies, where attention to and a critical engagement with evolutionary theories has always been central to the agenda, a more sceptical note is being struck. Thus, in their recent and quite powerful critique of evolutionary theories, Hilary and Steven Rose (2000) critique their profound misogyny and their complicity with imperial and colonialist projects of white, Eurocentric pseudo-science. These scholars are well positioned to issue a cautionary tale considering their lifelong involvement with radical critiques of science. They also track down the increasing interdependence of contemporary biological research and commercial as well as industrial concerns, which are far from politically neutral. I do think it crucial to the politics of nomadic subjectivity that these critical notes are heard and taken into account. Thus, a return to Darwin that would result in de-contextualizing and disembedding the power-effects of these theories in contemporary culture would be disastrous. I think that a new, constructive dialogue could be set up between philosophers and geneticists, not with a view to seek a consensus on the fuzzy area known as 'bio-ethics', but rather for the more rigorous task of exploring fully the implications of the radical de-centring of the subject which contemporary bio-sciences have brought about.

Deleuze's concept of the becoming-animal is a radical conceptual version of the anti-anthropocentrism that marks his generation of philosophers. Donna Haraway shares the spirit of this dislocation of the centrality of the human, in favour of the post-human and of bio-centred egalitarianism even though she rests on different conceptual foundations. Both Deleuze and Haraway refuse to underplay the contradictions and discontinuities between the human and the non-human environment. They also refuse to romanticize the interaction between them. This sentimental glorification of humans' proximity with animals is especially problematic in contemporary culture. This is due firstly to the social climate of resurgent socio-biological determinism, such as Hilary and Steven Rose denounce. This results in overemphasizing the 'animal nature' of humans, and usually quite simply of human males as the pretext and justification for social inequalities. A book that can bear the title *A Natural History of Rape: Biological Bases of Sexual Coercion*[4] is indicative of the social and political implications of this neo-deterministic, profoundly discriminatory trend. A second reason for refusing a romantic blurring of the human into the animal is the awareness of the deeply constructed nature of both the non-human and the human environments. I have emphasized throughout this study the rejection of essentialism as one of the key features of philosophical nomadism. Implicit in my position is also the awareness of the artificial nature of our own lived habitat.

This feature has been intensified in late post-industrial cultures by the integration of ecological and environmental concerns into the market economy of the globalization era. 'Bio-products' and organically grown products constitute a central concern in the consumption habits of technologically developed societies. Bryld and Lykke read this as a simultaneous act of sacralizing and cannibalizing the idea of 'real', that is to say, untamed and uncontaminated nature in post-industrial culture. Paradoxically, 'wild' nature has become: 'now a resource for technoscientific, military or commercial projects, now a site for the inscription of nostalgic desires for a sacred, motherly Eden' (Bryld and Lykke 1999: 5). It is against such Romantic re-packaging of nature, as well as against the consumeristic consumption of 'Earth-others' and, more especially, against the politically nostalgic position that I want to turn, as an alternative, to Deleuzian processes of becoming-animal.

Haraway gives constant examples of the becoming-animal of humans: simians and other upper primates are our next-door neighbours, genetically speaking. That is such a welcome relief from the qualitative distinctions that were made between species in earlier biological discourses. Human interaction with animals is being redefined by the techno-sciences of today: oncomouse and other experimental animals and insects (such as the fruit-fly); dogs and other genetically recombined 'pets' are the fodder for the bio-tech laboratories which construct contemporary techno-bodies. Multiple four-legged clones, or silicon-pumped Dollys crowd our social horizon.

Moreover, there is a deep anti-Oedipal sensibility at work in Haraway, as in Deleuze, though in her case and by her own admission it comes close to resistance against psychoanalysis (Penley and Ross 1991a). I agree with Haraway that the imaginary surrounding psychoanalytic definitions of the unconscious is deeply conservative, family-bound and heterosexist. But then, speaking as a cartographer, I think this is a perfectly adequate reflection of our culture and its dominant norms, so I would never blame psychoanalysis for bringing the bad news that we live under a phallogocentric regime. I will quarrel with psychoanalysis, however, when it argues for the historical necessity and immutability of the phallogocentric regime. In opposition to this political conservatism, I choose the transformative politics which feminism best exemplifies, and philosophical nomadism helps to theorize. Thus, Haraway's feminist cyborg project aims at dislodging the Oedipal narratives from their culturally hegemonic positions and thus diminishing their power over the construction of identity. Firmly located inside the belly of the beast of contemporary techno-culture and its mutant or hybrid social imaginary, Haraway wants to fight back by positing affirmative and empowering figurations for the new interaction with animals, mutants and machines, which is constitutive of our historical era.

The strength of Haraway's project is its inspirational force: she wants to invent a new discourse for the unconscious, one that can 'produce the unexpected, that can trip you, or trick you. Can you come up with an unconscious that escapes the familial narratives; or that poses the familial narratives as local stories, while recognizing that there are other histories to be told about the structuring of the unconscious, both on the personal and collective levels' (Haraway 1991: 9). The counter-figurations for this non-Oedipalized unconscious trace a sort of becoming-animal: the cyborg, the coyote, the trickster, the onco-mouse produce alternative structures of otherness. Just like Deleuze, Haraway has little patience for the linguistic paradigm within which the unconscious has been conceptualized, with its intrinsic binarism and the laws of displacement, condensation and exclusion. Haraway prefers instead multiplicities and multiply displaced identities. Non-linearity, non-fixity and non-unitary subjectivity are the priority, and they are situated in close proximity to woman, the native, the dispossessed, the abused, the excluded, the 'other' of the high-tech clean and efficient bodies that contemporary culture sponsors. This is comparable to Deleuze's attempts to rethink the becoming-animal as a figuration for the humanoid hybrids we are becoming.

Anti-Oedipal animality

I have argued so far that the question of the interaction between embodied practices – symptoms, emotions, desires, perceptions and sensations and the forms of expression available to them, mostly through the dominant model of consciousness – is not adequately represented in psychoanalytic theories of the imaginary. Thus, Deleuze's theory of becoming-animal also brings to a crux his and Guattari's quarrel with psychoanalysis, more specifically its reliance on the mechanisms of metaphor and metonymy as hermeneutical keys. The imaginary is not conceptualized along the semiological axis and the logic of latent and manifest meanings. That is to say, the 'meaning' – of a symptom, a text, a piece of music – is not indexed on the power of the signifier. What matters instead is the organization of the multiple elements that compose it – the symptom, the text, the music – in excess of language.

Deleuze's philosophy of radical immanence explodes the linguistic cage and proposes affectivity as a set of heterogeneous and multiple variations that require more complex schemes of analysis.

I said in the previous chapter that, for Deleuze and Guattari, Freud ended up closing the very door he had opened. In other words, Freud voices a fundamental insight about the affective and sexual structure of human subjectivity, but he then goes on to conceptualize it in a dualistic mode that serves the purposes of the culture of his times. Significantly, animals occur quite frequently in Freud's case-histories, from the phallic horse that haunts Little Hans's castration anxieties to the Wolf-Man's anal obsessions, not to mention the phantasmagoria of President Schreber. In psychoanalytic thinking, however, each animal signifies a repressed or disavowed aspect of the patient's remembered experience, now festering silently into pathology. It is a gateway to his or her unconscious and a significant lead into his or her secret fantasy-life. Animals are metaphoric representations or metonymic displacements of unprocessed traumas. As a 'cure' psychoanalysis rests on the linguistic method of interpretation: to access the unprocessed material brings it to resolution. This resolution is conceptualized as the unveiling of 'manifest' meanings, according to the linguistic-semiological paradigm.

Thus, Freud ends up 'humanizing' the kind of drives or desires that intimately associate humans with animals or blur the boundaries between them. I think that Freud does so in order to make these drives and yearnings more manageable, that is to say – to give to psychoanalysis at least some semblance of respectability as a therapy, a 'cure'. In other words, the animal part, like all the other 'dark continents', needs to be managed and clearly differentiated from the civilized subject one is to become. It is a matter of taste as much as of morality. These non-human drives for multiple encounters, wild bodily motives, heightened sensory perception and unbridled sexual activity, therefore, have to be assimilated or incorporated into a well-organized and functioning organism and by analogy, into well-regulated and normal orgasms. Out of the heterogeneous and complex pleasures and desires potentially available to one – the original 'polymorphous perversity' – a new kind of tolerable order has to be carved. The erotogeneous zones are coded as the areas of intense concentration of bodily sensations and pleasures: a sort of Fort Knox of the Libido. I often visualize them as a luna-park, where specific types of fun are made available, at a cost, at special times, in socially accepted ways, and usually scheduled during bank holidays.

Freud's theory of the drives articulated bodily functions with sensory perceptions and sensations and then attached them to 'proper' objects of desire. As I suggested earlier, translated into Deleuze's and Guattari's schizoanalysis, this produces a series of assemblages that seem 'natural', like mouth, hunger, food or breast = suck, swallow, eat! The anorexic/bulimic, among others, gets the instructions wrong, which is a matter of good health, as much as of good manners and morality. Similarly in sexual morality, the 'proper' object of desire (a human of the opposite sex) needs to be targeted for the fulfilment of the drive and the suitable assemblage of sensation needs to be grafted onto the appropriate organs. The long march through the Freudian phases, anal, oral, genital, is the road-map for that kind of journey. The beast in you has to be tamed: you may suck, just don't bite!

Moreover, the object of desire has to be made digestible, that is to say that it must facilitate and work within the process of assimilation of the darker and less desirable aspects of one's libido. The selection of 'proper' objects in fact requires the elimination of others as improper or 'abject'. The distinction between proper and abject objects of desire is fundamental for psychoanalysis and is used for policing the borders between the normal and the pathological, which is one of the prerequisites for gaining entry into civilized behaviour and therefore the social order. It is a matter for the Law, the Church and the medical profession.

Last, but not least, the animal drives have to be processed and tamed in order to be made tolerable. Their raw intensity needs to be turned down: howling to the moon in despair or bliss is not proper behaviour. The release of such levels of intensity – apart from being too wild for polite company – actually brings about pain: it is 'too much'. Clearly unaware of Mae West's world-famous *dictum*: 'Too much of a good thing can be wonderful', Freud believes that too much (of anything) can never be wonderful and that a dose of self-moderation is intrinsic to the definition of 'a good thing'. 'Too much' here means excessive levels of affectivity that transgress, upset or – in the case of the schizophrenic – explode the boundaries of the body. Being 'beside oneself' with emotion, passion, grief, pleasure or all of these combined is considered unhealthy and potentially pathological. These are unsustainable states, which one had better avoid, or dose with care. As Nietzsche pointed out, most humans live in fear of and longing for that intensity which is alternatively labelled 'passion' and 'ecstasy' or 'trauma' and 'anguish'; fear and desire for being transported beyond one's self towards an outside, an outsider, an other whom one hopes will be kind and nurturing. Even that Oedipal fantasy of care and nurture, however, needs to be qualified by what Freud called the death drives and Nietzsche expresses in terms of the ruthlessness or violence of life. If the life in me is not mine, it may rip me apart without any concern for my well-being. The outside/r need not be always reassuring, however familiar she or he may be. The notion of the 'becoming-animal' therefore throws open the doors of perception towards impersonal, uncaring, dangerous, violent forces. Wo/man is other wo/men's woolf, thus reaching out for that outside/r can also be an invitation to a walk on the wild side.

Todorov's analysis of the figure of the animal in the literary imagination is emblematic of the semiological and psychoanalytic approach which Deleuze has rejected. It occurs in the context of his work on the genre known as the fantastic (Todorov 1975). Starting from the assumption that the fantastic is an intermediary genre situated between the marvellous (unknown phenomena) and the uncanny (slightly familiar, though unsettling phenomena), Todorov argues that the power of the fantastic resides mostly in being able to produce literal representation of figural or metaphorical states. Metamorphoses and mutations are thus the staple diet of fantastic literature and their power of appeal rests on the collapse of the mind–matter distinction. Todorov adds that in the nineteenth century this kind of transgression was the trademark of madness or psychosis and the characteristic of children, mystics, mythical thinking, drug-users and other producers of genres that loosen up bonds and categorical distinctions. According to Todorov it is the erasure of these distinctions that makes the representations of metamorphoses not only implicitly transgressive, but also pan-erotic in an almost infantile way. That is to say that they become the targets of a system of unconscious impulses. The figure of the animal is a crucial element of this play of the fantastic imagination. Psychoanalytic discourse has contributed to replacing the literature of the fantastic in the contemporary imagination. We no longer need to refer to the devil to explain excessive sexual desire or to vampires to express the attraction exerted by corpses. The psychic realm has incorporated the fantastic dimension and has Oedipalized it. As Kafka shows, the irrational is like a generalized fantastic in which we are all caught. The supernatural has fused with the literary to produce a psychic unsettling literary genre based on mutations, as the prototype of hallucinations, psychic disorders or mental breakdowns.

Todorov's classical accounts of the kind of mutations, metamorphoses and transformations that occur in the literary genre of the fantastic, which also includes science fiction, is revealing. It reiterates a fundamentally humanistic belief in the need to uphold those categorical distinctions between Man and His others, which nomadic thinking is committed to dislodging. In so doing Todorov demonstrates another crucial point: that the blurring of boundaries or distinctions is often perceived as threatening or dangerous. The emphasis Todorov places on the analogy between metamorphoses and madness or narcotic hallucination is significant. It exemplifies the belief in the utter simplicity of the power of One signifier and it reasserts the familiarity of the binary distinctions which it upholds. Todorov is ultimately uninterested in the 'here and now' of the historical context which produces genres like the postmodern fantastic or science fiction – to which I will return in the next chapter. He has a moralistic purpose and is much more concerned with containing the potential damage made by these texts, rather than in interrogating their complex interaction with social realities where changes, transformations and mutations are ubiquitous. Politically, this is a very conservative position that aligns neo-humanistic beliefs with a nostalgic denial or distaste for historicity.

Historically, the dangerous tendencies or intense drives towards blurring of categorical distinctions or boundaries have been discursively packaged under the heading of 'passions'. The term passion, of course, is of the same etymological root as the notion of pathology. Both of them, in western culture, bear connotations of a disease that shatters the balance of the subject. Since the eighteenth century especially, the pathologization of the passions has led to the modern regime of sexuality that Foucault analyses in terms of the split between *ars erotica* and *scientia sexualis*. It marks a gradual impoverishment of human intensity under the double burden of medicalization of the emotions and the reduction of sexuality to genitality. This historical process has also invested primarily the female gender as a high-risk, 'emotional' category. The hysterical body of women in some ways marks the threshold of this process of pathologizing human affectivity (Ehrenreich and English 1979).

I have grown very dissatisfied with the idea of one master-code, a central symbolic sytem, that would administer the forms of cultural mediation. Irigaray challenges the univocity of the masculine saturated phallogocentric symbolic and opposes to it the possibility of a virtual feminine symbolic, as a project for feminist women to actualize. Deleuze – following Bergson and Nietzsche – redefines the imaginary as a transformative force that propels multiple heterogeneous 'becomings', or repositioning of the subject. The process of becoming is collectively driven, that is to say relational and external; it is also framed by affectivity or desire, and is thus ec-centric to rational control. Both acknowledge the constitutive force of unconscious affects, drives or desires. The imaginary is one of the vehicles of the unconscious. More importantly even for my work has been the impact of feminist theory and practice. This has convinced me that processes of change and transformation, however difficult and at times painful, are also empowering and highly desirable events.

Resting on the above, I want to suggest that the 'imaginary' refers consequently to a set of socially mediated practices which function as the anchoring point – albeit unstable and contingent – for identifications and therefore for identity-formation. These practices act as interactive structures where desire as a subjective yearning and agency in a broader socio-political sense are mutually shaped by one another. Neither 'pure' imagination – locked in its classical opposition to reason – nor fantasy in the Freudian sense, the imaginary for me marks a space of transitions and transactions. Nomadic, it flows like symbolic glue between the social and the self, the outside and the subject; the material and the ethereal. It flows, but it is sticky: it catches on as it goes. It possesses fluidity, but it distinctly lacks transparency. I have used the term 'desire' to connote the subject's own investment – or enmeshment – in this sticky network of interrelated social and discursive effects. Sexual difference plays an important role in structuring the imaginary. The network of social relations constitutes the social field as a libidinal – or affective – landscape, as well as a normative – or disciplinary – framework.

The social imaginary has a rather long and respectable pedigree in both modernist and poststructuralist philosophies. Louis Althusser's influential definition of it as the process of mediation between one's real-life conditions and one's representation of these conditions to oneself is extremely useful. In its classical Althusserian sense, the 'imaginary' blurs the split between the self and society, or between the 'inside' and the 'outside' of the subject. The link is provided by the psychoanalytic notion of 'identification', which describes the mechanisms by which one is captured, or 'captivated' by social and cultural formations. For both Lacan and Althusser the imaginary is governed by the mastercode that is beamed down by the symbolic system: phallogocentrism. Their interaction provides the motor for the process of becoming-subject (or *assujetissement*) in terms of being-subjected-to visible and invisible webs of social relations.

The most immediate term of reference for this definition of the 'imaginary' is the classical notion of 'ideology' in Marxist theory. Althusser's 'imaginary' innovates on what I consider as the binary Marxist opposition between 'ideology' and 'scientific truth', with the corrollary of 'alienation' as opposed to 'authenticity'. More importantly, the 'imaginary' provides a constructive answer to the dilemma of how ideology 'gets' its subject. I was never convinced by theories of 'internalization' of ideological or cultural codes and by the opposition between self and society which they imply. The imaginary offers the added advantage of inscribing the process of subject-formation into a multi-layered web of socio-political relations. Althusser, however, remains attached to the Lacanian structure and locates one master-code – phallogocentrism – at the heart of this operation.

The poststructuralist generation, starting with Foucault, challenges this central master-code on which the forms of mediation are supposed to hinge. As I mentioned before in the discussion about power, it is rather the case that self and society are mutually shaped by one another through the choreography of entitlements, prohibitions, desires and controls which constitute the socio-symbolic field. The subject is enmeshed in this network of interrelated social and discursive effects. This network constitutes the social field as a libidinal – or affective – landscape, as well as a normative – or disciplinary – framework. The important point for poststructuralists is to stress that one's relation to this complex network of power relations is always mediated, that is, it is caught in a web of imaginary relations.

In order to mark the separation from psychoanalytically-invested readings of the imaginary, I try to avoid references to 'metaphors' as significant mechanisms in psychic life. The law of metaphor and metonymy, condensation and displacement, was posited by Lacan and is reiterated by orthodox Lacanians as the central mechanisms of the unconscious. I would rather approach the unconscious as a nomadic process of creativity, with Deleuze, rather than as an essential 'black-box' allegedly containing the central data-flow of our psychic life, as Lacan would have it.

In my perspective, the shift away from the psychoanalytic scheme is justi-fied in several ways, the first of which is indeed historical: in the age of globalization and high-tech societies where speed and simultaneity are key factors, we need to create figurations of the subject that are suitable. The idea of adequate forms of expression of the kind of subject that we have already become is crucial to the neo-materialist philosophy I am outlining here. There is also, however, a conceptual necessity; and this is related to the limitations of psychoanalysis as an ethics of the self. Post-Lacanian in many ways, Deleuze considers a great deal of psychoanalytical practice as complicitous with the kind of over-inflation of the bourgeois individual, of which 'ego-psychology' is the ultimate example. The 'humanization process' which psychoanalysis pursues re-inscribes the subject in a semiological cage controlled by Law, Lack and Signifier. The theory of becoming aims to re-inscribe subversion at the heart of subjectivity and to make it operational. The becoming-animal undoes one of the major borders of the metaphysics of the self, scrambling the distinction between human and non-human. It opens up the borders to encounters of the third and even the Nth kind: the becoming-animal turns into the becoming/insect/molecular/imperceptible. It not only engages in dialogue with the classical 'other' of Man – the mon-ster within, the Dr Jekyll, the beast – but it also frees the animal from the anthropocentric gaze altogether. The 'other' dissolves into a series of non-dualistic and non-oppositional entities, organic and inorganic, visible and not – all powerful matter in the sense of *potentia*, all stretching beyond death and finitude. It is Ovid together with Kafka, assisting in redrawing the cartography of the subject by releasing His (the gender is no coincidence) others from his monological grip.

> Becoming-animal means precisely making the move, tracing the line of escape in all its positivity, crossing a threshold, reaching a continuum of intensities that only have value for themselves, finding a world of pure intensities, where all the forms get undone, as well as all the significations: signifiers and signifieds, in favour of matter yet un-formed, of deterritorialized flows, of a-signifying signs. (Deleuze and Guattari, 1975)

This raises ethical questions about how far to go in pursuing changes and stretching the boundaries of subjectivity. The issue of 'too much' also raises the question of pain, even of violent emotions or excess. Deleuze's becoming-animal leads to his re-appraisal of a Spinozist ethics of sustainability. It is a call for experimenting with limits and with possible levels of subversion. It is also a way of challenging a conceptual creativity so that we can find non-negative and non-pathological ways of expressing the intensities we experience 'within'. In this respect, it offers an alternative theory of desire and a re-definition of affectivity, as the starting-point for a transformative ethics.

The message of dominant morality is clear: 'too much' – too intense a level of experienced intensity – is bad for one's health. As the ethics of psychoanalysis are based on reducing the patient's suffering, the pain of heightened intensity becomes a problem to be eliminated. Freud translates his problem into an economy of excess and lack, aiming at equilibrium. Deleuze, on the other hand, rejects this dualistic scheme, resting on the Spinozist brand of monism, and therefore on the notion of immanence. He starts from an already exploded, non-unitary subject and then renders the problem in terms of variations of intensity and alternative assemblages that would allow one to experience complex, multiple and heterogeneous flows, or affects. As a criterion of framing the process, I would single out sustainability, that is to say, the capacity to sustain and to endure. Considering the emphasis philosophical nomadism places on experimentation and interrelationality, cultivating the capacity to last and to endure is a major priority (Gatens and Lloyd, 1999). The becoming-animal points to this kind of re-organization of one's sensory and perceptive field of action. It stands in direct opposition to the process of humanizing the drives, which is so central to psychoanalysis. More important for Deleuze is to turn this into a post-human process whereby levels of undifferentiated, pure sensations could be expressed and lived out – is something beyond good and evil and beyond pain and pleasure – which I visualize as sets of variations of intensity.

For philosophical nomadology it is not the case that intensity is intrinsically dangerous, excessive or pathological. Deleuze's reversal of Platonism means that he calls into question this framework of interpretation. It is thus plausible to argue that it is the historically-established notion of consciousness that is inadequate, not the kind of intensities, flows or passions that constitute the human being and which have historically become available to us through technological, scientific, especially bio-molecular and genetic, and other forms of development. Without forgetting for one moment the power differentials and patterns of exclusion that are constitutive of advanced societies, it is important for me to stress that such a society is the result of human endeavours. That is to say that technological changes are the effect of complex, interactive webs of collective efforts, from the mental or scientific to the manual or labour, with many in-between steps. Technophobia consequently seems an inadequate position in that it denies the enormous investment of human energy, intelligence and imagination that went into designing the new technologies. Moreover, it reinstates the rhetoric of humanism in constructing the machines as antithetical to human evolution. The hypocrisy of this position is untenable. I want to argue consequently that an in-between position needs to be opened up, neither technophobic, nor naively technophilic, but rather sober enough to address the complexities engendered by our historicity; more of this in chapter 5.

Deleuze questions, through the interaction with animals or machines, the imaginative poverty of the kind of figurations that are available to express the contemporary forms of ethical subjectivity. Continuing to apply to ourselves the mental habits and theoretical frames of representation that we have inherited from the past is as lazy and as inadequate as describing the Concorde as just another flying object. Surely more of an effort could be made to account for the kind of subjects we have become. To avoid such self-defeating moves, we need to think complexities also and especially in terms of affectivity.

Given that in the materialist philosophy of immanence that I favour there is only one matter – and it is enfleshed or embodied – the process of becoming is a transformation in terms of a qualitative increase (in speed, intensity, perception or colour) that allows one to break into new fields of perception, affectivity, becoming; nothing short of a metamorphosis.

As I suggested earlier in this chapter, the ultimate frame or horizon for the processes of becoming is cosmic, the infinity of the 'becoming-imperceptible'. This used to be rendered in the old language of holism, fusion with the universe, or a sort of oceanic feeling that Freud associated with female *jouissance*. Deleuze wants to recast this sense of intimate interconnectiveness as an ethos of ecological empathy and affectivity which also cuts across different species, that is to say different levels of *bios* and *zoe*. The axes of this trans-species transferral and continuity are information-based: they come down to a question of memory, of the genetic as well as the more human or genealogical kind. Bio-centred egalitarianism is therefore an ethics of affirmation which steps out of the nihilistic gloom. Deleuze and Guattari conceptualize it in the mode of a depersonalized, transgenic mutual reliance upon a living environment or territory: an eco-philosophy framed by geo-political concerns. In this perspective the human is absolutely off-centre and, very often, off the point.

Very much a thinker of the outside, of open spaces and embodied enactments, Deleuze encourages us not to think in terms of within/without, but rather as levels of expression and sustainability of unfamiliar forces, drives, yearnings or sensations; a sort of spiritual and sensory stretching of our boundaries; an immanent sort of happening. In other words, a qualitative leap is needed and it is neither a suicidal jump into the void, nor a fall into moral relativism. Nor does it amount to a romantic re-appropriation of the schizophrenic, non-human elements of the self *per se*. I see it rather as a way of making the contemporary subject slightly more familiar with and consequently less anxious about the yet untapped possibilities that his or her living, embodied and embedded self can empower him or her for; a way of living more intensely, on increasing one's *potentia* and with it, one's freedom and understanding of complexities, but also an ethics that aims at framing, sustaining and enduring those very complexities.

Becoming insect

Insects also have a very respectable literary pedigree in European culture and are very coded culturally. In the post-nuclear historical context, they have become the sign of a widespread repertoire of angst-ridden fears and deep anxiety. Prior to this commodification as phobic objects, however, they enjoyed a much richer and more varied repertoire. Creepy mutants; vermin emerging from the sewerage; resilient survivors; tentacular left-overs from a previous evolutionary era; one of the seven plagues in Saint John's Apocalypse; signs of the wrath of God as the biblical locusts; insects cover a number of staggering signifying practices. On the positive side, from Aesop to La Fontaine to contemporary Hollywood animation films, ants are the prototype of the industrial robot, or the industrious factory worker. Capable of lifting fifty times their own body weight, they are resistant to pesticides and enjoy fast reproductive cycles. Crickets may be the lazy hedonists lying in the sun, but they have amazing destructive powers. Thomas (1979) estimates that crickets can reach a density of two thousand per square metre; they can also cover ten kilometres a day and thus can destroy something like four thousand tons of greens every twenty-four hours. With maniacal precision Thomas also adds that there are five million different species of insects. At the average weight of two and a half milligrammes, they make their presence on the earth felt! After all, they have lived on it for more than three hundred million years. Bees are, historically, the sophisticated industrial engineers. In his *Natural History* Pliny marvels at them as real-life factories. They produce honey, make wax, serve a thousand practical purposes; they work hard, follow their leaders and respect their governmental organization. Collectively minded, they are ideal members of the polity though, like ants, they tend to be obsessive. Derrida (1987) resorts to the metaphor of bees to express his disapproval of academic feminists and to condemn our allegedly regimented and authoritarian ways of thinking. Bees also, however, believe in individual enterprise; they produce their own medicine – the *propolis* – and are perfectly integrated in their own environment in that they hibernate in winter and are superbly well-organized. Great military minds, business people and engineers, bees leave Pliny gasping for air and Derrida wishing for more.

Pliny himself highlights the features of insects which, in my opinion, are crucial to understanding the becoming-insect which Deleuze defends in his philosophy of bodily materialism and becoming. First, the shift of scale and the paradoxes of vision that follow; in something like infantile wonder about their sexuality, Pliny asks: 'where did Nature find in a flea room for all the senses?' (Pliny 1983: 433). Again: 'at what point in its surface did she place sight? where did she attach taste? where did she insert smell? and where did she implant that truculent and relatively very loud voice?' (Pliny 1983: 436). Secondly, their extremely economical and efficient anatomy:

> They have no internal organs except, in the case of quite a few, a twisted intestine. Consequently when torn asunder they display a remarkable tenacity of life and the separate parts go on throbbing because whatever their vital principle is, it certainly does not reside in particular members but in the body as a whole – least of all in the head, and this alone does not move unless it has been torn off with the breast.

Insects exacerbate the human power of understanding to the point of implosion. Tiny miniatures, they exercise the same immense sense of estrangement as dinosaurs, dragons or other gigantic monsters. Improbable morphological constructs, they challenge and titillate and are hybrid par excellence.

Other qualities that make insects paradigmatic are their power of metamorphosis, the parasitism, the power of mimetism or blending with their territory and environment and the speed of movement. Shaviro argues (1995: 47) that 'insect life is an alien presence that we can neither assimilate nor expel'. As such it dwells between different states of in-between-ness, arousing the same spasmodic reactions in humans as the monstrous, the sacred, the alien. This is a reaction of simultaneous attraction and repulsion, disgust and desire. They pose the question of radical otherness not in metaphorical but in bio-morphic terms, that is to say as a metamorphosis of the sensory and cognitive apparatus. In this regard, the insect provides a new paradigm for discontinuous transmutations without major disruptions. The key elements of this are: larval metamorphoses; the speed of their reproductive system; the propensity to generate mutations; the faster rate of genetic recombination. Moreover, not having any major neuronal reservoir, insects are free from the hold of memory and of the socially enforced forms of sedimented memory, known as institutions. In Deleuze's terminology, they are multiple singularities without fixed identities. All of these have been amply explored and documented in literature, cinema and culture.

Of bugs and women, of lice and men

In what follows I want to approach insects as indicators and figurations of the decentring of anthropocentrism and point to post-human sensibilities and sexualities. In order to do so, I will have to explore some popular literary genres such as science fiction and horror. Although I will return to a more detailed analysis of these genres in the next chapter, I want to start here with a cartographic reading of the women–insects nexus. I will consequently interrogate the social imaginary to see how this interconnection is represented in post-industrial technocultures. Pursuing further the line of becoming-insect/woman/imperceptible I will take the insect as a figuration of the abject, a border-line figure, capable of bearing different meanings and associations. It is a generalized figure of liminality and in-between-ness, which shares a number of structural features with the feminine. I would situate it rather on the horizon of the 'post-human', in closer connection to the technological than to the actual animal 'kingdom'.[5]

Contemporary science-fiction texts trace numerous lines of affinity and co-extensivity between women, technology, and animals or insects. Whereas commentators usually focus on one of these aspects, however, I think they should be kept together as a block of becomings. More specifically, following Deleuze, I see them as a variation on the paradigm 'woman = monster or alien other', which I will return to in the next chapter. They are assimilated within the general category of 'difference', which facilitates a deep empathy between women and aliens and also favours exchanges and mutual influences. This points in the direction of a very genderized approach to the different processes of becoming and the metamorphoses that mark science fiction. Science-fiction horror films often draw explicit parallels between the woman's and the alien's animal or insect bodies. Barbara Creed argues that there is a privileged relationship between the becoming-insect and becoming-woman. For instance Cronenberg's *The Fly* displays a Kafka-like metamorphosis of the scientist. The film draws parallels between the woman and the fly, which are reinforced in the nightmare scene where she gives birth to a giant maggot.

As often in Cronenberg's work, the asymmetry in the process of becoming between the sexes is respected and it becomes explored visually in different (de)compositions of embodiment. More importantly, the difference is not only in the starting positions of the two sexes, but also in the end results of the processes of transformation. Further examples of this asymmetrical gendered rendition of the becoming-insect can be found in the classical science American-fiction films from the 1950s, which express a deep-seated anxiety about the nuclear age. This anxiety is coated very often in the form of the destructive powers of the either females or aliens, or possibly both. This fear has been likened to the tradition of the 'Virago' theme in classical literature,[6] and an example of it is the film *The Attack of the Fifty-Foot Woman* (1958). The film features a very angry young woman who, exposed to atomic radiation, grows out of all proportions and terrorizes her husband and then the local town. Exactly like insect-films such as *Tarantula* (1955) and *Them* (1954), which features gigantic post-nuclear ants, this blown-up, larger-than life female figure is a screen on which all sorts of other anxieties are projected. This point can be demonstrated also with reference to another cult-film from the fifties: *The Incredible Shrinking Man* (1957), which acts almost as the counter-point to *The Attack of the Fifty-Foot Woman*. In this film the male hero – shrunk to miserable proportions after exposure to nuclear radiation – falls victim to a giant black spider. His encounter with the hairy beast is visually compared, through cross-cutting, with images of his own wife, who by now has grown proportionally gigantic. In an effect reminiscent of the most misogynist passages in Jonathan Swift's *Gulliver's Travels*, the female body emerges from this as a monstrous other. In *The Fly* (1958) when the mad scientist looks at his wife through his insect-eyes, we have another blow-up phenomenon of the female multiplied ten-fold. In a gesture which anticipates Cameron's *The Terminator* (1984), she mercifully kills him under an industrial press.

The asymmetry in the representation of the visual destiny of the two sexes when exposed to the same devolutionary forces (atomic radiation) is striking; the process unfolds along gender lines: the woman blows up into a terrifying force and the poor man shrinks out of sight. Visually, the effects of this asymmetry are even more striking, resulting respectively in gigantic close-ups of female genitalia on the one hand, and on the other in the heroic celebration of minute human males in their deadly encounters with hairy giants. The same technique is used in the film *Tarantula*, with the close-up of the giant spider's face through a window frame of the house where the suburban white woman watches the hairy cavity in horror. This is not only a classical *vagina-dentata* shot, but it also enacts an opposition black–white; human–non-human, with uncouth hairiness as a major differential. *Tarantula* is a spectacular text, where the becoming-woman and the becoming-insect intersect constantly, so as to appear almost interchangeable. They express the deep-seated anxiety about social and cultural mutations. The text functions by magnification (Carroll 1990) of the abject body of the spider, which has grown abnormally as a result of nuclear radiation. The internal alterations of the genetic code – a standard item in post-Hiroshima science-fiction films – both reflect and engender external chaos and anarchy. The tarantula is worse than the worst she-wolf: insidious, mighty and scary in its archaic hairiness, she cannot be killed by the traditional modernist means of purification – electricity.[7] The only way to exterminate the brute is by calling in the US Air Force and have it napalmed to ashes, from the sky.

The evidence gathered so far suggests that, in the contemporary social imaginary, an association is established between women, technology and insects. Three categories of otherness turned into one axis of titillation, horror and cultural consumption. The central question I want to raise in relation to this phenomenon is how it relates to Deleuzian processes of becoming. The interrelation between images as projection of the paranoid imaginings and fears of the Majority and the creative quest for figurations that evoke the patterns of becoming-minoritarian is so complex that I will devote the next two chapters to the discussion. For the moment, let me add this element to my cultural cartography and return to my discussion of insects as technological artifacts, or entities that stand in between the organic and the inorganic.

As Bukatman put it, in his analysis of Bruce Sterling's cyberpunk novels (1993: 277): 'Insects are only the most evident metaphorical process conflating a number of irreconcilable terms such as life/non life, biology/technology, human/machine.' As such, insects signal a high degree of imbrication of the organic with the technological; this can be evidenced in the insectoid and arachnoid terminology that is so often used to describe advanced technologies, especially robots and virtual reality artefacts. This kind of imagery stresses the interdependence of technology on other social and environmental forces. Cyber-feminists like van Oldenberg (1999) argue that the Internet or computer-mediated future can only be arachnoid, or spider-like: it functions via lines, knots, connections, relations in a manner that is also analogous to the human brain. Thus, the discourse of arachnomancy can be used to explore possible evolutions of information technologies.

How are the insect and the technological linked in a process of becoming that dislodges the human from his or her naturalistic foundations, thus inflicting a final blow to any notion of 'human nature'? Shaviro rightly suggests (1995) that in so far as the becoming-insect in science fiction is an effect of devolutionary practices, it is linked – albeit negatively – to the technology that triggers them off. In the 1950s it is nuclear technology and in the 1990s it is molecular biology, but the two are linked both historically and conceptually.

In biology, it is the speed and efficiency of its molecular structure and more especially of its reproductive cycle that has made the fruit-fly into the most important experimental site in modern molecular research (Fox Keller 1985). Haraway also hints at an 'insect paradigm' in contemporary molecular biology, which has moved beyond the classical opposition of 'vitalistic' to 'mechanistic' principles, to evolve instead in the direction of serial repetitions. Haraway takes this as a serious indication that we have already left the era of 'bio-politics' to enter that of 'the informatics of domination'. As the text by Clarice Lispector (1978) will demonstrate, in such a universe, the insects will most definitely inherit the earth.

Insects have also gained widespread prominence and star billing in contemporary culture. An evident insect and also a spider paradigm is in full display in recent cinematic exploits in the genre of cyberpunk and science fiction. Gigantic metal-framed imitation-insects crawl all over the surface of films as *Star Wars III: The Return of the Jedi* and *Robocop*, as well as in the digital nightmare-worlds of *The Matrix*. Insect aesthetics reaches its

apotheosis in the digital images of *Antz* and *Bug-story*, which merely official-
ize a *topos* that is firmly instilled in the contemporary imaginary: the
post-human mix of organic and inorganic organisms. The film *Kosmopolis*
also highlights this point: it celebrates with splendid imagery the almost-
imperceptible but all-pervading presence of insect-life: 'Beyond anything
we could imagine, almost beneath our notice.' The following properties of
insects get star billing: their enormous powers as music-makers and producers of sounds, the speed of the vibrations they produce, their capacity to
defeat gravity and crawl vertically as well as horizontally, their hyper-active
sexuality, with highly accelerated rhythms and made up of many rhizome
trans-species copulations with plants and flowers as well as entities of the
same species (a life cycle can be completed in twenty-four hours).

There are other aspects of the becoming-insect, however, that, read in a
Deleuzian perspective, point towards technology and away from humanism: *homo faber*, rather than *homo sapiens*. Deleuze signals out some quite
explicitly in *Mille Plateaux*: insects are essentially about the becoming-
imperceptible, the becoming-molecular mostly because of the speed of their
lifespan. Their significant traits in terms of a Deleuzian mapping of forces
are dryness, hairiness, metal-like body-frames, great resilience. They are
environment-bound, thus elemental, either because linked to the earth and
to its underground/crust (*chthonic* forces) or defying its gravity thanks to
aircraft-like bodyframes (remember the exhilaration of Kafka's Gregor when
he discovers that he can crawl up on the ceiling).

Of great importance are the shifts in sensory and spatio-temporal
co-ordinates that make the insects genuinely admirable organisms. The power
of vision of some of them, for instance the fly's eye, can be considered as a
masterpiece of evolution. Kurt Newmann highlights this perfectly in his
1958 film *The Fly*, in the spectacular scene where the guilt-ridden scientist,
already altered by his mutation into a fly – is shown advancing towards his
wife and seeing her through his insect-eye, as through a kaleidoscope that
multiplies her infinitely. Again, the genderization of the scene is telling.

Acoustic environments

In all these regards, the insects are a very perfect machine-like organism
which is as other from the mammals and therefore the humans as biologically possible. What interests Deleuze particularly about the speed of the
insects' bodies, however, is their technological performativity. Insects are
fantastic music-makers. Deleuze distinctly warns us that he does not mean
the usual bodily noises that one makes in moving about the planet, but
rather the specific capacity to produce sounds that have speeds, variations
and intensities worthy of human compositions. Insects – as well as other
animals – offer convincing examples of non-linguistic communication and

modes of thought, ranging from visual apprehension to sonar and other acoustic technologies, including an acute sense of internal time. It is probably on this score that insects constitute a real challenge for humanity; they deprive the human of his or her alleged monopoly over music-making: 'Birds are just as important, yet the reign of birds seems to have been replaced by the age of insects, with its much more molecular vibrations, chirring, rustling, buzzing, clicking, scratching and scraping' (Deleuze and Guattari 1980: 379). It would be interesting to analyse contemporary music by techno-artists like Meredith Monk and Diamanda Galas along these lines; the latter is especially comparable to Carmelo Bene for her vocal virtuosity and the capacity to capture the sound-like inner core of words, pushing the phonemes to the point of implosion. Techno-acoustic aesthetics undo not only the priority of the human voice in music-making, but also the centrality of the human as a sensible means of achieving rhythms and sounds that reflect our era. The virtuality of D. J.s' hybrid mix has replaced the virtuosity of performers.

Most dwellers of the post-industrial urban space have developed a paradoxical relationship to their own acoustic space. As Harry Kunneman astutely observes in his analysis of the 'walkman subject' (1996), technology has endowed us with the capacity to create and to carry around in our own embodied self our own musical habitat. This may or may not coincide with the mass-produced saturation of commercial sounds, or the Gothic pastiche of the MTV scene. Of all technologies we inhabit, the musical, acoustic or sound ones are the most pervasive, yet also the most collective. They thus summarize the paradoxes of nomadic subjectivity as simultaneously external and singular.

The interconnection of sounds, technology, insects and music, however, prompts another remark: namely, how rare it is to encounter music or sound that reflects the acoustic quality of the environment most of us inhabit. That is to say, a very crowded, noisy, highly resonant urban environment where stillness and silence are practically unknown. I think that a great deal of music or sound production of the alternative kind today aims precisely at capturing the intense sonority of our lived-in spaces, and yet to empty it of its representational value. Techno-sounds, and the technological performances of Deleuze-inspired music colourists like Robin Rimbaud, also known as Scanner, or D. J. Spooky, or of contemporary artists like Soundlab, Cultural Alchemy is a gamble with this apparently contradictory aim: to map out the acoustic environments of here and now, while undoing the classical function of music as the incarnation of the most sublime ideals of the humanist subject.

In music, time can be heard. It is a pure form of time through the mediation of rhythm. This, in a nutshell, is its relevance for nomadic subjectivity. Technologically mediated music de-naturalizes and de-humanizes the time-sequence. It can push speed and pitch to post-human heights, but it can also fade them to pre-human depths of inaudibility. How to make us hear the inaudible, the imperceptible, that roar which lies on the other side of silence, is what at stake in this process. How to impose an audible form upon the amorphous mass of sounds we inhabit is, for Deleuzian composers, the challenge. The method of composition is in keeping with Deleuze's criteria of selection, process, and in-between transitions. In music one can hear the transitions in the form of intervals. In nomadic music, the interval marks the proximity but also the singularity of each sound, so as to avoid synthesis, harmony or melodic resolution. It is a way of pursuing dissonance by returning it to the external world, where sounds belong, always in transit, like radio-waves moving ineluctably to outer spaces, chatting on, with nobody to listen.

Why bother? Because this is an adequate, historically accurate and culturally relevant acoustic map of the world we are living in. Remember, however, dear reader, the pact we made in chapter 1, and our dialogical contract: do we live in the same world? Do you recognize yourselves in the cartography I am drawing here? Does this tune speak to your ears? Does it resonate? If not, skip this passage, move on and waste no time.

There is also a political side to this, as to all cartographies, given that vision as a sense has been historically privileged as a hegemonic element in the constitution of the subject, and considering also that the scopic is dominant in contemporary epistemology and psychoanalysis. And keeping in mind that visualization techniques are central to contemporary formations of power as domination, I can only conclude that the visual regime is dominant, or molar, in the political economy of postmodernity. As such, it is saturated with power-relations. This is not the case for sounds or the acoustic regime. They are more subversive, because they are less codified by power. Sound is more abstract, less prone to immediate commodification into an economy of language. Since the events of 1968, in Europe the counter-culture has invested the production of alternative acoustic environments and forms of sound-transmission as central elements of cultural and political activism, from the free radio stations of the seventies to the techno-music of today. The coming of the new information technologies and cyber-feminism have merely intensified this trend.

Traditionally, music is expected to be linear, sequential, based on mathematical order. This order is created by repetition, that is to say melodies constructed by rhythm. It can express the memory of the majority subject, or the web-like genealogies of the minoritarian ones. Pick your tune. Whereas classical music, including pop, rock and their off-shoots, aims at resonances, and the constitution of alternative resisting, counter-cultural subjectivities, technologically-based experimental music of the rhizomatic kind attempts to make us hear the inaudible. It aims at what Achim Azepanski (Force Inc.

Music Works 1996: 18) calls 'a virtual sound space'. This is a space of de-territorialization of our acoustic habits through the production of unexpected, speedy, hostile sounds that 'tear up the forms that the memory has stored as music, in a whirl of absolute speeds that are like a swelling and receding of sound streams, but also a flowing into one another of microstreams, small whirls create microscopic jumps and strange concentrations . . .' (1996: 18).

In fact, the example of insects suggests that we inhabit unfamiliar, posthuman acoustic environments all the time. We just do not hear them – we are not used to 'taking them in', or to tuning into them. Rhizo-music forces this encounter by re-creating it technologically, in the best musical tradition. As such, it represents a space of becoming. The key notion in becoming-insect as in rhizo-musicology is that of an environment, an acoustic territory, a position of spatio-temporal co-ordinates where rhythms are produced, remembered or stored and eventually produced. Hence the connection to animals and insects, territories, or habitats are constituted through the composition and the organization of refrains or rhythms understood as patterns of repetition and occupation and marking of a space; invisible signatures, so to speak.

Bogue sums up as follows the function of these refrains or patterns of repetition: 'They may (1) mark or assemble a territory; (2) connect a territory with interval impulses and/or external circumstances; (3) identify specialized functions; (4) or collect forces in order to centralize the territory or go outside' (Bogue 1991: 91). The function of the refrain is to create spaces of transition or becoming-in-between passages that destabilize the linearity of recorded time, packaged as musical sounds. Deleuze's vision of the becoming-minoritarian of music offers a way of reconstructing the subject's relationship to his or her environment, earthly and cosmic, in a non-mathematical mode. Deleuze's 'abstract machines', best expressed in his becoming-insect, are rhythmic and abstract. Deleuze challenges the representational function of music as expressing the harmony of the spheres, in opposition to the dark chaos of unaccounted-for space. The accountability of space is ensured by mathematical ordering; in Plato's philosophy this results in a time-honoured connection between music, mathematics and cosmology. It is this cosmic quality of music that makes it relevant for philosophical nomadism, in that it points to the infinite in a very grounded, embedded fashion.

In their committed anti-Platonic mode, Deleuze and Guattari want to de-link the representation of the cosmos from its reliance on the rationality of a mathematical order. They approach it instead as an open system, uncontainable and incommensurable with the human capacity to count. Music is accordingly liberated from its human constraints and turned into a transversal space of molecular becomings. Rhythms acquire a singularity and autonomy of their own. As many contemporary artists from Laurie

Anderson to Sterlac have pointed out, the sheer materiality of the human body and its fleshy contents (lungs, nerves, brains, intestines, etc.) are as many sound-making, acoustic chambers. Enhanced technologically, these internal sounds can confront the listener with as shocking a sensation of unfamiliarity as the external rumbles of the cosmos.

The becoming-animal or insect has nothing to do with imitating the sounds of animals or insects. That mimetic staticity has been amply used up in classical music. It has produced flat and mostly banal renditions of animal sounds that make a mockery of themselves. As Deleuze suggests, Art does not imitate: it steals and runs; the painter does not imitate the bird: it captures it as line and colour. This is a process of becoming that deterritorializes both the artist and his or her object. Against imitation, rhizomatic music aims at deterritorializing our acoustic habits, making us aware that the human is not the ruling principle in the harmony of the spheres.

Grossberg (1997) sees acoustic refrains as crucial elements in framing space-creating sound-walls that encircle and contain the subject, sonic bricks that allow for stability, albeit temporarily. Under the impact of molecular becomings, however, they can split open all boundaries, tear down the walls and re-join the cosmos. It is a case of mobility versus the 'disciplined mobilization' of social space (Grossberg 1997: 97). The becoming-minoritarian of music produces a practice of expression without a monolithic or unitary subject that supervises the operations and capitalizes upon them.

Music increases the intensity of becoming: it is about crossing as many thresholds of intensity as the subject can sustain. All becoming is transgressive; it also aims at approaching the imperceptible, the unthinkable, the audible. Just as writing, for Deleuze, can engender becoming by being intransitive, so music can express affectivity, immanence and dissolution of boundaries. Music is constant becoming in its refrains and rhythmic narrations. It makes audible the irreducibility of in-between spaces, polyphonic hybridization, multiple sonic interferences.

In-sects/sex

The transformative speed as well as an immense power of adaptation is the force that makes insects the entity most closely related to the becoming-molecular and becoming-imperceptible. The fact that most of their life cycle is made of metamorphoses through different stadia of development is a manifestation of the same principles. As the title of this essay suggests, however, I would rather speak of met(r)a-morphoses, that is to say of a general becoming-minoritarian that does not erase sexual difference. I will return to this. I think that in a Deleuzian perspective the evidence points to a powerful link between the insect and the electronic technology: the ticking away of incessant bytes of information at the speed of light. I think this destabilizing post-human speed is the source of Deleuze's connection to writers like Burroughs, but also to others, whom he inexplicably ignores, like Kathy Acker and Angela Carter; more on this in the next chapter.

For Aristotle, insects have no specific sex, for Pliny, their sexuality is undecidable as their sex is invisible. Elizabeth Grosz, on the contrary, sees the insect as a highly sexualized 'queer' entity, capable of titillating the collective imagination especially on the issue of sex and death (1995b). She focuses on the fascination of humans for insect sexuality. She concentrates on two insects particularly, the black widow spider and the praying mantis, especially in the work of Roger Caillois and Alphonso Lingis. She finds in these the prototype of a post-human philosophy. In their mimicry and camouflage abilities, insects enact the psychoanalytic phenomenon of psychasthenia, that is to say a disintegration of the bounds of consciousness and the relinquishing of its ties to the body so that the distinction between the inside and the outside becomes difficult to hold. Accordingly, the sexual connotation of this orgiastic dissolution of the boundaries of decency in insects leads Caillois to a semi-delirious set of associations between the praying mantis–religion–food–orality–vampires–the vagina dentata–automatism–the female android. What emerges loud and clear from the series of associations is the insect-paradigm as a model for polymorphous anti-phallic sexuality. Lingis argues that the orgasmic body cannot be reduced to the organic body but to an organic assemblage of forces that exceeds and challenges the boundaries of morphology which finds an interesting resonance in the sexuality of insects.

In terms of their reproduction, insects have perfected hybridity. They point to a disturbingly diverse sexual cycle, when compared to mammals; in facts, insects are non-mammals that lay eggs. As such, they are likely to feed into the most insidious anxieties about unnatural copulations and births, especially in a 'post-humanist' culture obsessed with artificial reproduction. Moreover, because of their rapid life cycle, there is no question of caring for their infants, mostly because they are not born prematurely (like humans). In a Deleuzian vein, these relatively obvious differences from the human lay out the grid of a new set of spatio-temporal co-ordinates, which translate into affective typologies and speed or rhythms.

The queer sexuality of insects, spiders, invertebrates, fish and nocturnal animals has been filmed with magnificent creativity by Jean Painlevé in the 1920s and 1930s. He was a pioneer of scientific filming who experimented extensively with new techniques, such as underwater filming, as well as with eccentric or unusual subject-matters. For instance, his short exploration of the seahorse displays real virtuosity in imaging what can only be described as an alternative life and sexual system. Among others, the hippocampus offers a male birth scene in which the male of the species carries the embryos, fertilized by the female, nurtures them in a special pouch endowed with blood vessels and then delivers them with due spasms and contractions. Painlevé manages to turn the filmic images into a permanent challenge for the spectators. The hippocampus is one of those invertebrates that challenges our anthropocentric expectations of what the animal or organic other should look like. It displays the dignity of verticality and evokes with uncanny elegance the style of bipeds. All eyes and no mouth, it looks like an extra-terrestrial life-form which is puzzled by our peculiar terrestrian habits. The same aim is pursued in the documentaries about natural vampires, preda-tors and wild animal forms on earth, in the air or underwater, bats, insects, crickets, sea-stars, octopuses, worms, parasites, locusts, blood-sucking urchins that sink their fangs into the unsuspecting limbs of human bathers, shrimps that look like a pair of eyes fitted on stilts which float around like fragments of crystal carried by the tide. Their sexuality is enough to make pure mockery of any Christian eulogy of 'nature': bisexuality, same-sex sex, hermaphroditism, incest and all other kinds of unnatural sexual practices are part of the animal kingdom. Painlevé records and shows them all, so as to demolish any Romantic or essentialistic assumptions about a natural order. It is a queer world out there!

As I argued before in my exegesis of Deleuze's case against the humanism of psychoanalysis, the organic body functions in unified alignment of organs and functions according to the normative matrix of dialectical heterosexual desire (for the desire) of the other. Both agree that the greatest pleasure is obtained through subversion of this order, that is to say, through the unex-pected, the construction of unprogrammed surfaces of pleasure. Disrup-tions, rather than the unfolding of the predictable old scenario of heterosexual seduction, is the key to trigger the desire in these post-human times. Trans-formations and metamorphoses are the true site of desire, asymmetrically embodied ecstasy in and of difference, not the articulation of the libidinal economy of the same. Lust and pleasure in the nomadic mode melt down the cohesion and unity for the body, allowing for the cricket in you to sing, and the cockroach in you to endure: something that David Cronenberg has understood completely. This sexual theme links insects to technologies in the contemporary social imaginary in a way that also triggers ethical and political implications.

Considering this 'queer', or unsettling, quality of insexts, let me raise again the questions of how sexual difference affects their representation in the contemporary social imaginary. As suggested earlier in my analysis of how contemporary popular culture promotes the link between women, insects and technology, we need to diversify the process of becoming-insect. It can simultaneously express the anxieties of the majority (dominant subject-position) and the aspirations of the minoritarian subject-position. In order to explore the latter, I now want to argue that there is a specific pattern of becoming woman/insect, which has features of its own and cannot be reduced to the undifferentiated becoming postulated by Deleuze, as I will show next.

Clarice Lispector as the anti-Kafka

'Every woman is the woman of all women, every man is the man of all men and each one of them could present her/himself wherever the human is at stake.'

Clarice Lispector, *La Passion selon G. H.*, p. 193

The main character in *Passion According to G. H.* is the image of post-emancipation female subject: a sculptress, living on the top floor of a luxurious apartment-block in a modern South-American metropolis. She represents the advantages of class: elegance, leisure, economic independence and creativity. Moreover, she has gained the right to a room of her own, both financially and sexually. She is the sole owner of this space, having neither husband nor children.

The plot of the story is a met(r)a-morphosis that consists in her crossing a series of boundaries which become thresholds, like steps in a process of unravelling the levels of her subjectivity. This voyage across the multi-layered structure of her subjectivity is a process of affirmative deconstruction, or mimetic repetition, that opens up for the protagonist unsuspected paths of becoming. This process also involves the questioning of her relationship to otherness, according to a series of differentiating variables: class, race, life-style, the inhuman, the animal, the inorganic and the cosmic. It also results in the progressive loss of her identity until its dissolution into a cosmic becoming. The catalyst for the whole process is her intimate encounter with an insect, to which I will return.

The first threshold she crosses is the class boundary, which also stands for her public personality or social self, and is closely connected to race or ethnic identity. The action takes place on the maid's day off: the maid is a native Brazilian woman, dark-skinned and absolutely not as Eurocentric as G. H. Prompted by the desire to tidy up what she expects to be a messy room, G. H. enters her maid's quarters. The whiteness and cleanliness of it will blind her and confront her with her own culture-specific colour-blindness. This room is at the far end of her luxurious apartment, in the furthest section of the house, at the back of the kitchen. The inner space of the house is, in this text, a projection of the female body, and the back of the kitchen is an area lying on the margins of the conscious space of the rest of the house. This room is the negation and the counterpoint of the calm comfort of the flat. It lifts out or strips the ironical sense of distance which

G. H. has wrapped up around herself. The process she undertakes is therefore a plunge into the depths of her own self. This is a space of multiple becomings, where sexual difference will come into play. The second threshold marks the collapse of the barriers between the human and its animal and inorganic others. Through a series of structural analogies with insects, these barriers are systematically dissolved. This begins with the description of her house as 'the top of a bee-hive', solid but aerial, and culminates with her encounter with the roach. Becoming her own piece of flesh, G. H. plunges ever more deeply into the folds of her own materiality, becoming animal, insect, mineral. She experiences it in the mode of desire and adoration of the life which, flowing through her, does not belong to her alone. Seduced by a force that she cannot name because it inhabits her very deeply, she consumes this cannibalistic act that consists in assimilating the roach. This gesture transgresses a number of thresholds and breaks many taboos: human–non-human, fit to eat–unfit to eat, cooked–raw, etc.

This wealthy white woman progressively loses her socially-defined identity; the result is an epiphany beyond words. G. H. will come to realize that she is part of a deeply interlocked system of space and time. She can almost hear the imperceptible flow of time going past; she remembers events that have not taken place yet, compressing the spatio-temporal continuum so as to inhabit simultaneously different time-zones. She thus expands her consciousness to encompass the multiplicity of possibilities that dwell within her. No longer an individual, a person, she turns into a particle of living matter: intelligent flesh that can think and remember; a living example of radical immanence; de-human, post-human and all too-human at the same time. The point around which the whole event is unfolded is G. H.'s confrontation with the abject body of a roach. It is first by staring at, and then by gradually incorporating the co-ordinates of this ancient, age-less portion of living matter that G. H. 'becomes' her own material embodied section of space and time: an immanent, sentient being.

Let us reflect on this point: an insect is non-human, but also somewhat non-animal, a 'drop of pure matter' (p. 60). It is rather a border-line being, in between the animal and the mineral. Roaches, in particular, are as ancient as the crust of the earth and endowed with astonishing powers of survival – like being resistant to nuclear radiation. They are also, by definition, objects of disgust and rejection. The insect as a life-form is a hybrid in so far as it lies at the intersection of different species: it is a winged sort of fauna (p. 62); it is also microcosmic. The insect also lies in between the imaginary and the scientific: a full bestiary is included in this list of abject beings that are comparable to this bug in their power to cross and blur human boundaries. A list of impure animals follows, drawn from the Bible or other folklore.

As Kristeva points out in her commentary on Mary Douglas's work on the abject, this is a figure of mixity and intermediary states (Kristeva 1980).

Most abject beings, animals or states are also sacred, because they mark essential boundaries. First and foremost among them is the boundary of origin, that is to say the interface between life and death. The mother as life-giver is an abject figure: a symbolic signpost marking the road to sunny daylight and thereby also the way to dusty death. It is no wonder that most primitive religions are mother-based and fertility-bound. Abject beings are eternal in the sense of being the same as they were when they were created: they are essential and therefore sacred, feared, totemic. They correspond to hybrid and in-between states and as such they evoke both fascination and horror, both desire and loathing.

G. H.'s 'becoming' consists firstly in a sort of awakening: she comes to experience with the intensity of simultaneous pain and joy the commonality of matter between herself and this particular portion of living matter, half-animal and half-stone, living on quite independently of the gaze of the human beholder. By a gradual set of shifts, G. H. realizes the non-centrality of the human to life and to living matter. What follows is an experience of transcendence in and through the flesh. Akin to sexual ecstasy, this experience is one of utter dissolution of boundaries of self, species and society. And it is precisely at the moment when she is both pre-human and all too human, that she experiences the femaleness of her embodied portion of being. Her female materiality consists precisely in the capacity for, or tendency towards, concomitance with other living matter and the experience of desire as adoration.

In an extraordinarily intense passage, G. H. discovers, however, that at the very point where she parts from her human envelope, to discover her material one-ness of being with all that is, she also experiences – with the force of an evidence – that she is a portion of matter sexed female. She is exactly that: a *she*, even and especially in the ecstatic experience of transcendence through the flesh. And in that instance, she is one and the same as the abject body she has swallowed, and incorporated. She becomes imperceptible matter.

In the next step, the linearity of time is dissolved. The process of becoming is described externally, through a series of analogies between the individual, intimate time of her being (*Aion*) and the historical, external time (*Chronos*). Thus, G. H. remarks that one day the foundations of the present civilization will sink in, as in an earthquake, exposing its hidden foundations. This marks the return to a primordial state beyond or prior to the civilized veneer; the room is a microcosm, where time implodes into a continuous present. Progressive, linear time is short-circuited by the circular times of her own process of becoming. The cyclical temporality of her becoming-minoritarian combines with a basic re-shuffling of her constitutive elements, to produce new terms of reference for a post-human consciousness. This leads the character to encounter, beyond the dissolution of time, to a point of ascesis, or of opening out. The microcosmic room is the tip of a minaret, the heart of the desert, a space of its own that defies euclidian geometry. It is a space where anamorphosis and optical illusions accompany the collapse of linear time. As ancient as the earth, it is a pre-historical space: the frescos left by the maid are primitive figurines that create the sense of ancient rituals; the writing on the wall is a sarcophagus's inscription. It is on the other side of the civilized space of the self.

Like a mystic on top of some sacred mountain, she gazes into the depth and soon starts seeing: she experiences the interconnectedness of beings: buildings are bodies, both are made of living matter. Nature is the unity of matter and this unity is not natural, but handcrafted by human endeavour among other forces. It is worked through by the crafty hands of builders: of pyramids, temples, high-rise flats, acropolises and sewerage systems. What she becomes aware of is not only the insect but also her becoming-inanimate, her being-an-insect-too. In this recognition of her materiality she steps beyond good and evil, she is flesh: embodied, thinking, sensible matter, reaching out cosmically, that is to say becoming imperceptible.

Clarice Lispector acknowledges that she wrote *La Passion selon G. H.* following the experience of an abortion; the whole story can be read as a ritual whereby she cleanses her memory of the traces of her encounter with the organic matter that generates within a female body. It also clearly marks the confrontation with the maternal as an abject but unavoidable site of female identity. The encounter with the portion of being that is the roach brings about a return of her repressed. It firstly reminds her of her child-hood as a poor child living in insalubrious surroundings, in the company of rats and cockroaches.

The realization of the co-extensivity of her being with that of all sort of organic matters marks her becoming-alive, in the manner of living matter. Beyond humanity, G. H. experiences drives and desires that are alien to the civilized human being. She de-programmes the humanization of the drives or affects which I analysed earlier. This description of the becoming-insect is comparable to Deleuze's definition. In their analysis of another memorable encounter between a human and an insect, Kafka's *Metamorphosis*, Deleuze and Guattari develop a full theory of the becoming-animal as a form of universal deterritorialization, which is never just reproduction or imitation. The becoming-animal entails movements, vibrations, and threshold-crossings. The becoming is a question of connections, alliances, symbiosis: it is a question of multiplicity. In this respect, the chain of becomings goes on: becoming-woman or child or animal or insect or vegetable or matter or molecular or imperceptible.

As in other stages of the argument about the process of becoming, how-ever, Deleuze and Guattari do not take into account the variable of sexual difference in their analysis. In their commentary on the Kafka story, the process of metamorphosis is not at all related to the embodied male subjectivity which provides the corporeal field for this transformation to occur. In Clarice Lispector's story, on the other hand, the entire process of becoming, down to the crux of the encounter with the insect, is specifically marked as sexed female. References to female sexuality, to motherhood, to body fluids, to the flow of blood and mucous are unmistakably female. At the same time, however, the structure of the successive becomings experienced by G. H. is in keeping with Deleuze's analysis of becoming as a symbiotic metamorphosis.

La Passion selon G. H. is such a rich text that it deserves more attention than I can devote to it here. I have simply used it as an illustration of how the perspective opened by sexual difference allows for notions such as genderized becoming, or gender-specific forms of transcendence. These contrast sharply with the sexually undifferentiated patterns of becoming that are advocated by the philosophers of difference, like Deleuze. In her philosophical commentary on this text, the Italian philosopher of sexual difference Adriana Cavarero (1990), sees in it the affirmation of a feminist brand of radical materialism. The life which, in one, does not bear one's own name, is a force that connects one to all other living matter. Cavarero reads this insight as the woman's attempt to disconnect her sense of being from the patriarchal logos. By positing the connectedness of living matter as the foundation for an alternative system of thought, Lispector, according to Cavarero, dislodges one of the central premises of Western thinking: that being and language are one. With G. H., life as a raw force is in excess of the logocentric grid. Moreover, following the insight of Irigaray, Cavarero criticizes the assimilation of the universal to the masculine and defends the idea of a female-specific notion of being. That the living matter may not require the thinking 'I' in order to exist results in more emphasis being placed on the centrality of the sexed nature of the 'she-I'. One's sexed identity is primordial and inextricable from one's being. Sexual difference is definitional of the woman and not contingent: it is always already there.

In a very different reading of the same text, the French writer Hélène Cixous (1986b) reads the event as a parable for women's writing: 'écriture féminine' meant as a process of constitution of an alternative female symbolic system. G. H.'s passion is for life without mastery, power or domination; her sense of adoration is compared to the capacity for giving and receptivity, not for Christian martyrdom. Cixous connects this faculty to the ability both to give and receive the gift, that is to say to receive the other in all of his or her astounding difference. In her ethical defence of the politics of subjectivity, Cixous defines the ability to accept otherness as a new science, a new discourse that is based on the idea of respectful affinity between self and other. G. H.'s passion is about belonging to a common matter: life, in its total depersonalized manner. The term 'approach' defines for Cixous the basis of her ethical system: it designates the way in which self and other can be connected in a new world-view where all living matter is a sensitive web of mutually receptive entities. The key terms are affinity and receptivity. The other-than-human at stake here is that which, by definition, escapes the domination of the anthropo-logocentric subject and requires that he or she accepts his or her marginality. More specifically, the divine in all humans is the capacity to see interconnectedness and empathy. For Cixous this heightened sense of being is the feminine, it is the woman as creative force: poet and writer. The divine is the feminine as creativity. This is in keeping with the philosophy of radical immanence I mentioned earlier, especially the idea of the sensible transcendental.

As a counterpoint to that, let me spell out instead a possible nomadic reading of the passion play performed by G. H. Her encounter with the insect marks a change of space and speed in her experiential field: we are not dealing here with metaphors of insect-like sub-cutaneous sensibility, but rather about growing into different bodies, or growing different organs. G. H. becomes the insect itself; this occurs in different phases, which also correspond to different degrees of evocation of new fields of forces, or sensations, or flows. What is at stake is not the representation of a different consciousness, but its shattering into a dynamic field of transformations. Just like Deleuze, G. H. defines the process of becoming as the encounter of 'haecceities' (Deleuze and Guattari 1987b), single individualities that share certain attributes and can merge with each other because of them. This process is described as a becoming-inorganic, primordial matter, the 'inexpressive', 'the demonic', 'the diabolical', the 'pre-human' (p. 112).

The void encountered by G. H., contrary to the Sartrian nothingness, is a site of interconnectedness and mutual interdependence: 'Life, my love, is one big seduction where all that is alive is seducing each other. This room which used to be deserted becomes life in its primary state. I had reached the void and the void was alive and moist' (Lispector 1978: 73). The space of this void has female sexual connotations, it is a vision of the void as a mucous space, 'alive and moist'. The encounter with the abject bug reveals a deadly sort of organic affinity between the two forms of matter: G. H. and the roach, linked in their mutual ferocity. G. H. will kill, and the killing will be as much a gesture of connecting as of destruction. After she kills the roach, a white substance oozes out from its crushed body: like primitive magma, like impure discharges, this organic matter just pours out, ineluctably. This moment, which marks the transgression of all boundaries, pushes G. H. outside the perimeters of civilized behaviour and is described in a passage that reads like an extended commentary on Munch's painting *The Scream*.

Through this encounter, it is her own prehistoric materiality that is asserted. This sense of the non-humanity of all that lives and the off-centre position of the human to the living matter finds a counterpart in the structure of time which dissolves in the immediacy of the actual. This experience she describes as a metamorphosis: 'The world is not human' (81). This deeply-rooted affinity with the living matter is the amazing outcome of this revelation. The part of life that is in her is not hers. She used to be a sentimentalized, utilitarian, majority-bound, psychological entity culturally constructed as feminine. Now life claims her out of her civilized neutrality; life bursts out of her like a dyke that collapses and, in collapsing, sweeps everything aside. She is becoming-woman/minoritarian/insect/imperceptible, multiple and yet has never been more singular than in this process. The return of life is described as repetition: 'At times life returns' (82). This life which returns is simply a force that demands to be expressed, but it is so intense that it sweeps everything aside. The realization that the human is superfluous to the life-flows scares her; the raw force of life is frightening; the 'sentimentalization' of life is necessary to cover up this rawness and disperse the fear. She loses all ideas, to become sensitive matter. G. H. uses metaphors of fertility for this process, in a manner that is reminiscent of Irigaray's definition of vision as caressing proximity, not as rapacious possession of the other. This redis-covery of the life in her takes the form of the transcendence of the human: anti-Kafka in her power of regeneration, female in her generative force, yet beyond the psycho-sexual identity of Woman.

This process of peaceful taking-in of the world is described as oratorio: pure expression of passions, without prayers or requests. This is the path to her transcendence: transcendence as radical immanence, so as to stay within that which is. This is what she calls 'Dieu': the divine is the pure expression of the joy of/in being; stronger than the guilt or the sense of sin. In this process, G. H. steps beyond Christian morality. Thus, she remembers her abortion and her being pregnant as ways of being in life, being neutral, becoming-matter: both joyful and horrible. The suspending of the new life in her is described as matter acting upon matter, it is value-free. At this point she melts into or becomes imperceptible. Faced with the immensity and the holiness of all that is, she bows down and she adores: adoration as the best mode of approach and perception of the other.

Lispector's 'becoming-insect/imperceptible' is analogous to the sensible transcendental of Irigaray, which I analysed in the previous chapter. It marks a process of radically immanent subjectivity acting on a gendered threshold of transcendence. This process results in a non-theistic redefinition of the sacred as life: *zoe* and *bios* reunited in becoming. I would analyse Lispector's novel *La Passion selon G. H.* in terms of the sequence becoming woman–animal–insect–imperceptible. I also emphasized the gendered nature of both the process of becoming and of the time-sequence that marks it. The encounter between the emancipated woman and this abject inhabitant of the entrails of space is resolved in her recognition of the co-extensivity of all living matter.

It is also an expression, however, of Deleuze's empirical transcendental: Deleuze's analysis of the latitudinal–longitudinal span of intensities that connect different layers of consciousness is highly relevant. What does not check, however, is his assertion of the undifferentiated trajectory of the becoming. For G. H. the progression is very gender-specific, as are the cross-references to body-parts and body-fluids that mark this process. It is radical immanence of and in the body. She moves towards becoming-molecular, but the becoming-imperceptible coincides with a sort of illumination that connects her to the pre-human, but also projects her inexorably towards a post-human interconnectedness. G. H. becomes one with the cosmos as a dynamic principle: she is but a point in it, burning with an intensity that makes her into an organizing principle. Faced with the immensity of this force which is in her but does not belong to her, G. H. simply bows down and honours this totality, in adoration. This living force is in excess of the phallogocentric hold, and by letting go to it G. H., far from dissolving into the undifferentiated, emerges as 'the woman of all women', one with the whole of that gendered humanity which she cannot represent otherwise than by partaking fully of its speed and intensity: after which there is only silence.

Conclusion

When compared with this analysis of the metamorphosis that takes place in Lispector's tale of becoming, however, Deleuze's analysis of the 'becoming-woman/insect' does come across as inadequate in its sexually undifferentiated approach. May I again be so bold as to suggest that is because Deleuze is 'located' elsewhere: close enough to the feminist claim to the empowerment of alternative female subjectivity, but distant enough to ignore it. Other followers of Deluze will not agree and may even turn my statement around to indicate my own Molar/Moral attachment to principles of identity and femininity which are but ideological formation, or the expression of the collective fantasies of our social order. Buchanan (2000) calls my attachment to sexual difference a matter of addiction. If this be so, I have no major objections. I find, however, that Buchanan's position, not unlike Deleuze's own, expresses quite clearly its own location and hence the partiality of his viewpoint. The difference is that he fails to acknowledge it.

Politics being no more than a theoretically informed map, Deleuze draws his own topology, and he is fully entitled to it. Speaking as a feminist I see this as confirming the importance of the 'politics of location' and of sexual difference as marking asymmetrical positions between the sexes. The positioning that comes from our embodied and historically located subjectivities also determines the sort of political maps and conceptual diagrams we are likely to draw.

Speaking as a Deleuzian who believes that desire is the effective motor of political change, as opposed to wilful transformation, I experience a genuine, positive contradiction in Deleuze's thinking. This contradiction supports my belief that the quest for points of exit from identities based on phallogocentric premises is affected by sexual difference meant as the dissymmetry between the sexes. Consequently, one must work on the assumption that the process of becoming may not be as unified and homogeneous as contemporary techno-culture and the philosophers of difference would want it to be. It can only be hoped therefore that the last word about women's radical processes of transformation, over the becoming-woman or becoming-insect, bugs and woman, may come from the *practice* of sexual difference as a conceptual and political project. Met(r)amorphoses are the conceptual core of these transformative practices.

However 'molar' this may appear, I do think it important to assert the asymmetry between the majority and the minority all the way to the specific forms of affectivity, time-sequences and the kind of plans of immanence they can engineer. As people who come *after* Deleuze, I also think it important that we take this up point seriously and develop it sequentially. It seems to me urgent to rescue Deleuze's work from the risk of falling into the banality of asserting that minorities – in all their diversity – constitute the perfect prototype for the generalized modes of asubjective consciousness that Deleuze is advocating. Or in the obscenity of suggesting that differences of power *and* entitlement do not matter. I think it simply is *not* the case for Deleuze that women, blacks, children, insects or plants are rhizomic *avant la lettre* or have been nomadic since the beginning of time. And yet this oversimplified notion is gathering momentum at the present stage of reception of Deleuze.[8] I think this is dangerous not only because it is a misreading of Deleuze's becoming, but also because it hinders serious conceptual criticism of his work, which in my opinion needs to be undertaken. I want to suggest that the only way to avoid the double pitfall of oversimplification and therefore banality on the one hand and dogmatic repetition of his master's voice on the other is to explore further the notion of how the asymmetry between the Majority and the minorities affects the entire process of becoming and not only its starting premises.

What is at stake in this is the definition of the political in the historical age of postmodernity. As Massumi put it:

> the boundaries of identity in advanced capitalism are shifting rapidly. So fast, in fact, that any crystallization of specific identities, even by marginal groups is at best an oasis of relative stasis in the global capitalist time: a local re-territorialization, guarded frontiers in an uncertain landscape. The collectivity consolidated by an identity politics is an instant archaism, if not in spite of then because of its success. (Massumi 1992: 209)

Arguing that any molar sedimentation of identities based on gender, sexual orientation, class, ethnicity, nationality or religion is constitutively doomed to be one step behind the reconfigurations of identity that are actually taking place in the social field, Massumi calls for more attention to be paid to the 'outside' of the re-territorialized grounds. In terms of temporality, the consolidation of identity is a coagulation of time and space which interrupts and interferes with the process of becoming.

Massumi however avoids the holier-than-thou conceptual purity that haunts so many other Deleuzians, and recognizes that the Deleuzian process of becoming need not be a normative standpoint. Consequently it does not entail the injunction to give up identity politics or to stop fighting for basic rights. Nor does it inevitably amount to a vote of no confidence in oppositional politics, from consciousness-raising to civil disobedience. The point is quite simply not to block the process at any one point, but rather to inject movement into politics.

Boundaries must be set and reset; boundaries become thresholds: 'it is less a question of abandoning the politics of specific identity than of supplementing and complicating it' (Massumi 1992: 210). This amounts to the recognition that processes continually go on, in an internally differentiating manner. This can also be fulfilled through the strategy of creative or strategic mimesis as positive simulation that does not essentialize an original. The point is to aim at the transformative impact of one's political processes. I have argued throughout this book that feminist politics of location have inaugurated the kind of in-depth transformative politics that philosophical nomadism seems to be preaching with such passion. The feminist strategy of affirming the virtual feminine by a collective revisitation of its multiple sites of visualization is one good example. The production of alternative figurations for the new singularities being produced collectively at the moment is another. These alternative subject-positions express the transformation they embody and act as the free-floating affectivity, which Massumi describes as a tendency without an end, or a non-self-consuming, non-capitalizing process.

My claim that the on-going transformations of our times do not erase sexual difference, but merely displace it, is simultaneously a conclusion and a new start. As the former, they bring to a peak the discussions about Deleuze and feminist theory, which has been central to this book till now. As a new hypothesis emerging from this first cluster of chapters, however, they shift the grounds of the debate towards an analysis of the contemporary social imaginary about changes, transformations or mutations. I have raised this hypothesis especially in my analysis of the axis women–monsters–insects–technology. In the next chapter I will expand on this axis and analyse it more globally. In so doing, I will pursue my stated conclusion about the potency and endurance of sexual difference against the trends that aim at gender neutrality or sexual indifferentiation, especially within technological culture. I will also argue however for technophilic and positive ways of associating women, insects and technology, in opposition to some of the decadent or nihilistic repertoire that circulates in post-industrial cultures.

That is no mean feat, considering how deeply ingrained in Western thought is the habit of constructing difference as pejoration. In psychoanalytic discourse and its feminist derivatives the unthinkable, monstrous other is usually rendered in the category of the 'abject'. As Kristeva argues, the abject is an unassimilable other that potentially threatens the stability of the subject. Whether these destabilizing elements are assessed negatively or positively as potential sites of subversion, what remains constant is the dialectics of otherness within which these others are constructed as simultaneously necessary and as indigestible, inappropriate(d), and thus alien. Deleuze's becoming-animal challenges all this and is a precious tool in the task of reconfiguring the subject and his or her imaginary towards becoming-minoritarian.

That the unholy marriage of *bios* and *zoe* with *technos* – which lies at the heart of the cyber-teratological social imaginary of late postmodernity – is bringing about dislocations of sensibility, subjectivity and agency is clear. Finding adequate representations for these changes is a challenge which, in my opinion, cannot be met through Oedipal loyalty to the master's voice, but rather by the joyful cacophony of many insect-like acoustic environments. I have made an unequivocal choice for conceptual creativity, that is to say for a qualitative leap forward, which, in the way of all enfleshed subjects, may well require taking two steps back.

Philosophical nomadism is a brand of post-humanism. Consequently I think it is right to suggest that, to enact a Deleuzian process of becoming, you are better off cultivating 'your inner housefly or cockroach, instead of your inner child. . . . And don't imagine for a second that these remarks are merely anthropomorphizing metaphors' (Shaviro 1995: 53). These changes of co-ordinates rather point to the political and conceptual necessity to change in depth and thus to extract from our enfleshed memory the repertoire of available images for self-representation. It is not a mere voluntaristic switch of identifications and it could not be further removed from wilful self-naming. I would rather describe it as a process of peeling off, stratum after stratum, the layers of signification that have been tattooed in the surface of our body and – more importantly – in its psychic recesses and the internalized folds of one's sacrosanct 'experience'. Like a snake shedding an old skin, one must remember to forget it.

By analogy, the process is one of de-familiarization: imagine for instance changing family albums, picking up one that belongs to a total stranger and looking for familiar traits in it: you will *always* find them. In the act of recognizing them, you will have changed: the generic actualizes the singular in a de-personalized mode of affectivity, or interrelatedness. As Virginia Woolf put it: 'it will have been a childhood, but not *my* childhood!' 'I' is not the owner of that portion of space and time that I occupy; 'I' is only a rubber stamp and 'I' is actually only passing through. *Zoe*, however, is in the driver's seat.

4

Cyber-teratologies

'In science fiction films, the hero just flies in at the very beginning. He can bend steel with his bare hands. He can walk in zero gravity. He can see right through lead doors. But no one asks him how he is able to do these things. They just say, "Look! He's walking in zero gravity." So you don't have to deal with human nature at all.'

Laurie Anderson, *United States*

'There's a quality of legend about freaks. Like a person in a fairy tale who stops you and demands that you answer a riddle. Most people go through life dreading they'll have a traumatic experience. Freaks were born with their trauma. They've already passed their test in life. They're aristocrats.'

Diana Arbus, *Diana Arbus*, p. 3

So far, I have been courting with assiduity two interrelated concepts: firstly the cartographic practice of critical theory; secondly the yearning and quest for new styles or figurations for the non-unitary or nomadic subject. The case I am building up is in no way linear, but rather multi-faceted and web-like in its ramifications. This style can be assessed as either admirable or totally opaque, depending on one's politics of location, that is to say on readers' situated and necessarily partial perspectives. I stipulated a different pact with my readers, in opposition to the definition of the author as the unitary notion that keeps the text together by actually owning the key to its meaning. What does this apparently complex dialogical exchange between readers and writer come down to? I would describe it as a mutual pact of tolerance for complexities on both sides. That being the case, internal differentiations must be allowed for. As the author, having passed the halfway mark, I feel torn between two equally powerful pulls: the first is towards self-explanatory transparency, in spite of my resistance to the clarity fetishism which I sarcastically commented on in chapter 1. The second pull, however, is for a nomadic and flexible approach that would allow readers to make up their own route through my text. I shall accordingly not take them by their virtual hand and guide them through a recapitulation of aims and intentions.

Lest this appeal to readers to fend for themselves be taken as rude, may I remind readers that, if this book were a CD-Rom or an Internet site, they would not hesitate to interfere with it, to manipulate it on the innermost level of techno-intimacy. They would simply take it over, scan it, pick it up, click it, down-load it, print it, cut it and glue it as if it were the most natural course of events. As an author based in the Gutenberg Galaxy, I feel at a double disadvantage. Firstly, I am stuck with the obligation of linearity of the reading process which militates against the joint author–readers' nomadic sensibility that I have been advocating since chapter 1. Secondly, I have to overcome my own frustration at the situation and cultivate the patience necessary to recapitulate, summarize and repeat. I shall consequently do so by providing a minimalist set of road-signs.

About figurations: they evoke the changes and transformations which are on-going in the 'g-local' context of advanced societies. Special emphasis has been given to the dislocations induced by the fast rates of change upon established notions of identity. Figurations are expressive of cartographic readings of the subject's own embedded and embodied position. As such, they are linked to the social imaginary by a complex web of relations, both of the repressive and the empowering kind. The idea of figurations therefore provides an answer not only to political, but also to both epistemological and aesthetic questions: how does one invent new structures of thought? Where does conceptual change start from? What are the conditions that can bring it about? Is the model of scientific rationality a suitable frame of reference to express the new subjectivity? Is the model of artistic creativity any better? How does it act upon the social imaginary? Will *mythos* or *logos* prove to be a better ally in the big leap across the postmodern void? What is the specific contribution of philosophical nomadism to this discussion?

About transitions: the nomadic or rhizomatic mode in critical theory aims to account for processes, not fixed points. This means going in between different discursive fields, passing through diverse spheres of intellectual discourse. Theory today happens 'in transit', moving on, passing through, creating connections where things were previously disconnected or seemed unrelated, where there seemed to be 'nothing to see'. In transit, moving, displacing also implies the effort to move on to the invention of new ways of relating, of building footbridges between notions. This mode of working, which Isabelle Stengers (1987) calls epistemic nomadism, can only work, in fact, if it is properly situated, securely anchored in the 'in-between' zones. It is therefore crucial to learn how to think about processes and not only concepts. The challenge is in how to represent in-between zones and areas of experience or perception.

About difference: it is both the problem and the solution. This implies a related challenge to the habit that consists in representing changes or transformations in pejorative terms. In this chapter, I will present my own cartography of the postmodern Gothic, that is to say the teratological social imaginary of post-industrial societies. I will also outline a number of standard readings of monstrous formations, in keeping with psychoanalysis and semiotics. In the next chapter, on the other hand, I will spell out a nomadic and rhizomic way to approach in a creative manner the cyber-monsters of high-tech societies. Through it all, I will evolve slowly from a cartographic to a more figural way of discussing the central concepts of philosophical nomadism, namely embodiment, materialism and sexual difference.

About sexually differentiated becomings   In the previous chapter, in my analysis of the axis women–insects–technology I raised the issue which is central to this chapter, namely: how to assess the social imaginary that produces such representations. Does it express the deep-seated anxiety of the Majority, or are there other patterns of subversive, becoming-minoritarian at work as well? What's the place of sexual difference in this cultural trend? Is there hope for the new monsters?

   With these sign-posts in mind, let us proceed.

The cyber-monsters of late postmodernity

Postmodernity is notoriously the age of proliferating differences. The devalued 'others' which constituted the specular complement of the modern subject – woman, the ethnic or racialized other and nature or 'earth-others' – return with a vengeance. They are the complement to the modern subject, who constructed himself as much through what he excluded, as through what he included in his sense of agency or subjectivity. Phallogocentrism as an apparatus of subjectivity works by organizing the significant/signifying differences according to a hierarchical scale that is governed by the standardized mainstream subject. Deleuze calls it 'the Majority subject' or the Molar centre of Being. Irigaray calls it 'the Same', or the hyperinflated, falsely universal 'He'. It is against 'Him' that the social and political movements of the postwar period have concentrated their critical efforts. As Canguilhem put it, normality is, after all, only the zero-degree of monstrosity.

Difference, however, has been rendered in theoretical discourse in negative terms of pejoration. Feminist theory describes this as a sort of 'metaphysical cannibalism' (Braidotti 1991) that feeds on its structurally excluded others. This function is crucial to figures of negative difference such as the deviant or monstrous others. In fact, as I will argue in this chapter, it is in the language of monstrosity that difference is often translated. Because this difference-as-pejoration fulfils a structural and constitutive function, it also occupies a strategic position. It can consequently illuminate the complex and dissymmetrical power-relations at work within the dominant subject-position.

This proliferation of 'differences' can no longer be fitted into a dialectical mode of opposition. For instance the women's movement has marked an indelible scar on the symbolic tissue of phallocentric culture; emergent subjectivities from the post-colonial horizon have displaced the Eurocentred world-view; various brands of fundamentalism as well as both communist and post-communist nationalism have created powerful images of 'threatening alien others'. This process confuses the distribution of values according to self–other dichotomies. To top it all off, ecological disaster spells the end of the drive towards mastery of nature, while the technological revolution makes it all the more urgent to resolve issues of access to and participation in a democracy that is threatened by the informatics of domination.

The emergences of the new critical discourses of psychoanalysis, linguistics and ethnology are both the symptom of a crisis in the classical philosophical discourse and a response to that crisis. They also express the emerging presence of the 'others' of classical humanism. For instance, the woman, as referent for embodied, lived experience, fantasy and desire is at the heart of the discourse and practice of psychoanalysis, much as the ethnic other is the focus of ethnology. And the environment as the non-verbal framework within which human subjectivity is constructed simply breaks through the classical scheme of representation that coded it as 'nature' and requires more subtle forms of mediation. Modern biology, linguistics and anthropology all struggle with the issue of what to do with 'human nature' and in some way organize a sort of division of discursive labour among them.

These discourses draw their disruptive and innovative force precisely from the fact that they embody and express the view of those pejorative, often pathologized and yet structurally necessary 'others' who constituted the boundary-markers of modernity. They are therefore both the symptom of the crisis of dominant subjectivity and the expression of altogether new subject-positions.

Moreover, late post-industrial societies have proved far more flexible and adaptable towards the proliferation of 'different differences', than the classical Left expected. These 'differences' have been turned into and constructed as marketable, consumable and tradable 'others'. The new scattered and

poly-centred power-relations of post-industrialism have resulted in the marketing of pluralistic differences and the commodification of the existence,
the culture, the discourses of 'others' in the mode of consumerism. Popular
culture is a reliable indicator of this trend, which sells 'world music', or a
savvy mixture of the exotic and the domestic, often in the mode of neo-
colonial romantic appropriation of 'difference'. Although ethnicity and race
continue to play a major role in organizing the consumeristic appropriation
of proliferating differences, the trend is so global as to leave no identity
untouched. Just take any product: chocolate-chip cookies or good old American ice-cream, and re-package it with a foreign-sounding name, and you
can get that 'global economy' feeling. Contemporary music and fashion fit
the bill just as neatly.

An important implication of this situation is that in late postmodernity,
advanced capitalism functions as the great nomad, the organizer of the
mobility of commodified products. A generalized sense of 'free circulation'
pertains, however, almost exclusively to the domain of goods and commodities, regardless of their place of origin, provided they guarantee maximum
profit. People do not circulate nearly as freely. It is therefore crucial to
expose the logic of economic exploitation that equates nomadic flux with
profit-minded circulation of commodities. Given that technologies are so
intrinsic to social and discursive structures of postindustrial societies, they
deserve special attention. From a critical perspective, the most salient aspect
of the technologies is the issue of access and participation: knowing that
barely twenty per cent of households in the world have electricity, let alone
telephone-lines and modems, well may one wonder about the 'democratic',
let alone the 'revolutionary', potential of the new electronic frontier. Thus,
access and participation to the new high-tech world is unevenly distributed
world-wide, with gender, age and ethnicity acting as major axes of negative
differentiation.

Massumi, in his political analysis of the historical condition of postmodernity (1998), describes global capitalism as a profit-oriented mix-and-match
that vampirizes everything. Contemporary capitalism functions by 'circulat-
ory stratification': 'It sucks value from pre-existing formations but in killing
them endows them with eternal after-life' (1998: 53). The media industry is
an integral part of this circular logic of commodification. Images constitute
a serious, never-ending, forever-dead source of capital: a spectral economy
of the eternal return. This implies also that a generalized sense of schizophrenia marks the social horizons of most cultures at the beginning of a new
century. I would argue that the postmodern condition rests on the paradox
of the simultaneous occurrence of contradictory trends; for instance, on the
one hand the globalization of the economic and cultural processes, which
engenders increasing conformism in lifestyle, telecommunication and consumerism. On the other hand, we also see the fragmentation of these processes,

with the concomitant effects of increased structural injustices, the marginalization of large sections of the population, and the resurgence of regional,
local, ethnic, and cultural differences not only between the geo-political
blocks, but also within them (Eisenstein 1998). Technology is a major factor
here.

In fact the 'global' economy is a 'g-local' effect: it is a highly localized
and situated phenomenon that consists in packaging and marketing differences as consumable goods. It is this paradox of highly local manifestations
of more general trends that makes 'glocal' cultures so difficult to analyse.
They simultaneously blur, but also uphold the boundaries between 'home'
and 'elsewhere' in ways which call for new types of power analysis. Conceptual creativity is needed because technological postmodernity is also
and primarily about structural injustices and inequalities in 'post-industrial/
colonial/communist' societies. It is about the becoming-third-world of the
first world, while continuing the exploitation of developing countries. It is
about the decline of 'legal' economies and the rise of structural illegality as
a factor in the world economy – also known as 'capital as cocaine' (Land
1995). It is about the militarization of the technological space, and also
about the globalization of pornography and the prostitution of women
and children, in a ruthless trade in human life. It is about the feminization
of poverty and the rising rates of female illiteracy, as well as the structural
unemployability of large sectors of the population, especially the youth.
This social order is also about the difficulty of the law to cope with phenomena such as the new reproductive rights, ranging from copyright laws in the
use of photocopiers and video-recorders, to the regulation of surrogate
motherhood and artificial procreation, not to mention the problem of
copyright on Internet and environmental control, this extensive web of
micro-relations of power is at the heart of what Foucault calls 'bio-power',
that is to a system of diffuse and all-pervading surveillance and over-
regulation, that is centreless, and consequently all the more pernicious and
effective.

I take the spasmodic and slightly schizophrenic concurrence of these phenomena as the distinctive trait of our age. The proximity and quasi-familiarity
of differences has turned the 'others' into objects of consumption, granting
them alternatively a reassuring and a threatening quality that by-passes the
swinging doors of the dialectics. We have entered instead into a zigzagging
pattern of dissonant nomadic subjects. Keeping track of them is the harsh
challenge that critical theory is attempting to meet. Expressing the positivity
of difference in the age of its commodified proliferation is a conceptual task
that, however, keeps on bumping against the walls of dialectical habits of
thought.

The social imaginary of late urbanized Western postmodernity is in the
grip of teratological or monstrous others. The monstrous, the grotesque, the

mutant and the downright freakish have gained widespread currency in urban post-industrial cultures also known as 'postmodern Gothic'. In his classic analysis, Lesley Fiedler (1979) points out that since the sixties a youth culture has evolved that entertains a strong, albeit ironic and parodic, relationship to freaks. Feminist culture is no exception. Sontag (1976) has noted that the revival of cultural interest in freaks in the sixties' literature and cinema coincides with the outlawing of the famous freak show of Coney Island. The physical suppression of the freaky beings facilitated their metaphoric consumption. Just like other endangered species, the eviction of freaks from their highly policed territories functioned as a licence for their commodification as the subject matter of popular art and culture.

One of the sources of the great popularity of this genre is the fact that this structural ambiguity lends itself to multi-media applications: to visualization, dramatization, serialization, transformation into musicals (Andrew Lloyd Webber's *Cats* and *Phantom of the Opera*, to name but a few) and video-games of all kinds. Early cinema actually swarms with monstrosities of all kinds, like *Nosferatu* and *The Golem*. The shift away from marginality into the mainstream occurs in the seventies with W. P. Blatty's *The Exorcist* (1971) and Ira Levin's *Rosemary's Baby* (1967) and *The Stepford Wives* (1972). A new generation of accomplished film directors was ready to take up the challenge: Spielberg, Cronenberg, De Palma, Cameron, Lynch, Carpenter, Ridley and Tony Scott, Bigalow and others. The audience was primarily the baby-boomers, that is to say the first post-war generation that grew up with television and its endless re-runs of B-rate films. As Carroll points out (1990), they are also the generation of feminism, civil rights and other momentous social and political changes.

Freaks, the geek, the androgyne and the hermaphrodite crowd the space of multiple Rocky Horror Shows. Drugs, mysticism, satanism, various brands of insanity are also in the catalogue. Murder and cannibalism, made visible by Romero in *Night of the Living Dead* in the sixties, became eroticized by Greenaway in the eighties and made it into the mainstream by the nineties, with *Silence of the Lambs*. The analysis of the current fascination with the freakish half-human/half-animal or beast-figure alone would fill a volume. We may think, as an example, of comic strips (the Ninja Turtles), TV classic series like *Star Trek*, the covers of records, CDs and LPs, video-games and CD-ROMs, video clips and the computer-generated images of Internet and Virtual Reality, as further evidence of the same trend. They are connected to the drug culture, as much as to its spin-offs in music, video and computer cultures. A great deal of this culture is flirting with sexual indeterminacy, which has been rampant since David Bowie's path-breaking Ziggy Stardust.

Contemporary culture has shifted the issue of genetic mutations from the high-tech laboratories into popular culture. Hence the relevance of the new monsters of science fiction and cyberpunk, which raise metamorphosis to the status of a cultural icon. 'Altered states' are trendsetters: video drugs now compete with the pharmaceutical ones. This cyber-teratology also gives a new twist to the centuries-old connection between the feminine and the monstrous. There is indeed a distinct teratological flair in contemporary cyber-culture, with a proliferation of new monsters which often merely transpose into outer space very classical iconographic representations of monstrous others. Whether utopian (*Close Encounters*) or dystopian (*Independence Day*), messianic (*E.T.*) or diabolical (*Alien*), the inter-galactic monstrous other is firmly settled in the imaginary of today's media and of the electronic frontier. Lara Croft of the *Tomb Raiders* series inaugurates the genre of the digital heroine character, post-Barbarella but also post-Ripley (from the *Aliens* series) and thoroughly Gothic.

Quite significant is also the contemporary trend for borderline or liminal figures of sexuality, especially replicants, zombies and vampires, including lesbian vampires and other queer mutants, who seem to enjoy special favour in these post-AIDS days. This is not only the case as far as 'low' popular culture genres are concerned, but it is equally true of relatively 'high' literary genres, as testified by authors like Angela Carter, Kathy Acker, Martin Amis, Bret Easton Ellis and Fay Weldon. The established success of genres such as horror, crime stories, science fiction and cyberpunk also points to a new 'post-human' techno-teratological phenomenon that privileges the deviant or the mutant over the more conventional versions of the human. Becker argues that these forms of neo-Gothic also express some of the liberatory potential of the postmodern condition in that they place back on to the social agenda issues of emotion and of excess. She also argues (Becker 1999: 2) that 'one of the secrets of the Gothic's persistent success is gender-related: it is so powerful because it is so feminine.' Part of this feminine charge consists, according to Becker, as well as to Linda Hutcheon, in excess and boundary-blurring, all of which exceed the boundaries not only of the classical Gothic genre, but also of pulp, porn, parody and other eminent postmodern sub-genres. As such it constitutes a serious gender-laden challenge for cultural criticism.

On this score, feminism is very much part of this culture. Contemporary feminist culture is just as passionately parodically and paradoxically involved with the cyber-monstrous universe as any other social movements or cultural and political practice in late post-industrial societies. Feminism shares fully in and actively contributes to the teratological techno-imaginary of our culture, and with it an emphasis on hybrid and mutant identities and transgender bodies, as I argued in the discussion on alternative patterns of desire in chapters 1 and 2. Cyber-feminists play with body-boundaries and the contours of the corporeal, presenting graphical surfaces where theoretical questions mingle with visual montages that re-assemble familiar images into monstrously unfamiliar forms. This is a relevant expression of the contested location of femininity in postmodernity, which, as Griggers put it, is of the register of the unrepresentable:

> the unspeakable as all that accompanies the breakdown of rational conscious-ness flows constantly around us . . . the breakdown functions as the successful failure of feminine subjectification – the antiproduction of feminine subjectivities. Beyond the unspeakable, only morbid symptoms remain to be located, re-covered, mapped – the bulimic vomiting of the toxic maternal, the anorectic refusal to take in the phallus, the neurasthenic introjection of the social fem-inine as slow suicide, the autistic refusal of the social body as 'real' percept through sensory mutilation – mnemic signs providing both clues and impene-trable screens for affects and events but unrepresentable. (Griggers 1997: 104)

In her inimitable style, Griggers positions the embodied female in the highly turbulent zone that is the dissolution of classical subjectivity. The list of psycho-pathologies she provides functions as the frame for the pathetic/despotic location of (mostly) white femininity in advanced post-industrial cultures. For more on this, return to chapter 2.

Gender trouble, a sort of trans-sexual imaginary, rather than seventies-style lesbianism has entered feminist culture. 'Queer' is no longer the noun that marks an identity they taught us to despise, but it has become a verb that destabilizes any claim to identity, even and especially to a sex-specific identity. The heroine chic of Calvin Klein's advertising campaign and the success of anorexic top models like Kate Moss have fashioned the body in the direction of the abject: hybrid mutant bodies seem to be the trend. The anorexic and amenorrheic body has replaced the hysteric as the *fin-de-siècle* psycho-pathological symptom of femininity and its discontents. The abject drug-addicted bodies of Irving Welsh's *Trainspotting* have met with a huge cultural resonance and unprecedented success. The alliance between queer sexuality, drugs and cyber-technology was announced in the psychedelic, narcotic film *Liquid Sky* (1993), where the lethal alien-body machines spread like a virus through the post-industrial urban landscape. They seduce and induce cosmic orgasms and then they kill the humans at orgasm point, mak-ing them disappear. The aliens feed on the euphoria-producing chemicals secreted during orgasm.

A colder, more ironic sensibility with a flair for sadomasochism is the contemporary version of 'no more nice girls'. Mae West has replaced Rebecca West as feminist mother, as Madonna claims in her *Sex* album (1992). Cyber-feminism in all its multiple rhizomatic variables promotes a mon-strous or hybrid imaginary. Bad girls are in and bad girls carry or are carried by a teratological imaginary. As Warner puts it: 'in rock music, in films, in fiction, even in pornography, women are grasping the she-beast of demonology for themselves. The bad girl is the heroine of our times, and transgression a staple entertainment' (Warner 1994: 11). The iron-pumping giant Ninja mutant Barbies are upon us!

Mary Russo, in her important work on the female grotesque, sees the 1990's fascination with freaks as a reaction against the normalizing and normative elements of mainstream feminist culture, which is also linked to a generational shift. She argues that through the eighties – the period I analysed in chapter 1 in terms of the 'sex wars' – American feminism entered a process of normalization in response to the conservative backlash and the negative portrayal of feminist women in the media. For fear of being marginalized and excluded from the mainstream, feminists adopted reassuring strategies which led them to reject 'the strange, the risky, the minoritarian, the excessive, the outlawed and the alien' (Russo 1994: vii). This is how the freak or the monstrous comes to overlap with the grotesque in the political imaginary of today. The nineties' re-appropriation of these categories is a deconstructivist turn that 'parallels the powerful, historic detours of words like "black" or, more recently "queer", away from their stigmatizing function in the hands of dominant culture, a trajectory that is often described as moving from shame to pride' (Russo 1994: 76). Relying on the theoretical work of Kristeva and Bakhtin, Mary Russo defines the female grotesque as the site of transgression, 'the horror zone par excellence' (1994: 10). It marks the return of the repressed of the political unconscious of late postmodernity through the expression of a carnivalesque culture of the excessive, the risky and the abject. For Russo the freak overlaps with the grotesque as a bodily socio-political category.

The monstrous or teratological imaginary expresses the social, cultural and symbolic mutations that are taking place around the phenomenon of techno-culture (Penley and Ross 1991a). Visual regimes of representation are at the heart of it. From the panoptic eye explored by Foucault in his theory of 'bio-power' to the ubiquitous presence of television, surveillance video and computer screens, it is the visual dimension of contemporary technology that defines its all-pervading power. With the on-going electronic revolution reaching a peak, it is becoming quite clear that this disembodied gaze constitutes a collision of virtual spaces with which we co-exist in increasing degrees of intimacy. In this context, feminist analysis has alerted us to the pleasures but also the dangers of 'visual politics' (Vance 1990), and the politics of visualization, especially in the field of bio-technology (Franklin, Lury and Stacey 1991). Whereas the emphasis on the powers of visualization encourages some of the theoretical masters of nihilistic postmodern aesthetics (Kroker 1987; Baudrillard 1995) to reduce the bodily self to a mere surface of representation and to launch a sort of euphoric celebration of virtual embodiments, the feminist response has been more cautious and ambivalent. It consists in stressing both the liberating and the potentially one-sided application of the new technologies (Haraway 1991; Zoe 1992). They argue for the need to develop figurations of contemporary female subjectivities that would do justice to the complexities and the contradictions of our technological universe. I will return to this.

The contemporary science fiction genre

'Science fiction has gone through a whole evolution taking it from animal,
vegetable and mineral becomings to becomings of bacteria, viruses, molecules
and things imperceptible.'
                        (Deleuze and Guattari, *A Thousand Plateaux*: 248)

One needs to turn to 'minor', not to say marginal and hybrid genres, such as
science fiction, science-fiction horror and cyberpunk, to find fitting cultural
illustrations of the changes and transformations that are taking place at
present. I also think they provide an excellent field in which to test and
apply Deleuze's work on culture, embodiment and becoming. Deleuze
acknowledges the importance of the science fiction genre himself, when he
praises these texts for their nomadic force: science fiction is indeed all about
displacements, ruptures and discontinuities. As a 'low culture' genre, moreover, it is also mercifully free of grandiose pretensions – of the aesthetic or
cognitive kind – and thus ends up being a more accurate and honest depiction
of contemporary culture than other, more self-consciously 'representational'
genres (such as the documentary, for instance).

Furthermore, for the purpose of the argument that I am pursuing through
this book, namely the quest for positive social and cultural representations
of hybrid, monstrous, abject and alien others in such a way as to subvert the
construction and consumption of pejorative differences, I think the science-
fiction genre offers an ideal breeding ground to explore what Haraway
describes affectionately as 'the promises of monsters'. In this section I
will argue forcefully for the relevance of Deleuze's theory of becoming to
science-fiction texts and films,[1] while also arguing with him on the issue of
sexually differentiated nature of these processes. I will also challenge his
idea of sexually undifferentiated 'becomings' by pointing to significant evidence of gender-specific patterns.

Even the most conservative commentators (Smith 1982) recognize that
science fiction is a literature of ideas, with a serious philosophical content
and a distinct tendency to moralizing. The dividing line between conservative and other critics, however, concerns the relation between that fantastic,
the magical and the strict genre of science fiction. Thus Smith argues that
'absurdist, existentialist literature, the type in which human beings are inexplicably transformed into cockroaches, does not qualify as science fiction'
(Smith 1982: 9). I beg to differ from this reductive approach. This recalls the
traditional standards of judgement exemplified by Todorov, namely that
even fantastic literature must not seriously threaten the morphological
normality and the moral normativity of the humanistic world-view. Metamorphoses are fine, so long as they are kept clean and in control, that

is, anthropocentric and moralizing. All the rest does not deserve to be taken into serious consideration. I will defend instead the idea that science fiction enacts a displacement of our world-view away from the human epicentre and that it manages to establish a continuum with the animal, mineral, vegetable, extra-terrestrial and technological worlds. It points to post-humanist, bio-centred egalitarianism.

As Laurie Anderson wittily put it, the anti-anthropocentrism of this genre allows it to dispense rapidly with the question of 'human nature' and its psychological repertoire, so as to move on to the exploration of other possible worlds. The emotions commonly associated with humans are not eliminated so much as decentralized and diffused throughout the text. Robert Scholes (1975) has argued that this technique operates a de-familiarization or sense of estrangement that is potentially confusing but often also exhilarating. Thus science fiction has the means of mirroring and even magnifying the crisis of our culture and our times and of highlighting some of its potential dangers. Scholes places high value on the visionary and didactic role played by the imagination in times of crisis. He argues forcefully that science fiction is a genre that takes the risk of looking into the future and drawing cognitively significant and morally relevant conclusions, in keeping with the established tradition of 'fabulations'.

Scholes defines science fiction as a 'structural' fabulation, that is to say a sub-branch of the speculative mode (as opposed to the dogmatic) and close to the didactic romance. It is strongly influenced by science and tinged with clear moral tones, and demands quite a large imaginative effort of its readers. Science fiction is a genre that accepts full responsibility for its attempt to imagine things differently and thus enacts a sort of cognitive responsibility for its own imaginative flights. As such it is beneficial not only to society but also to science which needs to be imaginative and speculative in order to progress.

Teresa de Lauretis defends the positivity of science fiction in terms of very definite textual processes 'that coexist with narrativization and counter its tendency to totalize meaning' (1980: 160). In this respect, de Lauretis, quoting Foucault, suggests that contemporary science fiction has moved beyond the irreconcilable classical conflict between utopia and dystopia, moving instead towards heterotopia, the co-existence of mutually undermining meaning systems which point to the dissolution of the unitary notion of the subject.

Less high-minded but equally convinced of the seriousness of the science-fiction genre, Fredric Jameson values it precisely for the dominant role that the wild imagination is allowed to play in it. This allows science fiction to dramatize both the fears and the aspirations of our culture at the level of the plot itself. Relying on his idea of 'the political unconscious' (Jameson 1981) as a vast network of ideas, narratives, fantasies, memories and expectations – a web of 'narrative pensée sauvage' – Jameson argues that it has the power to structure the social field as well as its cultural production. Writing specifically about science fiction, Jameson (1982) praises the epistemological priority of imagination and fantasy not only in culture but also in 'high' theory and in science, thus challenging the separation of the two.

What distinguishes contemporary science fiction from the nineteenth-century versions is that, rather than offering utopian scenarios, it reflects back to us our sense of estrangement at the fast rate of changes that are taking place in the present. Science fiction, in other words, is the defamiliarization of the 'here and now', rather than dreams of possible futures. It both reflects and provokes unease. Jameson summarizes this as the 'unthinkability' of the future, or the death of utopia, which is a mark of late postmodernity understood as the cultural logic of advanced capitalism. The contemporary imaginary is impoverished and unable to think about difference outside the frame of deep anxiety. Science fiction therefore becomes a vehicle for the reflection on our own limits, on the cultural, ideological and technical closures of our times. By doing this, science-fiction texts become self-referential in that they reflect upon their own limits and circumstances. They reflect the fundamental sense of disbelief of an entire culture towards itself and thus echo the doubts of well-meaning progressive people confronted with the large-scale social transformations of today.

As an example, Fredric Jameson's influential idea of the political unconscious attempts to hold together a notion of 'cognitive mapping' of the present with a pedagogical political culture in such a way as to create a totalizing effect. The role of psychoanalysis in this is significant: Jameson tries to apply the Freudian methodological scheme and distinguishes between latent and manifests meanings in texts (be it social or literary ones). Thus, the political unconscious indicates the mass of underlying latency, that is to say an infrastructure of yet-untapped material that can and should be made manifest. Jameson then goes on to index these meanings on mechanisms of cultural narrative and the workings of the individual unconscious according to Freud's psychoanalysis. This lends a deep and secret unity to the collection of fragments that is the cumulated texts of a culture and which can be reconstituted in critical analysis. The legacy of Hegel and Marx casts a long shadow over Jameson's work and it tilts his notion of interpretation towards the classical dialectical method of unveiling latent meanings. Jameson's subsequent attempts to draw conceptual analogies between his 'antitranscendent hermeneutic model' (1981: 23) and Deleuze and Guattari's anti-interpretative model is, in my opinion, unconvincing.[2] Jameson is both praising the fragment and constructing it as a phobic object that needs to be recomposed within a more unitary plot and a single theoretical framework in which the parts indeed reflect the whole.

As a result, Jameson's 'political unconscious' becomes yet another master-narrative solidly indexed on the historicist reading of capitalist development. I find his uni-linear mode of thinking especially ill-suited to contemporary complexities. Given in fact that cartographies are politically informed maps of the present, it follows that they are not one-dimensional, but rather give rise to all sorts of contestations and dissonant readings. Major axes of dissonance are sexual difference, gender, ethnicity, age, religious and national identity and social class, as well as access to education. It is this proliferation of dissonant differences that makes the nomadic practice of philosophy into a complex and multi-layered which web of power-relations which breaks up bilateral and usually binary or dualistic modes of interrelation. I think Marxist modes of social analysis do not escape from binarism and in some ways, notably in the opposition between 'ideology' and 'science', re-assert it with distressing conviction.

Thus, Jameson claims to follow Deleuze's lead and yet he remains an unrepentant Marxist in his totalizing vision of the relationship between the fragments and the whole. I think with Deleuze that neither in science fiction nor in any other text is there a master plot to be unveiled or revealed by the simultaneous deployment of world history and individual psychic processes. There are only fragments and sets of hazard-meetings and *ad hoc* intersections of events, Deleuze's points of crossings, rather that Freud's libidinal predestination or Marx's teleological process.

Therefore, however close to Deleuze in terminology, Jameson's project is conceptually and affectively different from the nomadology. Jameson applies a modernist philosophy of time to the analysis of the socio-economic cultural conditions of late postmodernity. He adopts the lexicon of nomadology, not its syntax. Poststructuralism thrives on fragments and discontinuities without falling into the indulgence of relativism, the hysteria of panic or the dubious luxury of melancholia. Poststructuralism is a pragmatic philosophy that rejects the ghosts of metaphysical interiority, the 'hauntology' of missing presence. It specifically rejects the tyranny of a signifier that forever refers to something else, which is never 'there' and never 'that' anyway. What you see is what you get and what you see – as Walter Benjamin put it ever so lucidly before the Nazis pushed him to suicide – is but a heap of debris which they call progress.

The imaginary of disaster

If it is the case, as Noel Carroll (1990) argues, that the genre of science-fiction horror movies is based on the disturbance of cultural norms, it is then ideally placed to represent states of crisis and change and to express the widespread anxiety of our times. As such, this genre is as unstoppable as the transformations it mirrors.

The current manifestations of fascination with the monstrous can be linked with the historical phenomenon of the 'post-nuclear sensibility' (*Diacritics* 1984), often referred to as the 'post-human' predicament. Significant writers like Amis, Acker, Weldon, Russ and Carter, who in my opinion have provided some of the most illuminating accounts of the monstrous imaginary of contemporary culture, link it directly to the post-nuclear predicament. The historical factor that marks this shift is that science and technology – far from being the leading principles in a teleological process aimed at the perfectibility of the human – have 'spilled over', turning into sources of permanent anxiety over our present and future. The 'thinkability' of nuclear disaster makes for an almost trivialized popularity of horror, which is connected to the unthinkability of the future. An imaginary world filled with images of mutation marks much more than the definitive loss of the naturalistic paradigm: it also brings to the fore the previously unspeakable fact that our culture is historically condemned to the contemplation of its extinction. Barbara Johnson argues along similar lines, within a Derridian perspective. In her comments on Mary Shelley's *The Last Man* (Johnson 1980), Johnson thinks that the contemplation of the death of the future, the extinction of the last human, is the condition of possibility for contemporary literature. Being able to represent a future in which she or he will most probably not play a role confirms the reader in the enjoyment of the act of reading itself. The text projects us beyond the contemplation of our own death.

This 'apocalyptic imagination' (Ketterer 1976) thus plays with religious and moral themes. In her classical definition of this genre, Susan Sontag associates science fiction with the imagination of disaster and the aesthetics of destruction: 'The peculiar beauties to be found in wrecking havoc, making a mess' (Sontag 1976: 119). The more extensive the scale of the disaster, the better. Hence an in-built sense of cruelty which makes the science-fiction genre overlap with the horror movie. Sontag argues in fact that the spectacle of abject and abnormal bodies, 'the sense of superiority over the freak conjoined in varying proportions with the titillation of fear and aversion make it possible for moral scruples to be lifted, for cruelty to be enjoyed' (Sontag 1976: 122). In other words, science fiction offers the enjoyment of suffering and destruction in a very simplistic and highly moralistic frame. That usually singles out science and technology – especially the nuclear – as the source of anxiety and evil.

Though historically the actual event of a nuclear explosion has materialized only in selected parts of the globe, the build-up of nuclear weapons is a problem in itself. Meanwhile the toxic waste and other polluting side-effects of the nuclear situation have increased genetic defects and other congenital malformations. Teratoxicology (Glamister 1964) is the brand of molecular biology that deals with bio-chemically induced birth defects and mutations and monitors their progress since the Manhattan project.

In her in-depth analysis of the political economy of the postnuclear predicament and the thinkability of disaster, Sofia Zoe comments very wittily:
'The unthinkable has never been innocently unthought: the extinction question's conspicuous absence from all but the most recent American political
discourse has been maintained by the condensation of extinction anxieties
onto ambiguous symbols, and their displacement onto other political and
moral issues' (Zoe 1984: 47). Zoe reads science-fiction representations of
foetal life alongside the political campaigns of the Pro-Life militants of the
American New Right and their idea of foetal personhood. This eye-opening
comparative reading shows that one of the aims of cultural practices centred
on the foetus is to distract our attention from the practices of extermination
currently growing in the world as a result of the military-industrial complex.
Sofia Zoe points out the contradictions of contemporary culture, which is
so concerned with 'rights to life' in the case of abortion and reproduction
issues while it continues to neglect the culture of death in nuclear armament,
the pile-up of radioactive waste and other toxic material, and the environmental crisis. It is as if the much-publicized spectacle of the suppression
of a few unborn babies were allowed to obscure the far larger and more
dramatic possibility of the extinction of life on this planet as a whole. Again,
bios dominates *zoe* in political discourse to the right of the centre.

Part of the unsettling quality of science fiction – that mixture of familiarity and estrangement which has emerged as one of its main features – is
due to the fact that it combines macro-events with micro-instances, in a sort
of condensation of space and time which increases proportionally with the
levels of anxiety. Stewart argues that spatially science fiction, like the genre
of horror, plays on hybridity and liminality. The scenes often take place in
dungeons (part basement, part cave); swamps (part earth, part water); woods
(part garden, part wilderness) and most significantly, in the suburban household (part home, part hell). Susanne Becker puts it succinctly: 'Gothic horror
is domestic horror, family horror, and addresses precisely those obviously
"gendered" problems of everyday life' (1999: 4).

Massumi (1992), in his analysis of the political economy of advanced
capitalism, situates the management of anxieties and the ubiquity of fear as
key-elements. Quoting Deleuze and Antonio Negri, he defines this as the
'accident-form', which is the defining event of the contemporary subject's
position in the new world disorder. Massumi sums up the logic of fear and
anxiety in the background of the decline of ideologies, which does not mean
the defeat of one ideology (capitalism) over another (communism), but rather
the defeat of ideology itself. Since the end of the cold war in 1989 especially,
a new situation has risen which marks the decline of the binary opposition
between freedom and despotism, which Reagan and Bush hailed as the
struggle of democracy against the evil empire. The enemy is no longer outside, she or he is now within, and what we used to call war has moved into

the home-front: terrorism is the mode of contemporary domination. It works by random violence: the bullet shot that inflicts the fatal blow could literally come from anywhere, at any time and hit anybody. It is the random shot, the accident as catastrophe that defines the political economy of fear, that is to say the threat of imminent disaster striking at any point in space or time: planes crashing because of explosive engines artificially placed upon them, or, as in the case of the Concorde, because of a torn tyre.[3] Safety seems to have left our lives – what will become of our children?

The accident is imminent but, as Massumi astutely puts it, it is also immanent, it is here and now, blended with the most familiar and the most intimate: the macro and the micro coincide in the moment of the catastrophe. A general sense of disaster accompanies the breakdown of established patterns of identity and kinship. There is not one enemy any more, but the infinite possibility of enemies everywhere. In the economy of fear, the enemy has become virtual and as such it awaits actualization. It could be the child, the woman, the neighbour, the AIDS virus, global warming or the next computer crash. It is unspecified because it has become a generic category, a prototype that can fit many bills at once; the accident will happen, it is only a question of time.

> Fear is the translation into 'human' terms and onto the 'human' scale of the double infinity of the figure of the possible. It is the most economical expression of the accident form as subject-form of capital: being as being-virtual, virtuality reduced to the possibility of disaster, disaster commodified, commodification as spectral continuity in the place of threat. (Massumi 1992: 185)

Consumerism, the acquisition of property and purchases are the logic that best expresses the captivity of this kind of market economy. One which predicates forces outside its control as the perpetual threat to its or our survival. Thus elevating consumerism to the function of the orgiastic consummation of fear: in the West we have become our own monsters. The commodity encapsulates the contraction of space and time: each gadget or electronic appliance represents the promise of enjoyment and consequently also its deferral. It is therefore caught in the spectral economy of the ghostly presence–absence of fulfilment; as such it haunts us. The commodity embodies futurity, as time stored (future use) or time saved (a productivity enhancer). Massumi argues that the commodity has become co-extensive with the inner space of subjectivity, as well as the outer space of the market and of social relations. Post-industrial subjectivity is about consumerism, the constant management of 'crisis' and the exploitation of its contradictions.

Loyal to the bodily materialism of Deleuze, Massumi points out a qualitative difference between the winners and the losers of the present economic world-order. Whereas the winners only put their money on the line, the losers risk their bodies. The readers may remember at this point the discussion of chapter 1: that a subject-position like the cyborg simultaneously evokes an abstract image, or spectral commodification (Schwarzenegger) and a very embodied, concrete and actualized one, namely the mostly anonymous, under-paid exploited bodies of labourers – mostly ethnic, natives or immigrant – who fuel the technological revolution. The over-exposed anonymity of the latter makes them coincide with their exploited bodies and ends up making them invisible. The dominant subject-position, however, consists in reaching high definitions of identity, or singularity, that is to say in gaining access to visibility, albeit of the spectral kind. Whiteness, the colour of corpses and of zombies is, according to Dyer, a major factor in regulating access to visibility with high definitions of identity, as opposed to the over-exposed anonymity of the excluded and the losers. Power today is a matter of selection and control, entitlement and access: it is bio-power, centred on the body and on its imagined promises and horrific threats. As Foucault put it, that engenders a system of integrated and all-encompassing surveillance which postulates potential, virtual enemies everywhere, also and especially within its by now exploded boundaries. Politics today is the management of the terror evoked by this imminent and immanent threat. The media both relays and produces this fear and the panic attack with their fixation on live coverage of the next disaster before the next one which, at least cathodically, happens everywhere and at all times.

I think Massumi's superb analysis of the political economy of fear is in tune with the basic concepts of philosophical nomadism. It also helps us understand the mutual dependence of the issue of political theory with cultural, artistic and literary concerns. Philosophy takes place in the world: it is co-extensive with the cartographic practice that consists in taking stock of the social imaginary, the social positions it sustains and the desires it sponsors. On all these scores, therefore, I can only conclude that science fiction is a highly philosophical genre.

Feminist science fiction

As an adventure-minded and action-oriented tale of exploration, war, conquest and destruction, science fiction fits in with relatively traditional gender narratives: it is quite a male-dominated adventure story. As Sarah Lefanu put it, however, science fiction as an experimental genre came of age in the sixties, as a challenge to the stock conventions of both realistic and fantastic literature. Eminently political, in both a dystopian and a utopian sense, it destabilized authority in all its forms and, as such, it exercised a fatal attraction for feminist writers bent on challenging the masculine bias of literature and society. The number of female science-fiction writers has consequently grown fast (Lefanu 1988).

Science-fiction writers find their historical roots in the nineteenth-century Gothic tradition which is one of the few genres of the period that allows women to play active roles as travellers, murderesses, thieves, adventuresses of all sorts. That most Gothic heroines are eminently wicked is also a tribute to their intelligence and wit. One of the direct links between the Gothic and science fiction is the idea of travel through space and time: outer space travel allows for fantasies of escape into alternative systems. Nowadays, gender relations, sexuality, child-bearing and alternative ecological and technological systems are all part of the post-nuclear trip. The most direct point of reference, therefore, remains science and technology. Even at its most dystopic, as in M. Atwood's *The Handmaid's Tale* (1985), I think that feminist science fiction is structurally technophilic. It takes distance from the feminist tradition of opposition to bio-technology, best exemplified by Gena Corea's notion of 'the mother machine', also known as 'the reproductive brothel' (1985 a and b) where women are totally enslaved to mechanical procreation. Historically, Dorothy Dinnerstein (1977) launched the idea of technology as the subordination of the female humans to the mechanical powers of men. Adapting Mumford's idea of the 'megamachine' to the feminist movement, Dinnerstein denounces the gigantism, the bureaucracy and the general regimentation of society that accompany advanced technology. She opposes to the inorganicism of contemporary culture a more organic, life-giving female world-view.

This position contrasts with another clear strand within non-fictional feminist theory, which relates more positively to the utopian aspects of the culture of science and technology. The most telling case is that of Shulamith Firestone, whose masterpiece *The Dialectic of Sex* (1970) was to influence not only the theoretical and political practice of the second feminist wave, but also the fictional works of writers such as Charnas, Piercy, Russ and Gearhart. Firestone represents the 'technophilic' trend in feminism, which was to be a minority position until the late eighties, when more 'cyber-minded' feminists emerged. Cybernetic feminism relies on the use of technologies in every aspect of social interaction, including reproduction, in order to relieve women from the drudgery of paid work, the oppression of the patriarchal family and masculine violence. In Firestone's Marxist utopia the ultimate aim of technology is to relieve humanity of its enslavement to an obsolete natural order. The reproductive utopia of techno-babies is part of it, and it is connected to collectivist politics, social utopianism and seventies radical feminism.

Another important insight Lefanu brings to this discussion is that of a structural analogy between woman as the second sex – the 'Other of the Same', to quote Luce Irigaray – and the alien or monstrous other. They are assimilated within the general category of 'difference', understood as a term of pejoration. Lefanu extends this insight to speak of a deep empathy between women and aliens which, in science-fiction literature, favours exchanges and mutual influences. As a matter of fact, in science fiction written by women, women simply love the aliens and feel connected to them by a deep bond of recognition. This bond is played out differently, however, by different authors.

In this respect, the striking feature of feminist science fiction is less the affirmation of the 'feminine' in an essentialist and moralist manner than the questioning and the deconstruction of the gender dichotomy itself. It is a genre that erodes the cultural foundations of notions such as 'woman' and 'man'. In her work on feminist literary postmodernism and in a dialogue with Scholes, Marleen Barr coins the expression 'feminist fabulations' to include works of science fiction, utopia, and fantasy but also the mainstream fiction of Virginia Woolf, Gertrude Stein, Djuna Barnes and Doris Lessing, which share in restructuring patriarchal narratives, values and myths (Barr 1993). In Barr's assessment, these texts contribute to the postmodern undoing of master narratives and to challenging literary hierarchies.

Science fiction is about sexual metamorphoses and mutations. Angela Carter's 'New Eve' changes from man to woman, much as Woolf's Orlando. Joanna Russ's 'female Man' navigates between sexual polarities, opening up new possibilities; Ursula LeGuin's characters determine their sexual characteristics depending on whom they happen to fall in love with. Most of these mutations are ways of exploring sexuality and desire in situations of extreme duress, just before or after the collapse of civilization and the end of recorded time.

A great deal of these physical and morphological mutations are expressed in the language of monstrosity, abjection and horror; in fact, the whole Gothic repertoire is ransacked and recycled shamelessly in science fiction texts. What horror has to do with is the lifting of categorical boundaries between humans and their others: racialized or ethnic others, animals, insects or inorganic and technological others. The main function of horror, consequently, is to blur fundamental distinctions and to introduce a sense of panic and chaos. The monstrous body fulfils the magical or symptomatic function of indicator of the register of difference, which is why the monster has never been able to avoid a blind date with women. In the post-nuclear cybernetic era, moreover, the encounter between the maternal body and the technological apparatus is so intense that it calls for new frames of analysis. Contemporary 'monstrous others' blur the dividing line between the organic and the inorganic, thus rendering superfluous also the political divide between technophobia and technophilia. The issue becomes one of redefining the techno-body in such a way as to preserve a sense of singularity, without falling into nostalgic reappraisal of an essential self. The issue of the boundaries of identity raises its monstrous head.

Extra-uterine births

Several feminist critics (Creed 1990) have argued that the genre of science-fiction horror films is of great relevance to feminism because it is explicitly bent on the exploration of the maternal body and processes of birth. This genre uses the woman's body to explore the possibilities for the future, potentially destructive or positive as they may be.

All fans know that science fiction since *Frankenstein* has to do with fantasies about how science and technology manipulate the body, especially the reproductive body. Science fiction represents alternative systems of procreation and birth, ranging from the rather child-like image of babies born out of trees or of cauliflowers, to monstrous births through unmentionable orifices. Extra-uterine births are central to science fiction texts. Thus, woman as the mother of monsters and the monstrosity of female genitalia are a crucial element in science fiction. The theme of conception and birth is a constant to science fiction as a genre, but interest in it has increased in recent years. Barbara Creed argues that science-fiction horror films, for instance, play with fundamental male anxieties about procreation. They deal with these anxieties by displacing them – usually on the mother's body, which is represented as *the* site of horror: a monstrous vision. There has been a concentration of images connected with the female reproductive cycle: the giant foetuses of *Dune*, *Inseminoid*, *The Thing*, *Alien* and *Aliens*.

These texts externalize and therefore allow us to explore the insides of alien figures who are coded as female in so far as they reproduce, and yet remain threatening. These figures resemble the human but are represented as a source of horror and overpowering awe. A reading inspired by psychoanalysis, especially by Freud's essay on the Medusa-like powers of the female sex, sees these films as displaying a distinct preoccupation with the occult, monstrous powers of the maternal body and the unfathomable depths of female genitalia. The mother as monster becomes a powerful *topos* of this genre and it expresses a deep anxiety about the feminine and gender identity.

A great deal of these horrific effects are achieved through a change in scale which magnifies defects and bodily features. In an illuminating analysis of gigantism, Calame (1985) points out that the gigantic body is a sign of mis-measure, excess and consequently of deviation. It visibly transgresses the delphic principle of the right middle, which has been central to Western aesthetics since Antiquity. Bogdan (1988) emphasizes the importance of the phenomena of aggrandizement and dwarfness in freak shows since the nineteenth century. He points out that tallness is traditionally associated with exotic, orientalist and racist narratives – even the giraffe as an unusually tall animal is no exception. Dwarves, however, tend to fit in with the home-grown European tradition of miniatures and consequently are more acceptable (think of Tom Thumb). The contemporary fascination with insects and other microscopic actors also fits in with this.

Let me try to draw a cartography of the women–monsters nexus, as it is represented in films, depending on their relationship to human reproduction.

Firstly, there are films where science manipulates reproduction, producing machine-made humans. Here the classical example is the series of *Frankenstein* films, where the mad scientist gives in to the impulse to play God and create life in his image, producing only an aberration in the process. In *The Bride of Frankenstein*, the monster is so very ugly that even his fiancée rejects him. Films like these display a rather modernist view of the powers of technology and science, which are seen as a threat to the humanist spirit. This genre culminates in the masterpiece that is *Metropolis*, where the female body doubled up as a robot becomes the symbol of man's ambivalent technological future. In this film technology is embodied in a female robot, a machine-vamp who leads the workers on a rampage and is subsequently burned at the stake (Huyssen 1986). More on this in the next chapter.

A second common topos is the insemination of the female by aliens of all sorts. In *The Fly*, the female body becomes the site of the unknown, that is to say of a hybrid mix of human and non-human. *Inseminoid* shows the woman being impregnated by an alien who will destroy the earth. In Cronenberg's *The Brood* the woman gives birth to monstrous dwarves through a sack attached to the side of her stomach. This theme can be seen as a variation on possession by the devil, of which a major term of reference remains *Rosemary's Baby*. Films like *It's Alive!* are a variation on satanic births. Woman's intercourse with zombies is explored in *Village of the Damned*. A more light-hearted approach can also be found in fifties films such as: *I Married a Monster from Outer Space*.

Thirdly, machine–woman copulation and monstrous high-tech birth: *Xtro*, *Inseminoid*. Robots, born mechanically but 'becoming' human because of affectivity, love and desire: *Daryl*, *Terminator 2*, *The Man who Fell to Earth*, *The Man who Folded Himself*. In *Aliens* human bodies are nests for monstrous embryos that come to birth through the stomach. These films explore the inside of alien female figures who resemble the human and are coded as a source of abject horror and overpowering awe. The *Alien* series is marked by womb-like, wet and sticky interiors, fallopian tube corridors and small closed-in spaces full of unmentionable horrors.

Next, cloning, in movies such as *Clones* and *Seconds*. Some of the more serious films in this tradition show up the political dangers implicit in cloning. Thus *The Boys from Brazil* plays with the temptation to follow the Nazis' experiments with eugenics in the attempt to create a master-race. The all-time classic series in this genre, however, is *The Thing*; both the original and the many remakes illustrate this quite well. 'The thing' is the body of an alien creature, usually fallen from outer space or exploding from within one's unsuspecting body, creating havoc. In the original film version, 'the thing' is a vegetable substance with green fluid instead of blood; it reproduces by cloning: he carries spores in his wrists and reproduces from them as flowers do. In the modern remake 'the thing' is an amorphous blob of living death that squats in other people's bodies. 'The thing' which may appear as innocuous as a plant, however, needs animal blood as his basic food; so he kills and then drains the victims of all their bodily fluids. 'The thing' behaves like a vampire, it looks like a non-human and it splatters huge quantities of blood.

A variation on the theme of self-birth is the vegetable-born body-double in *The Invasion of the Body Snatchers*. This is a film from the late fifties, which shows the human race gradually being taken over by identical-looking androids devoid of all feelings and emotions. It is a typical paranoia-McCarthy-era film; the body doubles are born out of plants.[4]

Male births are also noteworthy. Here, the phantasmagoria is quite striking: in *Alien*, man gives birth to a non-human using his stomach as the incubator, in what can only be described as a blatant case of womb-envy, after having been inseminated through the mouth. In *The Thing* and *The Fly* man gives birth to himself transformed into another life form: a murderous monster or a gigantic insect. Actually, Spielberg is the master of male-birth fantasies. The film *Indiana Jones* is the perfect example of this: there is no mother in sight, ever, but God the father is omnipresent. In the series *Back to the Future* which he produced, the teenager boy's fantasy of being at the origin of himself is given full and prolonged exposure, using the device of time-travel to skip generations and even climb down the evolutionary scale. Constance Penley (Penley et al. 1991b) has argued that a film like *Terminator* enacts a primal-scene fantasy in the form of a time loop. One has to return to the past in order to generate an event that has already made an impact on one's identity. According to Freud, being present at the scene of one's conception expresses the fantasy of witnessing parental intercourse. The linearity of time (*chronos*) is split, allowing for the spatialization of time through time-travel. It also allows, however, for the contemplation of the possibility of disaster, namely the end of time and extinction. I will return to this time-loop paradox in technology in the next chapter.

Last but not least, the 'feminization' of man in the sense of a sex-change: the 'feminine' as 'effeminate' in trans-sexual or trans-gender films such as *Psycho* or *Dressed to Kill*.

Sexual anarchy or disorder is built into the monstrous imaginary and thus makes it analogous to the queer or deviant body, as in the trans-sexual imaginary which I analysed in chapter 2. For instance Hurley has noted (1995) that a great deal of the appeal of the *Alien* in the homonymous film-series has to do with its puzzling sexuality. It is both phallic and vaginal; it reproduces without heterosexuality or any sexual act; it produces extra-uterine births and it treats the human as mere host, in the best parasitic tradition. Human sexuality with its metaphysical dualism of the sexes is a highly inadequate paradigm to explain this 'horrific embodiment' (Hurley 1995: 218). This fantasmagoric of unnatural births and unrepresentable sexualities of the most hybrid kind plays with alternative body-forms, or morphologies. It thus offers a repertoire of virtual re-embodiments in the post-human mode which I explored in my analysis of the becoming animal/insect of chapter 3.

Thus, the alien's bodily morphology is suitably complex and it defies human comparisons: it resembles a spider, a crustacean, a reptile, an insect, a skeleton stripped of its flesh. This flesh, moreover, is made up of materials that may be popular on Mars but are considered inimical to human life on this planet: mostly acids and metal wiring. Hurley concludes that this horrific embodiment constitutes 'a collapsing of multiple and incompatible morphic possibilities into one amorphous embodiment' (1995: 219). This throws a terminal challenge towards a human identity that is commonly predicated on the One. Furthermore, the parasitic relationship the alien establishes with its human host cannot fail to contaminate the human organism, disgregating it from within. This destructive symbiotic relationship between the normal and the pathological, the human and the monstrous, is such as to blur the distinction between the human and other species. Categorical distinctions thus become erased and this marks the demise of the human subject: his body in ruins, his ontological security shattered, his identity in tatters. One could not find a more graphic rendition of the poststructuralist idea of the 'death of man'.

Meanwhile, however, this subject's mother had not fared very well at all: she has been taken over by the bio-technological corporate industrial system. It may be objected that most horror films are made by men and that the only pleasures or terrors on offer are male-defined. The horror film speaks to the contemporary social imaginary, revealing – perhaps more than any other genre – the unconscious fears and desires of both human subjects: male fears of woman's reproductive role and of castration and woman's fears of phallic aggression and violence. No doubt as women make more horror films, the latter area will be explored more fully. As things stand now, however, the science-fiction horror film is male-dominated and it is a privileged site of deployment of male anxieties about reproduction and consequently also about female power.

The material/maternal feminine as monster

Science-fiction horror films play with fundamental male anxieties and displace them by inventing alternative views of reproduction, thereby manipulating the figure of the female body. As I mentioned earlier, in these films a parallel is often drawn between the woman's and alien, animal or insect bodies. The female body emerges from this as a monstrous fetishized other, capable of breeding unmentionable and unpresentable misfits.

Preoccupation with the horror of the maternal feminine expresses a deeply-seated postmodern anxiety about the social and symbolic orders. The monstrosity of the female is a sort of paradox, which on the one hand reinforces the patriarchal assumption that female sexuality is evil and abject, on the other hand, however, it also states the immense powerfulness of the female subject. Creed (1993) is careful to distinguish from these texts the elements of male fear of the female castrator, while she also stresses the elements of affirmation of the feminine. Relying mostly on Kristeva's work, Creed links the ambivalent structure of the maternal feminine to religious taboos on perversions and abominations, which include decay, death, human sacrifice, murder, bodily wastes, incest and the feminine body. Creed breaks down the dominant topos of the monstrous mother into a number of recurrent images: the monstrous womb, the irresistibly repugnant lesbian vampire, the castrating mother. The 'horror' part of these films is due to the play with a displaced and fantasized 'maternal' function, as holding simultaneously the key to the origins of life and to death. Just like the Medusa's head, the horrific female can be conquered by being turned into an emblem, that is to say becoming fetishized.

Thus, it is no coincidence that in *Alien*, a classic of this genre, the master-computer that controls the spaceship is called 'Mother' and she is vicious, especially to the post-feminist heroine (Sigourney Weaver). The maternal function in this film is displaced: the alien reproduces like a monstrous insect by laying eggs inside people's stomachs, through an act of phallic penetration through the mouth. There are also many scenes in the film of ejection of smaller vessels or aircrafts from the mother-dominated, monstrous and hostile spaceship. Mother is an all-powerful generative force, pre-phallic and malignant: she is a non-representable abyss from which all life and death come (Penley 1986).

The other side of the coin of the monstrous maternal/material feminine is however the manifest failure of men to maintain paternal authority. As many science-fiction narratives make evident post-nuclear contexts of urban decay, they also highlight the failure of the father to keep up his political, economic and spiritual privileges. David Cronenberg is, in my opinion, one of the most interesting authors in this respect. Thus, the rage and frustrations of the mother and her rebellion against the patriarchal order are at the heart of the monstrous births of films like *The Brood*. Parthenogenetic births are always a sign of the potentially lethal powers of the undomesticated female. This *topos* resurrects an ancient set of beliefs about the monstrous powers of the female imagination (Braidotti 1996). They simultaneously also express, however, men's sense of impotence and of increasing irrelevance.

Modleski has pointed out that in contemporary culture, men are definitely flirting with the idea of having babies for themselves. Some of this is relatively naive, and it takes the form of experimenting with new and definitely helpful social forms of new fatherhood (Modleski 1991). In postmodern times, however, this male anxiety about the missing father must be read alongside the new reproductive technologies. They replace the woman with the technological device – the machine – in a contemporary version of the Pygmalion myth, a sort of high-tech *My Fair Lady*.[5]

Much feminist ink has been spilled in the attempt to analyse the link between the monstrous and the proliferation of discourses about 'the feminine' in late postmodernity. This discursive inflation concerns mostly male philosophers, artists, cultural and media activists. With the investment in this kind of 'feminine' as the site of virile display of a crisis, the topos of the monstrous female has proportionally gained in currency. I think it emerges as the expression of the fantasy of dangers that threaten postmodern, or 'soft', patriarchy. Thinking through this material with Deleuze, I think that the monstrous feminized other of science fiction expresses primarily the fear of the Majority-subject who sees them as a threat to their own patriarchal power. The imaginary in question is that of European men at a historical time of crisis. Lefanu's argument about the bonds of empathy that connects women, ethnic, technological and extra-terrestrial others in science-fiction texts written by women acquires a particular relevance here. It points to the alliance of the 'others' against the empire of the 'One'. Thus, I think that the first and in some ways foremost link between women, racialized, ethnic or technological others and monsters lies in the eyes of the Master colonizer. Only in His gaze are their respective differences flattened out in a generalized category of 'difference' whose pejorative status is structural to the establishment of a norm that is inevitably masculine, white, heterosexist and promoting of naturalistic and essentialistic beliefs. As I argued in chapter 1, both the feminine and the monstrous are signs of an embodied negative difference which makes them ideal targets for the 'metaphysical cannibalism' of a subject which feeds on what it excludes. Pejorative otherness, or 'monstrous others', help illuminate the paradoxical and dissymmetrical power relations within Western theories of subjectivity. The freak, not unlike the feminine and the ethnic 'others', signifies devalued difference. By virtue of its structural interconnection to the dominant subject-position, it also helps define sameness or normalcy among some types.

Noel Carroll (1990) argues that what demarcates the science-fiction genre from others, like the fairy tale or the myth and legend, is precisely the fact that the monstrous other is cast in the mode of a threatening otherness. They embody ontological impropriety. This negative difference causes a disturbance in the status quo and therefore evokes anxiety, the mixture of fascination and loathing in the spectators. We shrink away from them because their metamorphic powers are immense, as Diana Arbus knew all too well. That this is represented in a monstrous imaginary which is saturated with connotations of abnormality, deviancy, criminality, abjection and ugliness is, in my opinion, a legacy from the nineteenth-century discourse about monstrous races and deviant sexes. In the political economy of post-modernity, such as I outlined in chapter 1 and have been detailing through-out this book, the 'others' are simultaneously commodified into objects of material and discursive consumption. They are also, however, emerging in their own right as alternative, resisting and empowering counter-subjectivities. For the moment, let me concentrate on the former. Popular cultural practices like cinema were extremely quick in registering the return of the pejorative others as objects of consumption: marketable in their abjection. As an indication, let me offer a chronological sequence of film production of difference. It is my own very situated and consequently highly partial genealogy of the axis monster–native–robot–woman.

1920	*Caligari*	psychic possession by mad scientist
1923	*L'Inhumaine*	*femme fatale* merges with robot to produce Orientalist sexual delights and endless perdition
1926	*Metropolis*	virgin–whore split projected on to the fleshy woman–android divide with the aim of rescuing civilization from the abyss
1931	*Svengali*	demon lover cast as Oriental threat, endowed with divine powers as singing voice ruining single white female forever
1932	*White Zombie*	white paranoia in the Southern seas coupled with demonic possession
1932	first *Tarzan* film	
1932	first *Frankenstein* film	
1932	first *Jekyll and Hyde* film	devolutionary tale of genetic undoing by morally and sexually corrupt mad scientist

Einersen and Nixon (1995) single out two major figures of female aberration which express deep male anxieties about women: the 'Virago', masculine female, and the 'Lamia', who is hyper-feminine and even more lethal. As I argued in chapter 3, Fay Weldon's 'She-devil' is a good example of the former, Coleridge's 'Christabel' and her many re-incarnations down to A. S. Byatt's *Possession* are good examples of the latter. Also on the side of the

'Lamia' are the heroines of the *film noir* genre and other *femmes fatales* in cinema. Gilbert and Gubar have argued (1977) that the figure of the 'Virago' is a particularly strong presence in the eminently misogynist genre of satire, which functions by magnifying the physical and moral imperfections of women. Showalter (1990) points out that the misogynist repertoire is stable throughout history; for instance at the end of the last century female emancipation was blamed for the moral decline of culture and eventually the fall of Western civilization. Disapproval of the 'new woman' was expressed in monstrous images of depravity, mutation, degeneration and perversity.

A more contemporary version of the Virago *topos* is the over-ambitious female of the post-feminist era, usually a multi-talented super-bitch who causes havoc and needs to be put in the right place. Doane and Hodges (1987) provide an excellent analysis of this phenomenon in terms of monstrous amazons. Lefanu also echoes this concern, pointing out that the figure of the monstrous amazon, so popular in science fiction, comes directly from the Gothic tradition. It is a figure of loathing and fear who is generally forced into submission to the male order, although female science-fiction writers are resisting and reversing the trend. Generally, however: 'Amazons must be punished, nominally perhaps for their presumption in assuming "male" characteristics, such as strength, agency, power, but essentially for their declaration of Otherness' (Lefanu 1988: 33). Marina Warner (1994) concurs, and argues that the image of the destructive monstrous female is especially current in the ways in which contemporary culture portrays feminism. The monstrous female has turned into the monstrous feminist, whom conservatives hold responsible for all the evils of today's society. Especially targeted for criticism is the single mother. As Warner rightly points out, this is not only a prominent 'problem' for the enemies of the welfare state, but also a general threat to masculine authority. Reproduction without men triggers a deep malaise in the patriarchal imaginary, resurrecting the centuries-old myth of gynocracy (Warner 1994: 4–5). Women's bodies today are in the same position as monstrous bodies were over a century ago: a testing-ground for various brands of mechanized reproduction. Are Corea's nightmare world of 'gender-cide' (1985 a and b) or Atwood's dystopia of the techno-brothel (1985) likely scenarios?

To sum up: in the contemporary imaginary, the monstrous refers to the play of representation and discourses that surround the bodies of late postmodernity. It is the expression of a deep anxiety about the bodily roots of subjectivity which foregrounds the material/maternal feminine as the site of monstrosity. I view this as the counterpart and the counterpoint to the emphasis that dominant post-industrial culture has placed on the construction of clean, healthy, fit, white, decent, law-abiding, heterosexual and forever young bodies. The techniques aimed at perfecting the bodily self and at correcting the traces of mortality of the corporeal self – plastic surgery, dieting, the fitness craze and other techniques for disciplining the body – also simultaneously help it supersede its 'natural' state. What we witness in popular culture is almost a Bakhtinian ritual of transgression. The fascination for the monstrous, the freaky body-double, is directly proportional to the suppression of images of both ugliness and disease in contemporary post-industrial culture. It is as if what we are chasing out the front door – the spectacle of the poor, fat, homeless, homosexual, black, dying, ageing, decaying, leaky body – were actually creeping in through the back window. The monstrous marks the 'return of the repressed' of techno-culture and as such it is intrinsic to it.

As I mentioned earlier on, however, these monstrous representations do not express only the negative or reactive anxieties of the majority. They also, often simultaneously, express the emerging subjectivities of the former minorities, thus tracing possible patterns of becoming.

Thus while the monstrous feminist haunts the imagination of the operators of the backlash, a less destructive reappraisal of the monstrous other has been undertaken by feminists needing to redefine difference positively. Multiculturalism and the critique of Orientalism and racism have also contributed to a rethinking of the cultural and scientific practices around monstrous bodies. The need has emerged for a new epistemology to deal with difference in non-pejorative terms. In this case, the freak/monstrous other becomes emblematic of the vast political and theoretical efforts aimed at redefining human subjectivity away from the persistently logocentric and racist ways of thinking that used to characterize it in Western culture.

Confronted with such a discursive inflation of monstrous images, I refute the nostalgic position that reads them as signs of the cultural decadence of our times, also known as the decline of 'master narratives', or the loss of the great canon of 'high culture'. I am equally opposed to the paranoid and misogynist interpretations of the new monsters. The proliferation of a monstrous social imaginary calls instead for adequate forms of analysis. More particularly it calls for a form of philosophical teratology which Deleuze is in a unique position to provide. I argue that a culture, both mainstream and feminist, where the imaginary is so monstrous and deviant, especially in its cybernetic variants, can profit greatly from philosophical nomadology. The project of reconfiguring the positivity of difference, the philosophy of becoming and the emphasis on thinking about changes and the speed of transformation are a very illuminating way to approach the complexities of our age.

From a cultural angle, a nomadic approach to contemporary creativity, be it conceptual, scientific or artistic, casts a most significant light on some of the most unprecedented aspects of advanced post-industrial cultures. Among them I would list the disaggregation of humanistic subject-positions and values, the ubiquitous presence of narcotic practices and of cultural artifacts derived from the drug culture, the all-pervasive political violence and the intermingling of the enfleshed and the technological. These features, which are often referred to as the 'post-human' universe can be read in an altogether more positive light if they are approached from the angle of philosophies of radical immanence. Multiple patterns of becoming over-throw humanistic parameters of representation, while avoiding relativism by grounding practice in a tight spatio-temporal framework.

Beyond metaphors: philosophical teratology

I have argued that the reason why the monstrous is a dominant part of the social imaginary is that it offers privileged mirror-images. We identify with monsters, out of fear or of fascination. This may also help to explain the peculiarly reassuring function that the representation of freaky bodies fulfils in the anxiety-ridden contemporary imagination. As Diana Arbus suggests, freaks have already been through it and have come out at the other end. If not quite survivors, they are at least resilient in their capacity to metamor-phose and thus survive and cope. Many late twentieth-century humans may instead have serious doubts about their capacity to cope, let alone survive. In the case of monsters, the accident or catastrophic event, to paraphrase Massumi, has already taken place. This can afford us a welcome relief and a break from the generalized political economy of fear, precisely by incarnat-ing fully its destructive potential. They exemplify the virtual catastrophy by embodying it. The effect is cathartic, erotic and deeply emotional: with a sigh of relief the would-be suburban monsters rush to embrace their poten-tial other self. Contemporary horror and science-fiction literature and films show an exacerbated version of anxiety in the form of the 'otherness within': the monster dwells in your embodied self and it may burst out any minute into unexpected and definitely unwanted mutations. The monster is in your embodied self, ready to unfold. The monstrous growths spreading within one's organism, as Jackie Stacey (1997) reminds us, in the form of cancer or other post-nuclear diseases, are also variations on the theme of the 'enemy within'.

Monsters are 'metamorphic' creatures who fulfil a kaleidoscopic mirror-function and make us aware of the mutation that we are living through in these post-nuclear, post-industrial, post-modern, post-human days. For instance Sontag (1976) has argued that Diana Arbus's photos of human oddities are troubling not so much for their subject-matter, as for the strong sense of the photographer's own consciousness and involvement with them. The fact of Arbus's own suicide adds a tone of tragic authenticity to the images and it testifies to the metamorphic power of the freaks, that is to say the extent to which they captivate the artist and lay a psychic ambush for her. Arbus's representation of freaks embodies the paradox of the contemporary teratological imaginary: on the one hand they familiarize us with human oddities and thus lower our threshold of tolerance of the horrible. On the other hand they keep a cold and unsentimental distance from them, displaying them as unself-conscious and quite autonomous. In fact, these pictures of freaks have the utter lack of irony and the stiff respectability of Victorian portraits, so that they paradoxically end up reinforcing our sense of alienation from them. These pictures become neutrally self-referential and thus defeat any possible moral message.

The metamorphic power of monstrous others serves the function of illuminating the thresholds of 'otherness' while displacing their boundaries. As I argued earlier in this chapter, this process mobilizes issues of embodiment, morphology and sexuality, scrambling the code of phallogocentric, anthropocentric representation in which they are traditionally cast. For instance, Fiedler's analysis of the typology of contemporary monsters classifies them in terms of lack, of excess and of displacement of organs. Noel Carroll (1990) also points to hybridity and categorical incompleteness as defining features of monsters. This means that they superimpose features from different species, displaying alternatively effects of excess or staggering omissions. The detachability of bodily organs is crucial to this effect, and Carroll analyses it in terms of either complete lack of shape – as in the gelatinous blob-like entities – which effaces all meaningful morphological points of reference, or else by fusion and fission of body parts. The fusion blurs significant distinctions, such as living–dead, male–female, human–animal, insect–machine, inside–outside. Fission, on the other hand, displaces the attributes of these categories over other entities, creating body-doubles, alter-egos and other forms of displacement of familiar traits. A variation on this is the evocation of abject monstrosity by metonymy: vermin, skeleton, decaying body parts as ways of representing the monstrous entity without actually showing it.

This facilitates the analogy with the feminine. As psychoanalytic feminism has successfully argued (Wright 1992), the feminine also bears a privileged relation to lack, excess and displacement. By being posited as eccentric vis-à-vis the dominant mode, or as constantly off-centre, the feminine marks the threshold between the human and its 'outside'. This outside is a multi-layered framework that both distinguishes the human from and also connects it to the animal, the vegetable, the mineral and also the divine. As a link between the sacred and the abject, the feminine is paradoxical in its monstrosity. In other words, it functions by displacement and its ubiquity as a social or philosophical 'problem' is equal to the awe and the horror it inspires. Metamorphic creatures are uncomfortable 'body-doubles' or simulacra that simultaneously attract and repel, comfort and unsettle: they are objects of adoration and aberration. As I mentioned earlier, in science-fiction texts written by women, a sort of deep complicity runs between the other of the male of the species and the other of the species as a whole.

The other historically continuous analogy between women and monstrous beings has to do with the malignant powers of women's imagination. Ever since Antiquity the active, desiring woman's imaginative powers have been represented as potentially lethal, especially if pregnant. On the destructive powers of the pregnant woman's imagination the literature is vast.[6] Huet (1983) uses a psychoanalytic framework to read the fear of the maternal imagination as a variation of the male anxiety over castration. The pregnant woman literally has the capacity to undo the father's signature and uncreate life. Doane (1987) and Williams (1989) find the same mechanism at work in classical Hollywood cinema where, 'when the woman looks' with desire, trouble is never too far off. These feminist critics have argued that the lethal gaze of the desiring female expresses a general fear and mistrust of female desire and subjectivity in phallocentric culture.

Psychoanalytic feminist theory has also cast an interesting light on this aspect of the monstrous imaginary: women who are caught in the phallogocentric gaze tend to have a negative self-image and to dread what they see when they look in the mirror. One is reminded of Virginia Woolf and Sylvia Plath who saw monsters emerging from the depth of their inner mirrors. Difference is often experienced as negative by women and represented in their cultural production in terms of aberration or monstrosity. The Gothic genre can be read as female projection of an inner sense of inadequacy. In this perspective, the monster fulfils primarily a specular function, thereby playing a major role in the definition of female self-identity. *Frankenstein* – the product of the daughter of a historic feminist – is also the portrait of a deep lack of self-confidence and even deeper sense of displacement. Not only does Mary Shelley side with the monstrous creature, accusing its creator of avoiding his responsibilities, but she also presents Frankenstein as her abject body-double, which allows her to express self-loathing with staggering lucidity.

Gilbert and Gubar (1979) have argued that in English literature women have often depicted themselves as vile and degraded. Thus, they read Frankenstein as Mary Shelley's anti-Prometheus response to Milton and also as a tale of self-hatred. I think the latter is especially true of creative women, whom Virginia Woolf urged to 'kill the angel in the house' and confront the inner demons so as to stretch their resources to the limit. I read Mary Shelley's character of Frankenstein as mirroring the process of literary creation: he is isomorphic with the structure of Shelley's book – which is also rather badly structured and shapeless. Thereby it confronts the readers with the auto-referentiality that is the key to this genre's power to make us experience our limits. I find it a text that is affected by deep *malaise* which takes the form of an uneasy epistolary format with many flash-backs and

detours. The effect is one of unrest and torment also for the readers. Moreover, Mary Shelley on several occasions deliberately compares the text to
Frankenstein's monstrous body; a horrible, unfinished product, it portrays
the activity of writing as doomed to failure and basically unfulfilling.
Frankenstein is the becoming-writer of Shelley and he is a most imperfect
writing machine. His difficulties with comprehension and communication
reflect the circular logic of the process of writing, which delivers itself to
the pursuit of its own clarity. Graphic onanism, games of seduction and
repetition, writing is eroticized in the same way as the agony of longing, but
it offers little relief and even fewer rewards. The constant confrontation that
Shelley sets up between healthy normal human heterosexuality and the
sterile pleasures of the anthropomorphic monster stresses this point: that
creative writing does not pursue the sublime, but it rather courts disaster
and crime.

The metamorphic dimension fulfills another function. I argued earlier

Thus, Mary Shelley criticizes primarily the hubris of the scientists who
play God by creating artificial life: crazy little men locked up in their dungeons and masturbatory chambers, prey to matrix-envy and trying to turn
shit into gold or petrified matter into new life, swapping anatomy against a
new destiny. The ontological jealousy of the fallen angels working maniacally
so as to capitalize on time and space and achieve self-reproduction haunts
the writers also. A comparable folly inhabits also the creative spirit who
endlessly spills his or her fluids on the whiteness of the page in an endless
process of self-birth from which there is no escape. The circularity of the
writing process expresses a delirium of self-legitimation. All writing is simultaneously predatory, vampiristic and self-serving and no significant distance
separates the gloved hands of the creator from the hideous claws of the
monster. Through *Frankenstein*, Mary Shelley becomes herself such a writing
device, a depersonalized entity, a 'bachelor machine'. Baldick has argued
that Mary Shelley's masterpiece achieves a double sort of self-referentiality:
'both in its composition and in its subsequent cultural status miming the
central moments of its own story' (1987: 30). In a remarkable case of 'bib-
liogenesis' the process of artistic creation, the status of motherhood and the
birthing process all mirror each other and overlap constantly. Remembering
that Mary Shelley's mother Mary Wollstonecraft died as a result of giving
birth to her, the text, the body and the mother become one ungovernable
heap of excessive meanings, which explode *Frankenstein* outwards, into a
mythic dimension.

The metamorphic dimension fulfills another function. I argued earlier
that the monstrous as a borderline figure blurs the boundaries between
hierarchically established distinctions (between human and non-human,
Western and non-Western, etc.) and also between horizontal or adjacent
differences. In other words, the monstrous triggers the recognition of a
sense of multiplicity contained within the same entity, as Jane Gallop has

put it (1989). It is an entity whose multiple parts are neither totally merged with nor totally separate from the human observer. Thus, by blurring the boundaries of differentiation, the monstrous signifies the difficulty of keeping manageable margins of differentiation of the boundaries between self and other.

This problem with boundaries and differentiation is at the core of the mother–daughter question, following the analyses of Irigaray, Hirsch and Chodorow. Any daughter, that is, any woman, has a self that is not completely individuated but rather is constitutively connected to another woman – her mother. The term mother is already quite tangled and complex, being the site of a symbiotic mix-up, which – according to Lacan – requires the ordering power of the Law of the Father in order to restore the boundaries. This is also the line pursued by Barbara Johnson in 'My monster/My self' (an allusion to Nancy Friday's popular *My Mother/My Self*). Who is the monster? The mother or the self? Or does the monstrosity lie in the undecidability of what goes on in between? The inability to answer that question has to do with the difficulty of negotiating stable and positive boundaries with one's mother. The monstrous feminine is precisely the signpost of that structural and highly significant difficulty.

It is worth noting that in the eighties, feminist theory celebrated both the ambiguities and the intensity of the mother–daughter bond in positive terms – 'écriture féminine' and Irigaray's paradigm of 'the politics of sexual difference' being the epitome of this trend. As I argued in chapter 1, by the late nineties the maternalist/feminine paradigm was well under attack, if not discarded. This shift away from gynocentric psychoanalytic feminism towards a definitely bad attitude to the mother coincides, as often is the case in feminism, with a generation gap. Kolbowski argues (1995) that Melanie Klein's 'bad' mother has replaced the Lacanian-inspired 'vanilla sex' representation of the M/other as object of desire. Accordingly, parodic politics has replaced strategic essentialism and other forms of affirmative mimesis in feminist theories of difference. Nixon reads the anti-Lacanian climate of the nineties, best illustrated by the revival of interest in Melanie Klein's theory of the aggressive drives, 'in part as a critique of psychoanalytic feminist work of the 70's and 80's, privileging pleasure and desire over hatred and aggression' (Nixon 1995: 72).

I would like to situate the new alliance that is currently being negotiated between feminists and Deleuze in this context of historical decline of Lacan's theory of desire as lack and the revival of Klein's theory of the drives. Although a colder and more aggressive political sensibility is dominant in the nineties, I do not share in either the rejection of the mother, or in the denigration of the material/maternal feminine, which it entails. This does not mean that I am thrown back into the murky depths of uterine essentialism. My rejection of a position allegedly beyond gender, or of sexual indifferentiation, is rather framed by philosophical nomadism. That means that I value the processes of change and transformation as ways of actualizing a virtual feminine in a network of interconnections with other forces, entities and actors. Like Massumi, I do not take Deleuze as an incitement to drop politics, even basic emancipatory politics, but as a way of complexifying it by introducing movement, dynamism, nomadism into it. In chapters 2 and 3 I also called this open-ended, multi-layered virtual feminine met(r)amorphosis. The matrix is neither flesh nor metal, neither destiny nor teleology: it is motion, in spatial as well as temporal terms.

Hal Foster argues that in the late postmodernism of the 1990s advanced technological cultures have moved beyond the notion of the death of the subject, into a kind of 'traumatic realism' (Foster 1996: 131). There is a return of the 'real' subject, in opposition to the excessive emphasis placed in the 1980s on the textual models of culture or conventional notions of realism. A growing disillusionment with the psychoanalytic celebrations of desire as experimentation and mobility is also palpable, in reaction to the AIDS crisis and the general decline of the welfare state at the end of the millennium. What is significant, argues Foster, is that this cultural dissatisfaction is expressed as a return to the shocked subjectivity of a traumatized subject. Given that, as Arbus noted, freaks are born with their traumas written all over them and that they embody the actualized catastrophe, they emerge as a revived cultural paradigm. Cindy Sherman's artistic trajectory is telling in this regard: from the early romances through the history portraits to the abject disaster-pictures of today, she signifies the shift from a fascination with signs and the effects of representation on reality to the realization that the whole body is being cannibalized by a gaze that is disengaged from any signifying system.

Hence the return of horror, in Kristeva's sense of the blurring of boundaries, that is to say a cultural fascination with the amorphous, the shapeless, the obscene. This takes the negative form of the cult of wounded, diseased, traumatized bodies. Foster describes it as a contemporary form of advanced melancholia which expresses a real fatigue with the politics of difference and an equal attraction for indistinction and death. Aesthetically, it produces both the ecstatic fascination for a body that is invaded by the technological gaze and the horror of this invasion which leads to real despair and to a sense of loss.

In other words, in this historical context of late postmodernity, difference returns not merely in the classical postmodern format of the counter-subjectivities of women, blacks, on technological others. It now returns as the abject body and, ultimately, as the last frontier for traumatized subjects, namely as the corpse. This is a forensic twist to the crisis of the humanist subject: it provides experiential grounding and hence authority to the subject as scarred and scared witness, heroic and damaged survivor, that is to say something that cannot be contested. 'For one cannot challenge the trauma of another; one can only believe it, even identify with it, or not. In trauma discourse, then, the subject is evacuated and elevated at once' (Foster 1996: 168). The accident has happened and there is no going back: the scar is its signature. It is neither negative, nor positive: it simply points to our historicity. This paradox reconciles the conflicting movements of the crisis of the Majority and the reconstitution of emergent counter-identities by the minorities. For me, the critical question remains whether this aesthetic of trauma is the epitome of the cultural impoverishment of today, or an alternative formulation of possible forms of resistance.

I want to argue that, given the importance of both the social imaginary and the role of technology in coding it, we need to develop both forms of representation and of resistance that are adequate. Conceptual creativity is called for, and new figurations are needed, to help us think through the maze of techno-teratological culture.

What has also emerged from a closer analysis of the cyber-teratological imaginary of advanced cultures is the crucial and highly strategic role played by the maternal feminine within it. There is especially one aspect of the quasi-isomorphic relationship between the technological tool and the maternal body that I find quite significant. This has less to do with the classical technophobic objection that the machines are 'taking over' the uterus (Corea 1985a), than with a shift in the position of female reproductive powers. In a context of disruption of the time–space continuum of humanism and of generalized post-nuclear anxiety, what is being highlighted in popular culture is the threat of collapse of paternal authority under the impact of the excessive growth of female power. This singles out the suburban nuclear family as the privileged stage of the horror show (Greenberg 1991). This has been the case in popular culture ever since *The Exorcist*, and it is explicit already in Hitchcock's *Psycho*, not to speak of Romero's *Night of the Living Dead* and *Alien*, of course. Monstrous gestations are a way of upsetting the monotonous normativity of the suburban family.

Where does this leave the woman, however? She is not only reduced to maternal power, but that power is also displaced on to technology-based, corporate-owned reproductive production systems. In some ways, the corporations are the real moral monsters in all the popular science fiction and cyberpunk films: they corrupt, corrode, exploit and destroy ruthlessly. The global incubators in the cyber-nightmare of *The Matrix* speak for themselves.

In other words 'Mother' has become assimilated into the techno-industrial system; reproduction, especially the reproduction of white, male babies, is a primary asset in the post-capitalist cash-nexus, which also bred its own youngsters. The maternal body therefore is at the heart of the political economy of fear in late postmodernity. She simultaneously reproduces the possibility of the future and must be made to inscribe this futurity within the regime of high-tech commodification which is today's market economy. To hold the maternal/material feminine in this double bind creates an area of great turbulence. This costs empirical females, as Griggers pointed out, in a high degree of discontent, pathology and disease, which I analysed in chapter 1.

The immediate effect of this *topos* is to disengage the child, the foetus, the embryo and even the ova from the woman's body. Much has been written about these 'foetal attractions' (Petchesky 1987; Franklin 1997) and the appearance of the foetus as an independent item in popular imagery. These images are also instrumental to the anti-abortion campaigns of intimidation and terrorism, as the propaganda film *The Silent Scream* demonstrates. Sofia Zoe (1984) has analysed the embryological images attentively, and recommends that they be kept in the context of nuclear technology and the threat of extermination. According to Zoe, the extra-terrestrial embryological imagery which abounds in science-fiction films expresses the intense uterus-envy that is built into technological culture.

In *2001*, for instance, the spaceship's main computer is coated in maternal imagery including the umbilical cord that links the astronaut to the ship. Zoe defends the hypothesis that there is a clear displacement from female uterus to paternal brain via the male belly. This produces a modern-day version of the myth of the birth of Athena in classical Greek mythology: fully armed, from the father's head, bearing on her breastplate the image of the Medusa's head, forever frozen in her horrific gaze. Zoe also notes the recurrence of the father–daughter dyad in science fiction, from Rotwang and Maria in *Metropolis* to Dr Morbius's girl, Alta, in *Forbidden Planet*, to Rachael, the brainchild of the corporation in *Blade Runner*. There is a real trend for Athena-like figures of young warriors at the service of the system on whom the father or scientist or corporation projects the animated remains of what used to be the female mother–nature, by now cannibalized into the company-owned techno-matrix. The brain-womb of the corporation produces the 'star child' in a crystalline Cartesian geometrical space: high-tech super-mums integrated in advanced computer circuits. There is no sticky or messy 'wetware' here. The pure light of reason fortunately also produces its nightmares, the slimy bad alien creatures that the shiny warriors fight to the bitter end, like Ripley in *Alien*.

Confronted with such maternal-corporate-hightech powers, and with such ominous examples of women's free will, men are represented as the heroic resistance fighters. In *Terminator 1* the male prophet descends to earth in order to pave the way for the saviour and to ensure that the elected female does reproduce the future Messiah, thus saving the humans. A deeply-seated anxiety about re-establishing the paternal line of filiation translates into a new masculine determination to make women do the right thing. Spielberg and Lucas are the main authors in this fundamentally conservative approach to the corporate-run vision of reproduction, with the technological apparatus safely tucked away in a maternal role. Fortunately, there are exceptions. Cronenberg is the author who highlights the vulnerability of the male body – more on him in chapter 5.

Conclusion

The contemporary social imaginary, in a twist that strikes me as rather misogynist, places squarely on women the blame for the crisis of identity in postmodernity. In one of those double binds that occur so often in the representation of those who are marked off as different, women are simultaneously portrayed as the unruly element that needs to be straightened-out, cyber-amazons in need of some governance, and also, however, as already complicitous with and integrated into the industrial reproductive complex. 'Mother the bitch' is also 'serial mum', using and abusing her powers over life. Sofia Zoe puts it admirably: 'Superman has incorporated and taken over female functions to become a high-tech Supermom, who feeds and fertilizes us with junk food, spermatic images and silicon chips, and who tempts us with terminal apples' (Zoe 1984: 51).

Translated into the Deleuzian language of the becoming-woman, the maternal/material feminine is simultaneously the despotic face of the Majority and the pathetic face of its minorities. On her increasingly contaminated body, post-industrial culture fights the battle of its own renewal. To survive, advanced capitalism must incorporate the mother, the better to metabolize her offspring. This is also known as the 'feminization' of advanced cultures, in the sense of what I would call the becoming-woman of men.

Tania Modleski (1991) notes this tendency in contemporary post-feminist American culture as a whole. For instance women are identified with the most popular, i.e. low-brow, cultural consumeristic habits (talk-shows, soap-operas, etc.) thus leading to a 'feminization of culture' as a synonym for lack of high culture. Men however continue to be represented as the creative and autonomous spirits. In some ways, this continues a glorious nineteenth-century tradition of structural ambivalence towards women. Huyssen analyses it lucidly in the paradox of the masculine identification with women at the turn of the last century. Flaubert's 'Madame Bovary, c'est moi' goes hand-in-hand with the effective exclusion of real-life women from the literary enterprise. It also takes the form, in Flaubert then as in soap-operas today, of representing women as avid consumers of pulp – symbolizing the vulgarity of mass culture – while creative high culture and tradition remain firmly the prerogative of men.

The *Alien* film series operates a welcome feminist intervention in this area. It turns the 'new female monsters' engineered by late post-industrial techno-societies, into the heroic subjects who are most likely to save humanity from

its techno-activated annihilation: the feminist as the last of the humans.
J. H. Kavanagh (1990) argues that *Alien* in fact celebrates the rebirth of
humanism in the shape of progressive feminism. The struggle is internal to
the feminine and it takes place between an archaic monstrous feminine
represented by the alien and the postfeminist emancipated woman represented by Ripley/Sigourney Weaver. The alien is a *phallus dentatus* born
from a man's stomach, grotesquely erect most of the time and prone to
attempt oral rapes with its phallic tail. Ripley emerges by contrast as the
life-giving post-feminist principle. A warrior with a heart of gold, rescuing
pets and little girls as well as life in the galaxy as a whole, she is the new
humanist hero: woman as the saviour of mankind.

I think it would be far too predictable an ending, however, were an inter-
galactic Joan of Arc bearing Sigourney Weaver's ghostly white face[7] to
represent all feminism can do for a species in advanced state of crisis. Not
that saving humanity be an unworthy cause, but it is a role that historically
women have often been called upon to play – especially in times of war,
invasion, liberation struggles or other forms of daily resistance. They have,
however, seldom drawn any real benefits for their status in society from
these episodes of heroism. By the dawn of the third millennium, women's
participation in ensuring the future of humanity needs consequently to be
negotiated and not taken for granted. As Barbara Krueger put it: 'we don't
need another hero'.

Moreover, in the frame of the feminism of difference that I have defended
throughout this book, it would be a defeat to have the dialectics of the sexes
merely reversed to the benefit of women – mostly white, highly-educated
women – while leaving the power structures practically unchanged. I think it
would be more beneficial to all concerned if the tensions that are built into
the end-of-century crisis of values were allowed to explode also within feminism, bringing its paradoxes to the fore. Because I think that feminism is
definitely not about a quest for final authenticity, for the golden fleece of
truth, I believe that at the dawn of the new millennium we need to acquire a
flair for complicating the issues, so as to live up to the complexities of our
age. I would like feminists to avoid repetitions without difference and the
flat-out recomposition of genderized and racialized power differences on the
one hand, or on the other the equally unsatisfactory assumption of a morally superior triumphant feminine showing the one-way road to the future.

There is another consideration which can also help us understand the
relevance of a feminist nomadic approach. In late postmodernity, various
brands of nihilism are circulating. A whole philosophical style based on
'catastrophe' is popular among several prophets of doom, who contemplate
the implosion of humanism with tragic joy.[8] Nothing could be further
removed from the ethics of affirmation, and the political sensibility of
nomadic subjects, than the 'altered states' proposed by those who celebrate

the implosion of sense, meaning and values for their own sake. They end up producing histrionic renditions of that delirious megalomania against which I propose firmly and rigorously a sustainable definition of the self. It seems clear to me that a culture that is in the grip of a techno-teratological imaginary at a time of deep social and historical change is a culture that badly needs *less* abstraction and less hype. This has also to do with the economy of the spectral, that is to say the forever living dead of the media representation system: images live on forever, specially in the age of their digital manipulation. They circulate in a continuous present in a ghastly/ ghostly economy of vampiric consumption. This postmodern Gothic element is consequently overwhelming in today's highly mediamatic societies. The revenant icons of the stars live on, Marylin and Diana always already young and dead and returning endlessly to our attention.

I believe that, in such a context, a concretely embodied and embedded reading of the subject as a material, vitalistic, anti-essentialist but sustainable entity can be a profoundly sane reminder of the positive virtualities that lie in store in the crisis and transformation we are currently going through. This is a question of style, in the sense of a political and aesthetic sensibility. It is crucial to nurture a culture of affirmation and joy, if we are to pull out of the end-of-millennium stagnation. Cultivating the art of complexity – and the specific aesthetic and political sensibilities that sustain it – I plead for working with an idea of the subject as the plane of composition for multiple becomings. It is against the contemporary forms of nihilism that a critical philosophy of immanence needs to disintoxicate us and to re-set the agenda in the direction of affirmation and sustainable subjectivity. In this project, the metamorphic company of monsters – those existential aristocrats who have already undergone the mutation – can provide not only a solace, but also an ethical model.

5

Meta(l)morphoses: the Becoming-Machine

'In the city now there are loose components, accelerated particles; something has come loose, something is wriggling, lassoing, spinning towards the edge of its groove. Something must give and it isn't safe. You ought to be careful. Because safety has left our lives. It's gone forever. And what do animals do when you give them only danger? They make more danger, more, much more.'

Martin Amis, *Einstein's Monsters*, p. 32

'Can you hear us ?
– Yes.
– What do we sound like?
– You sound like machinery.
– Is it nice?
– It is beautiful.
– What kind of machinery ?
– Ordinary, eternal machinery.'

Leonard Cohen, *Beautiful Losers*, p. 204

Introduction

In the last chapter I surveyed some aspects of the contemporary social imaginary with regard to technology, embodiment and sexual difference. I can now proceed with the issue of cyber-technology directly. As usual, I will run a non-linear, rhizomatic argument. On the one hand I will suggest that feminist and other critics can use theories of becoming in order to overcome the conservative or nostalgic accounts of contemporary culture and societal transformations. On the other hand, firm feminist interventions are needed within philosophical nomadism in order to re-inscribe the politics of location and of sexual difference in the sense of a dissymmetry between the sexes, so as to allow for a critique of the power differentials that are grafted on those differences.

As I argued in chapter 4, the challenge that the hybrid, the anomalous, the monstrous others throw in our direction is a dissociation from the sensibility we have inherited from the nineteenth century, one which pathologized and criminalized differences. Conservative cultural critics even today tend to view anomalies or deviant differences as dangerous signs of decadence, that is to say both morally inadequate and epistemologically bankrupt. This is for me one of the clear signs of that deficit of imaginary energy, or downright symbolic misery, which is one of the defining features of postmodernity. I have argued that to overcome such a crisis, new conceptual creativity is necessary. In this chapter I would like to argue that we approach the anomalous and monstrously different others not as a sign of pejoration, but as the unfolding of virtual possibilities that point to positive developments and alternatives. Reformulated in Deleuze's language, this would mean that the contemporary cyber-technological imaginary, which I analysed extensively in the previous chapter, expresses simultaneously two contradictory tendencies, yearnings or political passions. As a reactive or negative reaction, it expresses the fear and the anxieties of the Majority, embodied in the dominant subject-position of the male, white, heterosexual, urbanized property-owning speaker of a standard language, at a historical time when His certainties are crumbling. As an active, or affirmative and empowering, act, it expresses the political passions of all the subjects, Majority-based or minority-inscribed, who have opted for transformative politics and processes of becoming. Contrary to most orthodox Deleuzians, I think the simultaneity of these patterns of becoming, which are dissymmetrical in their starting positions, also engender equally dissymmetrical expressions. The political economy of fear and terror, therefore, does not affect the Majority and his minorities in the same manner.

In this chapter, I will turn more closely to an aspect of contemporary culture which has been present throughout this book: the relationship of body and technology and more specifically the ways in which the human is now displaced in the direction of a glittering range of post-human technological variables. This is both exhilarating and painful to the collective anthropocentric hubris which thinkers have inherited from centuries of Western humanism. I will track down some of these phenomena and try to point out both the usefulness of a nomadic approach and the necessity of reconnecting it to feminist practices of sexual difference.

By emphasizing the notion of transformative changes, mutations and metamorphoses, I have tried to rethink the unity between these classical, polarized binaries. References to the bodily materialism and the notion of immanence in Irigaray and Deleuze have supported me in this task. I have quarrelled with Deleuze for his absence of attention to the extent to which sexual difference affects and invests also the patterns of becoming that he presents as complex and multiple, but sexually undifferentiated. I will pursue this line in this chapter, by arguing for parallelism and resonances between the sexualized (male and female) bodies and the machine or technological other. Moreover, in the discussion of Haraway's cyborgs alongside Deleuze's rhizomes, I will suggest that it is crucial to invent conceptual schemes which allow us to think the unity and the interdependence of the human, the bodily and of its historical 'others' at the very time when these others return to dislocate the foundations of the humanistic world-view. While pursuing this critical enquiry, however, I will never stop arguing that it is equally important not to forget the empowering aspects of the dissymmetry between the sexes, or the fundamental non-coincidence of the feminine and the masculine, that is to say their incommensurability.

In between what's between bodies and machines

We have already seen in the previous chapter that the contemporary imaginary about the bodily self or the embodied subject is techno-teratological, as shown by popular culture and especially cinema. This associative link, however, is also fostered by negative representations of different 'others' which recycle themes and images from the Gothic tradition and project them on to the techno-monsters of late post-industrial popular culture. An essential element of its monstrosity is an element of hybridity – that is to say the blurring of categorical distinctions or constitutive boundaries. Primary among them is the distinction between different species – the human, the animal, the organic other, the inorganic other, the technological.

The blurring of these categorical divides between self and others creates a sort of heteroglossia of the species, a colossal hybridization. Technology is at the heart of this process which combines monsters, insects and machines into a powerfully post-human approach to what we used to call 'the body'. To say that identity, sexuality and the body are transformed by this is at best an understatement. Arthur Kroker (1987: 181) sums up the situation of postmodernity in arguing that humans are

> No longer the Cartesian thinking subject, however, but a fractal subjectivity
> in an ultramodern culture where panic science is the language of power: no
> longer ratiocination to excess, but parallel processing as the epistemological
> form of postmodern consciousness . . . ; no longer the geometrically-focussed

and self-regulating body, but technologies of the body immune as key features of a libidinal economy that produces toxic bodies and designer aesthetics as its necessary conditions of operation; and no longer univocal (grounded) perspective, but the fatal implosion of perspective into the cyberspace of virtual technology.

How did it get to this? Let me attempt a cartography.

That machines should imitate and replace the human is by now common knowledge. How that works exactly and what its implications actually are, however, is not nearly so simple. Georges Canguilhem (1966) argues that a sort of primitive anthropomorphism is implicit in the technological artifact and is written into the whole history of technology. This assertion of the primacy of the living, biological organism over the technological implies that the mechanical or technological other imitates the organic or living organism. To be fair, Canguilhem argues also that the living organism is more than the sum of its organic parts. This is one of the reasons why the discourse about the interaction between the human and the technological, the organic and the inorganic, challenges the powers of theoretical reason. For Canguilhem, the technological other exceeds philosophy's capacity to represent it theoretically, because it marks a relation, a process, and representing processes is not something that philosophical reason excels at.

This applies with special force to the technological body-double, automaton or anthropomorphic machine. Canguilhem studies the history of such machines and their attempt to reproduce the functions and structures of the human organism. All technologies become bio-technologies. Especially since the nineteenth century, Western culture has been faced with the promise or threat of meta(l)morphoses, that is to say a generic becoming-machine. The great advantage of Canguilhem's technophilic bio-philosophy is that it paves the road for re-thinking the symbiotic relationship between the human and the technological. Thus, I would argue that Canguilhem's pioneer work on scientific teratology is one of the genealogical sources for contemporary cyborg-thought. One of the implications of this approach is that technology is not just the expression of the desire for mastery, but also an object of desire, curiosity and affective involvement. I will argue later on in this chapter, therefore, that this technophilic anthropomorphism has two side-effects: the eroticization of the technological other as a sexual surrogate and the Oedipalization of the human–machine interaction.

The automaton is a machine with the outward appearance of the human, capable of generating its own energy and following a pre-established programme. It thus combines and embodies distinctive features of the techno-monstrous other: it is inorganic but functional, and that means that it interacts with humans in terms of usefulness and productivity. Programmability and functionality are the key terms of these anthropomorphic machines and distinguish them from all others. They have haunted the human imagination since Antiquity and well before the mechanical realization of perfectly functional body-doubles. In Greek myths, for instance, technological skill is represented with the greatest ambivalence, as something divine but also daemonic. This is the case of the god Hephaistos, the blacksmith who is physically deformed and doomed to manufacture in the earth's entrails, like some insects, the tools and weapons that will change the face of the earth forever more. Half-god and half-slave, as Fiedler points out (1996), the master craftsman is an object of both admiration and aberration.

Though the term 'monster' must be reserved for animate or organic entities, I would argue for a structural analogy between the organic monster and the technological or anthropomorphic other. Body-doubles, robots or automates have in fact the same metamorphic effect on the human observers as the freaks I analysed in chapter 4. They are objects of wonder and terror, loathing and desire. As body-doubles, they represent a re-assembly of organic parts, often arranged in a new order. This arrangement follows the rule of organizing organs on monstrous bodies by excess, lack or displacements.

Quite often, for reasons of convenience as well as playfulness, the re-arrangement of organic parts in the mechanical body-double expresses a fantastic array of alternative body-shapes, bodily functions, morphologies and sexualities. As such, the technological anthropomorphic machine is an object of imaginary projections and fantasy. It is half insect and half metal, as in the worst science-fiction horror movie. The automaton lends itself to such fantasmatic usages and it therefore plays a paradoxical role within scientific discourse. On the one hand it exemplifies the potency of scientific rationality to master life and the living, on the other hand it defies rational understanding. While being very much itself, the mechanical body-double is also irrevocably other. It is consequently positioned in ways that are analogous to the classical 'others' of modernity, which I outlined in chapter 1: the sexual, the ethnic and the natural others. As such it embodies the paradox of an irreducible singularity that serves as the model of expression for the innermost human faculties, while it renders them as external functions autonomous from the subject.

This level of complexity creates analogies between the automaton and the monstrous others. Like the Frankensteinian body-double, the automaton is a mixture of detachable parts and organs, a collage or montage of pieces. As such it is deceptively functional: the product of the imagination as much as of reason, the automaton is marked by ambiguity and polyvalence. It appears to go as far as humans in its imitation of living matter, and yet it is only a rationalistic scheme, closed upon itself and basically useless. It is linked to the monstrous through the mixture of fascination and horror which it provokes by being such a liminal borderline figure. It triggers a free play of the imagination, not unlike the Medusa's head of Freud and other figurations of the monstrous maternal feminine. The early historical versions of the robot were regarded as semi-magical and thus prompted reactions of both love and fear. The automaton is monstrous because it blurs the boundaries, it mixes the genres, it displaces the points of reference between the normal – in the double sense of normality and normativity – and its 'others'.

The simulation of the human is especially strong in the extent to which the technological other imitates sexual organs, activities and energies. Machines fulfil a fundamental libidinal structure, which mimes the workings of sexual energy. They question the boundary between the functional and the gratuitous, productivity and waste, moderation and excess. Machines make connections, cogs and spikes and tubes penetrate each other with fierce and mindless energy. From Eisenstein to Cronenberg the erotic power of the machine has not failed to impress film-makers, artists and activists. Some of them have not hesitated to stress the theatricality of the machines, their pure, un-productive representational value as 'bachelor machines', that is to say pure objects of play and pleasure, utterly deprived of functionalism. Anybody who has admired the Tanguely-designed fountain outside the Centre Pompidou in Paris, or any of the 'objects' of the surrealists, will recognize that sensation. This gratuitousness is central to the erotic power of the machine. The decorative function of machines has also been explored and exploited in clockwork machinery, music boxes, street organs, 'tableaux vivants' of all sorts, then the dolls and toys of the rich and powerful from the seventeenth century onwards. Like freaks, automata are for display and the delight of children of all ages.

Moreover, anthropomorphic machines, being eroticized as objects of imaginary projection and desire, titillate our sexual curiosity and trigger off all kinds of questions about sexuality and procreation. For instance, in the Renaissance, given the absence of clear demarcation lines between the human and the exact sciences, the automaton was explicitly involved in the discussion about the artificial procreation of life. The two issues, the machine and artificial reproduction, are linked intuitively in the alchemical imagination. Thus Paracelsus' theories of the 'homunculus' is the most explicit expression of this moment in the scientific imagination. Based on the notion of the priority of the sperm as a conceiving agent, these are theories of extra-uterine birth which support the fantasy of self-engendering. The eighteenth century marks the beginning of the philosophical period of reflection on machines: Descartes, Leibnitz and Pascal were among the first to build automates and be fascinated by them. The mechanical double of the human is both the exemplification of human qualities and their transcendence: it is both the rigorous application of scientific rationality and a model for it, as its logic is vastly superior to the human. Perfect artifact, the automate is artificial ruse that unveils and enacts the rules of human intelligence. It marks the troublesome proximity of the organic and the inorganic, the inanimate and the animate. Body without soul, it is at the heart of the problem of Cartesian dualism. The materialist rationalism of the eighteenth century sides the automaton with the soul-less animals, but it also makes it ask the key questions of the boundaries and therefore the limits of demarcation between the human and its others, animal or machine.

These lines of demarcation are re-shuffled and blurred in the age of modernity. Following Foucault's genealogy, I want to suggest that modernity challenges the classical, rationalist distinctions between mind and body and poses instead the issue of the structure of human embodiment as a problem in its own rights. The structures and functions of the living organism (*bios*) emerge as a specific item that calls for new tools of analysis. Recognized intrinsic qualities of the living organism *Zoe* challenge traditional discursive hierarchies. Darwin, Freud and Nietzsche join forces, albeit in radically different ways, in decentring the equation of subjectivity with rational consciousness. Psychoanalysis accomplishes the 'splitting' of the subject, by drawing a formidable line of demarcation between conscious and unconscious processes. The technological artifact comes to be inscribed in this contested, in-between area.

Thus the steam-engine provides Freud with the fundamental metaphor for libidinal desire. In keeping with nineteenth century mechanics and the laws of thermodynamics, the view of the libidinal subject as a steam-engine simultaneously announces the crisis of humanism and open up the dimension of the unconscious as untapped energy. Wiener (1948) in his influential classification of technological artifacts, defined the nineteenth century as a whole as the age of the steam-engine. The psychoanalytic discourse on the libido as the hidden motor of the subject connects desire to the machinelike, or technological, in both internal and external ways: internally, as the built-in energy and source of motion of the subject, externally, it points instead to an increasing standardization of human existence, which translates into the tensions and neuroses that Freud's patients bring into psychoanalysis. In both cases, the technological factor acts as a powerful bridge-maker or in-between player in designing the context of modernity.

As I argued in the previous section, in so far as the technological body–other has both a metamorphic and a paradigmatic function in representing the human organism, it also fulfils the role of sexual metaphor. The technological or mechanical other is libidinally charged in that it represents a connection, a link or an in-between. Such transition zones are heavily genderized. Thus, in a classical image of modernist utopia, the film *Metropolis* represents technology as embodied in a female robot. This 'machine-vamp' (Huyssen 1986) embodies a fundamental ambivalence towards technology: on the one hand it stresses its destructive potential, on the other its progressive and euphoric force. That the android be given a female form, while her creator is male, is such an obvious topos, argues Huyssen, that the director Lang does not even feel the need to explain the female features of the robot: it is the other, like woman and nature, firmly under male control and fully subjected to male desire. As virgin-mother or prostitute-vamp, the robot recycles basic male fantasies about woman.

One of the sources for the female robot Maria in Fritz Lang's *Metropolis* is the female android Hadaly in Villiers de l'Isle-Adam's masterpiece *L'Eve future* (1977), which exemplifies the modernist aesthetics of the machine in a number of ways. Firstly it casts the technological other in the female mould and the feminine mode. Contrary to Mary Shelley, who refuses to reproduce the female body-double, thus condemning Frankenstein to the ungrateful role of sterile 'bachelor machine', the nineteenth-century technological imaginary had no problems in actualizing the invention of the perfect female robot.

Secondly, modernist anthropomorphic machines function by the aesthetics of resemblance. Hadaly is the exact body-double of the all-too-human Alicia Clary. She is doubly monstrous in her perfect likeness and also because her birth is unnatural and man-made. The gap between the original and the copy, nature and culture, plays to the detriment of the former. Alicia, the embodied female, is endowed with sumptuous beauty but a very mediocre mind. In his longing for perfection, the creator-engineer Edison, like a modern Prometheus of reason, manufactures through a special technique called 'photo-sculpture' (p. 259) a soul that is suitable to Alicia's divine beauty. The empirical female is thus photo-cast and projected on a man-made android, Hadaly. As Wollen argued (1989), in the nineteenth century the mechanical other is still a very unique and personalized artifact, which lends itself to erotic fantasies.

Thirdly, this very sexualized and genderized operation is presented as integral to the logic of the nineteenth-century market economy. *L'Eve future* expresses the desire to perfect the female sex as fetishized, commodified, mechanical body-other, a topos that is dominant in the social imaginary of modernity. As Raymond Bellour (1991) has pointed out, Hadaly is the pure manifestation of industrial culture, which will invent the term robot in 1920 to designate the new class of industrial slaves:[1] she is made in the image of the Man who is made in God's own image. It is just, it is biblical and it is the principle of mechanical reproduction in that it redefines the relationship betwen the original and the copy. This also entails as a corollary the loss of the 'aura', that is to say that wonder and fear for that mixture of evil and magical powers traditionally associated with the body-doubles (cf. W. Benjamin 1968: 217–51).

Fourthly, the robot is actually better than the human; the copy is superior to the original. This superiority is defined not only in aesthetic but also in moral terms. The machine-like body-double has been perfected: it is the artifice elevated to the highest possible degree of sophistication. Industrial civilization is far superior to nature and the automaton represents a surface that awaits activation, just as in Christian thought the body awaits the mind in order to start living. *Bios* triumphs over *Zoe*. The closest parallel here is between the corpse and the robot, in so far as they both beg the question of finding a source of energy which would allow them to function. Like a soul that seeks incarnation, like a piece of metal ignited by the divine force of electricity, the (female) robot is a potential life longing to be actualized. The metaphysics of substance and the question of energy and motion are played out through the mediation of the technological body-double.

Fifthly, this is all related to the question of female identity, or the 'dark mystery' of femininity. The idea of woman's alienation from herself was fairly common in 1889 and scientists, led by Charcot and his student Freud, were seeking for an answer to the mystery. In *L'Eve future* the question of identity is linked to the fulfilment of desire in man; just like Pygmalion, the android female is an emanation of the male unconscious and the new spirit of the age and of mankind. Although Hadaly's genesis is well known to us, as she is an artifact, we still end up by losing sight of the father's mark. By replacing Alicia Clary, Hadaly successfully dismisses Edison's labour, his power and his knowledge. The work of art is erased, and in its place appears a subject. This emancipated subject abolishes the father's signature, and his very identity, in a move which shifts the play of uncanny resemblances into the domain of monstrosity (Huet 1983). Villiers acts out the nineteenth century's dream, giving a new twist to the image of the body-machine, but he plays a tricky game with sex. While she may be equipped with a sublime body, Hadaly remains completely ideal. Her overwhelming sensual attraction, borrowed from Alicia's beauty, is spiritualized: she is also an angel of fire and of light, a symbol of electricity, she is simultaneously sexless and highly eroticized. The idea is in one respect a simple one: Hadaly is a bodiless body. Genitality and the capacity to procreate are impossibilities for a machine, as they are for the monstrous Frankenstein. Edison is proposing to Lord Ewald a blend of hypnosis and love, or rather, a state of love under hypnosis. Freed from all sexuality, fixing love in the heat of its first moment, the android induces a transcendental form of eroticism.

Felicia Miller Frank (1995) stresses one of the paradoxes of the female techno-body. Crucial to Hadaly's power is the sublime female voice: in fact Hadaly is a acoustic body-machine, or an anthropomorphic music-box, she is phonograph-woman, 'the artificially incarnated bearer of a disembodied voice' (Miller Frank 1995: 5). The objectification of her voice mirrors the continuing objectification of woman in society. As such, it is the site of great ambivalence, echoing the affective plenitude of the mother's body, but also undermining the possibility of female subjectivity. She also signals quite powerfully, however, the advent of a new era in which technological innovation will challenge the human.

Constance Penley (1985: 39) argues that from about 1850 to 1925 numerous artists, writers and scientists imaginatively or in reality constructed anthropomorphized machines to represent the relation of the body to the social, the interrelationships of the sexes, the structure of the psyche, or the workings of history. Characteristically, the bachelor machine, as it is often called, is a closed, self-sufficient machine. Its common themes include frictionless, sometimes perpetual, motion, an ideal time and the magical possibility of its reversal, electrification, voyeurism and masturbatory eroticism, the dream of the mechanical reproduction of art, and artificial birth or reanimation. But no matter how complicated the machine becomes, the control over the sum of its parts rests with a knowing producer who therefore submits to a fantasy of closure, perfectibility and mastery. Penley also suggests that the bachelor machine's strict requirements for perpetual motion, the reversibility of time, mechanicalness, electrification, animation and voyeurism has characteristics that reminds us of another modernist apparatus: the cinema.

The configuration of the technological body-double alters considerably in postmodernity and especially since the post-nuclear predicament. As I argued in chapter 4, with nuclear power and its related environmental and genetic side-effects, science and technology have ceased to be the enactment of a future of liberation and spell out instead the new political economy of fear for the accident or the imminent catastrophe. The imaginary of disaster comes to mark advanced societies; since the 1950s, horror movies show the sequence: alien–monster–other as a technologically-driven process of devolution or disaster. Nuclear radiation, as well as a range of contaminations that are viral in structure and environmental in their expressions, cause human evolution to regress. The human organism implodes under the strain, exposing the vulnerability of the species. An explosive link is thus established between the human, technology, the natural environment and the evolutionary traits of humanity, enhanced and challenged by the new technologies. The historical era of postmodernity is marked by a new and perversely fruitful alliance with technology which stresses the proximity, familiarity and increased intimacy of the relation between the human and the technological universe. At such a time of important relocations for cultural and political practices of interaction with the technological universe, I would plead for resistance to both the fatal attraction of nostalgia and the fantasy of techno-utopias. I shall return to this.

I find that in opposition to these regressive trends, 'minor' cultural genres cultivate an ethics of lucid self-awareness. Some of the most moral beings left in Western postmodernity are the science-fiction writers who linger on the death of the humanist ideal of 'Man', thus inscribing this loss – and the ontological insecurity it entails – at the (dead) heart of contemporary cultural concerns. By taking the time to symbolize the crisis of humanism, these creative writers push the crisis to its innermost resolution. In so doing, they also strip the veneer of nostalgia that covers up the inadequacies of the present cultural (dis)order. I would like to suggest that some of the most innovative interventions on the contemporary crisis are feminist cultural and media activists such as the riot girls and other 'cyber-feminists'. Some of these creative minds are prone to theory, others – feminist science-fiction writers and other 'fabulators' (Barr 1987) like Angela Carter, Laurie Anderson and Kathy Acker – choose the fictional and the multi-media mode.

It would be a mistake, however, to think that the cyber-imaginary of techno-bodies is merely a symptom of fear, or cultural trend, a literary or utopian figuration lacking substantial social, economic and political implications. I rather think that the cyber-imaginary is powerfully active throughout the social fabric and in all the modes of representation prompted by our culture at present. Claudia Springer (1991) argues that a discourse celebrating the union of humans and electronic technology is currently circulating with equal success among the scientific community as in popular culture.

I want to start therefore from the assumption that the cyborg as a technologically-enhanced body-machine is the dominant social and discursive figuration for the interaction between the human and the technological in post-industrial societies. It is also a living or active, materially embedded cartography of the kind of power-relations that are operative in the post-industrial social sphere. Thus, Chasin (1995) argues that electronic technology, mostly the computer, disrupted in a creative manner the centuries-old distinction between human and machines, or humans and non-humans. Electronic machines are, from this angle, quite emblematic, as they are immaterial: plastic boxes and metal wires that convey information. They do not 'represent' anything, but rather carry clear instructions and reproduce clear information patterns. They work and in so doing sum up to perfection the genealogy of machines as industrial slaves.

Contemporary information and communication technologies, however, go even further in that they exteriorize and duplicate electronically the human nervous system, which has prompted a shift in our field of perception: the visual modes of representation have been replaced by sensory-neuronal modes of simulation. Images can be shot into the cortex and not merely projected into the retina. This shift is not without implications for human consciousness and its relations to sensory data perception. As Cecil Helman put it:

> Now there are prosthetic organs of plastic, metal, nylon and rubber. There are artificial heart valves and bones, synthetic arteries, corneas and joints, larynx and limbs, teeth and oesophagus. There are machines implanted inside the body, and outside on its surface. The heart beats now to the electrical rhythms of a tiny pacemaker. There are hearing aids and iron lungs, dialysis machines and incubators. In this century, a new body has been born, an ancestor of the cyborgs. (Helman 1991: 25)

Cyber-entities and techno-organisms proliferate in the age of artificial intelligence. Scott Bukatman argues (1993: 259) that: 'the computer alone is narrated as a prosthetic extension, as an addictive substance, as a space to enter, as a technological intrusion into human genetic structures and finally as a replacement for the human in a posthuman world'. The escalation of the interface between the human and the electronic machine is telling: from juxtaposition to superimposition until finally the technology supersedes the human. Bukatman argues that this projection of the physical self into an artificial environment feeds into a dream of terminal identity outside the body, a sort of 'cybersubject' (1993: 187). This exemplifies the worst tendencies of postmodern disembodiment and new-age fantasies of cosmic redemption via technology (think of the 'Starchild' of the film *2001*). Ultimately, these different ways of escaping from the body tend to suggest or yearn for the abolition of death, in an evolutionary perspective of more-than-the-human.

I find that a rather complex kind of relationship has emerged in the cyber universe which we inhabit: one in which the link between the flesh and the machine is symbiotic and therefore can best be described as a bond of mutual dependence. This engenders some significant paradoxes, especially when it comes to the human body. The corporeal site of subjectivity is simultaneously denied, in a fantasy of escape, and strengthened or re-enforced. Balsamo stresses the paradoxical concomitance of effects surrounding the new techno-bodies:

> even as techno-science provides the realistic possibility of replacement body parts, its also enables a fantastic dream of immortality and control over life and death. And yet, such beliefs about the technological future 'life' of the body are complemented by a palpable fear of death and annihilation from un-controllable and spectacular body-threats: antibiotic-resistant viruses, random contamination, flesh-eating bacteria. (Balsamo 1996: 1–2)

One explicit way in which contemporary culture has fulfilled the Frankensteinian fantasy is in the proliferation of transplants and implants, in the 'spare-part' surgery or prosthetic body-technologies. In fact, how realistic is the fantasy of cybernetic fusion between the human body and the technological support-system? R. M. Rossiter (1982) analyses the human–machine interaction in the case of dialysis patients before and after organ transplant. He stresses the dependency conflicts as well as the psychosexual disfunctions connected to the sense of intrusion and mutilation of one's body. The transplanted organ (the new kidney) tends to become the site of a conflict: it is fantasized as a malignant other, or on the contrary as a baby that needs to be nurtured; it also promotes identification with the donor or the donor's corpse. More poignant still is the extent to which the donated organ is constructed as an intruder that interrupts or definitely terminates the patient's relationship to the dialysis machine. That life-support system had become a maternal and reassuring site of semi-magical safety and also suspension of responsibility and judgement. The life-giving organ can therefore be perceived as an invader and a destroyer.

Celia Lury (1998) also analyses the rise of 'prosthetic culture', which challenges possessive individualism and some of the traditional properties of the human: consciousness, embodiment and unity. They are now replaced by experimentation, negotiations and artificial environments. The political economy of commodification promotes organ-snatching on a global scale. The 'mother-machine' I described at the end of chapter 4 marks the fusion of the womb with the computer network; the cortex and the spinal column are the ultimate 'axial cable' (Hayward and Wollen 1993: 6). The body is fully immersed in a flow of technological effects.

Vivian Sobchack (1995), speaking from her experience of undergoing major cancer surgery on her thigh with the eventual need for amputation and the addition of a prosthetic leg, literally brings us back to our senses by reminding us of the pain of actually becoming a cyborg. The wounds and deprivation imposed on the corporeal subject are such as to deflate any fantasy of being superseded by the machine. Sobchack offers instead a powerful and sobering reminder:

> What many surgeries and my prosthetic experience have really taught me is that, if we are to survive into the next century, we must counter the millennial discourses that would decontextualize our flesh into insensate sign or digitize it into cyberspace. . . . Prosthetically enabled I am, nonetheless, not a cyborg. Unlike Baudrillard, I have not forgotten finitude and naked capacities of my flesh nor, more importantly, do I desire to escape them. (209–10)

Sobchack is not alone in finding the fragility of her enfleshed self significant, both as a way of resisting the hype that surrounds the new technologies, and as the basis for an ethics of recognition of a common – albeit technologically enhanced – humanity and our common condition of mortality. The ethical issue is crucial to the whole discussion of non-unitary subjects, of bodies without organs and organs disengaged from bodies. I would like to add to this list the question of the status of sexual difference, to which I will return in a later section.

Bios/zoe meets technos

Against metaphysics

Philosophical nomadism acknowledges the techno-cultural status of contemporary corporeality, but it also challenges some of its self-destructive or nihilistic tendencies with reference to the key concepts of bodily materialism and immanence. I will argue that Deleuze's emphasis on anti-essentialist vitalism and complexity is not a recipe for cybernetic fantasies of escape from the body, but rather a rigorous call for re-thinking human embodiment in a manner that is co-extensive with our technological habitat. Deleuze shows that both the established ideas of the Organic and those of the mechanical world are equally Molar, or sedentary – or Majority – based. In terms of technology, they result in the humanistic vision of assembled parts working together to create a harmonious and well-functioning whole. In opposition to this holistic view of the mechanical world, Deleuze will defend a molecular, machine-like one, which is about becomings, without ultimate purpose or finality, a kind of generalized 'becoming-bachelor-machine'.

The starting-point for Deleuze is analogous to that of the becoming-animal, namely that the Western idea of the machine is impregnated with Platonic assumptions about a fundamental divide between the human and its others – technological or biological, racialized or sexualized as they may be. Between the human and the machine there is an ontological divide which is constitutive of human subjectivity. Heidegger puts this clearly (1993: 244):

> Technology is in its essence a destiny within the history of being and the truth of being, a truth that lies in oblivion. . . . As a form of truth technology is grounded in the history of metaphysics which is itself a distinctive and up to now the only perceptible phase of the history of Being.

Heidegger both humanizes technology and makes it part of the human's capacity for ecstatic ex-centricity (standing beside oneself in conscious self-reflexivity) which he sees as constitutive of the human subject. Go back to chapter 3 for this point: postmodernity is the historical time when such ontological distinctions collapse, much to Heidegger's chagrin. The 'others' return in the form of renewed concerns, alternatively experienced as sources of anxiety or as possibilities for new subject-positions. Again, philosophical nomadism takes its distance from this view.

The ordinary sound of well-oiled machinery spells out the rhythms of eternity – it paraphrases and mimes the notion of living organisms and thus functions as a metaphor for life. In this respect, the 'machine', understood in the abstract sense proposed by Deleuze, bears a privileged bond with the becoming-imperceptible, in the sense of an empirical transcendental yearning for dissolution into and merging with one's environment. I discussed this in relation to the becoming-animal of chapter 3. The merger of the human with the technological, or the machine-like, not unlike the symbiotic relationship between the animal and its habitat, results in a new compound, a new kind of unity. In the perspective of philosophical nomadism which I defend, this is neither holistic fusion nor Christian transcendence – it rather marks the highlight of radical immanence. It is not a biology but an ethology of forces – an ethics of mutual interdependence.

This present situation brings out to the extreme the contradictions of the 'post-nuclear' situation. Nuclear power historically also inaugurates the debate about genetic mutations. It combined the classical theme of human hubris – the fantasy of omnipotence – with the biblical theme of the wrath of God that destroys the earth and returns it, cleansed, to the cosmic soup from whence it had emerged over centuries of evolution. The evolutionary theme is consequently built into the discussion of mutations, hybrids and post-humanist conditions. This means that issues of ethics, ecological sustainability and bio-centred egalitarianism are especially relevant here. In opposition to the nostalgia and conservatism of the 1950s, throughout the 1990s post-industrial culture fell in love with its own techno-monstrous others also and especially with the 'monsters within'. Eric White (1995: 252) argues that contemporary evolutionary thinking posits the body as a composite that contains the traces of its long and painful biological history: 'the body is not a perfectly resolved unity endowed with a unique and everlasting essence but an evolutionary makeshift, a historically contingent contrivance whose genealogical affiliation with every other kind of organism is manifest throughout.'

This points to an ancestral continuity between the human and its previous incarnations at different stages of its evolution, a kind of genetic legacy, a trans-species proximity, which bio-technologies bring out and exploit cleverly. Exit Heidegger and enter instead the private horror museum depicted in *Alien IV*, where the heroine is able to see the earlier versions of herself, dutifully conserved in a bio-technological laboratory which traces her evolutionary history as a perfect clone of herself. I cannot think of a better image for the post-human predicament than this set of duplicates or simulacra, which have fed upon the original organism, consuming it like parasites; horrific, unholy technologically-mediated births of copies from copies, cells multiplying from cells in a DNA-driven display of life as a multiplicity of force that encompass both *zoe* and *bios*.

Post-human bodies

The model of the body proposed by the brand of philosophical nomadism I am defending is symbiotic interdependence. This points to the co-presence of different elements, from different stages of evolution: like inhabiting different time-zones simultaneously. The human organism is neither wholly human, nor just an organism. It is an abstract machine, which captures, transforms and produces interconnections. The power of such an organism is certainly neither contained by nor confined to consciousness.

Shaviro (1995) describes this shift in terms of a new paradigm: we are at the end of the post-nuclear model of embodied subjectivity and we have entered the 'viral' or 'parasitic' mode. This is a graphic way of explaining the extent to which today's body is immersed in a set of technologically-mediated practices of prosthetic extension. Read with Deleuze, this mode is anything but negative, expressing the co-extensivity of the body with its environment or territory, which is one of the salient features of the 'becoming-animal'. A body is a portion of forces life-bound to the environment that feeds it. All organisms are collective and interdependent. Parasites and viruses are hetero-directed: they need other organisms. Admittedly, they relate to them as incubators or hosts, releasing their genetically encoded message with evident glee. This expresses a selfish cruelty that horror movies capture perfectly, but it is a mere detail in a much broader picture. Although Shaviro plunges into what strikes me as a sentimental neo-Nietzchean celebration of the splendour of this relentless unfolding of *zoe*, I take the conceptually solid point here to be that the virus or parasite constitutes a model of a symbiotic relationship that defeats binary oppositions. It is a simulacrum that duplicates itself to infinity without any representational pretensions. As such it is an inspiring model for a nomadic eco-philosophy.

The analogy with human reproduction is picked up by Shaviro, who argues that it also involves 'vampirism, parasitism and cancerous simulation. We are all tainted with viral origins, because life itself is commanded and impelled by something alien to life. The life possessed by a cell, and all the more so by a multicellar organism, is finally only its ability to carry out the orders transmitted to it by DNA and RNA' (Shaviro 1995: 41).

I find this a rather problematic version of an otherwise important point about the primacy of life: Shaviro seems to abdicate all responsibility before the alleged dictatorship of the viral, proliferating class (no metaphor intended). Mindful of the warnings of Sobchack, I resist this hasty dismissal of the complexities of the corporeal self. This is for me a form of bio-centred nihilism which borders on moral irresponsibility. It also misunderstands the state of contemporary science, attributing to DNA immense powers which it does not possess. I therefore want to disagree with this kind of over-simplified glorification of raw, 'animal' life. I am as opposed to this hype about genetic determinism as I am to all other hypes surrounding new technologies: a new mix, a more balanced combination of elements, needs to be negotiated. Complexities are all very well, but the unity of matter cannot lead to bio-based cynicism and nihilistic dismissal of the paradoxes which define the human species.

The human body is fully immersed in systems of reception and processing of information: that which emanates from its genetic structures, as much as that which is relayed by satellites and wired circuits throughout the advanced world. As Hurley points out, however, the significant thing about post-human bodies is not only that they occupy the spaces in between what is between the human and the machines, that is to say a dense materiality, post-human bodies are also surprisingly generative, in that they stubbornly and relentlessly reproduce themselves. The terms of their reproduction, as I pointed out in the previous two chapters, are slightly off-beat by good old human standards, in that they involve animal, insect, and inorganic models. In fact they represent a whole array of possible alternative morphologies and 'other' sexual and reproductive systems. The paradigm of cancerous proliferation of cells is mentioned as an example of this mindless self-duplicating capacity of generative or viral life. Critics like Halberstam and Livingston are quick to point out how this generative disorder in contemporary molecular biology and genetics is both echoed and implemented by the everyday 'gender trouble' going on in societies where sexed identities and organic functions are in a state of flux.

Consequently, the post-human body is not merely split or knotted or in process: it is shot through with technologically-mediated social relations. It has undergone a meta(l)morphosis and is now positioned in the spaces in between the traditional dichotomies, including the body–machine binary opposition. In other words, it has become historically, scientifically and culturally impossible to distinguish bodies from their technologically-mediated extensions. Halberstam and Livingston conclude (1995: 19): 'Queer, cyborg, metametazoan, hybrid, PWA; bodies-without-organs, bodies-in-process, virtual bodies: in unvisualizable amniotic indeterminacy, and un-fazed by the hype of their always premature and redundant annunciation, posthuman bodies thrive in the mutual deformations of totem and taxonomy.' Whereas contemporary culture tends to react to the cyber-world according to the double-pull I have criticized throughout this book, on the one hand the hype and on the other hand the nostalgia, I would plea for a more 'passionately distant' approach. A form of neo-materialist appreciation of the body would be helpful here, to think through the kind of techno-teratological universe we are inhabiting. Rethinking the embodied structure of human subjectivity requires an ethics of lucidity, as well as powers of innovation and creativity. I wish to avoid references to paradigms of human nature (be it biological, psychic or genetic essentialism) while taking fully into account the fact that bodies have indeed become techno-cultural constructs immersed in networks of complex, simultaneous and potentially conflicting power-relations. I do not want to fall, however, into either moral relativism or the suspension of ethical judgement.

I would define this approach as a nomadic evolutionary thought which contrasts openly with contemporary bio-technological determinism. What comes especially under scrutiny in this perspective is the anthropocentrism that is in-built in so much evolutionary, biological, scientific and philosophical thought. Radically immanent philosophical nomadism, on the other hand, sponsors a subject that is composed of external forces, of the non-human, inorganic or technological kind. It is territorially based, and thus environmentally bound. The 'machine-like' in Deleuze's thought refers to this dynamic process of unfolding subjectivity outside the classical frame of the anthropocentric humanistic subject, re-locating it into becomings and fields of composition of forces and becomings.

This is as far removed from the advanced capitalist hype about technology as the future of humanity as can be. The latter constitutes an all-pervasive master-narrative of flight from the human embodied self, into the fake transcendence of a machine that strikes me as molar, Oedipalizing, despotic and exploitative. It is against this social imaginary of techno-transcendence that I want to argue for a more dissipative, eroticized and flowing interaction between the human and the bio-technological: an evolution of the non-teleological but nomadological kind.

The next step is a question about fast-growing and often contradictory discourses about techno-bodies circulating in post-industrial societies: how do they relate to and intersect with the bodily materialism and philosophy of radical immanence? Before I can approach such a question, however, I need to re-open another window, which not surprisingly is related to the all-too-human practice of sexuality.

Sexual difference in cyber times

Following the poststructuralist redefinition of bodily materialism, I want to take as the starting-point the paradox of the simultaneous over-exposure and disappearance of the body in the age of postmodernity. This results in a proliferation of discourses about, and practices of knowledge over, the body. Balsamo (1996: 5) states: 'A range of new visualization techniques contributes to the fragmentation of the body into organs, fluids and gene codes, which in turn promotes a self-conscious self-surveillance, whereby the body becomes an object of intense vigilance and control.' This engenders the simultaneous explosion of the body into a network of social practices (dieting, medical control and pharmaceutical interventions), as well as an implosion of the body as the fetishized and obsessive object of concern and care. I discussed this in chapter 2.

Bio-power constructs the body as a multi-layered entity that is situated over a multiple and potentially contradictory set of variables. Within the philosophical tradition, the genealogy of the embodied nature of the subject can be ironically rendered as Descartes's nightmare, Spinoza's hope, Nietzsche's complaint, Freud's obsession, Lacan's favourite fantasy, Marx's omission, a piece of meat activated by electric waves of desire, a text written by the unfolding of genetic encoding. Neither a sacralized inner sanctum, nor a pure socially-shaped entity, the enfleshed Deleuzian subject is rather an 'in-between': it is a folding-in of external influences and a simultaneous unfolding outward of affects, a mobile entity, an enfleshed sort of memory that repeats and is capable of lasting through sets of discontinuous variations, while remaining faithful to itself. The contemporary body is ultimately an embodied memory.

The techno-bodies of late post-industrial societies can and should be understood in the light of the increasingly complex amount of information that contemporary science has been able to provide about them. With reference to molecular biology, genetics and neurology – to mention just a few – the body today can and should be described adequately and with serious credibility also as a sensor, an integrated site of information networks. It is also a messenger carrying thousands of communication systems: cardio-vascular, respiratory, visual, acoustic, tactile, olfactory, hormonal, psychic, emotional, erotic. Co-ordinated by an inimitable circuit of information transmission, the body is a living recording system, capable of storing and then retrieving the necessary information and processing it at such speed that it can react 'instinctively'. Fundamentally prone to pleasure, the embodied subject tends towards the recollection and repetition of experiences which pleasure has 'fixed' psychically and sensually on the subject (to remember, after all, is to repeat, and repetition tends to favour that which gave joy and not that which gave pain). The body is not only multi-functional but also in some ways multilingual: it speaks through temperature, motion, speed, emotions, excitement that affect cardiac rhythm and the like.

To account for the embodied self in such ways exemplifies the type of vitalistic materialism which I want to defend. It does not amount, however, to a reduction of the subject to such functions alone; it merely aims to prevent avoiding them, as is too often the case in social theory. Taking seriously and thinking alongside the findings of scientific knowledge in the age of techno-bodies, in fact, runs against a well-established tradition of criticism, if not of actual rejection of the 'hard' sciences in social theory, both mainstream and feminist. A kind of mistrust of the 'hard' sciences on the part of the 'soft' (human, social or cultural) ones has dominated post-war critical theory.

I have argued that conceptual creativity is needed in order to re-think this kind of embodiment. I believe in a theoretical style that allows one to think processes, transitions, in-between zones and flows. This may require unconventional figurations and fast-changing maps of the various itineraries and locations. In any case, they will entail what I consider a healthy disregard of disciplinary and other corporatist academic boundaries. Philosophical nomadism is trans-disciplinary. This does not make it a cognitive vacuum or a form of moral relativism, but rather a quest for a new conceptual style. In his important work on postmodernist aesthetics, Huyssen (1986: ix) put the contemporary critic's dilemma as follows: 'to make quality distinctions remains an important task for the critic, and I will not fall into the mindless pluralism of anything goes. But to reduce all cultural criticism to the problem of quality is a symptom of the anxiety of contamination.' I would like to focus my attention on the contamination effects and the anxiety they provoke in contemporary culture, as well as on their creative potential.

This type of conceptual style, the nomadic shifts from embedded and embodied perspectives, viral politics and the paradoxes and intense provocation they engender, is very strong also in contemporary feminism. As a form of expression, it is especially favoured by cyber-feminists who are intent on challenging and re-figuring gender in cyberspace. Computer-mediated technology allows indeed for major redefinitions of identity (Turkle, 1995) and also of sexuality (Hall 1996) in a mode that is parodic, humorous, passionately political and occasionally angry. In all cases, sexual difference plays a crucial role in this new type of embodiment. Hayles (1999: xii) asks, 'What do gendered bodies have to do with the erasure of embodiment and the subsequent merging of machine and human intelligence in the figure of the cyborg?' In a similar vein, Balsamo, who believes that bodies are always and already marked by gender and race, asks (1996: 6): 'When the human body is fractured into organs, fluids and genetic codes, what happens to gender identity? When the body is fractured into functional parts and molecular codes, where is gender located?'

Claudia Springer (1996) argues that the social imaginary around cyborgs, or technobodies, is masculine, militarized and eroticized. It supports images of hyper-masculine killing machines, with wired circuitry both replacing and reinforcing muscular power. Springer argues that these over-stated traits over-ride not only the distinction between humans and non-humans, but also the question of sexual difference. Cyborgs, especially in contemporary cinema, assert a phallic metaphor for sexuality, as opposed to feminine fluidity or passivity. It is against such stereotypical images that Haraway opposes her idea of the cyborgs as hybrid, mix and multiple-connector.

I have suggested that in modernity the woman's body functioned as the site of inscription of the artificial or mechanical other, as in *Metropolis* and *L'Eve future*. In turn this coded as feminine the technological artifact, which functioned as the projection of male fantasies and desires and, as such, was highly personalized.

In late postmodernity, on the other hand, the female body remains a privileged site of re-inscription of the natural, not of the technological: the wetware is feminine. I pointed this out earlier on, in the analysis of the artificial uterus and the mother-machine. The strategic position of the maternal/material feminine inscribes it as the heart of conflicts of interests of post-industrial techno-sciences. Susan Squier (1995) sums it up in three key images: the extra-uterine foetus, the surrogate mother and the pregnant man. Inspired by Foucault, Squier reads the metaphorical break between mother and foetus as the simultaneous effect and production of contem- porary power, mostly in favour of the consolidation of the power of man. These images embody powerful social and economic interests, but also fulfil different functions depending on the politics of location, that is to say on the institutional and other power-relations of those who practice them. The extra-uterine foetus, the surrogate mother and the pregnant man, in other words, are not unilinear images, but complex, contradictory and often over- lapping locations. In answer to any possible charge of relativism, I refer the readers to my previous discussion of the politics of location, which as I argued earlier, is not relativistic: it is a politically informed account of the present.

The trend towards a blurring if not a downright erasure of sexual differ- ence, due to the impact of cyborgs or technobodies, is also evident in the tendency of mainstream postmodern philosophies to efface the feminine by making it express the anxieties and fears of the hystericized male subject- in-crisis. The work of Marilouise and Arthur Kroker on hysterical male discourse and its feminization as the signifier of the crisis comes to mind here. Bukatman has commented on the notion of 'body panic' in the work of the Krokers (1993: 247):

> The Krokers create a science fiction of conflation in which Walkmen, artificial insemination, computer functions, and body scanners are all operating at once upon the same body. As with Baudrillard, all meanings are imploded; all social practices are equal and equally dispersed throughout the technocultural system. . . . It has fallen to feminist and gay forces to confront the politics of reproductive technologies and viral containment, while postmodern metaphors and discourses madly multiply around them.

I think Bukatman is pointing out something very important here: on the issue of techno-bodies and the marvel of technologically enhanced bodies, our culture has gone into such a spin that a sober account of the state of the arts is impossible. Significantly, it is up to the minorities to try to ground, or to provide an accountable location for, a subject that has entered terminal hysteria about his technologically-supported potentialities. One result of this is the eroticization of the technological. This continues the modernist tradition, pushing it to implosion by collapsing the boundaries that historic- ally had separated organic from inorganic matter. Trust women, gays and other alternative forces, with their historically 'leaky bodies' (Grosz 1994a) to re-assert the powers, prerogatives and beauty of the 'wetware'.

The corollary of this is that technology in postmodern culture is no longer feminized, as it was in modernity, but rather neutralized as a figure of mixity, hybridity, interconnectiveness, in-between states such as trans-sexuality. If the machine is prosthetic and transgender and the maternal is mechanized, the female body has nowhere to go. I would say that it is in free fall outside classical sexual difference, into a sort of undifferentiated becoming-other. I want to argue that in this context, a feminist appropriation of Deleuze's becoming-machine, can act not only as an analytical tool, but also as a powerful reminder of alternative forms of re-embodiment. As such it constitutes a significant intervention on the social imaginary of late post-industrial societies.

The same post-industrial culture that is undergoing such transformations of the practices, the social status and the representations of subjectivity is also simultaneously in the grip of a techno-teratological imaginary. That is to say it simultaneously fears and desires the machine-like self/other. The terms of the paradox are such that all sorts of positions can co-exist within it. I think that this state of internal dissonance calls for a neo-materialist philosophy of an enfleshed self. The techno-hype needs to be kept in check by a sustainable understanding of the self: we need to assess more lucidly the price we are prepared to pay for our high technological environments. This discussion in some way juxtaposes the rhetoric of 'the desire to be wired' to a more radical sense of materialism, and there is no doubt that Deleuze's philosophy lends precious help to those – including the feminists of sexual difference – who remain to the end 'proud to be flesh'.

This positions contemporary culture in a sort of paradox. On the one hand an eroticized fetishization of the technological has pervaded through the imaginary of our societies, on the other hand, the technological is not associated with any sex, let alone the feminine, but rather with a trans-sexual or sexually undecided position. It coincides with a sort of flight from the body, which in my opinion confirms the most classical and pernicious aspect of Western phallocentrism. Evidence of this can be found in the extent to which gender boundaries and gender differences become exaggerated in both cyberpunk and the cyborg film genre.[2] In such a context, the female body is constructed as the site of the natural, of *bios* and *zoe*, hence also of procreation. In this respect, the highly sophisticated discourse of high-tech postmodernity leaves the female subject where it was before modernity, namely assimilated to nature, identified with reproduction and inimical to civilized progress. In what I consider a paradoxical reversal of the emancipatory ethos of modernity, the cyber-technological imaginary seems to yearn to push women back to a form of techno-primitivism that is regressive at best, profoundly reactionary at worst. Fortunately, however, women happen to know better, so the game is not over yet.

Dissonant becomings

In the previous chapter I explored the privileged links that exist between the female body and monstrous others. An analogous hypothesis can be formulated if we analyse the metamorphoses in the sense of becoming-machine in science-fiction texts. Contemporary culture offers overwhelming evidence that there is a privileged bond between the male and the machine. On the other hand, the woman is not tied to the machine in the same manner at all. Let me demonstrate my case.

Examples of male metamorphoses into machines:

1 by metallization or robotization of the male body: see Jarry (1993), *Le Surmâle*, as an example; *Terminator*, *Robocop*, and also the classic *Videodrome*. Body-building is also a form of eminent aggression, from the muscular circuitry of Schwarzenegger to the techno-primitivism of *The Matrix*.

2 The male body as speed or means of transportation, including zero-gravity travel: here the classic topos is the man and his car in the tradition of 'on the road' movies. James Dean and the 'scratch cars' revisited by J. G. Ballard: heterogeneous assembly of recycled pieces, a sort of 'patchwork on wheels', automated hybrid which is one of the trademarks of lower-class masculinity. But the series goes on with Superman and the male body as rocket or missile.

3 The male body as weapon: the penis as lethal instrument in all pornography, snuff films and various kinds of horror movies. Susan Brownmiller has argued that the use of male genitalia as a weapon to rape women and others is one of the crucial elements of society since pre-historic times. Made very explicit in *Peeping Tom*, but also, to a lesser degree, in *Terminator* and *Videodrome*.

Both in mainstream culture and in texts written by women, the woman seldom if ever metamorphoses into a machine; this path seems to be a male prerogative. Critics like Lefanu and Bukatman have remarked that women science-fiction writers seldom fall for the hyped celebration of escape from the body that marks so many male-authored cyberpunk and science-fiction texts. Maybe because the machine – except for the 'bachelor machine' – is culturally coded as active and productive and pertains to the public sphere? This resistance to associating the female with the inorganic may spring from the classical association of woman with life-giving forces and motherhood: a woman's becoming is through her children and she is not One. Though this is in patriarchal ideology a tool of oppression, feminists have revindicated the positivity of this multiple structure as a strategy of empowerment (think of Irigaray on sexual difference as the 'not one' from chapter 2). Balsamo argues that all cyborgs challenge the interrelation of human and machine, because technology is culturally coded as masculine, however, male cyborgs fail to challenge the distinction between human and machine. Because women are culturally coded as emotional, sexual and maternal, on the other hand, female cyborgs – whether hyper-built in the gym or prosthetically enhanced – 'embody cultural contradictions which strain the technological imagination' (1988: 335). Thus, meta(l)morphoses are not sexually undifferentiated, but rather heavily marked by gender, ethnicity and sexual difference.

Thus, the woman seldom metamorphoses into an android or a robot and if she does, the consequences are as devastating as in science-fiction horror movies. Films such as *Blade Runner* (1982) show female robots/cyborgs as killing machines as lethal as the males. The film *Eve of Destruction* (1991) features a female cyborg; here both the heroic and the liberatory notes are dropped in favour of a more traditional Frankensteinian approach. The cyborg Eve is the exact double of the female scientist who created her and even programmed her with her memories. Once she escapes, the cyborg proceeds to act out all of the scientist's repressed fantasies of revenge against men, causing death and destruction all round. The female cyborg contains a nuclear device inside her uterus, which is duly activated and puts the survival of the planet at risk. No cyborg saviour figure in cinema so far has been cast in the mould of the feminine.

I argued in the previous chapter that in the techno-teratological imaginary of post-industrial societies, the mother's body has already been assimilated to the technological industrial complex. This in turn engenders a number of powerful socially enforced images or figurations of post-human embodiment. Camilla Griggers (1997) points out a significant figuration of post-human femininity in the image of 'the process of becoming-lesbian in the public sphere and . . . the corresponding process of the public lesbian becoming killing-machine' (1995: 162). Wary as always of essentialism, Griggers does not want to argue that women are naturally pacifist, or that they have not participated indirectly in the war – the socially accepted killing machine. Nonetheless she can also safely argue that the military has been segregated for men only. Against this historical background, Griggers wonders why the topos of women who kill and more especially lesbians who kill is so popular in high-tech societies – the same societies that oppose abortion and women's status as soldiers. This also takes place at a time in history when war itself has become post-human, in that its advanced weapon-delivery system is technologically mediated. Resting on the historical precedent of Lizzie Borden, Griggers argues that female deviancy, in this case a criminally murderous woman, fits into a broader cultural repertoire of dangerous femininity. Like all deviancy, this is tainted with homoeroticism, as suggested by films like *Basic Instinct*, *Single White Female* and the classic *Thelma and Louise*. Women and lesbians who kill are simultaneously in excess of both punishment and protection by the law: they are elsewhere.

In the case of the technological 'other', or machine, even more than the animal, insect or abject and alien other, processes of intermingling or becoming show the same trends I noted in previous chapters, namely a simultaneous

degradation of the feminine and a reiteration of its importance as a threshold to processes of becoming which include both the Majority and the
Minority-subjects. Equally striking is the persistence of the nostalgic trend
which tends to represent these transformations or transgressive intimacies in
the mode of hyped-up 'new frontiers' or of neo-Gothic horror.

In the case of techno-bodies, the 'hype' is truly astonishing, considering
that machines and humans have been interacting at all levels since the first
industrial revolution. Cinema is one of the technologies that both embodies
and contributes to the representation of new body-machines. Parasitic upon
technology in many direct and indirect ways, cinema plays a crucial role in
the configuration of the new body-machines. It does so not only by focusing
on this *topos* thematically, but also by vampirizing other technologies, so as
to assimilate them into the cinematic apparatus. Thus, the cinematic image
is strategically positioned as a binding factor to represent the interaction
with technological body-others. Again, in this exercise in incorporation,
both sexuality and sexual difference play a crucial role, as I will argue in the
next section.

From 'Kustom Kar Kommando' to 'Crash'

The cult film-maker Kenneth Anger was Cocteau's assistant when he started
his film production in the late 1940s. His cinema explores the unbridled
intensity and dream-like world of male homoeroticism and sexuality. His
masterpiece *Scorpio Rising* (1964) zooms in on the neo-Gothic, neo-nazi
cultural revival in American society. *Kustom Kar Kommando* is Anger's
1965 eulogy of the motor-car as the ultimate fetishistic object of desire. It
celebrates with passionate delight the beauty of engines, chrome plates, pipes,
gears and dash-boards, all handled firmly by dashing young dandies. Oniric
and onanistic to the extreme, it is a piece of cyborg-art *avant la lettre*.

As A. Lingis suggested (1998), the privileged bond that ties men to their
automobiles and to speed in general is illustrated by a salient episode in
Leonard Cohen's *Beautiful Losers* (1966). In a section that reads like the
genealogy of Ballard's *Crash*, the two male characters go off for a drive that
is nothing short of the pure speed of sexual ecstasy. F., the main character,
enjoys an exceptional erection and massages his penis in full view of his
friends as he frantically drives into the night. The homoeroticism is palpable
(Cohen 1966: 92): 'How I was torn between the fear for my safety and the
hunger to jam my head between his knees and the dashboard!' The result is
deep interpenetration of men and their machines, a sort of blurring of their
sexuality with the metal-hard body of the automobile (Cohen 1966: 93):
'Two men in a hurtling steel shell aimed at Ottawa, blinded by a mechanical
mounting ecstasy . . . ; two naked capsules filled with lonely tear gas to stop
the riot in our brains.' As F. reaches orgasm, splashing his semen all over

the dashboard, and his friend loses his erection, the car swerves of the road and hits head-on a boarded-up hotdog stand. Nothing serious, and F. turns to his male friend and asks: 'Did you come?' Fear and danger are geared to hard-ons.

In the last scene of David Cronenberg's controversial *Crash* (from James Ballard's novel of 1973), after a hot car-chase in pursuit of his own lawfully-wedded wife, the male protagonist finally manages to bring about the meta(l)-morphosis he has been aspiring to all along, provoking a catastrophic car-accident. As the dust settles on a scene of twisted metal and bodily desolation, the husband turns to his wife and enquires: 'Did you come?' The female of the species, however, sadly remains contained within the confines of her skin-clad bodily organism. Not so much because of her biology, but of what was made of her biology by the phallic signifier, she has to admit, defeated, that no, she did not come. And then, in what I can only describe as a moment of sublime love, her husband strokes her ever-so-tenderly and promises: 'Maybe next time.' There is hope yet. Not the nostalgically-founded hope of old-fashioned humanism, not the perverse hope of psychoanalytically-phrased polymorphous perversity: just the hope for a qualitative transmutation of the human body into a post-human organism. This cybernetic interface with technology allows for speed and violent impact with other metal-clad humanoids.

There is a great deal of post-industrial and postmodern gloom in Ballard's techno-porn novel; as Bukatman put it (1993: 41): 'The cities, jungles, highways and suburbs of Ballard's fiction are relentlessly claustrophobic, yet empty; spectacular, but not seductive; relentlessly meaningful, yet resistant to logic. The repetition and obsessiveness of these works suspends temporality while it shrinks space.' The hope that is expressed by the already-(trans-)muted husband is that the woman, too, will manage to break out of this claustrophobic universe, its monotony and predictability. Breaking out of the straight-jacket of normal literally means breaking out of one's skin, ripping open the envelope of what used to be the border that framed the bodily humanism of the subject. Change hurts, transformations are no mere metaphors.

Throughout *Crash*, scars are the places where the flesh is re-composed, stitched-up and re-assembled after sustaining the impact of the metallic other. This type of interaction is celebrated as a new frontier, eroticized and transgressed. Scars mark the new topologies of bodies that are already meta(l)-morphosed into a new regime of pleasures and pains: 'sexual apertures formed by fragmenting windshield louvres and dashboard dials in a high-speed impact' (179). The bodies that have already undergone the trauma of the crash – much as the monsters described earlier by Arbus – are existential aristocracy. They have already gone through to a new stage of metamorphosis and as such they are the object of envy for the embodied subjects that have not yet gone through. In the film, as in the novel, scarred bodies are

intensely eroticized because they bear visible traces of their intercourse with
the technological other – they are tattooed via impact with the car body
(Ballard 1973: 28):

> As I looked down at myself I realized that the precise make and model-year of
> my car could have been reconstructed from the pattern of my wounds. The
> layout of the instrument panel, like the profile of the steering wheel bruised
> into my chest, was inset on my knees and shin-bones.

Every scar is consequently a border that can be trespassed – it is a border-
line zone, object of admiration and aberration, irresistibly attractive. Next
to scars, other forms of bodily modifications are equally charged with sexual
desire in *Crash*, notably tattooing, self-wounding and piercing. But the car
carries the day as instrument of shifts in perception, which pursue pleasure
to the utmost boundary: death.

As I said earlier, one very widespread feature of the contemporary technological imaginary is the extent to which it promotes practices of prosthetic extension and proliferation of bodily parts, organs and cells: a sort of
molecular promiscuity of bodies with organic and inorganic others is in
action. It transposes subjects latitudinally and longitudinally to a different
plane – beyond human nature and the imperatives of the genetic code.
Ballard captures perfectly this mutation (1973: 179):

> I dreamed of other accidents that might enlarge the repertory of orifices,
> relating them to more elements of the automobile's engineering, to the ever-
> more complex technologies of the future. What wounds would create the sexual
> possibilities of the invisible technologies of thermonuclear reaction chambers,
> white-tiled control rooms, the mysterious scenarios of computer circuitry?

Crash expresses a mutation in the order of human sexuality and sexual
difference that is as multi-layered as it is elementary. It is a shift of gears, a
change in speed, an acceleration that propels humans out of the last vestiges
of postmodern nostalgia for humanistic wholeness, or melancholia due to
its loss. It urges a qualitative leap over the last doubts and hesitations
that hold humans back from the concerted actualization of new virtual
embodiments, which contemporary technologies make possible. In this
evolutionary path woman is often represented as the resisting subject, not
easily prepared to make the jump towards disembodiment or virtual
re-embodiments. 'Maybe next time' sounds like the recognition of some impossibility, an uncrossable boundary, as well as the promise of repetition, of
eternal returns. The woman in *Crash* finds it difficult to become-minoritarian,
partly because of the far superior power of attraction and hence the competition of the machine, the motor-car, and the subject-positions it enables.

As Salman Rushdie pointed out in his commentary on Princess Diana's death (1997), our culture eroticizes and glamorizes consumers' technologies, starting from the automobile. Diana's death by car-crash was 'a cathartic event for millions' (Becker 1999: 282), related both to and by the media. As such, it brings out some of the central paradoxes of contemporary techno-culture, almost like a cruel illustration of everything Ballard and Cronenberg are trying to demonstrate. Princess Diana's crushed body acquires semi-religious significance, like a collective ritual on wheels, relayed cathodically all over the globe (Ballard 1973: 109):

> She sat in the damaged car like a deity occupying a shrine readied for her in the blood of a minor member of her congregation. Although I was twenty feet from the car . . . the unique contours of her body and personality seemed to transform the crushed vehicles . . . almost as if the entire car had deformed itself around her figure in a gesture of homage.

Rushdie argues that Ballard's novel blends together under the sign of a powerful new techno-sexuality the two dominant fetishes of our culture: consumers' commodities (the car) and celebrity (the star). The two are combined with almost obscene self-evidence in Princess Diana's death. The third party in the plot, crucial to the whole story, is the camera's eye – in Diana's case, the flashing lights of the papparazzi. Rushdie states (1997: 68):

> In Diana's fatal crash, the camera (as both Reporter and Lover) is joined to the Automobile and the Star, and the cocktail of death and desire becomes even more powerful than the one in Ballard's book. . . . The object of desire, in the moment of her death, sees the phallic lenses advancing upon her, snapping, snapping. Think of it this way, and the pornography of Diana Spencer's death becomes apparent. She died in a sublimated sexual assault.

Rushdie reads Diana's desperate last drive as her attempt to exercise some control over her status as collective object of desire, to emancipate herself from commodity to humanity, to acquire some subjectivity. In vain: she was not in the driver's seat.

By contrast, *Thelma and Louise*, the much-celebrated feminist version of road movies, uses the car as a vehicle of displacement or de-territorialization. It operates a shift of reality, a change of dimension. They are not just two runaway wives who have decided not to stand by their men, they also take turns at the wheel, swap places and drive on until they become increasingly depersonalized in the process. They disengage themselves from their social, sexual identity, go on a rampage, shoot and blow up. Finally, in the hyper-real space of the American roads, they melt into the landscape, merge with the speed of crossing it. Ultimately, they have nowhere to go, the destination is immaterial: all that matters is to be mobile, nomadic. They may as well be in the highways of *Crash*, or in a spaceship, heading outward and inwards simultaneously, until the apotheosis of their final leap into the void, that is to say their evaporation into myth. They do not signify anything, they become, transforming themselves and us as they go. Becoming-cyborgs may be virtual, but it is nonetheless socially enacted, materially grounded – embodied and embedded, to the end, enfleshed. And yet, all this information comes to us through the camera's eye – it is technologically transmitted. Cinema and TV are the main beneficiary of this process of becoming-machine of subjects. Their power of visualization has saturated the social sphere.

Cyborgs and nomads

This zigzagging itinerary of analogies and differences between feminist and other theories of the becoming-woman or animal or insect or machine leads me to restate my hypothesis. I want to raise the very real notion that the process of nomadic becoming, far from marking the dissolution of all identities into a state of flux where different connections will emerge, may itself be sex-specific, sexually differentiated and consequently take different forms and different senses of time according to different gendered positions.

A significant example of the often paradoxical affinity between feminist theory and philosophical nomadology is Donna Haraway's redefinition of materialism. I see Haraway as pursuing in a feminist way the line about bodily materiality, though she speaks the language of science and technology rather than that of post-metaphysical philosophy. She is an utterly non-nostalgic post-human thinker: her conceptual universe is the high-technology world of informatics and telecommunications. In this respect, she is conceptually part of the same epistemological tradition as Bachelard and Canguilhem for whom the scientific ratio is not necessarily hostile to humanistic approaches and values. Moreover, in this line of thinking the practice of science is not seen as narrowly rationalistic, but rather allows for a broadened definition of the term, to include the play of the unconscious, dreams and the imagination in the production of scientific discourse. Following Foucault (1977a), Haraway draws our attention to the construction and manipulation of docile, knowable bodies in our present social system. She invites us to think of what new kinds of bodies are being constructed right now: what kind of gender-system is being constructed under our very noses.

It is in this framework that Haraway proposes the figuration of the *cyborg*, which I mentioned in chapter 1. As a hybrid, or body-machine, the cyborg is a connection-making entity, a figure of inter-relationality, receptivity and global communication that deliberately blurs categorical distinctions (human and machine; nature and culture; male and female; Oedipal and non-Oedipal). It allows Haraway to think specificity without falling into relativism. The cyborg is Haraway's representation of a generic feminist humanity, thus answering the question of how feminists reconcile the radical historical specificity of women with the insistence on constructing new values that can benefit humanity as a whole, by redefining it radically. Her vision of the body is post-anthropocentric and pro-technology. Moreover, the body in the cyborg model is neither physical nor mechanical – nor is it only textual. As a counter-paradigm for the interaction between the inner and the external reality, it offers a reading not only of the body, not only of machines but rather of what goes on between them, as a new powerful replacement of the mind–body debate – the cyborg is a post-metaphysical construct. In my reading, the figuration of the cyborg reminds us that meta-physics is not an abstract construction, but rather a political ontology: the classical dualism body–soul is not simply a gesture of separation and of hierarchical coding, it is also a theory about their interaction, about how they hang together. It suggests how we should go about re-thinking the unity of the human being.

Balsamo (1996) stresses two crucial aspects of Haraway's cyborg, namely, that it corrects the discursive body with the materially constructed body. Secondly, that it bears a privileged bond to the female body. Woman as the 'other of the same' is in fact the primary artifact, produced through a whole social interaction of 'technologies of gender' (de Lauretis 1987). Translated into my own language, Haraway's figuration of the cyborg is a sort of feminist becoming-woman that merely by-passes the feminine in order to open up towards a broader and considerably less anthropocentric horizon. In this respect it is significant, as Pisters has astutely noted (1998), that Haraway describes the cyborg as a girl: a girl, that is to say not a fully grown woman, already caught in the Molar line of stratification. This on the one hand emphasizes the anti-Oedipal function of the cyborg. On the other hand, it perpetuates the tendency that is strong also in Deleuze and Guattari (Battersby 1998) to single out the little girl, Alice, as the marker of the moment of oscillation of identity, prior to entry into the Phallic symbolic. Pisters then goes on to argue that Haraway's cyborg can be compared to Deleuze's body without organs, and that Alice/the little girl's body can provide an illuminating lead into the discussion of technobodies in contemporary media and multi-information societies.

I find in Haraway an argument analogous to my plea for a more conceptually creative approach and more imaginative energy in the production of knowledge. We need new forms of literacy to decode today's world. Figurations also entail a discursive ethics: that one cannot know properly, or even begin to understand, that towards which one has no affinity. Critical intelligence for Haraway is a form of sympathy. One should never criticize that which one is not complicitous with: criticism must be conjugated in a non-reactive mode, a creative gesture, so as to avoid the Oedipal plot of phallogocentric theory.

The cyborg also challenges the androcentrism of the poststructuralists' corporeal materialism. Thus, while sharing a great deal of Foucault's premises about the modern regime of truth as 'bio-power', Haraway also challenges his redefinition of power. Supporting Jameson's idea that a postmodernist politics is made necessary by the historical collapse of the traditional left, and that it represents the left's chance to reinvent itself from within, Haraway notes that contemporary power does not work by normalized heterogeneity any more, but rather by networking, communication redesigns and multiple interconnections. She concludes that Foucault 'names a form of power at its moment of implosion. The discourse of bio-politics gives way to technobabble' (Haraway 1990a: 245, note 4). Two points are noteworthy here: firstly that Haraway analyses the contemporary scientific revolution in more radical terms that Foucault does, mostly because she bases it on first-hand knowledge about today's technology. Haraway's training in biology and the sociology of science are very useful here. By comparison with her approach, Foucault's analysis of the disciplining of bodies appears already out of date, apart from being, of course, intrinsically androcentric.

Haraway raises a point that Deleuze also noted in his analysis of Foucault, namely that the Foucauldian diagrams of power describe what we have already ceased to be; like all cartography, they act *a posteriori* and therefore fail to account for the situation here and now. In this respect, Haraway opposes to Foucault's bio-power a deconstructive genealogy of the embodied subjectivities of women. Whereas Foucault's analysis rests on a nineteenth-century view of the production system, Haraway inscribes her analysis of the condition of women into an up-to-date analysis of the post-industrial system of production. Arguing that white capitalist patriarchy has turned into the 'informatics of domination' (Haraway 1990a: 162), Haraway argues that women have been cannibalized by the new technologies, they have disappeared from the field of visible social agents. The post-industrial system makes oppositional mass politics utterly redundant: a new politics must be invented, on the basis of a more adequate understanding of how the contemporary subject functions.

Chela Sandoval expands Haraway's insight into a full analysis of the political economy of 'cyborgs', focusing on the human elements of exploitation of those underpaid workers who 'know the pain of the union of machine and bodily tissue, the robotic conditions and, in the late twentieth century, the cyborg conditions under which the notion of human agency must take on new meanings' (Sandoval 1999: 408). As the majority of this new underclass is composed of women, ethnic others, immigrants or refugees, Sandoval stresses the gender and ethnicity aspects of the cyborgs' social space, which are significantly neglected in most theories of globalization. 'Cyborg life: life of a worker who flips burgers, who speaks the cyborg speech of McDonalds, is a life the workers of the future must prepare themselves for in small, everyday ways' (1999: 408). Haraway's cyborg inserts an oppositional consciousness at the heart of the debate on the new technological societies currently being shaped, in such a way as to highlight issues of gender and sexual difference within a much broader discussion about survival and social justice. More than ever therefore, the question of power-relations and of ethical and political resistance emerges as relevant in the age of informatics of domination.

The cyborg theories emphasize that multiplicity need not lead necessarily to relativism. Haraway argues for a multi-faceted foundational theory for an anti-relativistic acceptance of differences, her cyborg is embedded and embodied and it seeks for connections and articulations in a non-gender-centred and non-ethnocentric perspective. I find the result liberating to the point of jubilation. Haraway's distinctive and idiosyncratic writing style expresses the force of the de-centring that she is operating at the conceptual level, forcing the readers to re-adjust or perish. Nowhere is the empowering force more visible than in Haraway's treatments of animals, machines, and the monstrous, hybrid 'others'. Deeply immersed in contemporary culture, science fiction and cyberpunk included, Haraway is fascinated by the difference embodied by reconstructed, mutant or altered others. Her techno-monsters contain enthralling promises of possible re-embodiments and actualized differences. Multiple, heterogeneous, uncivilized, they show the way to multiple virtual possibilities. The cyborg, the monster, the animal – the classical 'other than' the human – are thus emancipated from the category of pejorative difference and shown in an altogether more positive light. Haraway rejects the dialectics of otherness within which these others are constructed as simultaneously necessary and as indigestible, inappropriate/d, thus alien. The strength of Haraway's position is that she has relinquished this conceptual scheme altogether. She has already leapt over to the other side of the great divide and is perfectly at home in a post-human world. Haraway's intimate knowledge of technology is the tool that facilitates this qualitative leap; in this respect, she is a true cyber-teratologist.

My problems with the cyborg, however are conceptual. I believe that an alternative definition of the subject is necessary, even desirable, and consequently I cannot share in Haraway's preference for post-human agency. The same goes for sexuality and sexual difference: however much they may smack of metaphysics, I consider them as too structurally embedded in subjectivity to be merely laid aside as obsolete properties of a cybernetic self. It seems to me that Haraway's cyborg is unresolved not only on the issue of unconscious desires, fantasies and identifications, but also, on a more basic level, as to whether the cyborg is sexed at all. As I argued in chapter 2, I agree with Irigaray and cannot fathom a subject position outside sexuality, though I am in favour of nomadizing it and making it complex, multiple and internally contradictory. However complex the subject may be, however, she or he is neither undecided, nor indefinite.

Technobodies in the social-cyber space

I think that, far from abolishing or replacing the body, the new technologies strengthen the corporeal structure of both humans and machines. If you just think of the body of Arnold Schwarzenegger in the *Terminator* series, you will see that, however wired and metallic, it is still hyper-muscular, taut and fighting fit. The cyborg is a culturally dominant icon whose effects go well beyond those of cinematic or media seduction. They also affect the corporeal behaviour of 'real' humans the world over. For instance, I would want to argue that with their silicon implants, plastic surgery operations and athlete-like training, the bodies of Dolly Parton, Michael Jackson, or Jane Fonda, Cher and many other 'stars' are no less cyborg, or monstrous, than anything out of the *Aliens* film series. Pumping-iron mutants are here to stay.

All cyborgs, the majority as well as the minoritarian ones, inhabit a posthuman body, that is to say an artificially reconstructed body (Balsamo, 1993). The body in question here is far from a biological essence: it is a crossroad of intensive forces; it is a surface of inscriptions of social codes. Efforts are needed to rethink a non-essentialized embodied self after the decline of the naturalistic paradigm. As Francis Barker puts it (1984), the disappearance of the body is the apex of the historical process of its denaturalization. The problem that lingers on is how to re-adjust politics to this shift. Embodied subjectivity is thus a paradox that rests simultaneously on the historical decline of mind–body distinctions and the proliferation of discourses about the body. Foucault reformulates this in terms of the paradox of simultaneous disappearance and over-exposure of the body. Though technology makes the paradox manifest and in some ways exemplifies it perfectly, it cannot be argued that it is responsible for such a shift in paradigm. The issue of ethics raises immediately here: the crisis of humanism neither wipes out ethics, nor eliminates the need for it. It rather intensifies the necessity to elaborate values that are up to the complexities of our age. The first step is to reject nihilism.

The loss of the naturalistic paradigm entails that God is finally dead, driving many crazy with the fear of abandonment. The death of God has been long in coming and it has joined a domino-effect, which has brought down a number of familiar notions, such as the security about the categorical distinction between mind and body; the safe belief in the role and function of the nation state; the family; masculine authority; white privilege; the eternal feminine and compulsory heterosexuality. These metaphysically-founded certainties have floundered and made room for something more complex, more playful and infinitely more disturbing. Speaking as a woman, that is to say a subject emerging from a history of oppression and exclusion, I would say that this crisis of conventional values is not nihilistic, but rather a positive thing. The metaphysical condition in fact had entailed an institutionalized vision of femininity as a location of power, which has burdened my gender for centuries. The crisis of modernity is, for feminists, not a melancholy plunge into loss and decline, but rather the joyful opening up of new possibilities.

Thus, I want to argue that the hyper-reality of the cyborg or post-human predicament does not wipe out politics or the need for political resistance: it just makes it more necessary than ever to work towards a radical redefinition of political action. Nothing could be further from a postmodern ethics than Dostoevski's over-quoted and profoundly mistaken statement that, if God is dead, anything goes. This cynical *clin d'oeil* to moral and cognitive relativism is the opposite of the materialism and philosophical nomadism I have been defending in this book. The challenge for me is rather how to combine the recognition of postmodern embodied subjects with resistance to power but also the rejection of relativism and cynicism.

Secondly, post-human embodiment is written into the cash nexus, as Chela Sandoval also pointed out. Capital in these post-industrial times is an immaterial flow of cash that travels as pure data in cyberspace till it lands in (some of) our bank accounts. As Bukatman points out (1993), cyberspace is a highly contested social space that exists parallel to increasingly complex social realities. The clearest exemplification of the social powers of these technologies is the flow of money through computer-governed stock exchanges that always work and never sleep, the world over. This flow of pure data spells the decline of the master narratives of modernism, but as Bukatman astutely observes, it also constitutes a sort of master-narrative of its own, which spells the decline of humanism and the dawn of the age of post-humanity (1993).

Bukatman stresses the positive and potentially empowering impact of the new virtual, artificial environments and the extent to which they simultaneously dislocate and re-ground the bodily human subject. The point of origin of the subject is shifted to meaningful interiority and consciousness-driven stability to a complex and shifting techno-cultural configuration.

However, capital harps on and trades in body fluids: the cheap sweat and blood of the disposable workforce throughout the third world and the wetness of desire of first-world consumers as they commodify their existence into over-saturated stupor. Hyper-reality does not wipe out class relations: it just intensifies them. Postmodernity rests on the paradox of simultaneous commodification and conformism of cultures, while intensifying disparities among them, as well as structural inequalities. An important aspect of this situation is the omnipotence of the visual media. Our era has turned visualization into the ultimate form of control. This marks not only the final stage in the commodification of the scopic, but also the triumph of vision over all the other senses. It is also something of special concern from a feminist perspective, because it tends to reinstate a hierarchy of bodily perception which over-privileges vision over other senses, especially touch and sound. The primacy of vision has been challenged by feminist theories, which have inspiring things to say about scopophilia, that is to say a vision-centred approach to thought, knowledge and science. In a psychoanalytic perspective, this takes the form of a critique of the phallogocentric bias that is built into vision. Thus Irigaray (1974) links it to the pervasive powers of the masculine symbolic. Fox Keller (1985) reads it instead as a rapacious drive towards cognitive penetration of the 'secrets of nature' which bears a direct link to the social and psychic construction of masculinity. In a more socio-political framework, Haraway (1990) attacks the priority which our culture gives to the logocentric hold of disembodied vision, which is best exemplified by the satellite or eye in the sky. She opposes to it an embodied and therefore accountable redefinition of the act of seeing as a form of connection to the object of vision, which she defines in terms of 'passionate detachment'.

Across the board of contemporary electronic art, especially in the field of virtual reality, there are many women artists, like Catherine Richards and Nell Tenhaaf, who experiment with forms of technological creativity which challenge the in-built assumption of visual superiority which it carries. The real alternative to scopophilia, however, comes from the area of music and sound technology. As I argued in chapter 3, the sound environment offers far larger and more untapped resources for the subversion of dominant modes of representation. As visualization is the hegemonic regime, music or sound are seen as the most obvious alternative. It remains to be seen whether Internet-carried musical production will manage to make the 'sound colourist' or D. J. or acoustic engineers of today into a viable alternative to the vampiristic powers of the visual media.

Thirdly, the cyberbodies that gain simultaneously visibility and high-definition identity or singularity are prevalently white. Whiteness here does not designate any specific racial entity; it is rather a way of indexing access to power, entitlement and visibility with identity. In his perverse wit, hyper-real con artist Jeff Koons (ex-husband of the post-human Italian porno star Cicciolina) depicted Michael Jackson in a ceramic piece, as a lily-white god holding a monkey in his arms. With great panache, Koons announced that this was a tribute to Michael Jackson's pursuit of the perfectibility of his body. The many cosmetic surgery operations he has undergone testifies to Jackson's wilful sculpting and crafting of the self. In the post-human world view, deliberate attempts to pursue perfection are seen as a complement to evolution, bringing the embodied self to a higher stage of accomplishment. Whiteness being, in Koons' sublime simplicity, the undisputed and utterly final standard of beauty, Jackson's superstardom could only be depicted in white. Hyper-reality does not wipe out racism: it intensifies it and it brings it to implosion.

Another aspect of the racialization of post-human bodies concerns the ethno-specific values it conveys. Many have questioned the extent to which we are all being re-colonized by an American and more specifically a Californian 'body-beautiful' ideology. In so far as US corporations own the technology, they leave their cultural imprints on the contemporary imaginary. This leaves little room for any other cultural alternatives. The re-colonization of the social cyber-imaginary whitens out all diversity.

Confronted with this situation, that is to say with culturally enforced icons of white, economically dominant, heterosexual hyper-genderized identities – which simultaneously reinstate huge power differentials while denying them – what is to be done? The first thing I would recommend is to acknowledge the aporias and the aphasias of theoretical frameworks and look with hope in the direction of conceptual and artistic creation. There is no question that the creative spirits have a head start over the masters of meta-discourse, even and especially of deconstructive meta-discourse. This is a very sobering prospect: after years of theoretical arrogance, philosophy lags behind art and fiction in the difficult struggle to keep up with today's world. The point is to be able to create, invent and elaborate new conceptual frameworks. Creativity of thought is on the top of the twenty-first century agenda.

New masculinities or toys for the boys?

One of my arguments so far has been that the social imaginary around technobodies is tempted by a fantasy of flight from the body. This reduces the women to the site of reinscription of the natural, mostly in its material/maternal format. With the technological artifact situated in a trans-sexual space, and femininity associated, yet again, with the natural, the main sexualized body is male and it is around masculinity that the contested discussions about virtual identities are focused.

If you look at contemporary reconstruction of masculinity through media culture, you cannot help being struck by its familiarity. Take for instance masculinity in the alternative Cameron–Schwarzenegger or Cronenberg modes. Cameron and Cronenberg are the great reconstructors of the post-human masculine subject. They represent two opposed trends: Cameron takes a deep plunge into what Nancy Hartsock calls 'abstract masculinity' by proposing a hyper-real male body in the Schwarzenegger format.

Cronenberg, on the other hand, explodes phallic masculinity into two diverging directions: on the one hand the psychopathic serial killer and on the other, the hysterical neurosis of the over-feminized male: the transsexual and the hysteric.

Showalter (1990) describes Cronenberg as the director most explicitly concerned with male horror and masculine envy of the reproductive process. He plays the creativity of male scientists, engineers and technologies against the overwhelming and therefore uncontrollable and monstrous female reproductive capacity. This matrix envy is expressed in the insect-like foetus of *The Fly*, the extra-uterine sac of *The Brood*, the monstrous operating tools of *Dead Ringers* and the lovely hybrids of *Ex-istenz*.

While Cronenberg addresses the issue of the physicality of language in all his films, in *Videodrome* he fully addresses the issue of the construction of the body as text. In this film, the television takes over reality; there is a mutual imbrication of the real, the technologized and the simulated; the language is hyper-technologized, but anti-rational. Already in *The Fly* he had shown, through a series of genetic cut-ups, the breakdown of human hegemony. There is a pervasive anti-humanism in his films, 'as demonstrated by the recurrent fears of human contact, sexuality, or physicality in any form' (A. and M. L. Kroker 1987: 202).

The subject of the Cronenberg film is the limits of human action: the structures of external power and control to which the individual is subjected. This is connected to the rise of new technologies. In *Videodrome*, the male body undergoes a very different set of metamorphoses. Videodrome is a video channel specializing in snuff films. Through these scenes, they manipulate people's brains – including a brain tumour, which is described as an 'extra organ' that makes people receptive to the videodrome signal. What is interesting is that the boundary between reality and the televisional image is so blurred that it becomes undistinguishable from Rex's hallucinations.

As Professor O'Blivion put it, 'the battle for the mind of North America will be fought in the video arena' – the *Videodrome*. The television screen is the retina of the mind's eye. Therefore the television screen is part of the physical structure of the brain. This film shows a world where the television has taken over reality, so that you cannot tell the difference between the simulated image and the real. *Videodrome* explores the manipulative effect of video images and their direct impact on the mind: television programs its viewers, it makes them act in certain ways. It also induces tumours in their brains, causing hallucinations which are then recorded and used to blackmail the people involved. People are just programmed tapes, which are played back by manipulative hands. The tumours are described as a new evolution of the human brain, capable of provoking new sensations – mostly hallucinations and S/M fantasies. Their most immediate effect, however, is to domesticate the male body and to make it available, disposable, manipulatable, exactly as the female body has always been. The image Cronenberg chooses to represent this is that of the penetration of the male body through the stomach. The man gets an inner cavity through which he can be penetrated; what is deposited in him is a program, a message, an order. All the orders he gets are about killing. Feminist critics have argued that the wound that opens up in Wren's body when he becomes a video-recorder is a gaping, vagina-like one, thus representing his becoming-woman (Modleski 1986). Creed argues that this becoming-woman can be read critic-ally in a feminist perspective (1990): the dislocation of the categories of otherness is enacted, but no genuine alternative emerges. All we get is a man violating himself as a woman, and masochism is the dominant theme of *Videodrome*. In this respect, the becoming-woman of the Majority repeats the worst traits of the phallogocentric regime: it is an exercise in humiliation and an apprenticeship in self-mutilation. The man undergoes what women have had to suffer for centuries: this is the ultimate scenario of powerlessness and violation of one's body and it marks at best a generalized becoming-Sadean. His enemies can 'play him' – by inserting a videotape inside him which programs him to kill all their enemies. His 'memory system' is thus controlled by the majority and this embodied male becomes as much of an android as the *Blade Runner* 'replicants'. By becoming actively penetrable, his becoming-woman is complete. When compared to the high-tech machismo of *Terminator*, *Videodrome* is a more interesting film because it does not restate classical gender stereotypes, but rather questions the line of demarca-tion between them.

What makes *Videodrome* a classic is that it addresses the issue of the physicality and the corresponding malleability of the male body, while it also shows to what extent the body is constructed, thus striking an anti-humanist note. Of special relevance are the scenes where the video/TV screen comes alive, alternatively as an alluring female body, a bleeding, dying, tortured body, and at the end, a mass of bleeding organs. The plasticity of the screen, combined with the loss of depth or organic reality of the pro-tagonist's body, makes the interpenetration of the human and the machine and organic-inorganic possible.

The modernists hoped to perfect the human with the help of the machines, the postmodernists aim to replace the human with the machine meant as posthuman, that is to say of an altogether different quality than the human (Bergstrom 1991). This trend is intensified by the cultural production sur-rounding virtual-reality technology. This is an advanced brand of computer-designed reality, useful in its medical or architectural applications, but very poor from the angle of the imagination, especially if you look at it in terms of gender-roles. Computer-aided design and animation has the potential for great creativity, not only in professional areas such as architecture and medi-cine, but also in mass entertainment, especially video-games. It originates in technology to train air pilots to fly jet fighters. The Gulf War was fought by virtual reality machinery (it still resulted in the usual butchery); of late, the costs involved in producing VR equipment have decreased, so that people other than NASA are able to afford it.

Feminist researchers in this field have noted the paradoxes and the dangers of contemporary forms of disembodiment which accompany these new technologies. I am especially struck by the persistence of pornographic, violent, or humiliating images of women that are still circulating through these allegedly 'new' technological products. I worry about designing programs that allow for 'virtual rape and virtual murder'. For instance, *The Lawnmower Man* claims to be the first virtual-reality fiction film released in the market, though it is a film that makes a very mediocre use of powerful virtual-reality images. The subject of the film is a scientist who works for NASA and has devised very advanced mind-manipulating technologies, first using a chimpanzee as the object of a scientific experiment, later to be replaced by a mentally retarded man, whose brain is 'expanded' through this new technology.

The images of penetration of the brain are crucial to the visual impact of this film: it is about 'opening up' to the influence of a higher power. This can be juxtaposed to Cronenberg's 'invaginated' male bodies, penetrated by the cathode-tube radiations of *Videodrome*, and to the brain implants of *Johnny Mnemonic*. Thanks to this technology, the retarded man or *The Lawnmower Man* blossoms first into a normal boy, then grows into a superhuman figure. The reconstruction of masculinity in this film shows an evolution from idiot to little boy to adolescent to cow-boy to losing virginity to great lover to macho to rapist, murderer, serial killer and psycho. At an intermediate stage of his development, he claims he can see God, and he wants to share this experience with his girlfriend, to give her the ultimate orgasm. What follows is a scene of psychic rape, when the woman is literally blown apart and goes out of her mind. She will stay out of her mind from now on, as the boy progresses to become a god-like figure, a serial killer, a force of nature. This becomes almost a manifesto for evolutionary psychology.

Thus, alleged triumph of high-technologies is not matched by a leap of the human imagination to create new images and representations. Quite on the contrary, what I notice is the repetition of very old themes and cliches, under the appearance of 'new' technological advances. It just goes to prove that it takes more than machinery really to alter patterns of thought and mental habits. The fiction of science, which is the theme of science-fiction films and literature, calls for more imagination and more gender equality in order to approximate a 'new' representation of a postmodern humanity.

Springer argues that popular culture simultaneously strengthens and eroticizes the blurring of the boundaries between humans and machines. More importantly, it portrays this blurring exercise as an exciting and pleasurable experience. Springer argues that sexual metaphors abound in the discourse of cyborgs, as they did in classical modernist depictions of machinery. Cyborgs *incorporate*, rather than merely affect, humans, and thus promote the fantasy of fusion, the ecstasy of the merger between the organic and inorganic.

Deleuze's notion of the machine as a connector and distributor of energy makes the same point; machines are transformation engines: they transmit and produce – they create consistency (assemblages) and connection. As such, they are erotically charged and invested with desire. As Andreas Huyssen has argued, in the electronic era wires and circuitry exercise another kind of seduction than the pistons and grinding engines of industrial machinery. I think that the main thrust of micro-electronic seduction, as exemplified by the novels of Gibson, Sterling and Cadigan, is that of the fusion of one's consciousness with the electronic network: a sort of cosmic orgasm which generates the meltdown of the boundary between the self and the technological other, also known as 'melting into the matrix'. Celebrated by techno-nerds and cyber-feminists alike (Plant 1997), the fusion into the matrix is at the heart of what Springer (1991) calls 'the pleasure of the interface'. In turn, this rests upon the escape from the maternal site of reproduction of the enfleshed self, in favour of integration into the abstract circuit of a collectively-managed electronic matrix linked to a central point of consciousness. The film aptly called *The Matrix* gives a vivid illustration of this reproductive nightmare and the anonymous incubator cells in which single units of human flesh are nurtured and brought to maturity. As I argued in chapter 4, the maternal has already been integrated into the techno-industrial complex.

The eroticism of this kind of techno-imaginary is evident.[3] Whereas the orgasmic if not orgiastic undertones of this interface with the machine and the subsequent blurring of the self are obvious, paradoxically enough the gender-boundaries of this whole exercise remain surprisingly resilient in their familiarity. At the level of their cultural representation, Michael Jackson and Arnold Schwarzenegger, to mention but two opposite examples, appear as anything but gender-free. They are in fact hyper-genderized, almost to the point of exaggeration.

In his seminal work on masculinity, fascism and war, Klaus Theweleit has suggested that the 'metallization' of the male body expresses an increasing sense of fragility and a crisis of masculine identity. By way of compensation, and even at the risk of complete loss of humanity, the male subject protects his corporality with an armour of impenetrability. Bukatman picks up and expands this point, playing the armoured body of the masculinist cyborg against the malleability of the human. It is an uneven battle, but the human, however battered, is still hanging in there, fighting for validation and proud to be flesh!

The hyper-masculinity of the militarized aggressive cyborg is another panic response of the male human trying to counteract his growing obsolescence.

It is also a misogynist reaction to the potentially threatening role of electronic technologies that induce a sort of passive consumption which is culturally coded as feminine or feminized. The impenetrable metallic body defies the blurring of boundaries, is impenetrable and uncontaminated: a sort of techno-fascist fantasy of self-sufficiency. Constance Penley (1985) has argued that this reconfiguration of masculinity as an aggressive cyborg-killer indicates that patriarchy is more willing to dispense with human life altogether than with masculine superiority. In other words, a culturally-enforced paradigm such as the cyborg is also structurally ambivalent in terms of gender, but quite traditional in its politics.

Meanwhile, as this kind of re-negotiation of gender identity goes on, the gender gap in the use of computers, in women's access to computer literacy, Internet equipment and other expensive technological apparatuses, as well as women's participation in programming and in designing the technology, will continue to grow wider. Similarly, the gap between first and third worlds in access to technology will also go on (Eisenstein, 1998). It is always at times of great technological advance that Western culture reiterates some of its most persistent habits, notably the tendency to create differences and organize them hierarchically. Thus, while computer technology seems to promise a world beyond gender differences, the gender gap grows wider. All the talk of a brand new telematic world masks an ever-increasing polarization of resources and means, in which women are the main losers. There is strong indication, therefore, that the shifting of conventional boundaries between the sexes and the proliferation of all kinds of differences through new technologies will not be nearly as liberating as the cyber-artists and Internet addicts want us to believe.

One of the great contradictions of digital images is that they titillate our imagination, promising the marvels and wonders of a gender-free world while simultaneously reproducing some of the most banal, flat images of gender identity and also class and race relations. Virtual reality images also titillate our imagination, as is characteristic of the pornographic regime of representation. As if the imaginative misery were not enough, postmodernity is marked by a widespread impact and a qualitative shift of pornography in every sphere of cultural activity. Pornography is more and more about power-relations and less and less about sex. In classical pornography sex was a vehicle by which to convey power-relations. Nowadays anything can become such a vehicle: the becoming-culture of pornography means that any cultural activity or product can become a commodity and through that process express inequalities, patterns of exclusion, fantasies of domination, desires for power and control (Kappeler 1987).

The imaginative poverty of virtual reality is all the more striking if you compare it to the creativity of some of the women artists I mentioned earlier. By comparison, the banality, the sexism, the repetitive nature of computer-designed video-games are appalling. As usual, at times of great changes and upheavals, the potential for the new engenders great fear, anxiety and in some cases even nostalgia for the previous regime.

The most effective strategy remains for women to use technology in order to disengage our collective imagination from the phallus and its accessory values, money, exclusion and domination, nationalism, iconic femininity and systematic violence. For instance, Kathryn Bigelow's *Strange Days* both mimes and exposes the links between contemporary interactive technologies, visual culture, drugs and the pornography industry. In her film, the 'squid' is a wireless device that transfers psycho-sexual sensations. These can be replayed in CD format, producing hallucinatory experiences in the viewer. These images are drawn from real-life experiences of the most violent kind, akin to 'snuff films'. They can be simulated via neuronal sensory transmission, through the cortex. The retina is declared obsolete and so is the human gaze. Simulation and hallucination are stimulated by a technology that both mimes and externalizes the human nervous system.

The central point remains: there is a credibility gap between the promises of virtual reality and cyberspace and the quality of what it delivers. It consequently seems to me that, in the short range, this new technological frontier will intensify the gender-gap and increase polarization between the sexes. We are back to the war metaphor, but its location is the real world, not the hyperspace of abstract masculinity. And its protagonists are no computer images, but the real social agents of post-industrial urban landscapes.

From (baby)boom to bust?

The decline of the humanistic vision and social practices of the subject has favoured a post-humanist understanding of both the self and of its intellectual and artistic forms of expression. In this respect, technology as the 'outside' of the subject can be said to be constitutive of what it can nowadays become. Brad Epps calls this 'technoasceticism' and he defines it as a disciplinary art which implies that 'every construction, of self, space and society is at the same time a skillful and systematic exercise in control' (1996: 82). Technoasceticism implies a constructive mode of technophilia, with a deep sense of responsibility built into it; it also implies both the denial of the old humanistic self and the desire to reinvent it anew: both the renunciation and the reconfiguration of the desiring body and of its pleasures. Art as well as technology plays a role in this techno-redefinition of subjectivity in a decidedly post-human mode.

A culture whose social imaginary is structured like this needs to be grounded in a contemporary brand of materialism, which I locate in philosophical nomadism. I think the greatest misunderstanding about Deleuze and Guattari's body-machines is that they are often taken literally, as actual pieces of wires, silicon, metal and circuitry, or else they are taken figuratively, as if automata and cyborgs best exemplified the philosophical concept of body-machines. That in turn generates wild and wide associative readings of cyborgs, terminators and the like as expressions of nomadic becoming-machines. The point I want to make, however, is that the nomadic body-machines are no metaphors: they are engines or devices that both capture and process forces and energies, facilitating interrelations, multiple connections and assemblages.

I would recommend instead that we read Deleuze and Guattari's body-machines as simply yet another figuration for the non-unitary nature of the subject. The 'machine-like' part merely refers to the subject's capacity for multiple, outward-bound interrelations with a number of external forces or others. The machine stands for networks of interconnections, arranged along lines of flight or of becoming. These do not follow a linear path, they are not teleologically ordained, but rather zigzag across multiple, unexpected and often contradictory variables. The selection and dosage forces that are intermingled is essential to the whole exercise. The model is the same as the animal's proximity, intimacy and possession of its territory. It is about symbiotic alliances and fusion; more about viral or parasitic interdependence than anything else. Deleuze uses images like swarms of insects; the interdependence of the wasp and the orchid, the mutual dependence on territorial frames of reference, to express the notion of 'desiring machines'. A desiring machine is a productive assemblage of selected forces for the sake of becoming-minoritarian: it is a nomadic subject.

As Goodchild points out, the Deleuzian machines are planes of immanence, they are connecting devices that anchor the subject to a territory, a set of assemblages and encounters. They are not about signification, human intention or the Heideggerian meaning of being; they are assemblages that create pattern through repetition, abstract machines which express images of thought. The image is unconscious in that it precedes the actual activity of thought, or rather can only be grasped as that which comes before it, and is consequently always already presupposed. They express certain forces and infuse them through the thinking process. As such, the Deleuzian machines are desiring machines, but not because they are the objects of (consumeristic) desires: they rather express impersonal forces and intensive resonances between the psychic and the social. Goodchild proceeds to commit, in my opinion, a lapse in theoretical style by citing Cronenberg's *Terminator* as an example of this. Gender blindness knows no limits.

He is not alone. The fantasy of unlimited re-embodiments or radical transformation through the internet is central to the ideology of those for whom the desire to be wired is central. Sherry Turkle (1995) sees the net as experimental grounds for multiple and heterogeneous identities. How they would

connect to issues of embodiments and to that mixture of wisdom and cumulated pain, which goes by the name of experience and which Sobchack
reminds us of, is an open question.

The implications for sexual difference are not less daunting, considering
that with the coming of electronic technology the intimacy between bodies
and machines reaches higher levels of complexity. In so far as contemporary
technologies blur the boundaries between humans and others, they are transgressive. As such, they are often taken as a symbol for all kinds of other
transgressions, including sexual ones. For instance, in a piece pointedly
called: 'Birth of the cyberqueer', Morton (1999: 370) takes Deleuze and
Guattari's body-machines as pointing to a space of 'sexual deregulation',
where sexuality can be Oedipalized and return to its primary, ludic and polymorphous flows. Morton argues that Deleuzian bodies share in this queer
movement. In a similar mode Jordan (1995) adapts Deleuze's theory of
desire to his interpretation of rave parties and the culture of house music
and ecstasy. The machine-like assemblage of these events is crucial. 'This
undifferentiated state is a collective delirium produced by thousands of people
making the connections of drugs to dance, dance to drugs, drugs to time,
time to music and so on, and thereby gradually constructing the state of
raving and so the Bodies-without Organs of raving' (1995: 130). I always
find myself resisting these pop-interpretations of Deleuze's concepts, while
admiring the creativity of those who so freely kidnap these complex notions
and adapt them to their own ends. In the case of the drug culture, I doubt
very much that one needs or particularly gains anything by attempting to
frame it within a nomadic theory of desire. I remain sceptical of 'narco-
philosophers' of all kinds.

Richard Barbrook has written angrily against the sixties rhetoric of many
Internet gurus. Some of them embrace Deleuze and Guattari and attempt
the unholy alliance of digital elitism in the name of sixties libertarianism.
They thus end up with a form of aristocratic anarchism which is eerily
similar to Californian neo-liberalism. In the post-1989 context of decline
of revolutionary ideologies, the Internet prophets are the only ones still
pursuing dreams of change and social transformation. Barbrook argues that
the aesthetization of the sixties is central to the European approach to
Internet experiments, in opposition to the corporate ideology dominant in
California:

Deleuze and Guattari seem to provide theoretical metaphors which describe
the non-theoretical aspects of the net. For instance, the rhizome captures how
cyberspace is organized as an open-ended, spontaneous and horizontal network. Their Bodies-without-organs phase can be used to romanticize cyber-
sex. Deleuze and Guattari's nomad myth reflects the mobility of contemporary
net users as workers and tourists.

The techno-nomads control the Internet and have re-invented avant-gardism with techno-music spear-heading the revolution. For Barbrook, the alliance between liberal individualism, corporate ideology and this techno-primitivism is the worst possible connection. He argues that Deleuze's philosophy does not belong with such absurd bed-fellows and that a more rigorous approach is needed to theorize positively and not sentimentally the unique brand of electronic vitalism that is running through contemporary cyber-culture.

Bukatman agrees that the most serious problems arise from the unholy alliance of the cyber-ideology with individualism and the liberal market economy, and the sentimental attachment to a humanist definition of the subject as 'conscience and a heart'. After that, however, Bukatman goes on to provide a romanticized and inaccurate account of Deleuze as a techno-anarchist who can lead us to neo-transcendence through technology. 'Deleuze and Guattari are cyberpunks, too, constructing fictions of terminal identity in the nearly familiar language of a techno-surrealism' (1993: 326).

Again, I am rather sceptical of such affirmations and I would rather use Deleuze and Guattari's notion of 'bodies without organs' – a sort of organic bachelor machine – to deconstruct the myth of wholeness and organicism, but also to refuse the technocratic take-over of the human body. I agree with Bukatman, however, when he argues that the political resistance suggested by philosophical nomadism consists in working within the belly of the beast, situating the human as co-extensive and intimately connected to the technological, but also stressing the way in which the human occupies the threshold between technology and narration.

Hayles (1999: 286) also makes a powerful intervention in favour of a more sober and balanced account of contemporary technobodies:

> But the posthuman does not really mean the end of humanity. It signals instead the end of a certain conception of the human. . . . What is lethal is not the posthuman as such but the grafting of the posthuman onto a liberal human-ist view of the self. . . . Located within the dialectic of pattern/randomness and grounded in embodied actuality rather than disembodied information, the posthuman offers resources for rethinking the articulation of humans with intelligent machines.

Resting on Deleuze and on feminist epistemology, Hayles attacks the classical humanistic notion that subjectivity must coincide with conscious agency, and takes a firm stand in favour of a radical redefinition of the subject, in such a way as to avoid some of the mistakes of the humanist past, notably the liberal vision of an autonomous subject whose 'manifest destiny is to dominate and control nature' (Hayles 1999: 288).

None of this need be catastrophic but rather a way to allow for new life-forms and new forms of cohabitation between humans and technological others. Meta(l)morphoses need not be cast in the apocalyptic mode or mood.

I would recommend that we approach them nomadically – because we are indeed rooted, even though we go with the flow.

Conclusion

In relation to cyber-culture, I think it important to take distance equally from two related pitfalls. On the one hand is the euphoria of professional optimists who advocate proliferation of differences and the promise of electronic democracy for citizens affected by the 'desire to be wired' (John Barlow, Nick Negroponte and others) as an easy panacea; or the optimism of the techno-nerds who grab advanced technology and especially cyberspace as the possibility for multiple fantasies of expansion, ubiquity or escape. On the other hand I also disagree with the many prophets of doom who mourn the decline of the classical world and transform nostalgia into a political platform, not to speak of those, like the Unabomber, who fall into apoca-lyptic violence. This cautionary tone may well be the trademark of a genera-tion of intellectuals who still remember, with a wry smile, their first mechanical typewriter, as they play with the palm-tops of today. The speed of techno-logical change is such that many of us still treasure our 45 rpm records, let alone our LPs: dismayed and yet tenacious, we run the risk of turning our households into a museum of 'dead' media!

I would therefore rather keep a sober perspective on what I consider as the great challenge of contemporary social theory and cultural practice, namely how to make the new technologies enhance the embodied subject. This does not mean, however, that I will not also be critical of the cyber-teratological imaginary itself. My specific target in this regard is the tend-ency, which I consider nihilistic, that consists in declaring the superfluity of the body and its alleged irrelevance, or else to reduce it to 'meat', or to the status of a familiar parasite and the liquid unsubstantiality of the 'wetware'. This results paradoxically in both accelerating and denying its mortality, rendering bodily pain and suffering irrelevant in the process. Against such denials, I want to re-assert my bodily brand of materialism and remain to the end proud to be flesh!

Technology has become a challenge – it is the chance we have given ourselves, as a culture, to reinvent ourselves and display some creativity. Technology should assist human evolution. If the question is not: 'what we are?', but 'who do we want to become?', then the next step is: how can techno-culture help us achieve this? I would consequently reset the question of technology in the framework of the challenge of change or transforma-tion, which I see as central to both mapping the present and working towards a constructive future. We need instead to learn to think differently, more self-critically. The 'we' in question refers to those who occupy a centre

– any of the poly-located centres which situate most inhabitants of the north of the world in a position of structural advantage: some *more* than others, of course – but all more than most of the other dwellers of this planet. Acknowledging one's participation in and sharing of locations of power is the starting-point for the cartographic method, also known in feminism as the politics of location.

To sum up: while criticizing the imaginative deficit of our culture, that is to say our collective inability to find adequate representations of the kind of embodied nomadic subjects we have already become – multiple, complex, multi-layered selves, I have explored the kind of conceptual and representational shifts of perspective that would be needed in order for changes and transformations to be enacted at the depth of subjectivity, and thus make a lasting impact on the social and cultural spheres. I have quarrelled with the nostalgic tendency which accounts for changes, especially technological ones, in a paranoid mode that renders them as 'monstrous', pathological, decadent or threatening. I have also offered, both in this chapter and in chapter 4, counter-readings of these changes in such a way as to highlight their positivity and force.

One of the risks of the 'hype' that surrounds the meta(l)morphoses of cyber-culture is that of re-creating a hard core, unitary vision of the subject, under the cover of pluralistic fragmentation. In the language of philosophical nomadism, this would produce the deception of a quantitative multiplicity which does not entail any qualitative shifts. To avoid this pitfall, which fits in with the neo-liberal euphoria of much contemporary politics, I think it important to critique the unholy alliance of cyborgs with the classical bourgeois notion of individualism and the corollaries of commodification and consumerism which it entails.

A strong sense of embodied and embedded materialism is very relevant to the task of rethinking the symbiotic relationship between humans and machines, while avoiding the hype. I have taken a clear position, wanting to be equally distanced from both a hyped-up disembodiment and fantasies of escape, and a re-essentialized, centralized notion of liberal individualism. I have provided my own reading of technobodies and of the web of power-relations and effects they are navigating in. I have concluded that consumerism-minded techno-hype neither wipes out nor solves very traditional patterns of exclusion and domination. I do not see it as a guarantee for much progress in re-locating the traditional entitlements of a subject-position that is made to coincide with masculine, white, heterosexual, European identity. Nor does it help to re-configure either femininity as the classical *O*ther of Man, or of whiteness as a position of naturalized structural privilege. In some ways, as I argued in this chapter, techno-cultures even reinforce some of the worst traits of the traditional regimes of power, using the management of the insecurities triggered by the changes as the pre-test to the restoration of traditional hierarchies.

In my analysis of the social imaginary of late post-industrial societies, I singled out some trends in the identification of women with machines. One of these is that women and machines are closely associated. As a matter of fact, in modernity the machine often acts as a substitute for functions socially fulfilled by women. That goes as well for household appliances, as for the eroticized body-double of the film *Metropolis*. Because of this socially induced association, which is activated by popular culture and especially cinema, women and machines are presented as in competition with each other. What they compete for is, mostly, male attention, be it that of the father or the (hetero)sexual partner. It is not surprising then that women are often suspicious of technology and wary of machines. A slight touch of techno-phobia is understandable, given the close identification of the female body with the mechanically reproduced body-double.

This changes with the coming of postmodern machinery and electronics. The increasing degree of incorporation of technology by humans also shifts the grounds for the interaction between women and technology. I argued earlier in this chapter that whereas in modernity woman was associated with technology, in postmodernity the maternal/material feminine is represented as already incorporated into the technological complex. This incorporation has the effect of re-inscribing the feminine as the site of biological recreation, and of assimilating it into techno-industrial machinery. This also implies that the technological field is no longer the site of inscription of the feminine, but rather a space of sexual indeterminacy, which I rendered in terms of a trans-sexual imaginary. Read alongside the confinement of women back to a technologically-controlled reproductive role, this shift of perspective is problematic.

At first sight, in fact, the sexual undecidability of these new technologies, and the promises of endless restructuring and redefinitions of sexual identity which they entail, may appear attractive. Hence the tone of euphoria which marks a great many cyber-feminists. On closer scrutiny, however, I would argue that there is ample room for concern. As is often the case with promises of trans-sexual 'open-ness', in fact, the evacuation of the feminine is not far off. That would not be a problem in itself; I long for the by-passing of the dialectics of sexual difference understood as pejoration. The problem is that these shifts of perspective, changes and transformations are not taking place in a vacuum. Nor are they the mere effects of textual or discursive strategies. These transformations are rather embedded and embodied in the specific historicity of a social context which constructs technologies as liberating, while using them for the most confining, profit-making and sexually conservative ends. The example of bio-technologies, reproductive technologies and of women's access to information and communications technologies are significant in this respect.

Hence, my commitment to a materialist approach to the analysis of contemporary culture, which I have been defending throughout this book in

terms of the need for cartographic accounts of the changes that are occurring in post-industrial societies and in their imaginary. The implications of
my position are many-fold: on the theoretical front, I have grown very
dissatisfied with semiotically-based, psychoanalytically-oriented approaches
to 'cultural studies'. More especially, I am concerned by the disregard or
obliteration of material conditions, the materiality of structures of signification, which these linguistic methods imply. I am even more worried about
the widening gap between this 'cultural' approach and a socially-oriented
political one.

In reaction to this, and in order to attempt to bridge this gap, I want to
re-assert the need for a philosophical brand of embodied and embedded
nomadism. This implies that attention be given to the simultaneity and
mutual implication of issues of culture and power, political economies and
structures of signification. In order to think about the simultaneity of such
effects, I have argued for a new definition of the subject in keeping with
philosophical nomadism. This would be a subject that combines qualitative
shifts with a firm rejection of liberal individualism, and connects a distinct
sense of singularity with respect for complexities and interconnections. This
is a collectively-oriented, externally-bound, multiple subject whose singularity is the result of constant re-negotiations with a variety of forces.

Such a vision of the subject requires re-adjustments also in patterns of
desire. Sexualities are also being re-negotiated and re-configured along multiple, nomadic and hence potentially contradictory axes. Right across such
multiplicities, however, I have re-asserted the recurrence of a process of
'feminization' of the sensibility of nomadic subjects, in terms of affectivity,
fluidity, porosity of boundaries and constant interrelations. I have read such
a process of 'becoming-Woman' in terms of the idea of 'the sensible transcendental' proposed by Irigaray, and of Deleuze's notion of the empirical
transcendental.

This is a thorny issue, because it is clear that a generalized 'becoming-
Woman' of both male and female sexual identities and a relative blurring
of the boundaries between them is one of the features of post-industrial
societies. I have serious doubts as to whether this kind of becoming woman
is actually a step forward for all concerned. The point, however, is that such
a feminization process, with the subsequent blurring of the boundaries
of sexual difference, is culturally quite dominant. As I stated earlier, in the
techno-teratological imaginary of postmodernity, as well as in the hype
surrounding the machinic 'other', the feminine understood as the socially
constructed representation of *W*oman as the *O*ther of the Same finds itself
in a set of traditional positions. It is once again assimilated to biological
reproduction, though this is re-packaged under the cover of technologically-
driven sexual indeterminacy, or gender-bending. Read with Deleuze, this
tendency marks the becoming-Woman of Man and of the majority-based

vision of women. I have consequently argued that sharper differentiations are needed of the process of becoming-Woman/animal/insect/machines. The becomings of the majority are dissymmetrical with those of the minorities and they continue to produce strikingly different social imaginaries. While stressing this dissymmetry, I have praised the process of 'becoming-minoritarian' as an important re-location of subjectivity. In other words, it would be paradoxical if nomadic becomings were unilinear: they have to be rhizomatic, that is to say complex and dissonant. Sexual difference remains an axis of differentiation in this process.

The fantasy, the promise, the socially-induced yearning for sexual indeterminacy and a proliferation of gender-positions, which I have addressed throughout this book, are not, in my opinion, an actual progress in either the representation of the feminine or the real-life conditions of those who are the empirical referents for the feminine, namely women. Once again, therefore, I want to issue a very cautionary note about the impact of the new technologies and their potentially liberating force. My concern is increased by issues of ethnicity and by the obvious racialization of processes of access to and participation in the new technologies. As Eisenstein (1998) put it, the 'global obscenities' of continuing power-relations, structural exclusions and domination make a mockery of the liberatory promises of the new technologies.

At the same time, I do not want to fall back into the traditional technophobia that has marked so much of the feminist movement. I just want to argue for new forms of experimentation, discussion, and application of technologies to the needs, aspirations and to the imaginary of women, feminists, anti-racists, and other political subjects. On the political horizon of postmodernity, under the impact of the contradictory forces at work nowadays, I argued that the body has returned with a vengeance, but as is often the case with repetition, it does not return exactly to the same place. The youth rebellions of Seattle and other earth-related forms of political resistance have displayed half-naked embodied figures with the inscription: '*This* body is against genetically modified food.' The most photographed or filmed bodies were female. Their claim to the specificity of their body strikes me as a political form of strategic essentialism that inherits the feminist tactics of 'Our bodies, ourselves', but also opens them up to wider horizons.

Sexual difference, from being a boundary marker, has become a threshold for the elaboration and the expression of multiple differences, which extend beyond gender but also beyond the human. The emergence of the earth and of 'earth-others' as political subjects, is the surest indicator of this shift of perspective. I want to read this with the eco-philosophy of nomadism, as an attempt to re-think in a materialist manner the intricate web of interrelations that mark the contemporary relationship to one's environment. On the basis of Irigaray's theory of the 'virtual feminine' and of Deleuze's theory of the becoming-woman/animal/machine/imperceptible I would argue that this is a new kind of political subjectivity which no longer assumes the unitary, self-evident subject of modernity or of 'standpoint' feminism. This is rather a non-unitary, multiple, complex subject that inhabits several locations and moves between them, though not always with ease.

Such new political subjects move on the background of the post-industrial world-view and on the ruins of the post-nuclear condition. This subject moves in the political economy of terror or fear for the imminent and immanent accident, of the impending catastrophe of the disaster within and without. Technology is a powerful mediator for these fears, and a major factor in actualizing them. The nuclear refutes historically the Enlightenment promise of liberation through rationality. The post-nuclear predicament is marked by the fear of contamination, of viral attacks that result in an evolutionary catastrophe, a devolutionary crises, a metabolic breakdown. Art-works such as Ballard and Cronenberg's *Crash* are cathartic in that they exorcise the fear by actualizing it. They consequently enact the aesthetics of 'traumatic realism', the enfleshed point of no-return, the fatal impact of bodies in the lethal realm of pure speed. They also point to an ethics of neo-realist appraisals of risks and fears, which in turn expresses scepticism towards more grandiose meta-discourses such as Marxism and psychoanalysis. I have described this as a colder and slightly more cruel political sensibility.

Faithful to my initial promise that politics begins with our desires and that desires escape us, in that they are the driving force that propels us, I want to argue that we need to express political passions in ways that are adequate to our historical condition. This stresses the necessity of taking political affects of passions seriously. This means that, to account for them, cartographics are needed that map out different embodied and embedded positions. And intellectual dialogues need to be set up around exchanges of respective cartographies, in a new alliance with nomadic readers.

All this said, I remain deeply technophilic and extremely hopeful. Being a child of my time, I am in love with changes and transformations and very excited about the path-breaking developments I have witnessed in my lifetime. Neither nostalgia nor Utopia will do. We rather need a leap forward towards a creative re-invention of life-conditions, affectivity and figurations for the new kind of subjects which we have already become. In the meantime, we need to live with transitions and processes, in-between states and transformations. In terms of theoretical practice, I would recommend that we do not rush forward to hasty resolutions of complexities we hardly can account for. Let us instead linger a little longer within complexities and paradoxes, resisting the fear of imminent catastrophe. Let us take the *time* to go through with these processes. Time is all one needs.

There is consequently little time or space for nostalgia. Deleuze's hybrid nomadic selves, the multiple feminist-operated becoming-woman of women,

Irigaray's woman as not-one, Haraway's cyborgs, not unlike Cixous's new Medusa, are often rendered in the old-fashioned social imaginary as monstrous, hybrid, scary deviants. What if what was at fault here, however, were the very social imaginary that can *only* register changes of this magnitude on the panic-stricken moralistic register of deviancy? What if these unprogrammed others were forms of subjectivity that have simply shrugged off the shadow of binary logic and negativity and have moved on? Through met(r)amorphoses and meta(l)morphoses, the process of transformation of the subject goes on. So what if this new subject looks, feels and sounds unusual? S/he is monstrous, mixed, hybrid, beautiful and, guess what . . . ? S/he is laughing!

Epilogue

The only constant in today's world is change, but that is neither a simple nor a unilinear process. It rather operates with web-like sets of simultaneous shifts and contradictory trends. Bio-technologies, genetics and techno-sciences are major factors in the current social mutations. It is indeed the case, as Anne Fausto-Sterling points out, that 'we live in a geno-centric world' (Fausto-Sterling 2000: 235). The human has been subsumed in global relations of intimacy, complicity and proximity with forces of the inhuman and post-human kind: scientific, industrial and military complexes, global communication networks, processes of commodification and exchange on a global scale. These are complex networks of interface with technologies that have made 'Life' into their favourite control mechanism. The political economy of such a world in flux is the management of the insecurity and fears induced by the perennial state of change. In a Deleuzian perspective I would say that a constant state of crisis is what our system is all about. Be it a crisis of human 'Life', human rights, or human reproduction, post-industrial societies are confronted by the threat to the generic category of the human. This is a problem that defies the powers of analysis, let alone of redemption, by modernist political agency. Massumi puts it admirably: 'the "human" is more closely akin to a saleable virus, neither dead nor alive, than a reasonable animal standing at the pinnacle of earthly life-forms, one step below the divine on a ladder of perfection' (1998: 60).

Tracking the fluctuations of this new, post-human, disorder is the task of critical theory and it is a task which, as I argued throughout this book, meets with dense resistance, partly because of the illogical, self-contradictory nature of the realities it is trying to account for. I have stated time and again that reasoned cartographies are the starting point for the production of adequate accounts of the realities involved. The ultimate aim is the quest for resistance, but also creative and qualitative theoretical leaps across the uncertainties. I plead for pragmatic experimentations with sustainable models of nomadic subjectivity, in the hope that their vital structure will not be homologized into the system of commodification. In today's world more conceptual creativity is as necessary as an extra bit of audacity.

With this book I hope to have produced, albeit temporarily, an unprogrammed mutation in the order of our thinking, a momentary disruption, a reflexive pause and a point of resistance. The time frame in which I would want to express this is the future perfect, or anterior future, which links the present, past and future in connecting the propositional content of my ideas to sets of interrelated outside political forces. My political passion lies with positive metamorphoses, the kinds that destabilize dominant power-relations, de-territorialize Majority-based identities and values and infuse a joyful sense of empowerment into subjects bent on becoming. In so doing I have connected together the work of critical theory with that of the imagination, pleading for conceptual creativity and risk-taking as a way of thought.

Through it all I have argued that philosophical nomadism is not a heterogeneous brand of monism, but the actualization of multiple differences. Sexual difference as stating the principle of 'not-one' at the heart of subjectivity remains for me a relevant starting-point in the process of nomadic becomings. This is not a quantitative plurality within a one-dimensional and mono-directional system, but a qualitative multiplicity in an open-ended series of complexities. It is not an essentialist instinct or drive, but a vitalist tendency without an aim or an end, a non-self-enforcing and non-capitalizing entity. It is my conviction that this non-unitary, nomadic subject is the prerequisite for an ethics of complex but sustainable subjectivity in the age of the posthuman.

Let me sum up my main conclusions.

Against disembodiment

The radical bodily materialism of philosophical nomadic thought issues a firm warning against the fantasies of light from the body. Prosthetic enhancement is one thing, the fantasy of omnipotence another altogether. Rhizomatic or nomadic philosophy constitutes an anti-essentialist brand of vitalism that stresses radical immanence, or the bodily roots of subjectivity. This is, however, a technophilic position that opposes the abstractions of cyber-culture, while calling for new figurations of the subject in a manner that is co-extensive with his or her technological habitat. Nomadic body-machines are powerful figurations for the non-unitary subject-in-becoming that I consider as the most relevant alternative to the crisis of the humanist subject. It rests upon and brings to a positive resolution the painful historical process of disengaging theories of subjectivity from the concept of individualism. They also seal a new alliance between conceptual thought and creativity, reason and the imagination.

In praise of the principle of non-profit

In opposition to the metaphysical and the modernist vision of the machine as a harmonious assembly of parts working together to produce a socially desirable result (wealth, truth, etc.), nomadic machines are relentlessly gratuitous. They promote the principle of non-profit and function as unruly, disorderly, cacophonous, non-productive or sterile machines. They aim at resisting capital cumulation, at dissipative structures of gratuitous self-expression which therefore militate against self-destruction. Their flows of energy re-confirm the joy of creative wastefulness and resist the negative passion of greed. This is in direct opposition to the techno-hype that surrounds new technological developments in advanced post-industrial societies. As a dissipative, non-profit model of the technobody, nomadic subjectivity critiques liberal individualism and promotes instead the positivity of multiple connections. It also eroticizes interconnectedness, by emphasizing the role of passions, empathy and desire as non-self-aggrandizing modes of relation to one's social and human habitat.

In favour of viral politics

If we define human embodiment in accordance with philosophical nomadism, as a molecular organism, a bio-chemical factory, a neurological maze, an evolutionary engine endowed with its own temporality – both the time-sequence of the DNA and the more individualized or personal genealogy of memory – then we need to develop forms of politics that are suitable. Viral politics is one of these: it is a form of micro-politics that is embedded in the human body. It is territorially-based and environmentally-bound, much like an animal–machine compound. It is also a relentlessly generative organism that aims at living on. The 'machine-like' element here refers to the dynamic process of interaction between the human and non-human components of this subject. This is consequently an externally-directed, complex and collectively assembled subjectivity that disrupts the anthropocentrism of most human and social sciences and of critical theory. They cannot be dealt with through the modernist schemes of agency, but require a conceptual shift in the structures of political subjectivity.

Moreover, through this energetic intervention in the contemporary meta(l)-morphoses, nomadic body-machines as anti-representational, non-profit assemblages encourage us to think about the in-depth transformations of post-industrial culture as *just* changes. Just a set of mutations, emancipated from the monstrous and grotesque imaginary we have inherited from the nineteenth century and which tends to pathologize all that is new and different in the order of transformations of the human. Our politics begins with our desires to enact positive transformations on the environment we happen to inhabit. We need to think, resist and act the same way we live, that is to say, g-locally.

In favour of sexually differentiated cartographies

We need to think critically about the processes of change and mutation that both overwhelm our habits and expectations by saturating our social space and also fall short of their own over-inflated promises. Gender and ethnicity play a major role in controlling access to technological enhancement in these post-industrial and post-human times. This note of warning exposes techno-hype as a simultaneous process of titillation and disappointment about our own meta(l)morphoses. It would also attempt to re-embody it and re-embed it by injecting the principle of radical immanence into it and, with it, the politics of sexual difference in terms of the recognition of the continuing power of the dissymmetrical relations between the sexes.

Considering the normative role played by the genderized value-system, more attention to gender politics in the sense of sexual difference may also help us to provide more adequate figurations for the social transformations of our times. Against the centuries-old habit that consists in pathologizing and de-valuing all that is 'different', we may be able instead to re-configure transformations and processes of change positively. They would appear like sets of radical mutations acting on the 'g-local' stage, with much digitalized sound and fury but, for once and yet again, actually *signifying* nothing. Beyond signification, these transformations could be taken as the positive expression of nomadic, non-unitary subjectivity. However technologically enhanced and precisely because of its 'techno-natural' structure, nomadic subjects are radically embedded and embodied and therefore sexualized and accountable for their own spatio-temporal locations. This is only the first step towards a new ethics of accountability.

For an ethics of sustainability

Following Deleuze's re-reading of Spinoza and Irigaray's ethics of sexual difference, I am committed to grounding ethical accountability on a non-unitary vision of the subject. I want to stress the need for a new ethics for non-unitary cyborg-subjects that undergo met(r)amorphoses/meta(l)morphoses without altogether losing sight of the norms and values of the human condition. Contrary to those who argue against the need for a subject, I want to argue both for a dispersed form of affectivity, a flowing type of coherence and for the necessity of reconfiguring the subject. For me, alternative figurations of the subject are cartographic accounts of many, often contradictory, positions. What I yearn for is a high-tech, vitalistic, accountable figuration of border-crossings. Moreover, I wish to re-connect such transitions, transits and transformations to flesh and body and to a nomadic vision of the subject that, however much in process and in becoming, is still there.

Through emphasis on his or her embedded and embodied practices, however, I am interested in casting nomadic subjectivity in the mode of sustainability and endurance. I regret that I cannot pursue this further here.[1]

On bungee-jumping, or the art of hanging in there

In the last month of the last year of the last millennium I watched in London a performance by De la Guarda Company. They are bungee-jumping artist-athletes who perform lyrical, aggressive, fabulous movements of body and soul while hanging from ropes in mid-air, to the sound of extremely loud contemporary high-technology music.

Like the 'Sensation' exhibition this was a cultural event based on the concept of 'fusion': it is where the house-party meets 'Cirque du Soleil' and street fashion. This produced a state of flow that required high concentration as well as extreme physical and psychic daring. The result was a permanent challenge to the sensory apparatus. One was challenged by extreme levels of everything, from the volume of the music, to speed of the performers, the variations of the rhythm, the sharpness of the visual supports and the sheer volume of bodies one was surrounded by, and stimulated, titillated into extreme sensation also by the physical discomfort of having to stand up in a rain-soaked tent for the full duration of the performance. One's entire system was stretched to the extreme.

The impact of mood-enhancement technologies of the self – from the cult of fitness to drug-taking – was overwhelming: post-industrial culture seems to need deeper, faster, more thrilling kicks, more acceleration of sensory perception. The field of sensation is hungry for more, the doors of perception flung open more and more widely apart, seeking for proximity to danger. It is a state of intoxication that dematerializes the body while asserting it all the more firmly. It is almost a challenge to the limit of one's awareness, a constant clash with the senses. Who can endure and for how long?

The result was a simulated hallucination – consensual only in so far as I actually paid the ticket to get in there. Traditional modes of perception and acquired habits of spectatorship were peeled away and boundaries between the unfamiliar and the intolerable shifted. The effect was extraordinary: it was molecular, viral, mimetic, cosmic and ephemeral, sub-cutaneous and irresistible. It was the final crash of habits which had grown so close to our senses that we had thought them eternal. What are our 'habits' anyway? Just the cumulation of repeated experiences; the stock of predictable repetitions over a measurable stretch of time: habit is the in-built temporality of the obvious, the regular, the same. A habit is not really something other than the solemn preservation of experiences from the past, as expressed in the authoritative voice of the self, the nation, the family, masculinity in its hegemonic mode, his master's voice perpetuating the sound-bites of the same. Habits – even sensory habits – are micro-addictions applied to everyday life: 'we've always done it this way . . . it's always been like this.' One grows dependent on them: habits, customs, traditions become addictive. They are just your average legal drugs, life-support systems which are naturalized out of convenience.

Transformations of our sensory, perceptive and conceptual habits are everywhere in contemporary culture and because they are everywhere, they have become invisible. They have permeated the social and cultural spaces bringing about a collective fascination with speed, acceleration, intensities. Mood-enhancement is another word for cultural consumption: music pumped straight into the ears by walk- or diskmans to allow each one his or her acoustic environment; the beat of techno-music defying the heartbeat of even the fittest; fast driving; convulsive dancing induced by a number of acoustic and pharmaceutical stimulants. Singular modes of social behaviour are wiped out into a collective search for moods that can fix you. It is a feast of the sense-less, as Kathy Acker had so prophetically seen; it is the senses stretched to the extreme simulating the new, the unfamiliar, the unknown.

But it was all only a show, a simulation of this extreme stimulation. These athletes-artists were miming the consensual hallucination of cyberspace and virtual reality, although it was actually enhanced by the voluptuousness of extreme physical risk. The performers rained down on one from the ceiling, hanging on their bungee-jumping ropes; up and down they went, grabbing whoever they could as they bounced back up towards the top of the roof. What were the statistical probabilities of being the one who was picked out? or of crashing? The pattern was clear: ad hoc, random access, easy selection, no progression: this is the cruel law of the encounter between the techno-bodies falling from the ceiling and the gravitationally-bound ones still stuck to the ground. This was the traumatic return of the real bodies, muscular and post-human. Those two artists hanging on a bungee-jumping rope were walking horizontally across the side-walls like super-fit performers, not the wired-up fantasy of some computer programmer. Yet they looked just as unreal. This was the triumph of the technobody, in all its unexpected mutations. Like W.B. Yeats' long-legged flies on a stream, they pursued the most unlikely trajectory of humans turned into insects, into machines, gone out of our common co-ordinates. It was a transmutation of the senses and a transfiguration of the sense of self.

I was watching a collective metamorphosis. Those in it were no floating signifiers, but rather fleeting reminders of a humanity that has half-gone, and yet still endures: just hanging in there. Aren't we all?

Notes

Chapter 1   Becoming Woman, or Sexual Difference Revisited

1   I owe this witty formulation to the discussions with my colleagues in the European Network for Women's Studies, ATHENA, officially funded by the Socrates Programme of the European Commission.
2   The work of the European Network for Women's Studies within the official education and research programmes of the European Commission are of relevance to the project of building new bridges with the United States. For an overview, see Rosi Braidotti and Esther Vonk (eds.), *ATHENA Network: The Making of European Women's Studies* vol. I (Utrecht University, April 2000).

Chapter 2   Zigzagging through Deleuze and Feminism

1   See Rosi Braidotti (1981), 'Féminisme et philosophie: la critique du pouvoir et la pensée féministe contemporaine', doctoral dissertation, May 1981, Pantheon-Sorbonne University Paris; (1984) 'Femmes et philosophie: questions à suivre', *La revue d'en Face* 13, 23–33; (1985) 'Modelli di dissonanza: donne e/in filosofia' in Patrizia Magli (ed.), *Le Donne e i segni*, Urbino: Il Lavoro editoriale, 23–37; (1991a) *Patterns of Dissonance*, Cambridge: Polity, Jardine 1985; and Emerton 1986.
2   I am grateful to Roland Bogue for elucidating this point.
3   For a feminist analysis see Diamond and Quinby 1988, and McNay 1992.
4   Inventory, 'Intent on Dissent Survey Project n.2, 1999', of *Crash!* Exhibition, November 1999, London: Institute of Contemporary Arts.
5   See for instance the double CD, *In Memoriam: Gilles Deleuze*, Mille Plateaux 1996, Force Inc. Music Works, Frankfurt. I am grateful to Wander Eikelboom for this reference.

6   An example of this is the tendentious and misguided account of the failure of Deleuze-inspired 'Cultural Studies' in Miller (1993).

7   For a useful introduction to this aspect of Deleuze's work, see Bogue 1989.

8   See for instance: Stivale 1991 and Mills Norton 1986.

9   My translation.

10   My translation. (Wittig 1982: 116).

11   For an illuminating account of Hocquengem's theories, see Marshall 1997.

Chapter 3   Met(r)amorphoses: becoming Woman/Animal/Insect

1   Stivale distinguishes the following:

    1   becoming intense/child/woman: V. Woolf, D. H. Lawrence, H. Miller, Proust, Kafka;

    2   becoming animal: V. Woolf, Lovecraft, Hofmannsthal, Melville, Kafka, D. H. Lawrence, V. Slepian, H. Miller, Faulkner, Fitzgerald;

    3   becoming imperceptible: Castaneda, Lovecraft, V. Slepian, Hofmannsthal, Proust, P. Moran, Fitzgerald, Kerouac, V. Woolf, Kierkegaard, Michaux, Artaus, H. Miller;

    4   becoming hecceite in writing: C. Bronte, D. H. Lawrence, Faulkner, M. Tournier, Bradbury, V. Woolf, N. Sarraute, Artaud, Holderlin, Kleist, Proust.

2   For an attempt to explore the possible resonances between Deleuze and Jung, see Semetsky (1999).

3   I will develop this in a forthcoming study on sustainable ethics.

4   The authors are Randy Thornhill and Craig Palmer, for MIT Press, 2000.

5   For a very early outline of the 'becoming animal' see the special (1981) issue of *Polysexuality. Semiotext(e)*, 4, 1.

6   See for instance the enlightening collection edited by Dorrit Einersen and Ingeborg Nixon (1995).

7   Electricity as a source of life is central to *Frankenstein, Metropolis, L'Inhumaine* and *L'Eve Future*. It will remain so till the nineteen fifties, when it turns into a means of executionary death (*It Came from Outer Space*; *Attack of the Fifty-Foot Woman*) just as nuclear energy moves to centre-stage.

8   For a feminist critique of Deleuze's alleged philosophical orientalism, see Grewal Kaplan (1994).

Chapter 4   Cyber-teratologies

1   See also on this point White (1995).

2   On this point I disagree strongly with Ian Buchanan's hazardous attempts to graft Jameson on to the Deleuzian abstract machines, or diagrams.

3   For a very pictorial ilustration of this, see the film directed by Johan Grimonprez: 'Dial H.I.S.T.O.R.Y.' (1998), with musical score by David Shea.

4 It would be interesting to analyse this in the light of La Mettrie's philosophical masterpiece, *L'Homme machine*, and I regret I cannot pursue this here.

5 This is the case of the film *Weird Science*, where three teenage boys design their favourite woman on the computer, discussing at length the size of her breasts.

6 For a more detailed exposition see: R. Braidotti (1994a) 'Mothers, monsters and machines', in *Nomadic Subjects* and (1996) 'Signs of wonder and traces of doubt', in Lykke and Braidotti (eds.) *Between Monsters, Goddesses and Cyborgs*, London: Zed Books.

7 Anneke Smelik has commented on the analogy between Ripley and Joan of Arc, especially in *Alien III* (1996).

8 See for instance Kroker, A. and M. L. (1987).

Chapter 5 Meta(l)morphoses: the Becoming-Machine

1 The term 'robot' was coined by the Czech writer Karel Capek in 1917, from the Czech word for slave. In 1920 Capek published the futuristic *R.U.R.*

2 I am grateful to Anneke Smelik for the analysis of the cyberpunk and cyborg film genres.

3 For a more explicit discussion, see Rheingold (1990).

Epilogue

1 I am developing this idea in another study on sustainable ethics.

Bibliography

Acker, Kathy 1995: 'The end of the world of white men'. In J. Halberstam and Ira Livingston (eds), *Posthuman Bodies*, Bloomington: Indiana University Press.

Alcoff, Linda 2000: 'Philosophy matters: a review of recent work in feminist philosophy'. *Signs*, 25, (3), spring 2000, 841–82.

Amis, Martin 1987: *Einstein's Monsters*. London: Penguin.

Anderson, Laurie 1982: 'From the Air', *Big Science* CD, Warner USA.

Anderson, Laurie 1984: *United States*. New York: Harper & Row.

Appadurai, Arjun 1994: 'Disjuncture and difference in the global cultural economy'. In P. Williams and L. Chrisman, *Colonial Discourse and Post-Colonial Theory*. New York: Columbia University Press, 324–39.

Appiah, Anthony 1991: 'Is the post- in postmodernism the post- in postcolonial?'. *Critical Inquiry*, 17, Winter 1991, 336–57.

Arbus, Diana 1972: *Diana Arbus*. New York: Millerton.

Arendt, Hannah 1968: *Men in Dark Times*. New York: Harcourt Brace & Co.

Atwood, Margaret 1985: *The Handmaid's Tale*. Toronto: Seal Books.

Baldick, Chris 1987: *In Frankenstein's Shadow. Myth, Monstrosity and Nineteenth Century Writing*. Oxford: Clarendon Press.

Ballard, John G. 1973: *Crash*. New York: The Noonday Press, Farrer, Straus & Giroux.

Balsamo, Anne 1988: 'Reading cyborgs, writing feminism'. *Communication*, 10, 331–44.

Balsamo, Anne 1996: *Technologies of the Gendered Body*. Durham: Duke University Press.

Barbrook, Richard 2001: 'The holy fools'. In Patricia Pisters (ed.), *Gilles Deleuze: Micropolitics of Audiovisual Culture*, forthcoming, Amsterdam University Press.

Barker, Francis 1984: *The Tremulous Private Body. Essays on Subjection*. London: Methuen.

Barr, Marleen 1987: *Alien to Femininity: Speculative Fiction and Feminist Theory*. New York: Greenwood.

Barr, Marleen 1993: *Lost in Space. Probing Feminist Science Fiction and Beyond*. Chapel Hill and London: Chicago University Press and University of North Carolina Press.

Battersby, Christine 1998: *The Phenomenal Woman. Feminist Metaphysics and the Patterns of Identity*. Cambrige: Polity.

Baudrillard, Jean 1987: 'Nous sommes tous des transsexuels'. *Liberation*, 14/10/1997, 4.

Baudrillard, Jean 1995: *The Gulf War Did Not Take Place*. Sydney: Power Publications.

Beatty, John 1991: 'Genetics in the atomic age: the Atomic Bomb Casualty Commission, 1947–56'. In Keith R. Benson, Jane Malenschein and Ronald Rainger (eds), *The Expansion of American Biology*, New Jersey: Rutgers University Press.

Becker, Susanne 1999: *Gothic Forms of Feminine Fiction*. Manchester: Manchester University Press.

Bell, Vikki 1993: *Interrogating Incest. Feminism, Foucault and the Law*. London, New York: Routledge.

Bellour, Raymond 1991: 'Ideal Hadaly'. In Constance Penley, Elisabeth Lyon, Lynn Spiegel, Janet Bergstrom (eds), *Close Encounters. Film, Feminism and Science Fiction*, Minneapolis and Oxford: University of Minnesota Press, 107–30.

Benhabib, Seyla 1992: *The Situated Self*. Cambridge: Polity.

Benhabib, Seyla 1996: 'The reluctant modernism of Hannah Arendt'. In *Modernity and Social Thought*, 10, Rowman and Littlefield.

Benhabib, Seyla 1999: 'Sexual difference and collective identities: the new global constellation'. *Signs*, 24, 2, 335–62.

Benjamin, Jessica 1988: *The Bonds of Love*. New York: Pantheon.

Benjamin, Walter 1968: 'The work of art in the age of its mechanical reproduction'. In *Illuminations*, New York: Schollen Books, 217–51.

Bensmaia, Réda 1994: 'On the concept of minor literature: from Kafka to Kateb Yacine'. In Constantin V. Boundas and Dorothea Olkowski (eds), *Gilles Deleuze and the Theatre of Philosophy*, New York and London: Routledge, 213–28.

Berardi, Franco (BIFO) 1997: *Exit. Il Nostro Contributo all 'estinzione delle civilta'*. Milano: Costa & Nolan.

Bergstrom, Janet 1991: 'Androids and androgyny'. In Constance Penley, Elisabeth Lyon, Lynn Spiegel, Janet Bergstrom (eds), *Close Encounters. Film, Feminism and Science Fiction*, Minneapolis and Oxford: University of Minnesota Press, 33–60.

Berlin, Isaiah 1978: *Russian Thinkers*. London: Pelican Books.

Bettelheim, Bruno 1972: *The Empty Fortress: Infantile Autism and the Birth of the Self*. London: Collier-Macmillan.

Blasius, Mark 1994: *Gay and Lesbian Politics: Sexuality and the Emergence of a New Ethic*. London and New York: Routledge.

Boer 1996: 'The world beyond our window: nomads, travelling theories and the function of boundaries'. *Parallax*, 3, 7–26.

Bogdan, Robert 1988: *Freak Show. Presenting Human Oddities for Amusement and Profit*. Chicago: Chicago University Press.

Bogue, Ronald 1989: *Deleuze and Guattari*. London and New York: Routledge.

Bogue, Ronald 1991: 'Rhizomusicosmology'. *Sub-Stance*, 66, 85–101.

Bogue, Ronald 1993: 'Gilles Deleuze: the aesthetics of force'. *The Journal of the British Society for Phenomenology*, 24, 1, January, 56–65.

Boscaglia, Maurizia 1991: 'Unaccompanied ladies: feminist, Italian and in the academy'. *Differences* 2/3, 122–35.

Boundas, Constantin V. 1993: *The Deleuze Reader*. New York: Columbia University Press.

Boundas, Constantin V. 1994: 'Deleuze: serialization and subject-formation'. In Boundas and Olkowski (eds), *Gilles Deleuze and the Theatre of Philosophy*, New York and London: Routledge, 99–118.

Boundas, Constantin V. 1996: 'Gilles Deleuze (1925–95)'. Special issue of *Man and World*, 29, 3.

Boundas, Constantin V. and Olkowski, Dorothea (eds) 1994: *Gilles Deleuze and the Theatre of Philosophy*. New York and London: Routledge.

Brah, Avtar 1993: 'Re-framing Europe: En-gendered racisms, ethnicities and nationalisms in contemporary Western Europe'. *Feminist Review*, 45, 9–28.

Braidotti, Rosi 1991: *Patterns of Dissonance*. Cambridge: Polity; New York: Routledge.

Braidotti, Rosi 1993: 'Discontinuous becomings. Deleuze and the becoming-woman of philosophy'. *Journal of the British Society of Phenomenology*, 24, 1, January, 44–55.

Braidotti, Rosi 1994: 'Of bugs and women: Irigaray and Deleuze on the becoming woman'. In Carolyn Burke, Naomi Schor and Margaret Whitford (eds), *Engaging with Irigaray*, New York: Columbia University Press.

Braidotti, Rosi 1994a: *Nomadic Subjects. Embodiment and Sexual Difference in Contemporary Feminist Theory*. New York: Columbia University Press.

Braidotti, Rosi 1994b: 'Toward a new nomadism: feminist deleuzian tracks; or, metaphysics and metabolism'. In Constantin Boundas and Dorothea Olkowski (eds), *Gilles Deleuze and the Theatre of Philosophy*, New York and London: Routledge, 157–86.

Braidotti, Rosi 1996: 'Signs of wonder and traces of doubt: on teratology and embodied differences'. In Nina Lykke and Rosi Braidotti (eds), *Between Monsters, Goddesses and Cyborgs*, London: Zed Books.

Braidotti, Rosi 1997: 'Comments on Felski's 'The Doxa of Difference': working through sexual difference'. *Signs. Journal of Women in Culture and Society*, 23, 1, autumn 1997, 23–40.

Braidotti, Rosi 1998: 'Sexual difference theory'. In Iris Young and Alison Jaggar (eds), *A Companion to Feminist Philosophy*. Oxford: Blackwell, 298–306.

Bray, Anne and Colebrook, Claire 1998: 'The haunted flesh: corporeal feminism and the politics of (dis)embodiment'. *Signs*, 24, 1, Autumn 1998, 35–68.

Brennan, Teresa 1989: 'Introduction'. In T. Brennan (ed.), *Between Feminism and Psychoanalysis*. London: Routledge, 1–23.

Broadhurst, John (ed.) 1992: 'Deleuze and the transcendental unconscious'. In *Warwick Journal in Philosophy*, University of Warwick.

Brown, Wendy 1991: 'Feminist hesitations, postmodern exposures'. *Differences*, 3/1, 63–84.

Bruno, Giuliana 1990: 'Ramble City: postmodernism and Blade Runner'. In A. Kuhn (ed.), *Alien Zone*, London: Verso.

Bryld, Mette and Lykke, Nina 1999: *Cosmodolphins. Feminist Cultural Studies of Technology, Animals and the Sacred*. London: Zed Books.

Buchanan, Ian 1997: 'The problem of the body in Deleuze and Guattari, or, What can a body do?'. *Body & Society*, 3, 3, 73–92.

Buchanan, Ian 2000: *Deleuzism. A Metacommentary*. Edinburgh: Edinburgh University Press.

Buchanan, Ian and Colebrook, Claire (eds) 2000: *Deleuze and Feminist Theory*. Edinburgh: Edinburgh University Press.

Bukatman, Scott 1993: *Terminal Identity. The Virtual Subject in Post-modern Science Fiction*. Durham, NC: Duke University Press.

Burchill, Julie 1998: *Diana*. London: Weidenfeld & Nicolson.

Burger, Christa 1985: 'The reality of "machines", notes on the rhizome-thinking'. *Telos*, 64, 33–44.

Butler, Judith 1987: *Subjects of Desire. Hegelian Reflections in Twentieth-Century France*. New York: Columbia University Press.

Butler, Judith 1990: *Gender Trouble*. New York: Routledge.

Butler, Judith 1992: 'The lesbian phallus and the morphological imaginary'. *Differences*, 4, 1, 133–71.

Butler, Judith 1993: *Bodies that Matter: On the Discursive Limits of 'Sex'*. New York: Routledge.

Butler, Judith 1997: *The Psychic Life of Power: Theories in Subjection*. Stanford, CA: Stanford University Press.

Butler, Judith 1999: 'Preface 1999'. In *Gender Trouble. Feminism and the Subversion of Identity*. London and New York: Routledge.

Butler, Judith and Scott, Joan W. 1992: *Feminists Theorize the Political*. New York: Routledge.

Calame, Claude 1985: 'Les figures Grecques du gigantesque'. *Communications*, 42, 147–72.

Califia, Pat 1988: *Macho Sluts*. Boston: Alyson Publications.

Campbell, Beatrix 1998: *Diana, Princess of Wales. How Sexual Politics Shook the Monarchy*. The Women's Press: London.

Campbell, Marion 1985: *Lines of Flight*. Freemantle: Freemantle Arts Centre.

Canguilhem, Georges 1966: *Le Normal et le pathologique*. Paris: Presses Universitaires de France.

Canning, Peter 1985: 'Fluidentity'. *Sub-Stance*, 44/45, 35–45.

Carroll, Noel 1990: *The Philosophy of Horror: Paradoxes of the Heart*. New York and London: Routledge.

Carter, Angela 1985: 'The company of wolves'. In *Come unto These Yellow Sands*. Newcastle upon Tyne: Bloodaxe Books.

Castel, Robert 1976: *Le Psychoanlysme*. Paris: Union Générale d'Editions.

Castells, Manuel 1996: *The Rise of the Network Society*. Oxford. Blackwell.

Cavarero, Adriana 1990: *Nonostante Platone*. Rome: Editori Riuniti.

Caygill, Howard 1997: 'The topology of selection: the limits of Deleuze's philosophy'. In Keith Ansell Pearson (ed.), *Deleuze and Philosophy. The Difference Engineer*. London and New York: Routledge, 149–62.

Céard, Jean 1977: *Le Normal et les prodiges. L'insolite en France au XVIeme siècle*. Geneva: Droz.

Chanter, Tina 1995: *Ethics of Eros. Irigaray's Rewriting of the Philosophers*. New York and London: Routledge.

Chasin, Aleandre 1995: 'Class and its close relations: identities among women, servants and machines'. In J. Halberstam and I. Livingston, *Post-Human Bodies*, Bloomington, IN: Indiana University Press.

Chatelet, François 1970: *La Philosophie des professeurs*. Paris: Grasset.

Cixous, Hélène 1975: 'Le Rire de la Meduse', *L'Arc* 61, 245–64 English translation 1980: 'The Laugh of the Medusa'. In E. Marks and J. de Courtivron (eds), *New French Feminism*, Amsterst: University of Massachussetts Press.

Cixous, Hélène 1977: 'Le Sexe ou la tête'. *Les Cahiers du Grif*, 5, 5–15.

Cixous, Hélène 1986a: *Entre l'écriture*. Paris: Des Femmes.

Cixous, Hélène 1986b: 'L'Approche de Clarice Lispector'. In Cixous, *Entre l'écriture*, Paris: Des Femmes, 115–99.

Cixous, Hélène 1987: *Le Livre de Promethea*. Paris: Gallimard.

Clément, Catherine 1972: 'Les Petites filles', *L'arc*, 29, 1–2.

Clément, Catherine 1991: 'Lacan et l'Europe'. Le Magazine litteraire, 288, May.

Code, Lorraine 1991: *What Does She Know?*. Cambridge, MA.: Harvard University Press.

Cohen, Leonard 1966: *Beautiful Losers*. New York: Random House.

Colebrook, Claire 2000a: 'Introduction'. In Buchanan, Ian and Colebrook, Claire (eds), *Deleuze and Feminist Theory*, Edinburgh: Edinburgh University Press, 1–17.

Colebrook, Claire 2000b: 'Is sexual difference a problem?'. In Buchanan, Ian and Colebrook, Claire (eds), *Deleuze and Feminist Theory*, Edinburgh: Edinburgh University Press, 110–27.

Colombat, André 1996: 'November 4, 1995: Deleuze's death as an event'. *Man and World*, 29, 3, July 1996, 235–49.

Corea, Gena 1985a: *The Mother Machine: Reproductive Technologies from Artificial Insemination to Artificial Womb*. New York: Harper & Row.

Corea, Gena 1985b: 'The reproductive brothel'. In *Man-made Women: How New Reproductive Technologies Affect Women*, London: Hutchinson, 38–51.

Creed, Barbara 1990: 'Gynesis, postmodernism and the science fiction horror film'. In A. Kuhn (ed.), *Alien Zone*, London: Verso.

Creed, Barbara 1993: *The Monstrous-Feminine. Film, Feminism, Psychoanalysis*. New York and London: Routledge.

Davies, Jude and Smith, Carol R. 1999: 'Figuring white femininity: critique, investment and the example of Princess Diana'. In Heloise Brown, Madi Gilkes and Ann Kaloski-Naylor (eds), *White? Women. Critical Perspectives on Race and Gender*, York: Centre for Women's Studies/Raw Nerve Books.

Deleuze, Gilles 1953: *Empirisme et subjectivité*. Paris: Presses Universitaires de France. English translation 1991: *Empirism and Subjectivity. An Essay on Hume's Theory of Human Nature*. New York: Columbia University Press; translation by C. V. Boundas.

Deleuze, Gilles 1962: *Nietzsche et la philosophie*. Paris: Presses Universitaires de France. English translation: 1983: *Nietzsche and Philosophy*. New York: Columbia University Press; translation by Hugh Tomlinson and Barbara Habberjam.

Deleuze, Gilles 1964: *Proust et les signes*. Paris: Presses Universitaires de France. English translation 1972: *Proust and Signs*. New York: G. Braziller; translation by R. Howard.

Deleuze, Gilles 1966: *Le Bergsonisme*. Paris: Presses Universitaires de France. English translation 1988: *Bergonism*. New York: Zone Books.

Deleuze, Gilles 1968a: *Différence et répétition*. Paris: Presses Universitaires de France. English translation 1968: *Difference and Repetition*. London: Athlone.

Deleuze, Gilles 1968b: *Spinoza et le problème de l'expression*. Paris: Minuit. English translation 1990: *Expressionism in Philosophy: Spinoza*. New York: Zone Books; translation by M. Joughin.

Deleuze, Gilles 1969: *Logique du sens*. Paris: Minuit. English translation 1990: *The Logic of Sense*. New York: Columbia University Press; translation by M. Lester and C. Stivale.

Deleuze, Gilles 1972a: 'Les Intellectuels et le pouvoir. Entretien Michel Foucoult – Gilles Deleuze'. *L'arc*, 49, 3–10. English translation 1973: 'Intellectuals and power'. In D. Bouchard (ed.), *Language, Counter-memory, Practice*, Ithaca, New York: Cornell University Press; 205–17, translation by D. Boudiano.

Deleuze, Gilles 1972b: *Un Nouvel archiviste*. Paris: Fata Morgana. English translation: 'A new archivist'. In Peter Botsman (ed.) 1982: *Theoretical Strategies*. Sydney: Local Consumption.

Deleuze, Gilles 1973a: *La Pensée nomade*. Paris: Union Génerale d'Edition.

Deleuze, Gilles 1973b: 'La Pensée nomade'. In *Nietzsche Aujourd'hui*, vol. 1, Paris: Union Generale d'Edition, 159–74. English translation 1985: 'Nomad thought'. In David B. Allison (ed.), *The New Nietzsche: Contemporary Styles of Interpretation*, Cambridge MA.: MIT Press.

Deleuze, Gilles 1978: 'Philosophie et minorité'. *Critique*, 369 (Paris), 154–5.

Deleuze, Gilles 1981: *Francis Bacon: Logique de la sensation 1*. Paris: Editions de la différence.

Deleuze, Gilles 1983: *Cinéma I: L'Image-Nouvement*. Paris: Minuit. English translation 1986: *Cinema I: The Movement-Image*. Minneapolis: University of Minnesota Press; translation by Hugh Tomlinson and Barbara Habberjam.

Deleuze, Gilles 1985: *Cinéma II: L'Image-Temps*. Paris: Minuit. English translation 1989: *Cinema I: The Time-Image*. Minneapolis: University of Minnesota Press; translation by Hugh Tomlinson and Robert Galeta.

Deleuze, Gilles 1986: *Foucault*. Paris: Minuit. English translation 1988: *Foucault*. Minneapolis: University of Minnesota Press; translation by Sean Hand.

Deleuze, Gilles 1988a: *Le Pli*. Minuit, Paris. English translation 1992: *The Fold: Leibniz and the Baroque*. Minneapolis: University of Minnesota Press.

Deleuze, Gilles 1988b: *Périclès et Verdi: Le Philosophy de Fransois Châtelet*. Paris: Minuit.

Deleuze, Gilles 1989: 'Qu'est-ce qu'un dispositif?' In *Michel Foucault Philosophe*, Paris: Seuil, 185–95.

Deleuze, Gilles 1995: 'L'immanence: une vie . . .'. *Philosophie*, 47, 3–7.

Deleuze, Gilles and Guattari, Felix 1972a: *L'Anti Oedipe. Capitalism et Schizophrénie I*. Paris: Minuit. English translation 1977: *Anti-Oedipus. Capitalism and Schizophrenie*. New York: Viking Press/ Richard Seaver; translation by R. Hurley, M. Seem and H. R. Lane.

Deleuze Gilles and Guattari, Felix 1972b: 'Capitalisme énurgumène'. *Critique*, 306, Nov. 1972.

Deleuze, Gilles and Guattari, Felix 1975: *Kafka: pour une littérature mineure*. Paris: Minuit. English translation 1986: *Kafka: Toward a Minor Literature*. Minneapolis: University of Minnesota Press; translation by Dana Polan.

Deleuze, Gilles and Guattari, Felix 1976: *Rhizome*. Paris: Minuit. English translation: 'Rhizome', *Ideology and Consciousness*, 8, spring 1981, 49–71; translation by Paul Foss and Paul Patton.

Deleuze, Gilles and Guattari, Felix 1980: *Mille Plateaux. Capitalism et Schizophrénie II*. Paris: Minuit. English translation 1987b: *A Thousand Plateaus: Capitalism and Schizophrenia*. Minneapolis: University of Minnesota Press; translated by Brian Massumi.

Deleuze, Gilles and Guattari, Felix 1986: *Nomadology*. New York: Semiotexte; translation by Brian Massumi.

Deleuze, Gilles and Guattari, Felix 1991: *Qu'est-ce que la philosophie?* Paris: Minuit. English translation 1992: *What is Philosophy?* New York: Columbia University Press.

Deleuze, Gilles and Parnet, Claire 1977: *Dialogues*. Paris: Flammarion. English translation 1987a: *Dialogues*. New York: Columbia University Press; translation by Hugh Tomlinson and Barbara Habberjam.

Delphy, Christine 1975: 'Pour un materialisme feministe'. *L'Arc*, 61, 61–7.

Delphy, Christine 1984: *Close to Home*. London: Hutchinson.

Dement, Linda 1995: *Cyberflesh Girlmonster*, CD-ROM, Sidney, Australia.

Derrida, Jacques 1980: *La Carte postale de Socrate à Freud et au-delà Paris*. Paris: Flammarion.

Derrida, Jacques 1987: 'Women in the beehive: a seminar'. In Alice Jardine and P. Smith (eds), *Men in Feminism*, London and New York: Methuen, 189–203.

Descombes, Christian 1979: *Le Même et l'autre*. Paris: Minuit. English translation 1980: *Modern French Philosophy*. Cambridge: Cambridge University Press; translation by L. Scott-Fax and J. M. Harding.

Dews, Peter 1995: 'The tremor of reflection: Slavoj Zizek's Lacanian dialectics'. In *Radical Philosophy*, 72, July/August 1995, 17–29.

Diacritics: Nuclear Criticism (1984).

Diamond, Irene and Quinby, Lee (eds) 1988: *Foucault and Feminism*. Boston: North Eastern University Press.

Dinnerstein, Dorothy 1977: *The Mermaid and the Minotaur. Sexual Arrangements and Human Malaise*. New York: Harper & Row.

Doane, Janice and Hodges, Devon 1987: 'Monstrous amazons'. In *Nostalgia and Sexual Difference: The Resistance to Contemporary Feminism*, London: Methuen.

Doane, Mary Ann 1987: *The Desire to Desire: The Women's Film of the '40's*. Bloomington: Indiana University Press.

Donzelot, Jacques 1977: *Le Police des familles*. Paris: Minuit. English translation 1979: *The Policing of Families*. New York: Pantheon; translation by Robert Hurley.

Duchen, Claire 1986: *Feminism in France*. London: Routledge and Kegan Paul.

Dworkin, Andrea 1976: *Our Blood*. London: The Women's Press.

Ehrenreich, Barbara and English, Deirdre 1979: *For Her Own Good: 150 years of her Experts' Advice to Women*. London: Pluto Press.

Einersen, Dorrit and Nixon, Ingeborg 1995: *Woman as Monster in Literature and the Media*. Copenhagen: Copenhagen University Press.

Eisenstein, Hesker 1983: *Contemporary Feminist Thought*. Boston: G. K. Hall & Co.

Eisenstein, Zillah 1998: *Global Obscenities. Patriarchy, Capitalism and the Lure of Cyberfantasy*. New York: New York University Press.

Eliot, George 1973: *Middlemarch*. London: Penguin.

Emerton, Karin 1986: 'Les femmes et la philosophie: la mise en discours de la différence sexuelle dans la philosophie contemporaine'. Unpublished doctoral dissertation, Paris: Pantheon-Sorbonne University.

Epps, Brad 1996: 'Technoasceticism and authorial death in Sade, Kafka, Barthes and Foucault'. *Differences*, 8, 3, 79–127.

Eribon, Didier 1989: *Michel Foucault (1926–84)*. Paris: Flammarion. English translation 1991: *Michel Foucault (1926–84)*. Cambridge, MA: Harvard University Press; translation by Betsy Wing.

Essed, Philomena 1991: Understanding Everyday Racism. London: Sage.

Estés, Clarissa Pinkola 1992: *Women Who Run With the Wolves*. New York: Ballantine Books.

Fausto-Sterling, Anne 2000: *Sexing the Body. Gender Politics and the Construction of Sexuality*. Basic Books, Persens Books Group.

Fedida, Pierre 1980: 'Le philosophe et sa peau'. *L'Arc*, 49, 61–9.

Felski, Rita 1997: 'The doxa of difference'. *Signs*, 23, 1, 1–22.

Fiedler, Leslie 1979: *Freaks: Myths and Images of the Secret Self*. New York: Simon and Schuster.

Fiedler, Leslie 1996: *Tyranny of the Normal. Essays on Bioethics, Theology and Myth*. Boston: David R. Godine.

Firestone, Shulamith 1970: *The Dialectic of Sex: the Case for Feminist Revolution*. Toronto: Bantam Books.

Flax, Jane 1987: 'Postmodernism and gender relations in feminist theory'. *Signs*, 12/4, 621–43.

Flax, Jane 1990: *Thinking Fragments*. New York: Routledge.

Force Inc. Music Works 1996: Frankfurt, Mille Plateaux MP CD 22, EFA 00672-2, GEMA LC 6001.

Foster, Hal 1996: *The Return of the Real*. Cambridge, MA: MIT Press.

Foucault, Michel 1961: *Histoire de le Folie*. Paris: Gallimard. English translation 1965: *Madness and Civilization*, trans. Richard Howard, New York: Vintage Books.

Foucault, Michel 1966: *Les mots et les choses*. Paris: Gallimard. English translation 1980: *The Order of Things*. New York: Pantheon Books.

Foucault, Michel 1975: *Surveiller et punir*. Paris: Gallimard. English translation 1977: *Discipline and Punish*. New York: Pantheon Books.

Foucault, Michel 1976: *Histoire de la sexualité I. La volonte de savoir*. Paris: Gallimard. English translation 1978: *The History of Sexuality*, vol. I, trans. Robert Hurley, New York: Pantheon Books.

Foucault, Michel 1977a: 'Preface'. In Gilles Deleuze and Felix Guattari, *Anti-Oedipus*. New York: Viking Press (English original).

Foucault, Michel 1977b: *L'ordre du discours*. Paris: Gallimard.

Foucault, Michel 1984a: *Histoire de la sexualité II: L'usage des plaisirs*. Paris: Gallimard. English translation 1985: *History of Sexuality*, vol. II *The Use of Pleasure*, trans. Robert Hurley, New York: Pantheon Books.

Foucault, Michel 1984b: *Histoire de la sexualité III: Le souci de soi*. Paris: Gallimard. English translation: *History of Sexuality vol. III: The Care of the Self*, trans. Robert Hurley, New York: Pantheon Books.

Foucault, Michel and Cixous, Hélène 1979: 'A propos de Marguerite Duras'. *Cahiers Renaud Barrault*, 8–22.

Fouque, Antoinette 1982: 'Notre pays, notre terre de naissance, c'est le corps maternel', *Des femmes en mouvement/Midi Pyrennees*, 1, 9–15.

Fox Keller, Evelyn 1985a: *Reflections on Gender and Science*. New Haven, CT and London: Yale University Press.

Fox Keller, Evelyn 1985b: *A Feeling for the Organism*. New York: Freeman.

Fox Keller, Evelyn 1989: 'From secrets of life to secrets of death'. In Mary Jacobus, Evelyn Fox Keller, Sally Shuttle Worth (eds), *Body/Politics. Women and the Discourses of Science*, New York and London: Routledge.

Fox Keller, Evelyn and Grontowski, C. R. 1983: 'The mind's eye'. In Sandra Harding and M. B. Hintikka (eds), *Discovering Reality*, Dordrecht: Reidel, 207–24.

Frank, Manfred 1989: *What is Neostructuralism?* Minneapolis: University of Minnesota Press.

Frankenberg, Ruth 1993: *White Women, Race Matters: the Social Construction of Whiteness*. Minneapolis, University of Minnesota Press.

Franklin, Sarah 1997: *Embodied Progress: a Cultural Account of Assisted Conception*. London: Routledge.

Franklin, Sarah, Lury, Celia and Stacey, Jackie 1991: *Off-centre: Feminism and Cultural Studies*. London: Cornell University Press.

Fraser, Nancy 1996: 'Multiculturalism and gender equity: the US "Difference" debates revisited'. In *Constellations*, 1, 61–72.

Frye, Marilyn 1996: 'The necessity of differences: constructing a positive category of women'. *Signs*, 21, 4, 991–1010.

Fuss, Diane 1989: *Essentially Speaking. Feminism, Nature and Difference*. New York and London: Routledge.

Gallop, Jane (ed.) 1989: 'The monster in the mirror: the feminist critic's psychoanalysis'. In R. Feldstein and J. Roof (eds), *Feminism and Psychoanalysis*, Ithaca: Cornell University Press.

Gallop, Jane 1997: *Feminist Accused of Sexual Harassment*. Durham, NC: Duke University Press.

Gatens, Moira 1996: *Imaginary Bodies: Ethics, Power and Corporeality*. London and New York: Routledge.

Gatens, Moira and Lloyd, Genevieve 1999: *Collective Imaginings: Spinoza, Past and Present*. London and New York: Routledge.

Gedalof 1996: 'Can nomads learn to count to four? R. Braidotti and the space for difference in feminist theory', *Women: a Cultural Review*, VII, 2, 189–201.

Giddens, Anthony 1994: *Beyond Left and Right: The Future of Radical Politics*. Cambridge: Polity.

Gilbert, Susan and Gubar, Sandra 1977: 'The female monster in Augustan satire'. *Signs*, 380–94.

Gilbert, Susan and Gubar, Sandra 1979: 'Horror's twin: Mary Shelley's monstrous Eve'. In *The Madwoman in the Attic*, New Haven, CT: Yale University Press.

Gilman, Sander (ed.) 1985: *Difference and Pathology. Stereotypes of Sexuality, Race and Madness*. Ithaca: Cornell University Press.

Gilroy, Paul 1987: *There Ain't No Black in the Union Jack: the Cultural Politics of Race and Nation*. London: Hutchinson.

Gilroy, Paul 1993: *The Black Atlantic. Modernity and Double Consciousness*. Cambridge, MA: Harvard University Press.

Glamister, T. W. 1964: 'Fantasies, facts and foetuses. The interplay of fancy and reason in teratology'. *Medical History* 8, 15–30.

Goicoechea, David 1999: 'Irigaray's transcendental sensuotics, between Deleuze's rhizomatics and Derrida's deconstruction', paper delivered at the conference 'Rhizomatics, Genealogy, Deconstruction', Trent University, May 1999.

Goodchild, Philip 1996: *Deleuze & Guattari. An Introduction to the Politics of Desire.* London: Sage.

Goux, Jean Joseph 1977: *Les iconoclastes.* Paris: Seuil.

Greenberg, Harvey R. 1991: 'Reimagining the Gargoyle: psychoanalytic notes on *Alien*'. In Constance Penley, Elisabeth Lyon, Lynn Spigel, Janet Bergstrom (eds), *Close Encounters. Film, Feminism and Science Fiction*, Minneapolis: University of Minnesota Press.

Greer, Germaine 1999: *The Whole Woman.* London: Doubleday.

Grewal, Inderpal and Kaplan, Caren (eds) 1994: *Scattered Hegemonies: Postmodernity and Transnational Feminist Practices.* Minneapolis: University of Minnesota Press.

Griggers, Camilla 1997: *Becoming-Woman.* Minneapolis: University of Minnesota Press.

Grossberg, Lawrence 1997: *Dancing in Spite of Myself. Essays on Popular Culture.* Durham, NC, and London: Duke University Press.

Grosz, Elizabeth 1987: 'Notes towards a corporeal feminism'. *Australian Feminist Studies*, 5, 1–16.

Grosz, Elizabeth 1994a: 'A thousand tiny sexes: feminism and rhizomatics'. In C. V. Boundas and D. Olkowski (eds), *Gilles Deleuze and the Theatre of Philosophy* London and New York: Routledge.

Grosz, Elizabeth 1994b: 'The hetero and the homo: the sexual ethics of Luce Irigaray'. In C. Burke, N. Schor, M. Whitford (eds), *Engaging with Irigaray*, New York: Colombia University Press.

Grosz, Elizabeth 1994c: 'The labors of love. analyzing perverse desire: an interrogation of Teresa de Lauretis' The Practice of Love'. *Differences*, 6, 2–3, 274–95.

Grosz, Elizabeth 1995a: *Space, Time and Perversion. The Politics of Bodies.* Sydney: Allen and Unwin.

Grosz, Elizabeth 1995b: 'Animal sex. Libido as desire and death'. In Elizabeth Grosz and Elspeth Probyn (eds), *Sexy Bodies. The Strange Carnalities of Feminism.* London and New York: Routledge.

Grosz, Elizabeth 1999: 'Darwin and feminism: preliminary investigations for a possible alliance'. York: Routledge. *Australian Feminist Studies*, 14, 29, 31–45.

Grosz, Elizabeth (ed.) 1999: *Becomings. Explorations in Time, Memory and Futures.* Ithaca: Cornell University Press.

Grosz, Elizabeth 2000: 'Deleuze's Bergson: duration, the virtual and a politics of the future'. In Ian Buchanan and Claire Colebrook (eds), *Deleuze and Feminist Theory*, Edinburgh: Edinburgh University Press.

Grosz, Elizabeth and Probyn, Elspeth (eds) 1995: *Sexy Bodies. The Strange Carnalities of Feminism.* London and New York: Routledge.

Gundermann, Christian 1994: 'Orientalism, homophobia, masochism: transfers between Pierre Loti's *Azyadé* and Gilles Deleuze's "Coldness and cruelty"'. *Diacritics*, Summer-Fall 1994, 151–67.

Halberstam, Judith 1991: 'Automating gender: postmodern feminism in the age of the intelligent machine'. *Feminist Studies*, 3, 439–60.

Halberstam, Judith and Ira Livingston (eds) 1995: *Posthuman Bodies*. Bloomington, IN: Indiana University Press.

Hall, Kira 1996: 'Cyberfeminism'. In Susan C. Herring (ed.), *Computer-mediated Communication. Linguistic, Social and Cross-cultural Perspectives*, Amsterdam: John Benjamins.

Hall, Stuart 1990: 'Cultural Identity and Diaspora'. In J. Rutherford (ed.), *Identity: Community, Culture, Difference*, London: Lawrence and Wishart.

Haraway, Donna 1988: 'Situated knowledges: the science question in feminism as a site of discourse on the privilege of partial perspective'. *Feminist Studies*, 14, 3, 575–99.

Haraway, Donna 1990a: *Simians, Cyborgs and Women. The Reinvention of Nature*. London: Free Association Books.

Haraway, Donna 1990b: 'A manifesto for cyborgs: science, technology and socialist feminism in the 1980's'. In *Simians, Cyborgs and Women. The Reinvention of Nature*, London, Free Association Books, 149–82.

Haraway, Donna 1991: 'Cyborgs at large: Interview with Donna Haraway'. In Constance Penley and Andrew Ross (eds), *Technoculture*, Minnesota and London: University of Minnesota Press, 1–20.

Haraway, Donna 1992: 'The promises of monsters: a regenerative politics for inappropriate/d others'. In L. Grossberg, C. Nelson and A. Treichler (eds), *Cultural Studies*, London and New York: Routledge.

Haraway, Donna 1997: *Modest_Witness@second_Millennium. FemaleMan8_meets_ oncomouseJ* London and New York: Routledge.

Harding, Sandra 1986: *The Science Question in Feminism*. London: Open University.

Harding, Sandra 1987: *Feminism and Methodology*. London: Open University.

Harding, Sandra 1991: *Whose Science? Whose Knowledge?* Milton Keynes: Open University Press.

Hardt, Michael 1992: *Gilles Deleuze. An Apprenticeship in Philosophy*. Minneapolis: University of Minnesota Press.

Hardt, Michael 1998: 'The withering of civil society'. In Eleanor Kaufman and Kevin Jon Heller (eds), *Deleuze and Guattari. New Mappings in Politics, Philosophy and Culture*, Minneapolis: University of Minnesota Press.

Hartsock, Nancy 1990: 'Foucault on power: a theory for women?' In L. J. Nicholson (ed.), *Feminism/Postmodernism*, New York and London: Routledge.

Hartsock, Nancy C. M. 1983: 'The feminist standpoint: developing the ground for a specifically feminist historical materialism'. In Sandra Harding and M. B. Hintikka (eds), *Discovering Reality*, Dordrecht: Reidel.

Hawkesworth, Mary 1997: 'Confounding gender'. *Signs*, 22, 3, Spring 1997, 649–86.

Hayles, Katherine 1999: *How We Became Posthuman. Virtual Bodies in Cybernetics, Literature and Informatics*. Chicago: The University of Chicago Press.

Hayward, Phillip and Wollen, Tana (eds) 1993: *Future Visions: New Technologies of the Screen*. London: British Film Institute.

Heidegger, Martin 1993: *Basic Writings*. San Francisco: HarperCollins.

Helman, Cecil 1991: *The Body of Frankenstein's Monster. Essays in Myth and Medicine*. New York and London: W.W. Norton Company.

Holland, Eugene W. 1998: 'From schizophrenia to social control'. In Eleanor Kaufman and Kevin Jon Heller (eds), *Deleuze and Guattari. New Mappings in Politics, Philosophy and Culture*, Minneapolis: University of Minnesota Press.

Holland, Eugene W. 1999: *Deleuze and Guattari's Anti-Oedipus*. New York and London: Routledge.

hooks, bell 1990: 'Postmodern blackness'. In *Yearning*, Toronto: Between the Lines, 25–32.

hooks, bell 1995: 'Representations of whiteness in the black imagination'. In *Killing Rage. Ending Racism*, New York: Holt.

Huet Marie-Helene 1983: 'Living images; monstrosity and representation'. *Representations*, 4, fall 1983, 73–87.

Hurley, Kelly 1995: 'Reading like an alien: posthuman identity in Ridley Scott's *Aliens* and David Cronenberg's *Rabid*'. In Judith Halberstam and Ira Livingston (eds), *Posthuman Bodies*, Bloomington, IN: Indiana University Press.

Huyssen, Andreas 1986: 'The vamp and the machine: Fritz Lang's Metropolis'. In *After the Great Divide. Modernism, Mass Culture and Postmodernism*, Bloomington and Indianapolis, IN: Indiana University Press, 65–81.

Irigaray, Luce 1974: *Spéculum. De l'autre femme*. Paris: Minuit. English translation 1985a: *Speculum of the Other Woman*, transl. Gillian Gill, Ithaca, NY: Cornell University Press.

Irigaray, Luce 1977: *Ce Sexe Qui N'en Est Pas Un*. Paris: Minuit. English translation 1985b: *This Sex Which Is Not One*, transl. Catherine Porter, Ithaca, NY: Cornell University Press.

Irigaray, Luce 1980: *Amante Marine. De Friedrich Nietzsche*. Paris: Minuit. English translation 1991: *Marcine Lover of F. Nietzsche*, transl. Gillian Gill, New York: Columbia University Press.

Irigaray, Luce 1983: *L'Oubli de l'air chez Martin Heidegger*. Paris: Minuit. English translation 1991: *The Forgetting of Air in Martin Heidegger*.

Irigaray, Luce 1984: *L'Éthique de la différence sexuelle*. Paris: Minuit. English translation 1993a: *An Ethics of Sexual Difference*, transl. Carolyn Burke and Gillian Gill, Ithaca, NY: Cornell University Press.

Irigaray, Luce 1987a: 'Egales à Qui?' In *Critique. Revue Générale des Publications Françaises et étrangères*, 43, 480, 420–37. English translation 1988: 'Equal to Whom?' In *differences. A Journal of Feminist Cultural Studies*, 1, 2, 59–76.

Irigaray, Luce 1987b: *Sexes et parentés*. Paris: Minuit. English translation 1993: *Sexes and Genealogies*, transl. Gillian C. Gill, Ithaca, NY: Cornell University Press.

Irigaray, Luce 1989: *Le Temps de la Différence. Pour Une Révolution Pacifique*. Paris: Hachette. English translation 1994: *Thinking the Difference. For a Peaceful Revolution*, transl. Karin Montin, London: Athlone Press.

Irigaray, Luce 1990: *Je, Tu, Nous, Pour une Culture de la Différence*. Paris: Grasset. English translation 1993b: *Je, Tu, Nous. Towards a Culture of Difference*, transl. Alison Martin, New York and London: Routledge.

Irigaray, Luce 1991: 'Love between us'. In E. Cadava, P. Connor, J. L. Nancy (eds), *Who Comes After the Subject?* New York and London: Routledge, 167–77.

Jagger, Alison Marion and Young, Iris Marion (eds) 1998: *A Companion to Feminist Philosophy*, Malden, MA and Oxford: Blackwell.

Jameson, Fredric 1981: *The Political Unconscious: Narrative as a Socially Symbolic Act*. Ithaca, NY: Cornell University Press.

Jameson, Fredric 1982: 'Progress versus Utopia, or: can we imagine the future?' *Science Fiction Studies*, 9, 147–58.

Jameson, Fredric 1992: *Postmodernism or the Cultural Logic of Late Capitalism*. Durham, NC: Duke University Press.

Jardine, Alice 1984: 'Woman in Limbo: Deleuze and his (Br)others'. *Sub-Stance*, 44–5.

Jardine, Alice 1985: *Gynesis*. Ithaca, NY: Cornell University Press.

Jarry, Alfred 1993: *Le surumâle*. Paris: A.D.L.

Jeffords, Susan 1989: *The Remasculinization of America. Gender and the Vietnam War*. Bloomington, IN: Indiana University Press.

Johnson, Barbara 1980: 'Le Dernier homme'. In P. Lacoue-Labarthe and J. L. Nancy (eds), *Le Fins de l'homme*, Paris, Galilee.

Johnson, Barbara 1982: 'My monster/My self'. *Diacritics*, 12.2, 2–10.

Johnson, Richard 1999: 'Exemplary differences. Mourning (and not mourning) a princess'. In Adrian Kear and L. Deborah Steinberg (eds), *Mourning Diana. Nation, Culture and the Performance of Grief*, London and New York: Routledge.

Jordan, Jim 1995: 'Collective bodies: raving and the politics of Gilles Deleuze and Felix Guattari'. *Body & Society*, 1, 1, 125–44.

Jung, Carl G. 1982: *Aspects of the Feminine*. Princeton, NJ: Princeton University Press ARK Paperbacks.

Kafka, Franz 1988: 'The metamorphosis'. In *The Collected Short Stories of Franz Kafka*. London: Penguin.

Kallas, Aino 1990: 'La fiancée du loup'. In *La fiancée du loup*, Paris: Viviane Hamy, 107–72.

Kappeler, Susan 1987: *The Pornography of Representation*. Cambridge: Polity.

Kavanagh, John H. 1990: 'Feminism, humanism and science'. In Annette Kuhn (ed.), *Alien Zone*, London, Verso.

Kear, Adrian 1999: 'Diana between two deaths. Spectral ethics and the time of mourning'. In Adrian Kear and L. Deborah Steinberg, *Mourning Diana. Nation, Culture and the Performance of Grief*, London and New York: Routledge.

Kelly, Mary 1984: *Post-partum Document*. New York: Routledge & Kegan Paul.

Ketterer, David 1976: 'The apocalyptic imaginary, science fiction and American literature'. In Mark Rose (ed.), *Science Fiction. A Collection of Critical Essays*, Englewood Cliffs, NJ: Prentice-Hall.

Kolbowski, Silvia 1995: 'Introduction' and 'A conversation on recent feminist art practices', *October*, 71, Winter 1995, 49–69.

Kristeva, Julia 1980: *Pouvoirs de l'horreur*. Paris: Seuil. Translated as 1982: *Powers of Horror*. New York: Columbia University Press.

Kristeva, Julia 1981: 'Women's time', *Signs* 7/1, 13–35; also reprinted in N. O. Keohane, M. Z. Rosaldo & B. C. Gelpi (eds) 1982: *Feminist Theory: a critique of ideology*. Chicago: Chicago University Press.

Kroker, Arthur 1987: 'Panic value; Bacon, Colville, Baudrillard and the aesthetics of deprivation'. In John Fekete (ed.), *Life After Postmodernism. Essays on Value and Culture*, New York: Saint Martin's Press.

Kroker, Arthur and Marilouise Kroker 1987: *Body Invaders. Panic Sex in America*. New York, St Martin's Press.

Kruger, Barbara 1983: *We Won't Play Nature to Your Culture*. London: ICA.

Kunneman, Harry 1996: *Van theemutscultuur naar walkman-ego: contouren van postmoderne individualiteit*. Amsterdam: Boom.

Laclau, Ernesto 1995: 'Subjects of politics, politics of the subject'. *differences*, 7/1, 146–64.

Land, Nick 1995: 'Meat (or how to kill Oedipus in cyberspace)'. *Body & Society*, 1, 3–4, November 191–204.

Larvelle, François 1986: *Les Philosophies de la différence: introduction critique*. Paris: Presses Universitaires de France.

Lauretis, Teresa de 1980: 'Signs of w(a)onder'. In Teresa de Lauretis, Andreas Huyssen, Karin Woodward (eds), *The Technological Imagination: Theories and Fictions*, Madison: Coda.

Lauretis, Teresa de 1984: *Alice Doesn't*. Bloomington, IN: Indiana University Press.

Lauretis, Teresa de 1986: *Feminist Studies/Critical Studies*. Bloomington, IN: Indiana University Press.

Lauretis, Teresa de 1987: *Technologies of Gender*. Bloomington, IN: Indiana University Press.

Lauretis, Teresa de 1990a: 'Eccentric subjects: feminist theory and historical consciousness'. *Feminist Studies*, 16, 1, 115–50.

Lauretis, Teresa de 1990b: 'Upping the anti (sic) in feminist theory'. In M. Hirsch and E. Fox Keller (eds) *Conflicts in Feminism*, New York: Routledge, 255–70.

Lauretis, Teresa de 1990c: 'Introduction'. In *Sexual Difference: A Theory of Socio-Symbolic Practice*, Bloomington, IN: Indiana University Press.

Lauretis, Teresa de 1990d: 'The essence of the triangle, or: taking the risk of essentialism seriously'. *differences*, 1/2.

Lauretis, Teresa de 1994: *The Practice of Love: Lesbian Sexuality and Perverse Desire*. Bloomington, IN: Indiana University Press.

Lefanu, Sarah 1988: *In the Chinks of the World Machine. Feminism & Science Fiction*. London: The Women's Press.

Lichtenberg, Ettinger Bracha 1992: 'Matrix and metramorphosis'. *differences*, 4, 3, 176–208.

Lingis, Alphonso 1994: 'The society of dismembered parts'. In Constantin V. Boundas and Dorothea Olkowski (eds), *Gilles Deleuze and the Theatre of Philosophy*, New York and London: Routledge.

Lingis, Alphonso 1998: Paper delivered at the conference of the Society for Phenomenology and Existential Philosophy. University of Colorado, Denver, 8–10 October 1998.

Lispector, Clarice 1978: *La Passion selon G.H.* Paris: Des Femmes. English translation 1989: *The Passion According to G.H.* Minneapolis: University of Minnesota Press; translation by Ronald W. Souse.

Llosa, Mario Vargas 1997: *The Notebooks of Don Rigoberto*. Harmondsworth: Penguin Books.

Lloyd, Genevieve 1985: *The Man of Reason*. London: Methuen.

Lloyd, Genevieve 1994: *Part of Nature: Self-knowledge in Spinoza's Ethics*. Ithaca, NY and London: Cornell University Press.

Lloyd, Genevieve 1996: *Spinoza and the Ethics*. London and New York: Routledge.

Lorraine, Tamsin 1999: *Irigaray and Deleuze. Experiments in Visceral Philosophy*. Ithaca, NY: Cornell University Press.

Lury, Celia 1998: *Prosthetic Culture. Photography, Memory and Identity*. London and New York: Routledge.

Lutz, Helene, Yuval-Davis, Nina, and Phoenix, Anne (eds) 1996: *Crossfires. Nationalism, Racism and Gender in Europe*. London: Pluto Press.

Lyotard, Jean-François 1979: *La Condition postmoderne*. Paris: Minuit.

Lyotard, Jean-François 1984: *Tombeau de l'intellectuel*. Paris: Galilée.

Lyotard, Jean-François 1986: *Le Postmoderne expliqué aux enfants: correspondance 1982–1985*. Paris: Galilée.

MacCormack, Patricia 2000: '*Pleasure, perversion and death: three lines of flight from the viewing body*', Ph.D. dissertation, Monash University, 31 January 2000.

Macintyre, Ben 1992: *Forgotten Fatherland: the Search for Elizabeth Nietzsche*. London: Macmillan.

Madonna 1992: *Sex*. New York: Warner Books.

Marshall, Bill 1997: *Guy Hocquengem: Beyond Gay Identity*. Durham, NC: Duke University Press.

Martin, Biddy 1994: 'Sexualities without genders and other queer utopias'. *Diacritics*, Summer/Fall 104–21.

Massumi, Brian 1992. *A User's Guide to Capitalism and Schizophrenia*. Boston: Massachussets Institute of Technology Press.

Massumi, Brian 1992a: *First and Last Emperors, the Absolute State and the Body of the Despot*. Brooklyn: Autonomedia.

Massumi, Brian 1992b: 'Anywhere you want to be: an introduction to fear'. In Joan Broadhurst (ed.), *Deleuze and the Transcendental Unconscious*, Warwick Journal of Philosophy.

Massumi, Brian 1998: 'Requiem for our prospective dead! (toward a participatory critique of capitalist power)' in Eleanor Kaufman and Kevin Jon Heller (eds), *Deleuze and Guattari. New Mappings in Politics, Philosophy and Culture*, Minneapolis: University of Minnesota Press.

McClary, Susan 1991: *Feminine Endings: Music, Gender and Sexuality*. Minneapolis: Minnesota University Press.

McNay, Lois 1992: *Foucault and Feminism*. Cambridge: Polity.

Miller, Christopher 1993: 'The postidentarian predicament in the footnotes of A Thousand Plateaus: nomadology, anthropology, and authority'. In *Diacritics*, Fall, 6–68.

Miller, Nancy K. 1986: 'Subject to change'. In T. de Lauretis (ed.), *Feminist Studies/Critical Studies*, Bloomington, IN: Indiana University Press.

Miller Frank, Felicia 1995: *The Mechanical Song. Women, Voice and the Artificial in Nineteenth-Century French Narrative*. Stanford: Stanford University Press.

Mills Norton, Theodore 1986: 'Line of flight: Gilles Deleuze, or political science fiction'. *New Political Science*, 15, 77–93.

Minh-ha, Trinh T. 1989: *Woman, Native, Other*. Bloomington, IN: Indiana University Press.

Modleski, Tania 1986: 'The terror of pleasure'. In *Studies in Entertainment*, Bloomington, IN: Indiana University Press.

Modleski, Tania 1991: *Feminism Without Women: Culture and Criticism in a 'Postfeminist' Age*. New York and London: Routledge.

Mohanty, Chandra 1984: 'Under Western eyes: feminist scholarship and colonial discourse'. In *Boundary*, 2, 3, 333–58.

Moi, Toril 1994: *Simone de Beauvoir: the Making of an Intellectual Woman*. Oxford: Blackwell.

Morrison, Toni 1993: *Playing in the Dark. Whiteness and the Literary Imagination*. New York: Vintage Books.

Morton, Donald 1999: 'Birth of the cyberqueer'. In Jenny Wolmark (ed.), *Cybersexualities*, Edinburgh: Edinburgh University Press.

Muecke, Stephen 1984: 'The discourse of nomadology: phylum in flux'. *Art & Text*, 14, 24–40.

Newman, Michael 1989: 'Revising modernism, representing postmodernism: critical discourses of the visual arts'. In *ICA Papers; Postmodernism*, London: Institute of Contemporary Arts.

Nicholson, Linda 1991: *Feminism/Postmodernism*. New York and London: Routledge.

Nixon, Mignon 1995: 'Bad enough mother'. *October*, 72, 71–92.

Nussbaum, Martha C. 1999: *Cultivating Humanity: a Classical Defense of Reform in Liberal Education*. Cambridge, MA: Harvard University Press.

Olkowski, Dorothea 1994: 'Nieztsche's dice throw'. In Constantin V. Boundas and Dorothea Olkowski, *Gilles Deleuze and the Theatre of Philosophy*, New York and London: Routledge, 119–40.

Olkowski, Dorothea 1999a: *Gilles Deleuze and the Ruin of Representation*. Berkeley, CA: University of California Press.

Olkowski, Dorothea 1999b: 'Writers are dogs'. Paper delivered at the conference 'Rhizomatics, Genealogy, Deconstruction', University of Trent, Peterborough, Ontario, 20–23 May 1999.

Olkowski, Dorothea 2000: 'Body, knowledge and becoming-woman, morpho-logic in Deleuze and Irigaray'. In Ian Buchanan and Claire Colebrook (eds), *Deleuze and Feminist Theory*, Edinburgh: Edinburgh University Press.

Patton, Paul 1984: 'Conceptual politics and the war-machine in *Mille Plateaux*'. *Sub-stance*, 13, 3–4, 51–80.

Patton, Paul 1994: 'Anti-Platonism and art'. In Constantin V. Boundas and Dorothea Olkowski (eds), *Gilles Deleuze and the Theatre of Philosophy*, London and New York: Routledge, 141–56.

Patton, Paul 1996: *Deleuze: A Critical Reader*. Oxford: Blackwell.

Patton, Paul 1999: 'Difference and multiplicity'. Paper delivered at the conference 'Rhizomatics, Genealogy, Deconstruction', Trent University, Peterborough, Ontario, 20–23 May 1999.

Patton, Paul 2000: *Deleuze and the Political*. New York and London: Routledge.

Pearson, Keith Ansell 1997: *Viroid Life. Perspectives on Nietzsche and the Transhuman Condition*. London and New York: Routledge.

Pearson, Keith Ansell 1999: *Germinal Life. The Difference and Repetition of Deleuze*. London and New York: Routledge.

Penley, Constance 1985: 'Feminism, film theory and the bachelor machines'. *M/F*, 10, 39–59.

Penley, Constance 1986: 'Time travel, primal scene and the critical dystopia'. *Camera Obscura*, 15, 67–84.

Penley, Constance and Ross, A. (eds) 1991a: *Technoculture*. Minneapolis: University of Minnesota Press.

Penley, Constance, Lyon, Elisabeth, Spiegel, Lynn and Bergstrom, Janet (eds) 1991b: *Close Encounters. Film, Feminism and Science Fiction*. Minneapolis and Oxford: University of Minnesota Press.

Petchesky, Rosalind P. 1987: 'Fetal images: the power of visual culture in the politics of reproduction'. In M. Stanworth, *Reproductive Technologies*, Cambridge:
  Polity.

Pisters, Patricia 1998: *'From eye to brain. Gilles Deleuze: refiguring the subject in film
  theory'*. Ph.D. dissertation: Amsterdam.

Plant, Sadie 1997: *Zeros and Ones: Digital Women and the New Technoculture*. New
  York: Doubleday Books.

Pliny: *Natural History*, vol. III, books VIII–XI. Loeb Classical Library, Cambridge,
  MA: Harvard University Press and London: William Heinemann Ltd 1983.

Plumwood, Val 1993: *Feminism and the Mastery of Nature*. London and New York:
  Routledge.

Polysexuality. Semiotext(e) 1981: IV, 1, special issue.

Post-human 1993: Catalogue of the exhibition at Deichtorhallen, Germany.

Probyn, Elsbeth 1990: 'Travels in the postmodern: Making sense of the local'.
  In Linda Nicholson (ed.), *Feminism/Postmodernism*, London and New York:
  Routledge.

Probyn, Elsbeth 1995: 'Queer belongings. The politics of departure'. In E. Probyn
  and E. Grosz (eds), *Sexy Bodies. The Strange Carnalities of Feminism*, New York
  and London: Routledge.

Propp, Vladimir 1968: *Morphology of the Folktale*. Austin: University of Texas Press.

Rheingold, Howard 1990: 'Teledildonics: reach out and touch someone'. Mondo
  2000, Berkeley, CA: Fun City Megamedia.

Rich, Adrienne 1977: *Of Woman Born*. New York: W. W. Norton.

Rich, Adrienne 1979: *On Lies, Secrets and Silence*. New York: W. W. Norton.

Rich, Adrienne 1985: *Blood, Bread and Poetry*. New York: W. W. Norton.

Rodowick, Darid N. 1990: 'Reading the figural'. *Camera Obscura*, 24, 10–45.

Rojola, Lee 1995: 'The body which is not one'. In Dorrit Einersen and Ingeborg
  Nixon (eds), *Woman as Monster in Literature and the Media*, C.A. Reitzel Publish-
  ing and the University of Copenhagen.

Rose, Hilary and Rose, Steven (eds) 2000: *Alas, Poor Darwin. Arguments against
  Evolutionary Psychology*. London: Jonathan Cape.

Rose, Jacqueline 1986: 'Femininity and its discontents'. In *Sexuality in the Field of
  Vision*, London: Verso, 83–103.

Rosler, Martha 1990: Catalogue of the 'Decade Show' at the New Modern Art
  Museum, New York.

Rossiter, R. M. 1982: 'Life with artificial organs: renal dialysis and transplantation'.
  In Eric Shepherd and J. P. Watson (eds), *Personal Meanings*, New York: John
  Wiley and Sons.

Rouch, Hélène 1987: 'La Placenta comme tiers'. In *Languages*, 85, 71–9.

Rubin, Gayle 1975: 'The Traffic in Women: Notes towards a Political Economy of
  Sex'. In Reiter, Rayner (ed.), *Toward an Anthropology of Women*, New York: Monthly
  Review Press.

Ruppersberg, C. 1990: 'Alien Messiah'. In A. Kuhn (ed.), *Alien Zone*, London:
  Verso.

Rushdie, Salman 1997: 'Crash. Was Diana's death the result of sexual assault?'. *The
  New Yorker*, September 15, 68–9.

Russ, Joanne 1985: *The Female Man*. London: The Women's Press.

Russo, Mary 1994: *The Female Grotesque. Risk, Excess and Modernity.* New York and London: Routledge.

Sandoval, Chela 1999: 'Women prefer a choice'. In Jenny Wolmark (ed.), *Cybersexualities*, Edinburgh: Edinburgh University Press.

Sassen, Saskia 1994: *Cities in a World Economy.* Thousand Oaks and London: Pine Forge Press and Sage.

Sawicki, Jane 1991: *Disciplining Foucault. Feminism, Power and the Body.* London and New York: Routledge.

Scholes, Robert 1975: *Structural Fabulations. An Essay on Fiction of the Future.* London and Notre Dame: University of Notre Dame Press.

Schor, Naomi 1987: 'Dreaming dissymmetry. Barthes, Foucault, and sexual difference'. In Alice Jardine and Paul Smith (eds), *Men in Feminism*, New York: Methuen.

Schor, Naomi 1995: 'French feminism is a universalism'. *differences*, 7, 1, 15–47.

Scott, Joan Wallach 1996: *Only Paradoxes to Offer: French Feminism and the Rights of Man.* Cambridge, MA: Harvard University Press.

Scott, Joan Wallach and Butler, Judith (eds) 1992: *Feminists Theorize the Political.* New York: Routledge.

Semetsky, Inna 1999: 'Reterritorialization: drawing an archetypal map'. Paper delivered at the conference 'Rhizomatics, Genealogy, Deconstruction', Trent University, Peterborough, Ontario, 20–23 May 1999.

Shaviro, Steven 1995: 'Two lessons from Burroughs'. In Judith Halberstam and Ira Livingston (eds), *Posthuman Bodies*, Bloomington, IN: Indiana University Press, 38–56.

Showalter, Elaine 1990: *Sexual Anarchy: Gender and Culture at the Fin de Siècle.* New York; Viking.

Silverman, Kaja 1992: 'The Lacanian phallus'. *differences*, 4, 1, 84–115.

Smelik, Anneke 1996: 'Middeleeuwse maillots en de passie van Ripley. Verfilmingen van Jeanne d'Arc'. In *Jaarboek voor Vrouwengeschiedenis*, 16. Amsterdam: IISG, 133–41.

Smelik, Anneke 1998: *And the Mirror Cracked: Feminist Cinema and Film Theory.* Basingstoke: Macmillan.

Smith, David W. 2000: 'The place of ethics in Deleuze's philosophy'. In Eleanor Kaufman and Kevin Jon Heller (eds), *Deleuze and Guattari. New Mappings in Politics, Philosophy and Culture*, Minneapolis: University of Minnesota Press.

Smith, Nicholas (ed.) 1982: *Philosophers Look at Science Fiction.* Chicago: Nelson-Hall.

Snitow, Ann, Stansell, Christine, Thompson, S. (eds) 1983: *Powers of Desire. The Politics of Sexuality.* New York: Monthly Review Press.

Sobchack, Vivian 1995: 'Beating the meat/surviving the test or how to get out of this century alive'. *Body & Society*, I, 3–4, November 1995, 209–14.

Sontag, Susan 1976: 'The imagination of disaster'. In Mark Rose (ed.), *Science Fiction. A Collection of Critical Essays.* Englewood Cliffs NJ: Prentice-Hall.

Spivak, Gayatri Chakravorty 1976: 'Translator's preface', *Of Grammatology.* Baltimore: Johns Hopkins University Press.

Spivak, Gayatri Chakravorty 1983: 'Displacement and the discourse of woman'. In Mark Kupnick (ed.), *Displacement: Derrida and After*, Bloomington, IN: Indiana University Press, 169–95.

Spivak, Gayatri Chakravorty 1988: 'Can the subaltern speak?' In Cary Nelson and Lawrence Grossberg (eds), *Marxism and the Interpretation of Culture*, Basingstoke: Macmillan. Reprinted in Patrick Williams and Laura Chrisman (eds) 1994: *Colonial Discourse and Post-colonial Theory*, New York: Colombia University Press, 66–111.

Spivak, Gayatri Chakravorty 1989a: 'In a word'. *differences*, 1/2, 124–56.

Spivak, Gayatri Chakravorty 1989b: *In Other Worlds*. New York: Routledge.

Spivak, Gayatri Chakravorty 1992: 'French feminism revisited: ethics and politics'. In Judith Butler and Joan Scott (eds), *Feminists Theorize the Political*, New York: Routledge.

Springer, Claudia 1991: 'The pleasure of the interface'. *Screen*, 32:3 (Autumn), 303–23.

Springer, Claudia 1996: *Electronic Eros: Bodies and Desire in the Postindustrial Age*. Austin: University of Texas Press.

Spurlin, William J. 1999: 'Exemplary differences. Mourning (and not mourning) a princess'. In Adrian Kear and L. Deborah Steinberg, *Mourning Diana. Nation, Culture and the Performance of Grief*, London and New York: Routledge.

Squier, Susan 1995: 'Reproducing the posthuman body: ectogenetic fetus, surrogate mother, pregnant man'. In Judith Halberstam and Ira Livingston (eds), *Posthuman Bodies*, Bloomington, IN: Indiana University Press, 113–34.

Stacey, Jackie 1997: *Teratologies: A Cultural Study of Cancer*. London and New York: Routledge.

Stanton, Domna C. 1980: 'Language and revolution: the Franco-American disconnection'. In Hester Eisenstein and Alice Jardine (eds), *The Future of Difference*, Boston: G. K. Hall & Co.

Stengers, Isabelle 1987: *D'Une science à l'autre. Des concepts nomades*. Paris: Seuil.

Sterbak, Jana 1991: *States of Being/Corps-a Corps*. National Gallery of Canada, Ottawa.

Stivale, Charles 1984: 'The literary elements in *Mille Plateaux*: the new cartography of Deleuze and Guattari'. *Sub-Stance*, 44/45, 20–34.

Stivale, Charles 1991: 'Mille/Punks/Cyber/Plateaus: science fiction and Deleuzo-Guattarian "becomings"'. *Sub-Stance*, 66, 66–84.

Tamblyn, Christine 1994: Paper delivered at the conference 'Seduced and abandoned: the body in the virtual world' at the Institute of Contemporary Arts, London, 12–13 March 1994.

Theweleit, Klaus 1987: *Male Fantasies I: Women, Floods, Bodies, History*. Minneapolis: University of Minnesota Press.

Theweleit, Klaus 1989: *Male Fantasies II: Male Bodies: Psychoanalyzing the White Tenor*. Minneapolis: University of Minnesota Press.

Thomas, Louis-Vincent 1979: *Civilization and its Divagations. Mort, Fantasmes, Science-Fiction*. Paris: Payot.

Todd, May 1995: *The Moral Theory of Poststructuralism*. Pennsylvania: Pennsylvania State University Press.

Todorov, Tzvetan 1975: *The Fantastic. A Structural Approach to a Literary Genre*. Ithaca, NY: Cornell University Press.

Tredell, Nicholas (ed.) 1986: *Conversations With Critics*. Carcanet: Sheep Meadow Press, 58–74.

Tucker, Marcia 1994: 'The attack of the giant Ninja mutant Barbies'. In *Badgirls*, Cambridge, MA: New Museum of Contemporary Art, New York and MIT Press, 14–46.

Turkle, Sherry 1995: *Life on the Screen. Identity in the Age of the Internet*. New York: Simon & Schuster.

Unabomber 1995: The Unabomber Manifesto: Industrial Society and its Future. Berkeley, CA: Jolly Rogers Press.

Vance, Carol 1984: *Pleasure and Danger. Exploring Female Sexuality*. Boston: Routledge & Kegan Paul.

Vance, Carol 1990: 'The pleasures of looking. The Attorney General's Commission on Pornography versus Visual Images'. In Carol Squier (ed.), *The Critical Image. Essays on Contemporary Photography*, Seattle: Bay Press.

Van Oldenberg, Helene 1999: 'From spider-to-cyberfeminism and back'. In Mariva Cezinic (ed.), *From Elsewhere to Cyberfeminism and Back*, Maribor, Slovenia, Festival of Computer Arts.

Verma, Jatinder 1999: 'Mourning Diana, Asian style'. In Adrian Kear and L. Deborah Steinberg (eds), *Mourning Diana. Nation, Culture and the Performance of Grief*, London and New York: Routledge.

Villiers de l'Isle-Adam, Augusto 1977: *L'Eve future*. Paris: José Corti.

Vinci, Leonardo da 1988: *Il Bestiario*. Milan: Marinoni.

Violi, Patrizia 1987: *L'Infito singolare*. Verona: Essedue.

Vuarnet, J.-N. 1980: 'Métamorphoses de Sophie'. *L'Arc*, 49 Gilles Deleuze, 31–8.

Walkerdine, Valerie 1999: 'The crowd in the age of Diana. Ordinary inventiveness and the popular imagination'. In Adrian Kear and L. Deborah Steinberg (eds), *Mourning Diana. Nation, Culture and the Performance of Grief*, London and New York: Routledge.

Walters, Margaret 1997: 'American gothic: feminism, melodrama and the backlash'. In Ann Oakley and Juliet Mitchell (eds), *Who's afraid of Feminism? Seeing Through the Backlash*, Penguin Books, London.

Warner, Marina 1994: *Managing Monsters: The 1994 Reith Lectures*. London: Vintage Books.

Warner, Marina 1995: *Six Myths of Our Time: Little Angels, Little Monsters, Beautiful Beasts, and More*. New York: Vintage Books.

Weed, Elizabeth (ed.) 1989: *Coming to Terms*. New York and London: Routledge.

Weldon, Fay 1983: *The Life and Loves of a She-Devil*. London: Coronet.

West, Cornel 1994: *Prophetic Thought in Postmodern Times*. Monroe MF: Common Courage Press.

White, Eric 1995: 'Once they were men, now they're landcrabs: monstrous becomings in evolutionist cinema'. In Judith Halberstam and Ira Livingston (eds), *Posthuman Bodies*, Bloomington, IN: Indiana University Press, 226–44.

Whitford, Margaret 1991: *Luce Irigaray, Philosophy in the Feminine*. London: Routledge.

Wiener, Norbert 1948: *Cybernetics: or Control and Communication in the Animal and the Machine*. New York: John Wiley.

Wilding, Faith 1999: 'Monstrous domesticity'. http://www-art.cfa.cmu.edu/www-wilding/monstr.html.

Williams, Linda 1989: *Hard Core. Power, Pleasure, and the Frenzy of the Visible*. Berkeley, CA: University of California Press.

Williams, Patricia J. 1993: *The Alchemy of Race and Rights*. London: Virago Press.

Wittig, Monique 1973: *Le Corps lesbien*. Paris, Minuit.

Wittig, Monique 1979a: 'La Pensée straight'. *Questions Feministes*, 1980, 7.

Wittig, Monique 1979b: 'Paradigm'. In George Stambolian and Elaine Marks (eds), *Homosexualities and French Literature*, Ithaca, NY: Cornell University Press, 114–21.

Wittig, Monique 1982: 'Postface'. In Djuna Barnes, *La Passion*, Paris: Flammarion, 111–21.

Wright, Elizabeth 1992: *Feminism and Psychoanalysis. A Critical Dictionary*. Oxford: Blackwell.

Wright, Elizabeth and Wright, Edmonds (eds) 1999: *The Žižek Reader*, Oxford: Blackwell.

Wolf, Naomi 1991: *The Beauty Myth*. London: Vintage.

Woolf, Virginia 1977: *The Waves*. London: Grafton Books.

Yuval-Daris, Nira and Floya, Anthias (eds) 1989: Woman, Nation, State. London: Macmillan.

Žižek, Slavoj 1992: *Enjoy your Symptom! Jacques Lacan in Hollywood and Out*. London and New York: Routledge.

Zoe, Sofia 1984: 'Exterminating fetuses: abortion, disarmament, and the sexo-semiotics of extraterrestrialism'. *Diacritics*, Summer 1984, 47–59.

Zoe, Sofia 1992: 'Virtual corporalities: a feminist view'. *Australian Feminist Studies*, 15, Autumn 1992, 11–24.

Index

aberration 198–9, 202
abject: body 180, 186; cinema 180;
    insects 150; Kristeva 54, 161–2, 170;
    monstrosity 170, 202; mother 162,
    163; sacred 202; spider 151
abortion 163, 187
abyss/mother 196
accident-form, Massumi 187, 188, 201
Acker, Kathy 11, 19, 85, 158, 179, 186,
    222, 269
acoustics 154, 156, 157; *see also* music;
    sound
Aesop 125, 148
aesthetics 92–3, 152–3, 154
affectivity 16, 147, 268: body 104;
    Deleuze 96, 125; expression 119;
    flows 70; forces 68; intellectuality 71,
    73–4; Massumi 91; moderation 141;
    nomadic subject 260; pathology 143;
    politics 20; subjectivity 97; vitalism
    77
AIDS 53
aion/chronos 162; *see also* time
Alcoff, Linda 9
Alien film 179, 192, 194–5, 196, 207,
    208, 209–10
Alien IV film 226

aliens 190–1, 193, 194, 195; *see also*
    monstrosity
Aliens films 192, 193, 244
alterity 59–60; *see also* Other
Althusser, Louis 40, 55, 144
amazons 199
Amis, Martin 134, 179, 186, 212
Anderson, Laurie 2, 156–7, 172, 183,
    222
androcentrism 242
android 218–19; *see also* robots
Anger, Kenneth 236
animals: anti-metaphysics 121–5;
    Deleuze 121; de-territorialization
    121; drives 141; Freud 140; humans
    121–5, 137–8; immanence 133;
    impurity 161; machines 126; memory
    129; metamorphoses 126; metaphors
    125–7, 140; nomadology 133;
    not-One 133; Other 120; pets 121,
    134, 138; technology 126; Todorov
    141–2; war machine 128; *see also*
    becoming-animal
animation films 148, 153
anorexia–bulimia 18, 104, 107, 110,
    140–1, 180
Anthias, Floya 14

Index compiled by Zeb Korycinska